D1301672

DEBATING CHINA'S EXCHANGE RATE POLICY

MORRIS GOLDSTEIN
NICHOLAS R. LARDY
EDITORS

PETERSON INSTITUTE FOR INTERNATIONAL ECONOMICS
Washington, DC
April 2008

Morris Goldstein, Dennis Weatherstone Senior Fellow since 1994, has held several senior staff positions at the International Monetary Fund (1970–94), including Deputy Director of its Research Department (1987–94). He is the author of *Managed Floating Plus* (2002), *The Asian Financial Crisis: Causes, Cures, and Systemic Implications* (1998), *The Case for an International Banking Standard* (1997), *The Exchange Rate System and the IMF: A Modest Agenda* (1995), coeditor of *Private Capital Flows to Emerging Markets after the Mexican Crisis* (1996), coauthor of *Controlling Currency Mismatches in Emerging Markets* (2004) with Philip Turner and *Assessing Financial Vulnerability: An Early Warning System for Emerging Markets* with Graciela Kaminsky and Carmen Reinhart (2000), and project director of *Safeguarding Prosperity in a Global Financial System: The Future International Financial Architecture* (1999) for the Council on Foreign Relations Task Force on the International Financial Architecture.

Nicholas R. Lardy, senior fellow at the Peterson Institute since 2003, was a senior fellow in the Foreign Policy Studies Program at the Brookings Institution from 1995 to 2003. He was the director of the Henry M. Jackson School of International Studies at the University of Washington from 1991 to 1995. From 1997 through the spring of 2000, he was the Frederick Frank Adjunct Professor of International Trade and Finance at the Yale University School of Management. His publications include *China: The Balance Sheet* (2006), *Prospects for a US-Taiwan Free Trade Agreement* (2004), *Integrating China into the Global Economy* (Brookings Institution Press, 2002), *China's Unfinished Economic Revolution* (Brookings Institution Press, 1998), *China in the World Economy* (Institute for International Economics, 1994), *Foreign Trade and Economic Reform in China, 1978–1990* (Cambridge University Press, 1992), and *Agriculture in China's Modern Economic Development* (Cambridge University Press, 1983).

WISSER MEMORIAL LIBRARY

HG 3978
.D43
2008
Copy 1

PETER G. PETERSON INSTITUTE FOR INTERNATIONAL ECONOMICS
1750 Massachusetts Avenue, NW
Washington, DC 20036-1903
(202) 328-9000   FAX: (202) 659-3225
www.petersoninstitute.org

C. Fred Bergsten, *Director*
Edward Tureen, *Director of Publications, Marketing, and Web Development*

Typesetting by BMWW
Cover by Peggy Archambault
Cover photo: Imagemore Co., Ltd./Getty Images
Printing by Kirby Lithographic Company, Inc.

Copyright © 2008 by the Peter G. Peterson Institute for International Economics. All rights reserved. No part of this book may be reproduced or utilized in any form or by any means, electronic or mechanical, including photocopying, recording, or by information storage or retrieval system, without permission from the Institute.

For reprints/permission to photocopy please contact the APS customer service department at Copyright Clearance Center, Inc., 222 Rosewood Drive, Danvers, MA 01923; or email requests to: info@copyright.com

Printed in the United States of America
10 09 08   5 4 3 2 1

Library of Congress Cataloging-in-Publication Data

Debating China's exchange rate policy / Morris Goldstein, Nicholas R. Lardy, editors.
    p. cm.
    Proceedings of a conference.
    Includes bibliographical references and index.
    ISBN 978-0-88132-415-0 (alk. paper)
    1. Foreign exchange rates—China—Congresses.   2. Foreign exchange—Government policy—China—Congresses.   3. Currency question—China—Congresses.   4. Monetary policy—China—Congresses.   I. Goldstein, Morris, 1944–   II. Lardy, Nicholas R.
    HG3978.D43 2008
    332.4'560951—dc22

                                2008006541

The views expressed in this publication are those of the authors. This publication is part of the overall program of the Institute, as endorsed by its Board of Directors, but does not necessarily reflect the views of individual members of the Board or the Advisory Committee.

Contents

PETER G. PETERSON INSTITUTE FOR INTERNATIONAL ECONOMICS
1750 Massachusetts Avenue, NW, Washington, DC 20036-1903
(202) 328-9000   Fax: (202) 659-3225

C. Fred Bergsten, *Director*

BOARD OF DIRECTORS

* Peter G. Peterson, *Chairman*
* Reynold Levy, *Chairman,*
   Executive Committee
* George David, *Vice Chairman*

  Leszek Balcerowicz
  The Lord Browne of Madingley
  Chen Yuan
* Jessica Einhorn
  Mohamed A. El-Erian
  Stanley Fischer
  Jacob Frenkel
  Timothy F. Geithner
  Maurice R. Greenberg
* Carla A. Hills
  Nobuyuki Idei
  Karen Katen
  W. M. Keck II
  Michael Klein
* Caio Koch-Weser
  Lee Kuan Yew
  Donald F. McHenry
  Mario Monti
  Nandan Nilekani
  Hutham Olayan
  Paul ONe ill
  David J. O'Reilly
* James W. Owens
  Frank H. Pearl
  Victor M. Pinchuk
* Joseph E. Robert, Jr.
  David Rockefeller
  David M. Rubenstein
  Renato Ruggiero
  Richard E. Salomon
  Edward W. Scott, Jr.
* Adam Solomon
  Lawrence H. Summers
  Jean Claude Trichet
  Laura D'Andrea Tyson
  Paul A. Volcker
  Jacob Wallenberg
* Dennis Weatherstone
  Edward E. Whitacre, Jr.
  Marina v.N. Whitman
  Ernesto Zedillo

  Ex officio
* C. Fred Bergsten
  Nancy Birdsall
  Richard N. Cooper

  Honorary Directors
  Alan Greenspan
  Frank E. Loy
  George P. Shultz

ADVISORY COMMITTEE

Richard N. Cooper, *Chairman*

Isher Judge Ahluwalia
Robert E. Baldwin
Barry P. Bosworth
Menzie Chinn
Susan M. Collins
Wendy Dobson
Juergen B. Donges
Barry Eichengreen
Kristin Forbes
Jeffrey A. Frankel
Daniel Gros
Stephan Haggard
David D. Hale
Gordon H. Hanson
Takatoshi Ito
John Jackson
Peter B. Kenen
Anne O. Krueger
Paul R. Krugman
Roger M. Kubarych
Jessica T. Mathews
Rachel McCulloch
Thierry de Montbrial
Sylvia Ostry
Tommaso Padoa-Schioppa
Raghuram Rajan
Dani Rodrik
Kenneth S. Rogoff
Jeffrey D. Sachs
Nicholas H. Stern
Joseph E. Stiglitz
William White
Alan Wm. Wolff
Daniel Yergin

* *Member of the Executive Committee*

Preface

A substantial portion of the Peterson Institute's research and publications over the years has focused on exchange rates of the major industrial economies. In the early 1980s, John Williamson developed the concept of the "fundamental equilibrium exchange rate," an idea elaborated in his edited volume, *Estimating Equilibrium Exchange Rates* (1994). The yen-dollar relationship was the subject of two studies. I coauthored the first, *The United States-Japan Economic Problem* (1985, 2d ed. 1987) with William Cline and the second *Reconcilable Differences: United States–Japan Economic Conflict* (1993) with Marcus Noland. Other studies followed.

In the first half of the this decade the Institute organized two major conferences, one in September 2002 and the other in May 2004, to analyze the growing strength of the US dollar in the second half of the 1990s and the subsequent emergence of very large trade and current account deficits of the United States. This led to two volumes that I coedited with John Williamson, *Dollar Overvaluation and the World Economy* (2003) and *Dollar Adjustment: How Far? Against What?* (2004). Both these conferences on the dollar gave some attention to the Chinese renminbi, though at the time China's external surplus position was modest and China was in a relatively early stage of accumulation of what would become an unprecedently high holding of foreign exchange reserves.

Morris Goldstein and Nicholas Lardy—in a steady string of op-eds, Peterson Institute working papers, articles in leading economic journals, and contributions to other Peterson Institute volumes on international economic issues—have been analyzing the growing misalignment of the renminbi since 2003.

The Institute decided to organize a conference on October 19, 2007 focusing on China's exchange rate policy for two reasons. The first was the massive expansion of China's trade and current account surpluses, which continued to accelerate after the introduction of a modified exchange rate regime in July 2005. By 2006 China's current account surplus was far and away the largest of any economy in the world in absolute terms, and relative to the size of its economy had reach a level unprecedented for one of the world's top ten trading countries. The second was the continuing controversy over the role of the exchange rate of the renminbi in the adjustment of China's external surplus. The result is this volume, which analyzes all of the critical issues faced by China's economic policymakers as they affect the currency policy decisions that country must address.

The Peter G. Peterson Institute for International Economics is a private, nonprofit institution for the study and discussion of international economic policy. Its purpose is to analyze important issues in that area and to develop and communicate practical new approaches for dealing with them. The Institute is completely nonpartisan.

The Institute is funded by a highly diversified group of philanthropic foundations, private corporations, and interested individuals. About 30 percent of the Institute's resources in our latest fiscal year were provided by contributors outside the United States, including about 12 percent from Japan.

The Institute's Board of Directors bears overall responsibilities for the Institute and gives general guidance and approval to its research program, including the identification of topics that are likely to become important over the medium run (one to three years) and that should be addressed by the Institute. The director, working closely with the staff and outside Advisory Committee, is responsible for the development of particular projects and makes the final decision to publish an individual study.

The Institute hopes that its studies and other activities will contribute to building a stronger foundation for international economic policy around the world. We invite readers of these publications to let us know how they think we can best accomplish this objective.

C. FRED BERGSTEN
Director
March 2008

Acknowledgments

This volume and the conference that preceded it would not have been possible without the enthusiastic support of many people. The contributors who wrote and commented on the papers and then revised prior to publication deserve thanks. At the Institute, C. Fred Bergsten gave the project his whole-hearted encouragement and support from the beginning, in addition to contributing to the volume. Jeff Cordeau, Renée Duncan, Michael Ennis, Teresa Kasper, Yvonne Priestley, and Laura Searfoss ensured that the conference ran smoothly. Madona Devasahayam, Marla Banov, Brian Slattery, and Ed Tureen efficiently transformed the revised papers and comments into the current volume. Doug Dowson and Giwon Jeong provided excellent research assistance in the preparation of our own contribution to the volume. We would like to extend a special thanks to the People's Bank of China Vice-Governor Wu Xiaoling. She led her country's delegation to the annual International Monetary Fund–World Bank meetings in Washington in the fall of 2007 but took time from her busy schedule to address our conference.

MORRIS GOLDSTEIN
NICHOLAS R. LARDY

China's Exchange Rate Policy: An Overview of Some Key Issues

MORRIS GOLDSTEIN and NICHOLAS R. LARDY

More than two and a half years have passed since China announced a number of changes to its foreign exchange regime on July 21, 2005. During this period, the debate on the pros and cons of China's exchange rate policy, which had begun in earnest several years earlier, intensified. In this introductory chapter, we seek to convey the flavor of that ongoing debate by identifying and discussing several key issues. We also provide a summary of the other contributions to this volume—a reader's guide, if you will. All of these contributions (papers, discussants' comments, and remarks made during the conference's wrap-up panel) were originally presented at a conference on China's Exchange Rate Policy held at the Peterson Institute on October 19, 2007.

This section summarizes developments since China's exchange rate regime change in July 2005. The next section discusses four key challenges facing the Chinese authorities in light of the increasingly undervalued exchange rate and the accelerating buildup of foreign exchange reserves, namely: (1) maintaining a gradual pace of currency reform while trying to use monetary policy as an effective instrument of macroeconomic management; (2) reducing excessive reliance on external demand to sustain

Morris Goldstein has been the Dennis Weatherstone Senior Fellow at the Peterson Institute since 1994. Nicholas R. Lardy has been a senior fellow at the Peterson Institute since 2003. The authors are indebted to Doug Dowson and Giwon Jeong for excellent research assistance.

economic growth; (3) preventing the defense of the present currency regime from handicapping unduly efforts to strengthen and transform the banks into truly commercial entities; and (4) containing the risk of protectionism abroad in response to China's very large global current account surplus. The last section offers a brief scorecard on the leading options for China's exchange rate policy going forward, contrasting the features of a "stay the course" policy with those of a bolder "three-stage" approach that seeks to reduce more rapidly the current undervaluation of the renminbi.

China's new currency regime ended the fixed nominal exchange rate vis-à-vis the US dollar, which the authorities adopted at the time of the Asian financial crisis.[1] The official bilateral rate appreciated 2.1 percent, moving the rate from RMB8.28 to RMB8.11 to the dollar. By September 2007 the renminbi-dollar bilateral rate stood at RMB7.53, reflecting a cumulative nominal bilateral appreciation against the US dollar of 10 percent.[2] On a real trade-weighted basis, the renminbi appreciated somewhat less, only 7.4 percent according to JPMorgan.[3]

China's global current account surplus has expanded substantially over recent years. It stood at $68.7 billion (3.6 percent of GDP) in 2004 but rose to $160.8 billion in 2005 (7.2 percent of GDP) and then $250 billion (9.5 percent of GDP) in 2006 (National Bureau of Statistics of China 2007, 95; State Administration of Foreign Exchange, Balance of Payments Analysis Small Group 2007, 8).[4] By 2006 China's absolute current account surplus was, by a wide margin, the largest of any country in the world. Based on annual data on trade in goods, we estimate that China's current account surplus in 2007 will approach $400 billion, about 11 percent of 2007 GDP. A surplus of this magnitude relative to GDP is "unprecedented for a country of China's size and stage of development" (McGregor 2007).

---

1. Many analyses assert incorrectly that China adopted a fixed exchange rate in 1994. On January 1, 1994 the authorities eliminated their dual exchange rate system by raising the official exchange rate to the then prevailing market rate of RMB8.7. However, the authorities then continually adjusted the official rate until it appreciated to RMB8.28 in October 1997. That remained the official rate until July 21, 2005.

2. In early February 2008 the renminbi-dollar rate was RMB7.118, reflecting a cumulative nominal bilateral depreciation against the dollar of 15 percent. On a real trade-weighted basis, the degree of appreciation was much smaller, 8 percent, according to JPMorgan. The rate of renminbi appreciation relative to the dollar has not been uniform over this period. If one takes the annualized one-month change, the rate of appreciation has varied from less than 2 percent (even going slightly negative at one point in 2006) to almost 20 percent in late 2007 and early 2008 (Anderson 2007c, 2008).

3. Between the dollar peak in February 2002 and January 2008, the renminbi has actually *depreciated* on a real effective basis by between 0.4 and 9.8 percent, according to measures of real effective exchange rates published by JPMorgan, Citigroup, and the Bank for International Settlements.

4. Again, if one goes back to 2001, the expansion of China's global current account surplus is much larger, as it stood at only 1 percent of GDP at that time.

The buildup of official holdings of foreign exchange reserves has accelerated since July 2005.[5] In the 12-month periods through June 2005 and June 2006, reserves rose by $240 billion and $230 billion, respectively. But in the twelve months through June 2007, reserves rose by $391 billion, about three-fifths more than in the previous two 12-month periods. At the end of December 2007, total reserves reached $1,530 billion (People's Bank of China 2008).[6]

It is important to note that the relative importance of the current and capital account surpluses as contributors to the reserve buildup has changed dramatically. In 2004 the capital account surplus was more than half again as large as the current account surplus and thus accounted for most of the reserve buildup. In 2005, however, the current account surplus was 2.5 times the capital account surplus (National Bureau of Statistics of China 2007, 95). By 2006 the current account surplus was 25 times the capital account surplus and accounted for the entire reserve buildup (State Administration of Foreign Exchange, Balance of Payments Analysis Small Group 2007).[7] Thus, for 2005 and 2006, it is incorrect to argue that China's rapid reserve buildup was due primarily to large capital inflows rather than a growing current account surplus.

Challenges Facing the Chinese Authorities under the Existing Currency Regime

Any methodology that defines the equilibrium exchange rate for the renminbi as the real effective exchange rate that would produce "balance" in China's global current account position, or in its basic balance, or in its overall balance-of-payments position, yields the qualitative conclusion that the renminbi is significantly undervalued and probably by an increasing margin over time. As noted earlier, an increasingly undervalued exchange rate and the concomitant accelerating buildup of foreign ex-

---

5. Increases in official holdings of foreign exchange reserves are a downward-biased estimate of the magnitude of official intervention in the foreign exchange market for three reasons. First, through the end of 2006 the central government transferred $66.4 billion in official foreign exchange reserves from the State Administration of Foreign Exchange (SAFE) to the Central Huijin Investment Company (Kroeber 2007). Huijin has used the funds to recapitalize four banks and four insurance companies. Second, SAFE has engaged in swap transactions with state-owned commercial banks that have removed large amounts of foreign exchange from its balance sheet. Third, starting in 2007, on several occasions when the central bank raised the reserve requirement, it required banks to deposit the additional amounts in the form of foreign exchange.

6. China's annual exchange market intervention was roughly 10 percent of its GDP during 2004–06 but substantially higher at 14 percent in 2007.

7. The capital account surplus was $10 billion, and errors and omissions reflected an unrecorded outflow of $13 billion.

change reserves pose several economic challenges for the Chinese authorities. In this section, we discuss those challenges for the independence of monetary policy, the "rebalancing" of economic growth, the continuing efforts to reform China's banking system, and China's external adjustment and its contribution to correcting global payments imbalances.

Independence of Monetary Policy

A fixed exchange rate regime typically imposes a substantial constraint on a country's monetary policy for the simple reason that if domestic interest rates diverge too much from foreign rates, the country could be subject to destabilizing capital flows. This is particularly likely to be the case for small countries that are price takers in international goods and capital markets. Capital controls, in theory, could prevent large inflows (outflows) when domestic interest rates are higher (lower) than foreign rates, but in practice it is difficult to maintain effective controls over time, particularly in an economy that is very open to trade. Even when controls are effective in limiting capital inflows or outflows, a country with an undervalued fixed exchange rate, and thus a large current account surplus, will face the challenge of sterilizing the increase in the domestic money supply resulting from the large-scale purchase of foreign exchange (i.e., sale of domestic currency). Otherwise, the growth of liquidity in the banking and financial systems will lead eventually to inflation, which will result in an appreciation of the real exchange rate. Even when the authorities use sterilization successfully to control the growth of domestic liquidity, when the currency is increasingly undervalued, they will need over time to sell greater quantities of bonds to acquire the funds necessary for sterilization. This, in turn, causes an increase in the interest rate the central bank must pay on these bonds. Eventually, the interest the central bank pays on these bonds could exceed its earnings from its holdings of interest-bearing foreign currency–denominated financial assets, imposing a substantial financial constraint on sterilization operations.

Views on the extent to which China's exercise of monetary policy actually is handicapped by its undervalued exchange rate vary widely. One school of thought argues that China diverges substantially from the small open economy in which a fixed exchange rate means that a country's monetary policy is determined abroad. According to Jonathan Anderson (2004), "China can run an independent monetary policy under any renminbi regime." He believes China's capital controls are relatively effective and that sterilization—implemented mainly via the sale of central bank bills and increases in the required reserve ratio for banks—has been successful and can be maintained indefinitely. Thus, increases in China's international reserves—whether generated via a growing current account surplus, via the capital account (motivated by the expectation of currency appreciation, rising Shanghai property prices, or a booming domestic stock market), or via errors and omissions in the balance of payments—". . . have had virtually no impact on domestic liquidity conditions" (Anderson 2006a, 19).

Stephen Green of Standard Chartered Bank holds a similar view. He has tracked carefully the sterilization operations of the People's Bank of China (PBC) and has shown that even in the first half of 2007, when capital inflows through various channels increased dramatically, the central bank had little difficulty in retaining control of the growth of the domestic money supply (Green 2007a, 2007b).

The alternative school of thought is that China's (quasi) fixed exchange rate already has diminished the effectiveness of monetary policy and that this erosion is likely to continue. Thus, increased currency flexibility is needed to reduce the risks of macroeconomic instability, whether of domestic or external origin (Goldstein and Lardy 2006; Lardy 2006; Prasad, Rumbaugh, and Wang 2005). There are several strands to this argument.

First, central bank control of the growth of monetary aggregates in some periods has depended on the reintroduction of credit quotas for individual banks and various types of "window guidance" on bank lending rather than the use of interest rates. These much blunter instruments, rather than market signals, may lead to a much less efficient allocation of credit (Goldstein and Lardy 2004, 7–8; Goodfriend and Prasad 2006, 24).

Moreover, this alternative school of thought believes that the resultant policy mix has left China with an interest rate structure that is far from optimum. On the lending side, real interest rates have been relatively low for a rapidly growing economy. For example, in late July 2007 the central bank adjusted the one-year benchmark bank lending rate upward to 6.84 percent. But inflation, as measured by the corporate goods price index, was running at 5.4 percent, making the real rate less than 1.5 percent in an economy expanding at more than 11 percent in real terms.[8] This contributes to the underlying excess demand for credit and rapid growth of lending from the banking system.

From the point of view of savers, deposit rates are also low. In late July 2007, demand deposits yielded only 0.81 percent and one-year deposits 3.3 percent, in the face of headline consumer price index (CPI) inflation of 5.6 percent and a 5 percent tax on interest income (reduced from the previous 20 percent rate at the same time as the upward adjustment in interest rates in late July). Low or negative real returns on bank savings have been a major contributor to the boom in the property market and, more recently, in equity prices on the Shanghai stock exchange. By late August 2007, the Shanghai stock index was up more than fivefold compared with

---

8. The corporate goods price index is a more relevant indicator of inflation for firms than the CPI, which in 2007 was pushed up largely because of rising prices for several food items. Food currently accounts for about one-third of China's CPI.

July 2005. Companies listed domestically were trading at a relatively lofty 38 times estimated 2007 earnings. Even more problematic, half the growth of earnings of listed companies in the first half of 2007 came not from core operations but from profits from stock trading (Anderlini 2007).

In short, China might be regarded as a prototypical example of the general pattern that keeping exchange rates low requires keeping interest rates low (Eichengreen 2004). As in other countries maintaining undervalued exchange rates, the Chinese authorities have frequently been slow to raise the general level of interest rates for fear of attracting higher levels of capital inflows that at some point could prove more challenging to sterilize. But one consequence is real estate and stock market booms that heighten financial risk.

A second strand to the argument that increased exchange rate flexibility would enhance the effectiveness of monetary policy is that while the PBC has successfully sterilized the increase in the domestic money supply associated with the buildup of foreign exchange reserves, this sterilization entails hidden costs or risks. These include the risk of a capital loss on dollar assets in the event of eventual appreciation of the renminbi (Goldstein and Lardy 2006).

Equally important, the sustained large-scale sale of low-yielding central bank bills and repeated increases in required reserves both have an adverse impact on the profitability of state banks, hindering their transition to operation on a fully commercial basis (Yu 2007a, 20). In 2003 the central bank, having sold all of its holdings of treasury bonds, began to issue central bank bills to sterilize increases in the domestic money supply associated with its foreign exchange operations. By end-June 2007, total outstanding central bank bills held by banks reached RMB3.8 trillion (People's Bank of China, Monetary Policy Analysis Small Group 2007, 8). From mid-2003 through September 2007, the central bank also raised the required reserve ratio for banks by 50 or 100 basis points on 12 occasions, taking the ratio from 6 percent of deposits to 12.5 percent. The increase in the required reserve ratio compelled banks to deposit with the central bank RMB2 trillion more than would have been the case if the required reserve ratio had remained at 6 percent. The yield on three-month central bank bills at mid-year 2007 was only about 3 percent, and the central bank pays only 1.89 percent on required reserves. Because the benchmark one-year lending rate at mid-year was 6.6 percent, the RMB5.7 trillion increase in bank holdings of these low-yielding assets represents a large implicit tax on Chinese banks; indeed, that tax in 2006 was two-thirds of the pre-tax profits of the entire Chinese banking system.[9]

---

9. Abstracting from the issue of risk and assuming holdings of these two categories of assets by the banks at mid-year is equal to the average holding of these assets during the year, the implicit tax on the banking sector can be estimated as the sum of RMB3.8 trillion times 3.6 percent (the difference between the 6.6 percent benchmark lending rate and the 3 percent

Last but not least, it is one thing to argue that sterilization operations can be continued indefinitely because the interest rate on China's reserve assets exceeds that on its sterilization bills.[10] It is another thing entirely to argue that sterilization can be continued indefinitely while simultaneously reducing China's large external surplus. This is because large-scale sterilization blocks the monetary, interest rate, and relative-price mechanisms that would otherwise operate (via their effects on the saving-investment balance and on net capital flows) to reduce China's external imbalance. For example, in chapter 8 of this volume, Michael Mussa argues that when large-scale sterilization produces a negative growth rate in the net domestic assets of the PBC while the demand for base money is growing briskly, then that demand for money will be satisfied solely through an increase of the net foreign assets of the central bank, which is of course equivalent to an increase in international reserves.[11] In short, China can either continue its large-scale intervention and sterilization operations or significantly reduce its large external surplus. It cannot do both.

In the end, there is no definitive methodology to measure which of the two alternative views on the independence of monetary policy is correct. It appears to be a matter of judgment. Supporters of the status quo point to studies showing that capital controls continue to provide some degree of independence to China's monetary authority (Ma and McCauley 2007). And they are not persuaded that the resulting interest rate structure leads to excess investment. Despite China's uniquely high rate of capital formation in recent years, some studies show no evidence of a decline in the rate of return to capital (Bai, Hsieh, and Qian 2006). Some go even further, arguing that financial repression is positive since it allows low-cost bank financing of infrastructure and other strategic public investments that underpin China's economic expansion (Keidel 2007).

In contrast, those who believe China should allow greater exchange rate flexibility acknowledge that sterilization so far has limited the inflation and credit growth consequences of large and rapid reserve accumulation but emphasize the negative aspects of the resulting financial repression. It contributes to growing risks in property and stock markets,

---

interest banks receive on central bank bills) and RMB2 trillion times 4.7 percent (the benchmark lending rate minus the 1.89 percent interest banks receive on required reserves) or RMB231.4 billion. In 2006 the pretax profits of the entire Chinese banking sector were RMB338 billion (Chinese Bank Regulatory Commission 2007, 33).

10. The central bank has traditionally earned a profit on its sterilization operations. However, the combination of the falling yields on short term US treasury bonds, because of recent large decreases in the federal funds rate, and the rising rates the central bank is paying on its own sterilization bonds means these profits are under pressure and could even turn into losses.

11. For further elaboration of the "monetary approach" to the recent evolution of China's balance of payments, see the discussion later in this section on alternative explanations for the post-2003 surge in China's net exports.

subsidizes capital-intensive industries with adverse effects on the environment and the pace of job creation, and, as will be discussed below, makes it more difficult to transition to a more balanced and sustainable growth path.

The state of the debate on the links between monetary policy independence and China's currency regime is well illustrated in chapter 2 of this volume. There, Eswar Prasad argues that a flexible exchange rate is required to deliver an effective monetary policy and further capital account liberalization, and without such a monetary policy and capital account regime, it is much harder to achieve stable macroeconomic policies and an efficient and well-functioning financial market. Going further, the latter two elements are essential to achieving the ultimate objective of balanced and sustainable economic growth. Hence, in Prasad's framework, a flexible exchange rate becomes almost a prerequisite for high-quality economic growth. In contrast, the two discussants of the Prasad paper, Jin Zhongxia and Shang-Jin Wei, conclude that the benefits that a more flexible exchange rate confers on monetary policy have been somewhat oversold in China's case.

Prasad emphasizes that maintaining a tightly managed exchange rate entails also maintaining a set of distortionary policies—including financial repression and a relatively closed capital account; such distortionary policies in turn are costly. These costs include, inter alia, a low real rate of return to savers, provision of cheap credit to inefficient state enterprises, less scope for using monetary policy to combat shocks, slower employment growth, and a higher risk of asset price bubbles. Moreover, capital controls are leaky and become less effective over time. He recommends that China adopt both an explicit inflation objective as well as increased flexibility for the renminbi. He does not see a one-off revaluation of the renminbi as a solution to China's monetary policy problem.

Jin points out that the renminbi exchange rate has in fact become more flexible over the past two and a half years and hence that China's central bank now has more scope to implement an effective monetary policy. He also reminds us that the effectiveness of monetary policy in China is constrained by a number of factors, including uncertainties about the monetary transmission mechanism, rapid development of financial markets, and technical difficulties with the aggregate price indices—and not just by the currency regime. He maintains that the composition of inflation in China can also result in an underestimation of the true appreciation of the renminbi.

For his part, Wei stresses that China's capital controls are still binding at the margin, that China's fiscal policy leaves room for countercyclical policy, and that the constraint that the de facto dollar peg imposes on China's monetary policy has the advantage of providing effective anti-inflationary discipline. He finds no empirical evidence to suggest that flexible exchange rate regimes are associated with faster current account adjustment than are other currency regimes. In this sense, he concludes that it is the level of the real effective exchange rate for the renminbi that matters for China's external imbalance (and the problems that go with that imbalance)—not the flexibility of China's currency regime.

Rebalancing Economic Growth

Since 2004, China's top political leadership has assigned a high priority to rebalancing the sources of domestic economic growth. They envision over time transitioning to a growth path that relies more on expanding domestic consumption and less on burgeoning investment and a growing trade surplus (Lardy 2006). Expanding personal consumption is consistent with President Hu Jintao's emphasis both on creating a "harmonious society" and on reducing the pace of growth of energy consumption (associated strongly with investment spending), thus curtailing emissions of greenhouse gases and sulfur dioxide.

China can promote domestic consumption demand as a source of economic growth through fiscal, financial, and exchange rate policies. Fiscal policy options include cutting personal taxes; increasing government consumption expenditures—i.e., outlays for health, education, welfare, and pensions; or introducing a dividend tax on state-owned companies. The first would raise household disposable income and thus consumption expenditures. The second would both increase consumption demand directly and, by reducing household precautionary demand for savings, lead indirectly to an increase in private consumption expenditure. A dividend tax would reduce corporate savings and investment and provide revenues to increase government outlays on social programs.

Financial reform would reduce the extent of financial repression in China by paying higher real deposit rates to savers, thus increasing household income and consumption as a share of GDP. Although household deposits in the banking system as a share of GDP almost doubled between 1993 and 2003, the stream of pretax interest earnings generated by these savings declined from an average of about 5 percent of GDP in 1992–95 to only 2.2 percent of GDP in 2003. The contribution of interest income to disposable income has declined even more since the government introduced a 20 percent tax on interest income in 1999. The declining contribution of after-tax interest income to household disposable income over this period accounts for about two-thirds of the 4.8 percentage point decline in household disposable income as a share of GDP. If interest earnings of households after 1995 had grown proportionately with the stock of household bank deposits and the government had not introduced a tax on interest income, the contribution of interest income to household disposable income by 2003 would have been 5.7 percentage points of GDP greater than the actual contribution (Lardy 2007, 13).

Finally, appreciation of the renminbi could contribute to China's desired transition to a more consumption-driven growth path for two reasons. First, currency appreciation would reduce the growth of exports and increase the growth of imports, reducing China's external surplus.[12] Second, as already discussed, a more flexible exchange rate policy would allow the central bank greater flexibility in setting domestic interest rates and would thus increase the potential to mitigate macroeconomic cycles by raising lending rates to moderate investment booms. That would presumably lead to a lower average investment rate and thus contribute to the leadership's goal of reducing China's dependence on investment as a source of economic growth.

Given the recent developments in China's global current account position, it is hardly surprising that China has become increasingly dependent on the expansion of net exports of goods and services to sustain high growth. Net exports jumped from $50 billion (2.5 percent of GDP) in 2004 to $125 billion in 2005 and then $210 billion (7.5 percent of GDP) in 2006. We estimate that in 2007 net exports of goods and services were $300 billion, about 9 percent of GDP.[13] As a consequence, the contribution of net exports to economic growth has increased dramatically, from an average of less than 5 percent (0.35 percentage points of GDP growth) in the four years from 2001 through 2004 to an average of more than a fifth (2.4 percentage points of GDP growth) in 2005–06 (National Bureau of Statistics of China 2007, 36). The contribution of net exports to economic growth in 2007 likely will be even higher.

Although investment growth moderated somewhat in 2005–06, these very large increases in net exports of goods and services have meant that the consumption share of GDP has fallen significantly. By 2006, government and personal consumption combined accounted for only half of GDP, almost certainly the lowest share of any economy in the world. China is particularly an outlier in terms of personal consumption, which in 2006 accounted for only 36 percent of GDP (National Bureau of Statistics of China 2007, 35).

In summary, China has yet to transition to a more consumption-driven growth path. Indeed, growth has become even more unbalanced, as reflected in the declining consumption share of GDP. This decline is not only because the authorities have not undertaken sufficient exchange rate adjustment but also because they have neglected to implement the fiscal

---

12. See the discussion later in this section on the effectiveness of renminbi appreciation.

13. The estimate is based on Ministry of Commerce data on trade in goods in 2007 and data on trade in services in the first half of 2007.

and financial policies that would support the transition to more consumption-driven growth (Lardy 2007).

In chapter 3 of this volume, Bert Hofman and Louis Kuijs explain why a more sustainable growth path in China will require more reliance on services and less on industry, more reliance on factor productivity and less on capital accumulation, and more reliance on domestic demand and less on net exports. To illustrate how key imbalances in the Chinese economy might evolve to the year 2035 under alternative policy packages, Hofman and Kuijs consider two scenarios. The first one broadly incorporates features of past growth (that is, investment-led and driven by industry) and simply extrapolates it forward. The results—be it in terms of the share of industry and investment in GDP, or the size of the current account surplus, or energy intensity, or job creation, or the rural-urban income disparity—are disappointing. In contrast, a second scenario that incorporates five types of policies to help rebalancing yields much better outcomes. The exchange rate plays only a minor role in this second scenario, in large part because price and tax measures are used instead of the exchange rate to alter the relative attractiveness of manufacturing (tradables) vis-à-vis producing services (nontradables).

In his comment on chapter 3, Kenneth Rogoff observes that even assuming a fall in China's growth rate to 8 percent for the next decade and to 7 percent thereafter, China would on unchanged policies require a seemingly incredible investment share of 60 percent of GDP just to keep up the growth pace. He regards the model simulation more as a speculative flourish than as a centerpiece of the analysis. In particular, he questions how Hofman and Kuijs can regard the exchange rate as unimportant when their model seems not to contain any meaningful monetary or financial sector; indeed, Rogoff argues that their analysis is more consistent with the conclusion that to obtain significant rebalancing without exchange rate adjustment, China would be required to perform what he calls "policy reform miracles" on numerous fronts.

In the second comment on chapter 3, Barry Bosworth regards the contribution of Hofman and Kuijs as the attention their paper directs to the domestic side of economic imbalances that have developed in China since 2005. He argues that the public discussion has so far focused too narrowly on exchange rate issues. He notes that the literature now contains conflicting estimates of the distribution of Chinese saving between households and enterprises, yet this distribution is central to the adoption of appropriate policy measures. For example, if the emphasis is on enterprise saving, then much of the problem is that only a small share of growth in aggregate income is being passed on to the households, whereas a focus on household saving leads naturally to an examination of how fears of illness and old age affect saving in the absence of a stronger social safety net.

Speakers in the wrap-up panel, whose remarks appear in chapter 9, spoke strongly in favor of rebalancing the pattern of China's growth. Andrew Crockett argued that it was clearly in China's interest to create a social safety net that met the needs and aspirations of its people and that doing so would also have the favorable dividend of reducing China's external imbalance. He also thought there was considerable scope for making more widely available to Chinese households a set of financial instruments that also would increase the rate of spending. C. Fred Bergsten took the view that appreciation of the renminbi—as important as it was—was not the only answer to China's external imbalance problem. It had to be part of the broader rebalancing strategy, as laid out by Lardy (2007) and others.

Potential Effects on China's Banking System

There is considerable agreement both inside and outside China on the evolution of China's banking system and on efforts to date to reform it. It is recognized, for example, that the high share of bank deposits in household financial wealth and the dominance of bank loans in enterprises' external financing make the performance of the banking system in China more important than in most other economies—with significant impact on, inter alia, the growth of total factor productivity, household consumption, size of public debt, transmission of monetary policy, and prospects for capital account convertibility. Most observers also regard the central elements of China's banking reform as having moved the system in the right direction—including large-scale (over $300 billion) public recapitalization of the state-owned commercial banks to remove a huge overhang of nonperforming loans from bank balance sheets; implementation of tougher asset classification and provisioning guidelines; creation of an energetic bank supervisor (China Bank Regulatory Commission); large reductions in the number of bank branches and bank employees; World Trade Organization (WTO) accession; listing of four big state-owned commercial banks on stock exchanges; and the sale of bank shares to strategic foreign partners.

But the banking system still has some serious deficiencies and faces a number of formidable challenges going forward. Wendy Dobson and Anil Kashyap (2006) bemoan the still dominant (albeit declining) share of state-owned banks in total bank lending and continuing government pressure on these banks to direct too much credit to less-profitable state-owned enterprises to support employment. Similarly, Richard Podpiera (2006) concludes that, despite the de jure removal of the ceiling on loan interest rates, pricing of bank loans remains largely undifferentiated and that large state-owned banks do not appear to take enterprise profitability into account when making lending decisions. And Anderson (2006b) emphasizes the still relatively low profitability of China's state-owned banks, the high dependence of bank profitability on the huge gap between lending and deposit interest rates, and the likelihood that this interest rate gap will narrow markedly in the period ahead as financial liberalization and globalization proceed.

What is much less widely agreed on is how a more appreciated and more flexible exchange rate for the renminbi would affect bank reform. Too often, the effects of currency reform have also been confused with the effects of further capital account liberalization.

One popular view is that going much beyond the existing gradualist approach to currency reform would be too dangerous for the still fragile banking system. Mindful of financial crises in other emerging economies over the past dozen years, proponents of this view argue that a large renminbi appreciation could generate serious currency mismatches for banks and their customers. They worry as well that appreciation could bring in its wake a sharp reduction in growth, making it much harder to maintain the trend decline in banks' nonperforming loans. They point out too that China's financial infrastructure does not yet possess hedging instruments adequate for protecting market participants against a marked increase in exchange rate volatility. Their bottom line is that further strengthening of the banking system—and of the financial system more broadly—is a necessary precondition for bolder currency reform.

Others take a nearly opposite tack, seeing bolder currency reform as the ally rather than the enemy of banking reform. They offer the following rebuttals.

China's banks and their customers are much less vulnerable to currency mismatches than were their counterparts in earlier emerging-market financial crises (Goldstein 2007b).[14] After all, China is a net creditor—not a net debtor—in its overall foreign exchange position. Exporters have lower debt-equity ratios than firms in other sectors. Most of China's largest exporters are foreign owned and do not raise the bulk of their financing in the domestic market. Where the authorities require bank capital to be held in US dollars, reports indicate that the associated currency risk is hedged.

Best estimates suggest that 10 to 15 percent appreciation in the real effective exchange rate would reduce real GDP growth rate by 1 to 1.5 percent a year over a two- to three-year period—hardly a disaster given that in 2007, economic growth was 11.4 percent, consumer prices rose by almost 5 percent, and China's average growth rate over the entire postreform (1978–2006) period was 9.7 percent (National Bureau of Statistics of China 2007, 23).

The excessive accumulation of international reserves that has accompanied the increasingly undervalued renminbi has put Chinese mone-

---

14. Prasad in chapter 2 of this volume reaches a similar conclusion: "There is little evidence . . . that Chinese banks have large exposure to foreign currency assets or external liabilities denominated in renminbi that would hurt their balance sheets greatly if the renminbi were to appreciate in the short run."

tary authorities in a no-win dilemma, with increasing risk to the banking system.[15]

If the authorities did not sterilize the large increase in reserves, the resulting explosion of bank credit and of monetary aggregates would probably have been so large as to generate a watershed surge in nonperforming bank loans and domestic inflation. Indeed, even with the ambitious sterilization efforts of the past five years, there were costly bank credit booms in 2003, the first quarter of 2004, and the first half of 2006. In 2007 consumer price inflation also hit nearly 5 percent, while producer prices by December 2007 rose by almost 8 percent compared with December 2006.[16] With sticky nominal interest rates on deposits and loans, sharp increases in inflation translate into low—and sometimes, negative—real interest rates. This, in turn, can fuel overinvestment, slow or even negative growth in bank deposits, and speculative runs in equity and property markets.

Alternatively, the authorities can take the high sterilization route. But then the increase in inflation—which would otherwise appreciate the real exchange rate—is cut off. Similarly, if the growth rate of net domestic assets of the central bank is kept too low in a fast growing economy, then the excess demand for money will induce the very expenditure patterns and balance-of-payments inflows that will perpetuate the economy's external imbalance. Also, as suggested earlier, the need both to place large amounts of low-yielding sterilization bills with the banks and to repeatedly raise bank reserve requirements (which likewise pay low interest rates) imposes a "tax" on the banks that is not captured in standard calculations of the "cost of sterilization." If the banks absorb this tax themselves, then their profitability—which is already low by international standards—is further compromised; if the banks instead pass on the cost of sterilizing to depositors in the form of lower deposit rates, then depositors have an incentive to put their money elsewhere. Without adequate growth of bank deposits, bank loan growth will ultimately be constrained unduly. And if the authorities rely on window guidance—instead of sterilization—to control how much and to whom banks lend, then the longer-term objective of teaching credit officers how to evaluate creditworthiness and of developing a "credit culture" in China's banks is undermined.

As indicated earlier, low flexibility of the exchange rate—even with remaining controls on capital flows—also means that interest rate decisions will often be delayed beyond what would be desirable for domestic stabilization purposes—for fear that more decisive interest rate policy would trigger large capital flows, which in turn would put undue pressure on

---

15. Yu (2007b) puts it succinctly: "In summary, to achieve simultaneously the objectives of the maintenance of a stable exchange rate, a tight monetary policy, and a good performance of the commercial banks is impossible."

16. In December 2007, the CPI in China was 6.5 percent higher than a year earlier; core inflation (i.e., excluding food), however, was much lower—on the order of 1 percent.

the exchange rate. This too is not good for banks. Much of good central banking today involves taking preemptive interest rate action to ward off both sharp growth slowdowns and inflation excesses. If, for example, the authorities wait too long to move interest rates in response to an over-heated economy, the dose of monetary tightening may have to be much larger than if they acted earlier; the more volatile the operating environment facing banks, the higher the risk that bank credit growth will be too rapid or too slow. Similarly, if the monetary authorities are constantly tinkering with export taxes, restrictions on capital inflows and outflows, and the pace and volatility of the exchange rate crawl—as substitutes for more independent monetary policy and a more market-determined exchange rate—it is highly debatable that the need for banks and their customers to hedge against this kind of wider policy uncertainty will be less costly than hedging against greater exchange rate volatility.

Champions of the view that bolder currency reform should not be held hostage to the pace of financial-sector reform do not maintain that the remaining fragility of the Chinese banking system is irrelevant for the sequencing of other reforms. But they contend that capital account convertibility—not currency appreciation and flexibility—should await further strengthening of the banking system (Prasad 2007, Goldstein and Lardy 2003b, Williamson 2003). Here the argument is that so long as restrictions on capital outflows are reduced gradually rather than precipitously, then the authorities will have adequate room for maneuver in countering, say, an unanticipated setback on bank reform or an unexpected large fall in China's growth rate. In contrast, if bank fragility is paired with the potential for large-scale capital flight, then, as other emerging economies have discovered, the management of such a crisis is inherently much more difficult. Yu Yongding (2007b) observes that if Chinese households and firms decided for whatever reasons, rational or irrational, to suddenly increase markedly the share of their assets invested abroad, capital outflow in a short time span could be as much as $500 billion, with very unpleasant consequences for the Chinese economy.

Under this view, the right sequencing of reforms is to continue with bank reform and to move now to reduce significantly both the undervaluation and inflexibility of the renminbi—but to wait until China's financial system is on stronger footing before opening up too widely the doors on capital outflows.

Looking ahead, the conundrum facing China's banking system can be summarized as follows. The authorities have indicated, quite sensibly, that they wish to expand the role of commercial paper, bond, and equity markets to diversify (away from banks) the sources of external financing available to firms. In addition, they have expressed an understandable intention to gradually lift restrictions on capital outflows—in part to offer savers a higher rate of return and in part—given China's large global current account surplus—to take upward pressure off the renminbi. Such moves in the direction of further financial liberalization and globalization are likely, however, to have the competitive effect of reducing over time the existing 350 to 400 basis point spread between deposit and loan interest rates—since Chinese investors and savers will then both have a wider set of alternatives to domestic banks. As Anderson (2006b) points out, even a 100 basis point decline in the deposit-loan spread would have wiped out all the profits of state-owned banks in 2005. So how to square this circle? Yes, maybe costs can be reduced further by larger cutbacks in the number of branches and bank employees. Yes, maybe Chinese banks can increase somewhat the share of profits coming from fees so as to offset partially the fall in interest income. But in the end, two things would seem to be required. First, credit allocation decisions will have to be improved so less income is spent on dealing with bad loans. This in turn would seem to imply that the influence of political factors on loan decisions has to be reduced vis-à-vis the influence of arm's-length, commercial considerations. Can this be done other than by further privatization of banks, including probably raising the limit on foreign ownership of banks? We doubt it. Second, the burden increasingly imposed on bank profitability by the sterilization requirements of defending a seriously undervalued renminbi will need to be lowered. Can this be done other than by reducing the amount of intervention in the exchange market? Again, we doubt it.

External Adjustment, Global Imbalances, and the Rising Risk of Protectionism

China's exchange rate policy also carries important implications for China's own external adjustment, the correction of global imbalances, public policy toward sovereign wealth funds (SWFs), the operation of the international exchange rate system, and efforts to maintain forward momentum on globalization. In this regard, among the most interesting issues in the ongoing debate are the following:

- Given the wide range of estimates of renminbi misalignment, can one be confident that the renminbi really is seriously undervalued?

- If China did implement a sizeable revaluation/appreciation of the renminbi, would it be effective in reducing substantially China's large global current account surplus?

- Would the costs of a large renminbi revaluation be prohibitively high?

- What explains the large surge in China's current account surplus between 2004 and 2007?

- Will the effect of renminbi revaluation on global imbalances be larger (smaller) than sometimes assumed because it will (not) lead to sympathetic revaluations in other Asian and emerging-market currencies?

- With China's reserves topping $1.5 trillion at year-end 2007 and with the recent establishment of its own SWF, what will be the impact, and what principles should guide the fund's operations?

- Should the IMF have regarded China's large-scale, prolonged, one-way intervention in exchange markets since 2003 as currency manipulation, and how should IMF exchange rate surveillance be conducted going forward?

- Are the several currency bills now before the US Congress a serious threat to open markets, or are they a "third best" policy response to a beggar-thy-neighbor exchange rate policy?

Renminbi Undervaluation

Some argue that China should not have been expected to appreciate earlier and more forcefully because no one really knows the "right" or "equilibrium" exchange rate.[17] They note that existing studies yield a wide range of estimates of misalignment. An IMF study by Steven Dunaway and Xiangming Li (2005), for example, maintains that estimates of renminbi undervaluation range from zero to nearly 50 percent.[18] Furthermore, Dunaway, Lamin Leigh, and Li (2006) argue that a more definitive answer is unlikely to emerge soon because of data problems, instability in the underlying relationships, and lack of consensus on the proper methodology.

Others (Goldstein 2004, 2007b) find the evidence in support of a large renminbi undervaluation increasingly robust and, by now, simply overwhelming. They note that China's global current account surplus has grown without interruption from 1 percent of GDP in 2001, to 9 percent of GDP in 2006, to an estimated 11 percent of GDP in 2007; that China's net capital account position has usually also been in surplus over this period, sometimes becoming even larger relative to GDP than the trade balance surplus; that China's real effective exchange rate through January 2008 has actually depreciated on a cumulative basis over this period (see footnote 3)—notwithstanding the 15 percent nominal appreciation of the renminbi relative to the US dollar; that China's monthly intervention in the exchange market has been persistent, one-way, and growing in size; and that China's domestic economy has been growing at or above its potential.

---

17. Some in this camp (Mundell 2004) also maintain that a fixed exchange rate has served China well, that it could continue to do so, and that claims of "overheating" of the economy are misguided.

18. Similarly, Ahearne et al. (2007) find that renminbi appreciation of 5 to 25 percent would be required to reduce China's global current account surplus by between 3½ to 6½ percent of GDP. Crockett, writing in chapter 9 of this volume, concludes that there is wide agreement that the renminbi is both undervalued and insufficiently flexible but finds little agreement either on the size of the undervaluation or on how the existing misalignment should be corrected (e.g., large jumps versus small, gradual steps).

Taking these developments together, any reasonable back-of-the envelope calculation aimed at finding the level of the renminbi that would eliminate China's global current account surplus would generate a large (and growing) estimate of renminbi undervaluation. A variety of studies suggest that each 10 percent change in China's real effective exchange rate is associated with a change of 2 to 3.5 percent of GDP in China's global trade balance (Goldstein 2007b). Thus eliminating China's global current account surplus would require a 30 to 55 percent real appreciation of the renminbi. Just to cut the surplus roughly in half (say, reducing it by 6 percent of GDP) would imply a 17 to 30 percent undervaluation. Of course, in earlier years (say, in 2003 and 2004) when China's global surplus was much smaller, the implied undervaluation would be lower—but still not small. The fact that China's large current account surpluses have occurred when the domestic economy has also been booming means that China is in what James Meade (1951) called a "nondilemma" situation, where exchange rate appreciation moves the economy simultaneously closer to both external and internal balance.

Those who claim that the renminbi undervaluation verdict is clear cut concede that the relevant empirical literature has spawned a wide range of estimates but argue that this reflects largely a lack of comparability across studies. Some studies (Goldstein and Lardy 2006) assume that the objective is to eliminate entirely China's external imbalance, while others (Ahearne et al. 2007) assume that only part of this imbalance should or could be eliminated within the specified period. Some authors assume that exchange rate revaluation would be undertaken on its own, while others assume that revaluation would be paired with a macro policy that maintained a constant level of aggregate demand; in the former case, the contractionary effect of revaluation reduces the demand for imports in the second round, while in the latter case, there is no second-round effect on import demand.

Some studies opt for modeling explicitly the high import content in China's exports, while others ignore it; when the import content in exports is taken into account, renminbi revaluation leads to a smaller export-price increase than when it is not so assumed. Some studies assume higher export and import price elasticities of demand for China's trade than do others. Because China's imports and exports have been growing faster than GDP, the size of its traded-goods sector is larger now than it was even half a dozen years ago. This means that a smaller exchange rate change will be needed, ceteris paribus, to achieve a given trade balance target than when the traded-goods sector was smaller. Studies done at different points in time (even when the same methodology is employed) can produce different estimates of renminbi misalignment.

Some authors obtain point estimates that show very large renminbi undervaluation but do not regard the confidence level on those estimates as sufficiently strong to warrant an undervaluation conclusion (Cheung, Chinn, and Fujii 2007); other authors obtain similar estimates and accept the point estimate. And finally, there are several methodologies for inferring exchange rate misalignments—ranging from the macroeconomic balance approach, to various structural models of exchange rate determination, to a whole family of purchasing power parity models—and different authors have not always chosen the same methodology—even if some of those are regarded as more reliable than others.[19]

The contention of the large undervaluation school is that were one to "standardize" the misalignment exercise and to restrict attention to the better methodologies and the more reasonable assumptions, the large undervaluation verdict would emerge more clearly. They also point out that some of the initial agnostics on renminbi undervaluation have recently come around. In its 2004 Article IV consultation report for China, the International Monetary Fund (IMF 2004, 12) concluded that "it is difficult to find persuasive evidence that the renminbi is undervalued." Two years later the Fund's conclusion was quite different, namely, that "All of these developments point to the currency (the renminbi) as being undervalued and that this undervaluation has increased further since last year's Article IV consultation" (IMF 2006a, 17).

In chapter 4 of this volume, William Cline and John Williamson survey many existing estimates of the equilibrium value of the renminbi. They find that the literature offers widely varying answers. At the same time, only one of the 18 studies in their survey concludes that the renminbi is overvalued. The average estimates indicate substantial renminbi undervaluation—on the order of 20 percent for the real effective exchange rate and 40 percent for the nominal bilateral renminbi-dollar exchange rate. Also, they find that renminbi undervaluation has been increasing over time, with a 17 percent real effective appreciation needed in studies using data for the 2000–2004 period versus 27 percent for studies based on data for the 2005–07 period.

In explaining why there is such a wide range of estimates, Cline and Williamson argue that the available methodologies for calculating and inferring equilibrium exchange rates differ significantly in their reliability. They regard the approach based on fundamental equilibrium exchange rates (and macroeconomic balance) superior to both the purchasing power parity (PPP) approach and the approach based on behavioral equilibrium exchange rates. They strongly suspect that the PPP estimates overstate the needed degree of renminbi appreciation; the approaches based on fundamental equilibrium exchange rates and behavioral equilibrium exchange rates tend to produce similar estimates of renminbi undervaluation.

In his comments on the Cline-Williamson paper, Jeffrey Frankel concludes that the lack of consensus on renminbi misalignment militates

---

19. See IMF (2006b) for a discussion of different methodologies for assessing misalignment of exchange rates.

against giving either the IMF or the US Treasury legal mandates to assess exchange rate misalignments and to levy penalties if corrections by the erring governments are not forthcoming. After making a plea for reporting estimates of percentage undervaluation in logarithms, Frankel examines the pros and cons of alternative methodologies for estimating equilibrium exchange rates. On the whole, he is less critical of the PPP approach and more critical of the other two approaches than are Cline and Williamson. While he shares the broad conclusion that the renminbi is undervalued, he notes that the new price data for China recently published by the United Nations' International Comparison Program (ICP) imply that the renminbi is far less undervalued under the extended PPP approach than previously thought. He maintains that the most plausible explanation for China's growing trade surplus is that it is the product of tumbling trade barriers against China's exports and a substantial pre-existing cost advantage.

In the second comment on the Cline-Williamson paper, Simon Johnson concludes that a balanced approach using two or three reasonable methodologies can move us a long way in the right direction and can often find a range of plausible estimates for the equilibrium exchange rate. He agrees with Cline and Williamson that PPP methods are most dubious when applied to China because until December 2007, there were no comparable price data for China—and even the new ICP data should be handled with caution. Johnson suggests that less weight should be placed on methods that do not explicitly adopt a multilateral framework. He also posits that the behavior of net foreign assets could be informative in deciding whether external payments are approaching equilibrium.

Effectiveness of Renminbi Appreciation

Another bone of contention is whether a renminbi appreciation would have much effect on China's global current account position. The pessimists cite low wages and high profit margins (which would allegedly permit exporters to absorb the cost of appreciation without raising export prices), a high import content in exports, and low price elasticities of demand for imports and exports as factors that reduce the effectiveness of exchange rate action.[20]

The optimists see it differently. They agree that manufacturing wages in China are very low relative to those in, say, the United States but point out that Chinese productivity is also very low vis-à-vis the US level—and it is the combination of the two (unit labor cost) that matters for competitive-

---

20. Some (Bosworth 2004) also argue that there is no obvious channel by which a renminbi revaluation would correct China's saving-investment imbalance.

ness (Lardy 2006). If wages alone mattered, why is Germany, with the highest wages, the world's largest exporter? Moreover, why are some very-low-wage countries extremely modest exporters? Profit margins in China's traditional export industries (e.g., textiles, electronics, machinery, toys, sporting goods, and furniture) are modest (i.e., in the low to mid-single digits), reflecting strong competition in domestic and external markets. True, profit margins are higher in the newer and faster-growing export industries (e.g., aircraft parts, autos, ships, and telecom equipment). But there is so far little evidence that profit margins move systematically to offset the effects of nominal exchange rate changes on export prices. Anderson (2007b) observes that broad indices of China's export prices have been rising over the past two to three years, in contrast to falling export prices over the previous three-year period.

The import content in Chinese exports is high—on the order of 30 to 35 percent. As suggested earlier, this implies that (unilateral) renminbi appreciation will lower the cost of imported inputs and produce a smaller increase in export prices than if exports had no import content. But this does not imply that renminbi appreciation would be ineffective—only that the exchange rate change needs to be larger to achieve a given trade balance objective. China's role as a regional processing center does distort the meaning of China's bilateral trade imbalances with some industrial countries like the United States, since goods previously exported directly from some supplier countries now get assembled in China and thus show up in China's exports. But these imported inputs wash out when one looks at China's global trade imbalance.

Because the manufactured goods that China exports are typically quite price elastic (around the world) and because the goods that China imports are also produced in China, it is highly likely that the Marshall-Lerner conditions for an effective revaluation are satisfied. Although econometric studies of China's trade flows are still limited and have to contend with poor price data, relatively short sample periods, and large structural and cyclical changes, more researchers are finding significant price elasticities of demand.[21]

Optimists also make the debating point that if the demand for China's exports really was price inelastic, then the authorities should hardly fear revaluation, since higher export prices would then increase—not decrease—export revenue.

---

21. See Goldstein (2007b) for a summary of the results of many of these studies. In view of the difficulties of estimating the price elasticities for China's trade, some analysts choose instead to simply assume reasonable values for those elasticities. For example, Cline (2005) assumes that the import and export elasticities of demand are each unity. Anderson (2006a) assumes that the sum of the elasticities is just slightly above one.

Costs of a More Appreciated Renminbi

Even if a significant renminbi appreciation/revaluation would be effective in reducing China's large external imbalance, some analysts—including many in China—claim that the internal cost of such a policy would be too high in terms of China's growth, employment, and social stability. In his comments on this chapter, Fan Gang points out that in gauging the impact of a large renminbi appreciation, Chinese leaders have to be sensitive to the employment prospects of 300 million underemployed rural laborers (who each earn about $500 per year), as well as to another 300 million immigrant workers (with average earnings of about $1,000 per year). The Chinese authorities may also be deterred, according to Fan, by the concern that even a large renminbi appreciation is unlikely to diminish foreign pressure on China, especially from the United States; after all, job losses in Chinese export industries are more likely to be made up by job gains in countries like Vietnam and Bangladesh—not the United States; the overall US current account position may not change; the US dollar will likely keep falling due to the subprime mortgage turmoil and other factors; and even if the renminbi were to be revalued by 30 percent today, Fan posits that the US Congress and the markets might well request another similar jump soon. As a poor country with many potential risks and shocks before it, it may be wiser for China to take small steps in exchange rate adjustment.

The counterargument that the costs of a large renminbi appreciation should be manageable stresses the following observations. The last time China's real effective exchange rate exhibited a large real appreciation, namely, between 1994 and early 2001, when it appreciated by nearly 30 percent, China's growth did fall but still averaged 9 percent per year and in no single year did growth drop below 7.5 percent. As mentioned earlier, recent estimates (Shu and Yip 2006, Anderson 2006a) point to a 10 percent real effective revaluation of the renminbi lowering economic growth by roughly 1 percent a year (over a two- or three-year period). If even this modest decline in growth were seen to be too contractionary, revaluation could be paired with an increase in government expenditure on health, education, and pensions, reducing the need for precautionary savings and contributing to a reduction in China's external imbalance.

Employment growth has been noticeably slower during the recent period when investment and export-led growth have been most pronounced than during the period when China's economic growth was oriented more toward consumption (Lardy 2007). Employment in China's export industries accounts for roughly 6 percent of total employment—not 30 or 40 percent (Anderson 2007d). Tens of millions of Chinese workers lost jobs when state-owned enterprises were reformed in the mid- to late 1990s; if there was no social meltdown during that reform, why should there be one after a renminbi revaluation? If the concern is with income losses in low-margin traditional export industries, why not introduce a trade adjustment assistance package along with a renminbi revaluation? Since China's exports are produced more in the high-income coastal provinces than elsewhere, exchange rate action that reduces profitability in export industries should not exacerbate income inequality in China. And if the concern is that farmers and other rural inhabitants will be hurt by the lower cost of food imports following a revaluation, why can't the authorities take fiscal measures to cushion the impact of revaluation on that sector's standard of living?

Explaining the Surge in China's Global Trade Surplus

One of the yet unsolved mysteries on the external front is what was primarily responsible for the upsurge in China's global trade (and current account) surplus between 2004 and 2007? How does one account for an almost quadrupling of net exports of goods and services as a share of GDP, from 2.5 percent in 2004 to an estimated 9 percent in 2007?[22] Several hypotheses—not mutually exclusive—have been put forward, with different implications for China's exchange rate policy.

One hypothesis, highlighted by Lardy (2007), is that differential growth in total factor productivity between traded and nontraded goods has made Chinese goods far more competitive in international markets than is suggested by conventionally calculated real effective exchange rates. In short, while China's conventionally calculated real effective exchange rate changed little over this period, appropriately measured, the renminbi appears to have depreciated significantly since June 2005. The "real" adjustment in the JPMorgan index is based on the rate of change of "core" prices for finished manufactured goods, excluding food and energy, for the country in question compared with its trading partners.

But this methodology appears to be a poor measure of the change in the prices of China's exports. Despite a 9 percent appreciation of the renminbi vis-à-vis the US dollar between June 2005 and August 2007, the price of Chinese goods imported into the United States was basically unchanged.[23] The available evidence does not support the view that Chinese firms producing exports cut their margins in order to avoid passing through the renminbi appreciation to US consumers. If anything, profit margins in Chinese industry, which produces almost all of China's exports, have increased (World Bank 2007, 7). The most likely explanation is that produc-

---

22. As noted earlier, the explosion of the global current account surplus was similar—from 3.6 percent of GDP in 2004 to an estimated 11 percent of GDP in 2007.

23. Prices of Chinese imports in August 2007 were 0.2 percent less than in June 2005, according to the estimates of the International Price Program of US Department of Labor, Bureau of Labor Statistics. These estimates are not based on unit values of imports but take into account the changing composition and quality of imported goods.

tivity growth in those industries exporting to the United States was sufficiently large that firms could more than absorb the adverse effect of the rising value of the renminbi on their earnings. The combination of a nominal appreciation of the renminbi vis-à-vis the dollar of about 9 percent and unchanged prices of Chinese imports in the United States suggests that total factor productivity growth in China's export industries was 9 percent between June 2005 and August 2007. Over this period US prices rose about 7 percent. Since the prices of Chinese exports fell 9 percent while prices in the United States rose 7 percent, the Chinese currency would have had to appreciate in nominal terms against the dollar by about 16 percent to maintain the initial level of competitiveness of Chinese exports in the US market. But the rate of nominal appreciation was only about half that pace, so Chinese goods became much more competitive vis-à-vis import-competing goods made in the United States. And the prices of imports into the United States from countries other than China rose 10.9 percent over the same period, so Chinese goods gained even greater competitiveness vis-à-vis alternative external suppliers to the US market than they did against US domestic producers (US Department of Labor, Bureau of Labor Statistics 2007). A key implication of this "hidden Chinese export productivity" story is that if recent productivity trends were to continue, the renminbi would need to appreciate by a much larger degree against the US dollar than in the recent past for exchange rates to contribute to a deterioration in China's competitive position vis-à-vis the United States.

Some find this hidden productivity story unpersuasive because it covers only China's exports to the United States (almost 30 percent of total exports), and these may not be representative (e.g., on product mix) of total Chinese exports. Anderson (2007b), for example, argues that China's export prices for both traditional exports (like clothing and toys) and IT electronics have been rising by 3 to 4 percent a year since 2004—whereas they were falling by 3 to 4 percent a year during the 1995–2003 period.[24] He also wonders why, if rising productivity is responsible for the net export surge, we have not seen more of a continuous move toward more domestic sourcing in labor-intensive export industries. He speculates that China's now large export market share in some products (toys, footwear, and other low-end products) permits Chinese exporters to pass on their increased costs to overseas buyers. This cannot go on indefinitely if rising wages and renminbi appreciation persist, but he thinks it has been going on recently.

Fan, in his comment on this chapter, expresses some support for the hidden productivity thesis. Specifically, he points out that rapid productivity growth helps to explain China's good inflation performance, why

---

24. Anderson's analysis is based on Chinese export price data and Hong Kong data on prices of goods of Chinese origin that are reexported from Hong Kong. Unlike the price data analyzed in Lardy (2007), both of these are calculated from unit values.

profitability in Chinese corporations has recently been high, and why import substitution has been such a prominent feature of the recent net export surge.

A second hypothesis is that the large and growing trade surplus is primarily cyclical, with little relation to exchange rate developments. Anderson, in his comment on this chapter, as well as in some earlier work (Anderson 2007c), argues as follows: Any good theory about China's surging trade surplus has to confront several facts, namely, that the shift in the trade balance occurred primarily in the heavy industrial products (aluminum, machine tools, cement, key chemical products, and especially, steel and steel products); that it involved more of a collapse in imports than a jump in exports; that the net export shift was highly correlated with domestic demand swings; that gross domestic saving grew much faster than gross investment; and that profit margins in heavy industry fell during the initial increase in the trade surplus.

His explanation is as follows: The 2000–2003 period witnessed a boom in property, housing construction, and auto sales, brought on by rapid structural changes in home ownership and new consumer finance instruments; with sharply rising profits in industrial materials and machinery sectors, local governments and state enterprises invested heavily in smelting, refining, and machinery production. The boom soon turned into a bubble, and by early 2004, the authorities drastically curtailed lending for real estate and construction; the central government, however, could not slow the pace of investment in heavy industry. As a result, productive capacity grew much faster than domestic demand for the next three years; as profits fell, China began to cut its surplus capacity aggressively by cutting way back on imports and becoming a sizeable net exporter in a few industrial categories.[25] In short, it is as if a large stock of new excess capacity sprang out of the ground and subsequently played havoc with China's balance of payments. Anderson expected the excess capacity problem to soon abate. Indeed, as late as March 2007, Anderson (2007a, 35) argued that "China's trade surplus is already peaking and should begin to fall by the latter part of the year." He saw China returning to a more balanced trade position in the course of 2008 and 2009.

But questions also arise about the "cyclical, excess capacity" view of the surge in China's trade balance. Most fundamentally, unless one understands what is driving investment decisions in what later become industries with excess capacity, it is difficult to either forecast when excess capacity will contract/expand or to apportion influence among many plausible factors. Illustrative of the former point, writing in July 2007, Anderson (2007c) acknowledged that there was no sign whatsoever of stabi-

---

25. Anderson in his comments on chapter 1 notes that the fall in profits in heavy industry reflected a dramatic rise in production volumes, which more than offset the fall in unit margins.

lization of the trade balance, that excess capacity in the steel industry (which accounted for about a quarter of the trade surplus surge) showed no sign of a slowdown, and that after-tax profit margins in overall heavy industry had risen—in part because Chinese firms were doing a better job of exploiting export opportunities. More striking, even though the exchange rate allegedly had practically no role in the origin of the net export surge, Anderson (2007b, 9) recently recommended renminbi appreciation ". . . as the only real tool left available to the authorities to offset the effects of excess capacity creation. . . ."

But then how do we know that Chinese producers did not take the expected level of the exchange rate into account when making investment in tradable goods industries? After all, an undervalued exchange rate offered the safety valve of better access to overseas markets if domestic demand proved less buoyant than they expected. Similarly, doesn't an increasingly undervalued exchange rate and the spur it gives to exports help explain why investment and profits have slowed much less in this investment cycle than in earlier ones? And why should the same Chinese producers who allegedly paid no attention to the exchange rate in 2004–06 in making investment decisions now do so if the renminbi appreciates faster this year and next?

Yet a third explanation for the post-2003 net export surge comes from Mussa, whose paper appears in chapter 8 of this volume. He employs the "monetary approach" to the balance of payments not only to explain the net export surge but also to elucidate the corresponding and seemingly bizarre improvement in China's national saving-investment balance despite exceptional growth in investment.

Mussa argues that several features of China's economy make application of the monetary approach relevant and fruitful:

- China has maintained both a fixed/tightly managed exchange rate and capital controls during this period.

- The monetary aggregates in China are very large relative to the size of the economy (e.g., broad money is 150 percent of GDP versus 50 percent in the United States, and the Chinese monetary base accounts for 37 percent of GDP versus 6 percent in the United States).

- With annual growth of nominal GDP running about 16 percent in China, annual growth of the demand for base money is also large (about 6 percent of GDP).

- There is a remarkably stable relationship between base money and nominal GDP in China.

- Unlike the US Federal Reserve, the Chinese monetary authorities do not automatically adjust their net domestic assets to meet fluctuations in the demand for base money—instead, they adjust the growth of net domestic assets to offset increases in the supply of base money resulting from excessive inflows of foreign exchange.

- Foreign reserve inflows have fluctuated widely over the past decade (ranging from 0.4 percent of GDP in 1998 to 14 percent of GDP in 2007).

A key equilibrium condition is that the demand for base money has to equal the supply of base money, where the latter is composed of the net domestic assets and net foreign assets of the monetary authority. In periods when the ex ante demand for base money is growing rapidly but the monetary authority chooses to meet only part of this growing demand by expanding its net domestic assets, then the remainder of that demand will be satisfied by the foreign component of the monetary base—that is, by an increase in the net foreign assets of the monetary authority (that is, by an increase in international reserves). The increase in international reserves is, in turn, equal to the current account plus the capital account in the balance of payments.

Mussa shows that a key prediction of the monetary approach tracks the evolution of China's balance of payments quite well over the 1994–2006 period, including the net export surge of 2003–06. In that latter period, China's nominal GDP increased cumulatively by 75 percent, and base money expanded by 72 percent. The increasing undervaluation of the renminbi during this period contributed to the expansion in China's current account surplus; increasing capital inflows added to upward pressure on the exchange rate. The authorities intervened massively in the foreign exchange market to hold their exchange rate target, and they engaged in large-scale sterilization to prevent the huge intervention from being fully reflected in the supply of base money and in the inflation rate. These sterilization operations resulted in a large fall in net domestic assets of the monetary authority. All this in turn meant that the rapidly growing demand for base money was satisfied via the balance of payments—including the explosion of China's net exports from 2002 through 2006. For the 1994–2006 period as a whole, Mussa demonstrates that there is a reasonably close and positive relationship between the excess of base money growth over the growth of net domestic assets on the one hand and China's current account surplus on the other (both expressed as a share of GDP). The relationship between them is not one-for-one because other factors (for example, the capital account) also affect the current account, but Mussa maintains that the similarity of large swings in the two series is unmistakable.

The main policy implication of the monetary approach is that so long as the authorities continue to engage in heavy sterilization while economic growth and demand for base money are increasing rapidly, they will perpetuate the large external surplus by creating a monetary disequilibrium.[26] If they want to reduce the large surplus, they should cut back both on sterilization and on their massive exchange market intervention.

The monetary approach too is not without questions. Anderson, in his comment on this chapter, offers four criticisms of the monetary approach, as employed by Mussa:

- The dominant line of causation should be from an increase in China's reserves to a drop in the central bank's net domestic assets (what he calls the "balance-of-payments approach to money")—and not the other way around.

- Neither the ratio of cash to M2 nor banks' base money multiplier have been stable over time in China—contrary to the assumptions of the monetary approach.

- There has been no obvious upward pressure on either money market interest rates or long-term bond yields, as there should have been if agents were scrambling for money.

- The monetary approach is incapable of explaining why the household saving rate has remained constant while the corporate saving rate has risen sharply.

Suffice it to say that Mussa finds these criticisms of the monetary approach unpersuasive.

Renminbi Revaluation and Global Imbalances

Another vigorously debated question is the contribution that a renminbi appreciation could or should make to the correction of global payments imbalances, particularly the large US current account deficit, which hit $811.5 billion (6.15 percent of GDP) in 2006 and is running at just a slightly reduced ratio this year.

One school maintains that China's potential and fair contribution to this international problem is quite limited. After all, China's weight in the Federal Reserve's trade-weighted index for the dollar is about 15 percent. A unilateral 20 percent renminbi appreciation against the dollar by itself therefore would translate into only a 3 percent depreciation in the trade-weighted dollar—a move that would perhaps reduce the US global current account deficit by roughly $40 billion to $55 billion—hardly a major

---

26. The thrust of the argument here is similar to the conclusion that large-scale sterilization of reserve increases perpetuates external disequilibrium for a country with a large capital inflow because it prevents that inflow from lowering the interest rate and thereby discouraging further capital inflows.

contribution. The United States should instead raise its own low national saving rate—and particularly decrease government dissavings over the medium to long run—if it wants to significantly improve future US current account deficits and future US net foreign indebtedness (Roach 2007). Claims that foreigners will at some point soon tire of adding dollar assets to their portfolios underplays the decline of "home bias" in investment decisions, the attraction of the US capital market, and the moderate size of the US external financing needs relative to the large stock of financial wealth in US trading partners (Cooper 2005).

The large bilateral US trade deficit with China should not be a matter of concern since it is a country's global current account position that matters; also, the share of the US global trade deficit with emerging Asia has not changed much over the past several years: The share with China has increased while the share with other Asian economies has fallen—just what one would expect from China's emergence as a major regional processing center. A renminbi revaluation will merely induce a substitution away from Chinese products toward other low-cost producers, with little effect on total US imports.

China's large global current account surplus and the current renminbi exchange rate cause no major damage to either the US or the global economy. The US economy has been operating at full employment; the trend decline of employment in US manufacturing has been long running (well before any evidence of renminbi undervaluation); US consumers benefit from low-cost imports from China; and US borrowers benefit from low interest rates, which would otherwise be higher if China were not purchasing as many US government and other dollar-denominated securities in its exchange-market intervention operations. If renminbi appreciation were to generate a wider and rapid depreciation of the US dollar, there might not be enough slack in the economy to accommodate the expansion in US net exports without generating inflationary pressures. If there is a competitive benchmark for currencies in Asia, it is more apt to be the Japanese yen than the renminbi (Park 2007). Other countries benefit from the rapid growth of their exports to China. And China also benefits from this so-called Bretton Woods II arrangement since the low value for the renminbi assists China in dealing with its formidable employment problem and in attracting enough foreign investment to build a world-class capital stock for tradable goods (Dooley, Folkerts-Landau, and Garber 2003).

The opposing view sees much less justification for complacency about global payments imbalances or the undervalued renminbi.

True, a unilateral revaluation of the renminbi would not much affect the real effective exchange rate of the dollar. But China is a competitive benchmark for many others and if other Asian economies follow China's lead by revaluing their currencies, the effects on the dollar and on the US current account deficit would be anything but trivial. Emerging Asia plus

Japan has roughly a 40 percent weight in the Federal Reserve's trade-weighted dollar index. A 20 percent real appreciation in all Asian currencies would translate into an 8 percent real depreciation of the dollar and probably a $100 billion to $140 billion improvement in the US current account deficit (Goldstein 2007b). This is not small potatoes if the objective is to cut the US deficit, say, roughly in half. If China and Japan do not act to remove the currently large undervaluation of their currencies, other Asian economies that have allowed their currencies to appreciate significantly (e.g., Korea) might reverse course and use large-scale intervention to lower the value of their currencies (Park 2007).

The dollar is still overvalued by a considerable degree (Obstfeld and Rogoff 2006). Failure of Asian currencies to share appropriately in the needed real effective depreciation of the dollar would imply either of two undesirable scenarios: either other nondollar currencies—like the euro, the Canadian dollar, and the Australian dollar—would have to appreciate unduly when they already have made an important contribution (having risen in real effective terms since the dollar peak in February 2002 by 26, 20, and 48 percent, respectively) or the total amount of dollar depreciation would be too small to produce a meaningful reduction in the US global deficit (Truman 2005). The fact that financing of the US global current account deficit has relied heavily on official lenders and on short maturity instruments—with much of the proceeds going to stoke consumption rather than investment—ought to be regarded as worrisome (Summers 2004).[27] Recent turbulence in global financial markets linked to the US subprime market illustrates both how quickly risk perceptions can change and how financial contagion can operate. A disorderly correction of the US dollar—coupled with a much lower demand for US equities—could push the Federal Reserve into a thorny dilemma where higher US interest rates were needed to defend the dollar while lower interest rates were called for to limit the contractionary effects of an increasingly weak housing market. And if the US economy does enter or get close to a recession, adverse effects on US trading partners would be widespread. A renminbi revaluation will not necessarily result in a switch of US imports to other low-cost emerging economies if those emerging economies also allow their currencies to appreciate.

Yes, the United States should implement a credible medium-term plan for fiscal consolidation that would help raise the low US national saving rate. But satisfactory resolution of the global imbalance problem should not be an "either or" choice. We need both US fiscal action and a better alignment of key exchange rates, including the renminbi, to obtain the correction of global payments imbalances in the least costly way in terms

---

27. Setser (2007), writing in early October 2007, reports that central banks in developing countries provided almost all of the financing of the US current account deficit over the past four quarters.

of economic growth or inflation for both deficit and surplus countries alike (Mussa 2005).

The market for US government securities is very large, deep, and liquid. When Japan suddenly ceased its exchange market intervention in the second half of 2004 after having intervened (cumulatively) to the tune of about $320 billion in 2003 and the first quarter of 2004, we did not see a major run-up in US interest rates.[28] Emerging economies that have an export basket broadly similar to that of China do suffer a competitive disadvantage from the "export subsidy" (to echo Federal Reserve Chairman Ben Bernanke's (2006) characterization) that a highly undervalued renminbi imparts to China; some US industries are adversely affected as well. Seeking to maintain a highly undervalued renminbi as a means of implementing an investment and export-led growth strategy is not a sensible development plan for China (Lardy 2007), and many of the assumptions made in support of the Bretton Woods II story (e.g., the importance of the export sector in growth and employment, the role of foreign direct investment in financing total investment, the share of the United States in total trade, and the ownership of export industries) simply do not fit the specifics of the Chinese economy (Goldstein and Lardy 2005a).

Recent experience with the effect of the renminbi on other countries' exchange rates in Asia would seem to contradict two alternative assumptions. In the Bretton Woods II thesis, it is argued that Asian economies as a group share a strong self interest in maintaining an undervalued fixed exchange rate (since, among other benefits, it supports employment in their export industries). But if one looks at the evolution of real effective exchange rates for Asian economies from the dollar peak in February 2002 through August 2007, the record is diverse. More specifically, whereas Indonesia (37), Singapore (27), Korea (22), Thailand (15), and the Philippines (20)—call them the "movers"—have registered large appreciations in their real effective rates (ranging from 15 to 37 percent), Hong Kong (–24), Japan (–15), Malaysia (–13), Taiwan (–6), and China (–2)—the "stickers"—have recorded real effective depreciations (ranging from 2 to 24 percent).[29] If self interest is revealed by behavior, the "movers" must have therefore decided that the benefits of resisting real exchange rate appreciation, emphasized in Bretton Woods II, were considerably less than the costs.

At the same time, the diversity of real exchange rate behavior within Asia also casts doubt on the alternative assumption that unless China allows the renminbi to appreciate, nobody else in Asia will do so. Clearly, there must be other factors (e.g., the strength of domestic demand, pres-

---

28. See Ito (2004) for a full discussion of the motives for Japan's large intervention during this period.

29. Percentage appreciation and depreciation calculated from JPMorgan real broad exchange rate indices.

NEW YORK INSTITUTE OF
TECHNOLOGY

sures from capital inflows, inflation threats, and costs of sterilization) besides remaining competitive with China that affect Asian exchange rate policy. Since we cannot observe the counterfactual, it could be of course that we would have seen even more real appreciation among the movers—and much more depreciation among the stickers—if the renminbi had appreciated substantially since February 2002. Still, estimates of the maximum induced effects of renminbi appreciation on other Asian currencies probably need to be lowered. For example, if one assumes that a 20 percent appreciation of the renminbi would elicit no further appreciation among the movers but a 20 percent appreciation among the stickers, then the weight of the appreciating currencies in the Federal Reserve's dollar index (inclusive of China) would be 31 percent (not 40 percent as in the earlier example), and this would lead to about a 6 percent real effective depreciation in the US dollar (about twice as large as for a unilateral renminbi revaluation).

Outside Asia, if one goes down the list of the 25 largest US trading partners and looks for economies that have had depreciating real effective exchange rates or only mildly appreciating ones (from the dollar peak in February 2002 through August 2007) and where this exchange rate behavior could possibly have been influenced by competition with China, Mexico (–8), Israel (–6), Argentina (–4), and India (+7) make the cut;[30] together, those four countries have a weight of 12 percent in the Federal Reserve's trade-weighted dollar index (with the lion's share of that, almost 10 percent, contributed by Mexico).

Looking ahead, Goldstein (2007b) has argued that China's currency policy could generate an unfavorable demonstration effect in other emerging economies. One reading of China's post-2002 experience is that countries should engage in huge, persistent intervention in the exchange market, plus large-scale sterilization, and they too will be able to generate and sustain a highly undervalued real exchange rate, which is advantageous for growth. Were that the message, one might then see in the future much less real exchange rate appreciation in surplus countries and a smaller role for exchange rates in the correction of external imbalances—both bad news. Others would say that such a demonstration effect is quite unlikely. There are many earlier (non-China) examples in Asia of an undervaluation strategy (if one wants such a role model). As noted above, since 2002 some emerging economies in Asia have strongly discouraged real exchange rate appreciation, but some others have not. And the Chinese economy has some features (e.g., a still predominately state-owned banking system that can be persuaded to buy large amounts of low-yielding sterilization bills), not shared by other emerging economies, that contribute to the sustainability of an undervaluation strategy.

---

30. Switzerland (–11) and Saudi Arabia (–23) also appear on the depreciation list, but their exports are much less competitive with those of China.

In chapter 7 of this volume, Takatoshi Ito examines the influence of the renminbi on exchange rate policy in other Asian economies. He shows that exchange rate regimes in East Asia are diverse and uncoordinated: Japan has recently followed a free float; Korea, Singapore, Thailand, Indonesia, Malaysia, and the Philippines have adopted managed floating regimes with varying degrees of basket currency features; and Hong Kong and China have adopted hard and (de facto) crawling pegs, respectively, to the US dollar.

Ito maintains that it would be in the interest of most Asian economies to allow faster appreciation of their currencies. Such currency appreciation is also needed to resolve global payments imbalances. But there is a coordination failure: Many Asian economies are reluctant to see their currencies appreciate too much—lest they lose undue competitive advantage to China, while China itself worries that much appreciation of the renminbi—if not matched by other Asian currencies—will result in excessive job losses in its export industries. Lack of communication and commitment thus prevent both sides from acting in the common interest. Ito proposes the establishment of an Asian currency unit (ACU), cum a commitment by each Asian economy to aim at a stable relationship between its currency and the ACU, as a possible solution to the regional coordination problem.

In his empirical work, Ito finds that whatever the official pronouncements, the renminbi does not behave as a basket currency; instead, it has become a de facto crawling peg against the US dollar. At the same time, other Asian currencies put a much lower weight on the US dollar in their exchange rate policies than does China. Also, the influence of the renminbi on other Asian currencies cannot be separated (econometrically) from the influence of the US dollar on these currencies. After comparing both the attributes of alternative currency baskets for Asia (based on either 3 or 13 currencies) and considering the currently weak political cohesion in East Asia, Ito concludes that all that can be done for now is to prepare the relevant economic tools that could be used if and when political forces make greater currency coordination feasible.

In commenting on Ito's paper in chapter 7, Yung Chul Park takes a critical look at the Asian regional currency unit as a means of promoting greater East Asian coordination on exchange rate policy. He notes that in 2006, policymakers from the ASEAN-plus-three economies agreed to explore steps to create regional currency units as a sequel to two other regional initiatives, namely, the Chiang Mai Initiative and the Asian Bond Initiative.

Drawing on the experience of European countries with the European currency unit (ecu) as a precursor to the euro, Park recalls that the ecu was not able to deliver symmetry in adjustment between weak and strong currencies. He notes that the absence of a regional currency unit has generally also not stood in the way of developing markets for bonds denominated in a basket currency. Park concludes that so long as the yen remains a free floating currency and so long as China remains reluctant to revalue significantly its currency, a regional currency unit will be of little use as a surveillance indicator for coordination of exchange rate policy.

In his comments, also appearing in chapter 7, Jean Pisani-Ferry observes that prior to the autumn of 2007, Europe largely adopted a posture of benign neglect toward the renminbi. In contrast, the United States has for a while now been a vocal critic of China's exchange rate policy. Pisani-Ferry considers the factors that could account for this difference in attitudes between the two sides of the Atlantic.

He rejects the notion that China does not matter much to Europe: EU exports to China exceeded US exports to China by almost half in 2006, whereas the EU imports from China as well as the weight of the renminbi in the euro's effective exchange rate were only slightly lower than the comparable figures for the United States. Similarly, he rejects the argument that appreciation of the renminbi has little effect on the value of the euro. While it is true that Europeans are divided on exchange rate policy, they have been no less divided on trade matters, but that has not prevented them from having a common trade policy. He speculates that a strongly worded communiqué of the euro area finance ministers in October 2007 and the decision to send a high-level EU mission to Beijing to discuss exchange rate policy probably signal the end of Europe's benign neglect toward the renminbi. In the end, Pisani-Ferry postulates that Europeans are probably slower to react to external developments than Americans but also that an increasingly active European stance on China's exchange rate policy is in the cards—especially with the euro's sharp appreciation against the US dollar.

The comments of the wrap-up panel in chapter 9 include some views on the renminbi and global payments imbalances. Lawrence Summers concludes that the Chinese economic policy strategy, with its emphasis on export-led growth and on using large-scale exchange market intervention to hold down the value of the renminbi, has been as large a contributor to potential economic instability and to strains in the global financial system as we have seen in many years. He feels that the real concern should be with China's large global surplus rather than with the (negligible) effect of the renminbi on America's workers. Consistent with that view, Summers maintains that it would be better to follow a multilateral—rather than a bilateral, US-led—approach to correcting global payments imbalances. He does not see China's exchange rate as the primary source of the US global current account deficit.

Bergsten argues that if a reasonable goal was to cut the US global current account deficit in half, then one should not downplay the contribution that Asian currency appreciation could and should make to that objective: Indeed, work done at the Peterson Institute suggested that such

Asian currency appreciation could represent one-quarter to one-half of the needed adjustment.

Bergsten, Crockett, and Summers also took the view that all things considered, it was strongly in China's interest to implement faster appreciation of the renminbi and to do it at a faster pace than had occurred over the past two and a half years. In this connection, it was mentioned that there were many more cases where highly managed exchange rates were too slow to respond to market pressures for change than there were cases where exchange rate adjustment occurred and was subsequently viewed as premature or erroneous. There was consensus too that in measuring progress on exchange rate adjustment, the Chinese authorities should look to the real, trade-weighted exchange rate of the renminbi—and not so much to nominal, bilateral exchange rates. All that said, the wrap-up panel also counseled that there be an appropriate degree of modesty in pushing economic policy advice to policymakers in a country that had delivered exceptional growth performance over several decades.

Management of China's International Reserves

In late September 2007, China formally established the China Investment Corporation (CIC) to manage a portion of its massive US$1.5 trillion foreign exchange reserves. Many questions have been raised about the implications of CIC's management of cross-border assets (Truman 2007). Will the CIC be motivated by political considerations rather than conventional risk and rate of return?[31] Because of its potentially large size and method of operation, could the CIC contribute to uncertainty and turmoil in international financial markets? These concerns led a leading economic official of the European Union to warn in September 2007 that the European Union was likely to take steps to restrict investments by sovereign wealth funds (SWFs) that are not transparent.

Although the CIC could become the world's largest SWF, it will at least initially be relatively small and will invest primarily within China. Indeed, the CIC is probably more accurately described as a holding company than an SWF. The latter typically invest entirely off shore. In contrast, the CIC will incorporate Central Huijin, which has existed for a number of years, the conduit through which the government has transferred foreign exchange reserves to a variety of domestic financial institutions as part of their recapitalization and restructuring. To date these injections amount to $66.4 billion (see footnote 5), and it is widely anticipated that the government soon will inject $40 billion into the restructuring of the Agricultural Bank of China and $20 billion into the China Development Bank. Since the

---

31. Summers (2007) contrasts the investment motives of sovereigns and private investors and discusses the potential problems that the motives of sovereign wealth funds could generate.

initial funding of the CIC is only $200 billion, these domestic investments will absorb about two-thirds of the CIC's resources.

In addition, the CIC will absorb China Jianyin Investment (Limited), which manages domestic assets, and will create a third arm responsible for international investments, both strategic and portfolio. Direct strategic investments will presumably be concentrated in energy, resources, and commodities. Some strategic investments may take the form of loans to Chinese domestic companies seeking to expand abroad. And the management of some if not most of the portfolio investments is likely to be outsourced.

The magnitude of these international investments is likely to be limited since there are no concrete plans to transfer additional funds from the state's official reserves to the CIC, and the ongoing flow of foreign exchange purchased by the central bank will continue to be added to state official reserves rather than to the CIC.

Those who do worry about the potential prospective size of the CIC argue that to limit potential economic and political conflicts with its trading partners, the CIC should reject the approach taken by many state-controlled investors in Asia and the Middle East of keeping information secret. The CIC should instead adopt the Norwegian model of full transparency and accountability.[32] Full transparency, it is argued, will ensure both that political intentions are known and fully communicated and that financial and economic disturbances are minimized.

Others argue that transparency is only secondary and could even pose a threat to other priorities. Disclosing essential information—so the argument goes—about assets, investment strategy, or performance could sacrifice some control over how an SWF is administered. Furthermore, CIC management may be concerned that, despite the success of Norway's Government Pension Fund, full transparency could lead to inferior returns or greater volatility in domestic financial markets. Similar state-owned investment firms like Singapore's Government Investment Corporation (GIC) have made these kinds of arguments. Senior officials at GIC have maintained for years that "it is not in the nation's interest to detail our assets and their yearly returns" (Lee Kuan Yew 2001) and that "publishing this information would make it easier for would-be speculators to plan their attacks" (Lee Hsien Loong 2001).

In chapter 5, Edwin Truman examines the future accountability and transparency of the CIC. Expanding on his earlier work (Truman 2007), he presents the results of research on 32 SWFs of 28 countries by scoring them on their structure, governance, transparency and accountability, and be-

---

32. El-Erian (2007) argues that in encouraging transparency and disclosure for SWFs, politicians in industrial countries should focus on issues of governance, process, and risk management.

havior. The highest maximum score is 25 points, and the average score is just over 10 points, with Norway's SWF at the top (with 24 points) and two Abu Dhabi funds at the bottom (with a 0.5 score). On this metric, China's Central Huijin Investment Company scores substantially below the average for all funds. Given the actual and potential size of the new CIC, as well as China's growing weight in the international financial system, Truman suggests that the Chinese authorities should aim to place the CIC at the top league of SWFs. He explains that for China the basic question is what to do with reserves once they are there. He argues that the preferable approach to managing excess foreign reserves is to apply strict economic and financial criteria and to maximize return over a relevant time horizon, subject to risk management constraints. The rest of the world will hold China responsible for its actions to a greater extent than it would a country with much smaller cross-border assets, and the Chinese authorities, so Truman opines, should get used to it. His scoreboard for SWFs is based solely on publicly available information and is intended as a benchmark for a set of best practices. He counsels that now is the time for China to take the lead in helping to develop a set of best practices for SWFs.

Also in chapter 5, Mohamed El-Erian and Brad Setser provide comments and reactions to Truman's paper. While acknowledging that Truman's methodology for rating SWFs has brought a much needed rationality to the debate, El-Erian delves into why several SWFs get poor assessments on Truman's scoreboard yet generate very favorable perceptions for market participants that interact regularly with them. He observes that if Truman's methodology were applied to hedge funds and to private equity groups, they would be rated as low if not lower than the SWF complex; of course, hedge funds and private equity groups are owned by the private sector, while SWFs have governments behind them—a factor that results in greater scrutiny of SWFs. He notes that the behavior, investment savvy, and systemic impact of some SWFs—such as the Abu Dhabi Investment Authority, Singapore's GIC, and the Kuwait Investment Authority—have been observable for a long time. He regards their deployment of their patient capital as a stabilizing influence on the global economy—contrary to the low scores on the Truman rating scale. As such, El-Erian concludes that the ranking of SWFs in the Truman paper reflect more the limited access to information rather than the realities of the marketplace. He also suggests that the Group of Seven (G-7) debtor countries should be cautious in lecturing SWFs and in putting forward an excessively broad agenda for reforms on governance, investment process, and risk management. He prefers a more targeted approach to these subjects within a holistic approach that would also address other legitimate deficiencies in the international system—including questions of representation in multilateral fora.

For his part, Setser shares Truman's view that an expansion of SWFs calls for an increase in their transparency since, among other reasons, citizens of countries with large cross-border assets should be able to assess how their money is being spent. He focuses on what the US data allow us to infer about the current composition of China's external portfolio and on how the creation of the CIC might change the composition of China's demand for US financial assets.

Setser reports that China currently has a large and concentrated bet on a relatively narrow segment of the US fixed-income market and that the case for including equities in China's external portfolio is very strong. The pace of Chinese asset growth is now so rapid that even a modest shift in Chinese demand for US equities could have a dramatic effect on the US market. He underlines that the current governance structure of the CIC is apt to magnify global concerns about the politicization of Chinese investment decisions, that there is a need for the CIC to coordinate with the People's Bank of China (so that the CIC's investment decisions do not undermine the central bank's exchange rate policy), and that the CIC's high cost of funding and its desire to avoid losses from renminbi appreciation could result in the CIC taking excessive risks.

Currency Manipulation and IMF Exchange Rate Surveillance

Another bone of contention is whether, as a member of the IMF, China has been living up to its obligation (as contained in Article IV, Section I of the Fund's charter) to ". . . avoid manipulating exchange rates or the international monetary system in order to avoid effective balance of payments adjustment or to gain unfair competitive advantage over other member countries," and similarly, whether the IMF itself is living up to its obligations to ". . . oversee the compliance of each member country with its obligations," and to ". . . exercise firm surveillance over the exchange rate policies of members."

Some observers have answered one or both those questions with a resounding "no." Bergsten (2005, 2007), Desmond Lachman (2007), Goldstein (2004, 2006a, 2006b, 2007a, 2007b), Goldstein and Mussa (2005), Mussa (2007), and Ernest Preeg (2003), among others, have argued that China's persistent, large-scale, one-way intervention in the exchange market since 2003—at the same time that China's global current account surplus was large and growing and its real effective exchange rate was depreciating—constitutes strong evidence of currency manipulation. Here, currency manipulation can be interpreted to mean persistent policy efforts either to push the real effective exchange rate away from its equilibrium or to prevent it from returning to equilibrium. Those same authors, along with Timothy Adams (2006), David Dodge (2006), Mervyn King (2005), and the IMF's Independent Evaluation Office (IEO 2007), among others, have also suggested that the IMF has been found wanting or worse in its implementation of exchange rate surveillance.

Some other economists—including Anderson (2006a, 2007c) and Frankel (2006)—regard the renminbi as misaligned (undervalued) but do not regard China's exchange rate policy as meriting a "manipulation" finding. In its semiannual Reports to the US Congress on International Economic and Exchange Rate Policies, the US Treasury has become increasingly critical of China's exchange rate policy but has declined to name China as a manipulator because it could not establish "intent" to manipulate.[33] In its recent consultation reports on China (see IMF 2004 versus IMF 2006a), the IMF has moved from criticizing China's currency regime as insufficiently "flexible" to acknowledging that the renminbi is (also) "undervalued"; it has never, however, accused China of manipulating the value of the renminbi. This view is consistent with IMF Managing Director Rodrigo de Rato's (2006) repeated statements that he does not think it would be appropriate for the Fund to serve as a global "umpire" for the exchange rate system. In June 2007 the Fund obtained agreement from the membership to revise its 1977 Principles for the Guidance of Members' Exchange Rate Policies (IMF 2007a, 2007b), which the Fund felt was out-of-date and did not give it enough authority to be more activist on discouraging antisocial exchange rate policy; while the antimanipulation principle was maintained without alteration as a membership obligation, a new principle was added, recommending that members avoid exchange rate policies that result in "external instability." This new principle was regarded as helpful because it is based on outcome not intent and because it would give the Fund the latitude to label a currency as "fundamentally misaligned" without going the full monty to manipulation.

While the ongoing debate on the consistency of China's exchange rate policy with IMF surveillance guidelines has many facets, the opposing main lines of argument for the defense and the prosecution can be summarized as follows.

China's exchange rate policy is being unfairly singled out for criticism. China is not the only country to have recorded large percentage or absolute dollar increases in reserves in recent years, or to have a large global current account surplus relative to its GDP, or to have had a depreciation in its real effective exchange rate (Keidel 2005). Analysis by the US Treasury (2005, appendix) shows that different single indicators produce different orderings of manipulated currencies. It is strange—as argued by Fan in his comment on this chapter—that the country accumulating surpluses is blamed as the manipulator, while the country accumulating deficits (the United States) is not. The international community ought to be concentrating instead on how to put some disciplines on excessive money creation by weak currency countries. The Fund's charter permits

---

33. The IMF did name China as a currency manipulator in 1992–94; see Lardy (1994, 86–90), Frankel and Wei (2007), and Henning (2007).

members a wide choice of currency regimes, including fixed exchange rates, and defense of a fixed exchange rate can involve heavy exchange market intervention. A country that maintains the same parity over an extended period, as China did from October 1997 until July 2005—even resisting pressures to devalue during the Asian financial crisis—cannot be "manipulating" since it has not taken any active measures to obtain an unfair competitive advantage. Requiring China to undertake a large revaluation of the renminbi would risk social instability and would infringe unduly on China's national sovereignty. The concept of currency manipulation itself is ill-defined and nonoperational since many government policies affect exchange rates and the intent of these policies cannot be identified clearly.[34] If a question arises on policy intent, the strong benefit of the doubt should go to the country. After having weighed the evidence, neither the IMF nor the US Treasury has found China guilty of currency manipulation.

The IMF was timely in its criticism of the inflexibility of the renminbi, and labeling China as a currency manipulator would only have discouraged reform. The IMF has no set of penalties (other than the extreme and unlikely one of expulsion from the Fund) for noncompliance with a member's obligations.[35] No country has yet been found in violation of its Article IV obligations since the second amendment of the Fund's Articles of Agreement in the early 1970s, and the requirement to prove intent under the 1977 guidelines on exchange rate surveillance would not have supported a more activist stance on China's exchange rate policies. The term "manipulation" has a conspiratorial connotation that makes it unworkable for negotiations involving sovereign nations. The Fund means the Fund's Executive Board, and there was no consensus among the Fund's major shareholders for a more aggressive stance toward China's exchange rate policy. The Fund should not seek to serve as global "umpire" for the exchange rate system because such a role would conflict with the Fund's role as trusted advisor to its members.

Critics of China's exchange rate policy and of Fund surveillance of that policy do not find such arguments persuasive.

China's exchange rate policy has come under increasing international criticism because that policy is thwarting external adjustment, because it runs counter to China's international obligations as a Fund member and because China is moving too slowly to change it. It is unprecedented for a country of China's size to run a global current account imbalance (of either sign) of 11 percent or more of GDP. There is no other case of a systemically important country that meets all four of the following criteria: It

---

34. Crockett (2007) argues that the macroeconomic policy mix can affect the exchange rate—just as exchange market intervention can.

35. Eichengreen (2007) notes that the Fund has long had only limited leverage with surplus countries that do not borrow from the Fund.

has been intervening in the exchange market to the tune of roughly 10 percent of its GDP for several years running; its global current account surplus relative to GDP has almost quadrupled between 2002 and 2007; its real effective exchange rate by various measures has actually depreciated over this period (see footnote 3); and its domestic economy has been booming. Unlike major oil exporters, China's rapidly rising international reserves do not reflect the conversion of wealth from nonrenewable resources underground into financial assets above ground (Truman 2007). The IMF charter and guidelines do not prohibit exchange market intervention, but they do discourage prolonged, large-scale, one-way intervention because that particular kind of intervention is symptomatic of a disequilibrium exchange rate, which is costly both to the home country and its trading partners. Depending on what is happening to a country's balance of payments, a misalignment of the real exchange rate can occur just as easily from nonmovement as from excessive movement of the nominal exchange rate; similarly, a given level of the nominal exchange rate may be fine when a country's global current account is in deficit or in small surplus but can be problematic when there is a persistent, very large surplus. Blocking needed real exchange rate movement by intervening to keep the nominal rate fixed or quasi-fixed can therefore legitimately be classified as currency manipulation (Goldstein 2004, 2006c, 2007a). Accepting the argument that currency manipulation should be permitted for domestic employment reasons would make it impossible to have meaningful international guidelines discouraging competitive depreciation. If one accepted the Fund's (or the US Treasury's) standard of proof for "intent" to manipulate, there could never be a violation, short of a manipulation "confession" by the country. Judging whether China's exchange rate policy qualifies as manipulation is not a close call that involves giving the benefit of the doubt to the country. It is as clear a case of manipulation as arises outside of textbooks.

The Fund has done serious damage to its reputation both by not identifying earlier the growing undervaluation of the renminbi and by refusing to enforce its regulatory responsibility for discouraging currency manipulation.[36] Had Fund management and staff been warning the Chinese authorities, say since 2004, that their persistent, large exchange intervention was thwarting external adjustment and was in danger of breaching China's obligations, the Fund would have enhanced its credibility inside and outside China as evidence mounted of the internal and external costs of an inflexible and increasingly undervalued renminbi. Major shareholders of the Fund could perhaps have been persuaded to support this policy line if Fund management and staff had made the effort. IMF Manag-

---

36. In recent years, the Fund's forecasts for China's global current account surplus have also been systematically too low—seemingly damaging the Fund's diagnosis and policy prescription for exchange rate policy.

ing Director de Rato gave the game away early on by characterizing the issue not as potential manipulation violation but instead solely as a difference of opinion on the optimal speed of renminbi appreciation.

Through its rulings, the WTO has helped to define what is and what is not internationally acceptable trade policy; by rejecting its regulatory role, the Fund can claim no such clarification on exchange rate policy. "WTO compatibility" means something; no one speaks of "IMF compatibility" because no one knows what it is. A finding of manipulation by the Fund would have exerted more pressure for a change in Chinese exchange rate policy than has a difference of opinion between China and the Fund on the optimal speed of adjustment to greater exchange rate flexibility—both because countries are sensitive to alleged breaches of their international obligations and because such a finding from the Fund could aid chances of success for cases taken to the WTO using exchange rate–related reasons (e.g., Article XV frustration cases). There was nothing missing in the 1977 guidelines for exchange rate surveillance that would have prevented the Fund from enforcing its principle against currency manipulation. The June 2007 revision of these guidelines has added a new principle on avoiding "external instability," but unlike the antimanipulation guideline, the new guideline is only a recommendation—not a membership obligation—and hence, may have little effect. One could easily substitute another (more neutral-sounding) term for manipulation—say, destabilizing exchange market intervention—without changing the substance of Fund surveillance.

Last but not least, the critics assert that by rejecting its regulatory role as global umpire for exchange rates and by not enforcing its guidelines on exchange rate surveillance, the Fund has set the stage for national legislatures (e.g., the US Congress) to step in to fill the breach, with a higher consequent risk of tit-for-tat protectionist trade policy. Perceived "fairness" in exchange rate policy is a sine qua non for a win-win "grand bargain" between the industrial countries and the emerging economies on market access and power-sharing in the governance of the international economy—but this perceived fairness will not take root without the Fund serving as an unbiased, competent global umpire (Goldstein 2006a).

In chapter 8, Mussa appraises Fund surveillance toward China's exchange rate policies. He contrasts the good job that the Fund has done in recognizing and addressing the problem of global payments imbalances (including the correction of the large US global current account deficit) with the "catastrophic failure" on surveillance of China's exchange rate policies. He emphasizes that since 2002, the Chinese authorities have used massive, largely sterilized intervention in exchange markets to resist substantial and warranted appreciation of the renminbi—while China's global current account surplus has exploded. He argues that the real exchange rate of the renminbi has become increasingly undervalued and is being kept in that position by Chinese policies that are intended to resist significant renminbi appreciation.

Mussa maintains that before the summer of 2006, IMF reports spoke only vaguely about the desirability of greater flexibility of the renminbi—without stressing the need for major appreciation—and that the Fund's managing director (de Rato) denied the Fund's regulatory role over members' exchange rate policy and failed to point out forcefully to the Chinese authorities their general and specific obligations on exchange rate policy. His bottom line verdict is that the Fund's application of surveillance to China's errant exchange rate policy qualifies as ". . . Gross misfeasance, malfeasance, and nonfeasance by the Managing Director and more generally by the IMF."

In making his case, Mussa explains that official intervention in the exchange market is always carried out for "balance of payments purposes," that China's holding of foreign exchange reserves has gone beyond any reasonable standard of prudence, that China has been the only major player in the world economy that is making a large and negative contribution to resolving global payments imbalances, that China's intervention has been too prolonged and massive to suggest anything but a consistent effort to resist renminbi appreciation, and that failure by the Fund to enforce its regulatory role on exchange rate policy only serves to prompt others—including national legislatures—to seek redress through other channels.

In his comment on chapter 8, Steven Dunaway responds to Mussa's criticism of IMF surveillance toward China. He notes that a significant part of the Fund's surveillance work—especially on a sensitive issue like exchange rate policy—is done out of the public eye and must be done that way in order for the Fund to maintain its role as a trusted policy advisor. He goes on to argue that the Fund has been pressing China to increase the flexibility of the renminbi since 1999 and that the Fund's managing director, in meetings with Premier Wen Jiabao, stressed the need for greater flexibility and appreciation of the renminbi. Dunaway saw the 2004–06 Fund staff reports for China as conveying a clear picture of evolving IMF staff views on China's exchange rate policy. The main difference between the IMF and the Chinese authorities was on the speed of implementation of policies for rebalancing the Chinese economy, including removing the distortions associated with the prevailing exchange rate regime.

Summers, in commenting on Fund surveillance in chapter 9, is—like Mussa—highly critical of the Fund's performance. He concludes that if anything, Mussa's indictment of their surveillance toward Chinese exchange rate policy probably "understates" the case against the Fund. He characterizes the job that the Fund had done on this matter over the past four years as ". . . indefensible" and argues that the Fund's "culture" on exchange rate surveillance clearly needs to change.

Congressional Currency Bills

Increasingly frustrated with the uninterrupted rise in China's bilateral (with the United States) and global trade surpluses and with the failure of bilateral negotiations to produce a faster and larger appreciation in the renminbi, the US Congress had signaled its intention to pass new currency laws that would penalize any US trading partners that have "manipulated" and/or "fundamentally misaligned" currencies. These bills would replace the Omnibus Trade and Competitiveness Act of 1988 with new legislation that both has more "teeth" to induce compliance and limits the discretion of the US Treasury to avoid a designation of manipulation by arguing that there is insufficient evidence to prove intent to manipulate.

The first such currency bill to gain attention was the bill introduced by Senators Charles Schumer (D-NY) and Lindsey Graham (R-SC) in the US Senate in the fall of 2003; this was a China-specific bill that would have authorized a 27.5 percent tariff on imports from China if negotiations were unsuccessful in eliminating the undervaluation of the renminbi. While 67 senators expressed their intention to vote for the Schumer-Graham bill, its sponsors never brought their bill to a formal vote—delaying a vote several times to see if new bilateral negotiations with China would produce evidence of greater progress and finally, in early 2007, agreeing to join with Senators Max Baucus (D-MT) and Charles Grassley (R-IA) in sponsoring new legislation. Since then, three prominent currency bills have been introduced. The Senate Finance Committee bill (S1607) is sponsored by Senators Schumer, Grassley, Graham, and Baucus (hereafter, SGGB bill), and the Senate Banking Committee bill (S1677) is sponsored by Senators Christopher Dodd (D-CT) and Richard Shelby (R-AL). There is also a House bill (HR 2942), sponsored by Representatives Duncan Hunter (R-CA) and Timothy Ryan (D-OH). The SGGB bill was voted out of the Senate Finance Committee by an overwhelming 20-1 vote; similarly, the Dodd-Shelby bill was endorsed by the Senate Banking Committee by a 17-3 margin. In March 2007, testifying before the Senate Finance Committee, Senator Schumer predicted that the SGGB bill would garner bipartisan support in this session and would be "veto proof."

In chapter 6 of this volume, Gary Clyde Hufbauer and Claire Brunel lay out and discuss the main features of these three bills. Here, it is sufficient to note that

- the US Treasury would continue to provide biannual reports to Congress, identifying countries with manipulated or fundamentally misaligned currencies;
- the criteria for judging a currency to be manipulated would draw heavily on the pointers identified in the 1977 IMF guidelines on exchange rate surveillance (and in the US 1988 Omnibus Act), with the

exceptions that proof of intent is not required and that the US bilateral trade imbalance with that country is an additional indicator;

- where (e.g., SGGB bill) fundamental misalignment replaces manipulation, a distinction is made between misalignment attributable to a list of specific government policy actions (like those used to identify manipulation) and misalignment attributable to other causes (presumably including market failure), with penalties much greater for the former than the latter;

- penalties for noncompliance are usually graduated (as the period of noncompliance get longer)—for example, these penalties may begin with negotiations with the US Treasury and a call on the IMF to initiate a "special consultation" with the country; later on (e.g., after 30 or 180 days), the US executive director at the Fund would be asked to oppose any rule change that benefits the country (e.g., an increase in its quota or any IMF financing), the country would not be able to qualify for "market economy" status, and the country's goods would not be eligible for purchase by the US federal government; further down the road (e.g., after 270 or 360 days), various trade policy measures would kick in (e.g., the Treasury could file a WTO Article XV frustration case, or a misaligned exchange rate would be actionable as a countervailing subsidy, and/or the United States would initiate a WTO dispute settlement case and would consider remedial intervention); and

- there is usually a presidential waiver of the penalties in cases of vital economic and security interests, although some bills (e.g., SGGB bill) provide for a congressional override.

Not surprisingly, these bills have provoked a heated debate about their desirability and likely effectiveness both within the United States and abroad.

Those opposing these bills offer the following arguments. Such national currency legislation will usurp the authority of both the IMF and the US Treasury to deal more effectively and less confrontationally with international disputes involving exchange rate policy. The IMF has just revised and strengthened its guidelines on exchange rate surveillance, and those new guidelines should be given a chance to work. Similarly, the Strategic Economic Dialogue (SED) with China is making progress the old fashioned way, through consultation and discussion. The US Congress has neither the objectivity nor the expertise to render sound judgments on other countries' exchange rate policies. Whatever their original intent, these currency bills will ultimately become instruments of protectionism—much like the US experience with antidumping legislation. Econometric analysis by Frankel and Wei (2007) finds that "political" variables like the bilateral trade imbalance and the US unemployment rate (in presidential election years) have played as important a role in earlier Treasury manipulation findings as have legitimate economic variables, like the global current account imbalance, the estimated degree of currency misalignment, and the size of changes in international reserves. Although the new currency bills (unlike the original Schumer-Graham bill) may be technically "WTO compatible," the odds that the United States will actually win these cases before a WTO panel is low because the bills pursue arguments of dubious legal merit. Inserting currency matters into the WTO adjudication process would also risk "politicizing" the WTO dispute settlement process and weakening support for it around the world.

Moreover, these new congressional currency bills will not be effective in producing a faster and larger appreciation of the renminbi or in reducing the US global and bilateral trade deficits. Those policymakers in China who favor bolder currency reform will find their influence weakened by US legislation because reform will then look like capitulation to the demands of the US Congress. The IMF will likewise find it harder to enforce its new currency guidelines because it will look as if it is acting as a surrogate for the US government rather than as an objective international umpire. These bills contain no measures to improve the US saving-investment imbalance. They also run the risk of igniting trade policy retaliation and copycat currency bills abroad, thereby producing a completely unworkable and inconsistent network of exchange rate policy guidelines.

Those defending these currency bills offer a different perspective. The currency oversight process is badly broken—both internationally and in the United States. The IMF has not sent even one special consultation to investigate exchange rate policy abuses in 20 years—much less made a finding of currency manipulation. The Fund has been asleep at the wheel in identifying and discouraging currency manipulation in China. In a similar vein, the US Treasury has not enforced the currency manipulation provisions of the 1988 Omnibus Act in the face of overwhelming evidence that China has been thwarting external adjustment. The quiet bilateral diplomacy championed by Treasury Secretaries John Snow and Henry Paulson has produced precious little progress on the renminbi—especially when measured, as it should be, in terms of real effective exchange rates—and the currency deliverables from the SED have also been meager to date. Yes, if both—or even either—the Fund and the US Treasury were exercising their currency oversight responsibly, congressional action would be unnecessary. But even a "third best" policy response to a serious problem is better than no response at all. Congress is not usurping anything. The US constitution gives Congress the authority over currency matters, and Congress has seen fit to delegate that authority to the executive branch (the Treasury)—but such delegation is conditional on the Treasury performing well (Henning 2007). If currency oversight is neglected, it is perfectly reasonable for Congress to reassert its authority in this area—at least temporarily—until the Fund and the Treasury show signs of better performance. It is not "protectionist" for Congress to complain that another country (China) is not taking seriously its obligations on exchange rate policy as a member of the Fund, any more than it is protectionist for the United States to complain about China's enforcement of intellectual property rights. Condoning currency manipulation and allowing a "free for all" in the global exchange rate system is not the friend of open markets.

Defenders of these bills might also argue that it remains to be seen whether congressional currency bills will be effective in inducing faster appreciation of the renminbi. The US government does not refrain from criticizing publicly China's human rights abuses for fear it will slow reform; what is different about exchange rate policy? Congressional currency bills are part of the negotiation on exchange rate policy, and they may alter (in the desired direction) the cost-benefit calculations in Beijing about how fast to move on renminbi appreciation.

Hufbauer and Brunel explain that the three leading currency bills have five features in common: They would eliminate "intent" in determining whether or not manipulation or misalignment has taken place; they invoke unilateral and multilateral trade remedies if the offending country does not act to correct the manipulation/misalignment; they instruct the US Treasury to make a forceful case in the IMF; they set out deadlines for action, ranging up to 360 days; and some of the bills contain waivers that delay or override US remedies.

Hufbauer and Brunel reach four main conclusions. First, as stand-alone measures, congressional currency bills are unlikely to have much effect in persuading Beijing to implement a faster appreciation of the renminbi; however, drawing on the literature on economic sanctions, multilateral pressure—of which such bills may be a part, along with pressure from the IMF and the European Union—could be more effective in inducing action in the right direction. Second, trade remedy measures, sought in the WTO or under US laws, are best justified as levers to induce more forceful IMF action and to focus Beijing's attention on currency issues. Third, if an enlarged congressional voice on currency issues is heard only in exceptional circumstances, it may be helpful; on the other hand, if congressional committees continually pressure foreign countries over matters like the size of US bilateral trade imbalances, they could severely disrupt the international system. And fourth, since congressional currency legislation could spawn copycat legislation abroad, Congress should limit trade measures to situations where the foreign country is a major commercial player, is manipulating its currency via large-scale, persistent, one-way intervention as determined by the IMF, and is both running a large global current account surplus and has accumulated international reserves beyond an adequate level for prudential purposes.

In his comment on chapter 6, Stephen Roach emphasizes that China's large bilateral trade surplus with the United States reflects the fact that China produces and assembles a broad set of products that satisfy US consumers. Eliminating China's bilateral surplus would still have left the United States with over a $600 billion global current account deficit in 2006; putting pressure on a bilateral exchange rate will not solve a multilateral trade deficit.

Roach argues that the root cause of the large US external imbalance is the extraordinary lack of US domestic saving, and this saving deficit must be addressed if the United States is to make genuine progress—beginning with the US government. He stresses that the unwillingness of the US body politic to embark on the heavy lifting of education reform and other human capital investments leads to China bashing. He worries that the US Congress has lost sight of what he regards as the true objective of globalization, namely, ". . . to trust in economic partners to act out of collective interests in making the world a better and more prosperous place."

The conference's wrap-up panelists also comment on issues related to these congressional currency bills (see chapter 9). Fan acknowledges that the size of China's global current account surplus is unprecedented, but he thinks it is insufficiently appreciated that several other features of China's current situation are also unprecedented, including the size and composition of China's labor force, the role that foreign direct investment and multinational companies play in China's foreign trade, and the prolonged US global current account deficit in a global monetary system based on the dollar standard. In relative terms, China's external imbalance is not out of line with those of its Asian neighbors.

Crockett points out that it is very difficult to define exchange rate manipulation because so many policies affect exchange rates. While he sees dangers in an incremental approach to eliminating the misalignment of the renminbi, he feels the concept of incrementalism is so deeply ingrained in the Chinese leadership's approach to reform and has produced such positive overall results in the past that it is very unlikely that China would opt for a large, sudden renminbi revaluation.

Summers concludes that any approach that seeks to blame the Chinese exchange rate for the concerns of US middle-class workers is based on flawed economic judgment. That said, it is perfectly appropriate to be deeply concerned about the adverse effects of China's exchange rate regime on global imbalances and global financial conditions. If the US Congress is to become more activist on exchange rate policies of other economies, any legislation should take the form of a sense-of-the-Congress resolution urging more aggressive engagement on China's exchange rate policies through the IMF.

Bergsten offers a different perspective. He agrees that China's integration into the world economy presents a variety of unprecedented challenges. He does not think it would be feasible to engineer a substantial reduction in the US global current account deficit without also achieving a sizeable reduction in China's global current account surplus. He argues that China is clearly violating key IMF rules of the game on exchange rate policy, and this combination of a large disequilibrium with "unfair" policies is motivating congressional proposals. He does not think any of the major currency bills now before the US Congress could properly be labeled as "protectionist." If neither China nor the IMF acted in a timely way to correct the large undervaluation of the renminbi, he would be in favor of a more activist WTO in helping to rein in unfair exchange rate policies. While this approach has pitfalls, it would be better in the end than doing nothing.

Policy Implications and Options

The preceding discussion illustrates that multiple considerations are bearing on how China should conduct its exchange rate policy in the period ahead. In order to clarify the options available, it may be useful to frame the choice in terms of two competing strategies. The first we call "stay the course." The second we call the "three-stage approach."

The stay-the-course strategy begins from the proposition that no one should care much about exchange rate policy for its own sake. It is basically a facilitating mechanism for more fundamental objectives. From this bottom-line perspective, China's existing exchange rate policy could be regarded by its supporters as quite successful. After all, the average annual rate of growth since the July 2005 reform has been above 10 percent. Core inflation has been low. The 2007 spike in the CPI is mainly attributable to an excess demand for pork and a few other food products and should prove temporary. Bank credit growth, after running way ahead of targets in 2003, the first quarter of 2004, and the first half of 2006, is back in a reasonable range. The listing of four large state-owned commercial banks and sale of minority stakes to foreign strategic investors has gone well. The investment share of GDP has leveled off after several years of rapid increase. Yes, there are pockets of overheating, but the recent series of increases in both interest rates and reserve requirements, along with the continuation of heavy sterilization and targeted window guidance, should be able to take care of them. The stock of outstanding sterilization instruments relative to GDP has, as indicated earlier, grown enormously in recent years but is still low relative to the shares in some other Asian economies.

Contrary to the predictions of many outside analysts, it has been possible to implement a gradual appreciation of the renminbi vis-à-vis the dollar and still conduct a reasonably independent monetary policy without being overwhelmed by foreign capital inflows; when those inflows have gotten large, it seems to be more because of the attractions of the booming equity and property markets than because of strong speculation on further renminbi appreciation. Some progress has meanwhile been made, both in liberalizing further the capital outflow regime and strengthening the structure of the foreign exchange market. Yes, external criticism of China's mushrooming global current account surplus and of the scant appreciation of the renminbi's real effective exchange rate is on the rise. But the George W. Bush administration is on record as opposing new currency bills cum trade sanctions in the US Congress, preferring instead to stick with negotiations within the SED framework. The IMF has a revised set of guidelines for exchange rate surveillance, but the new managing director, Dominique Strauss-Kahn, may not wish to begin his term with a confrontation on China's exchange rate policy when he is simultaneously trying to garner support for IMF reform in other areas.

Seen from this perspective, some would say that the sensible strategy is to make only minor modifications to China's existing exchange rate policy. The strategy going forward would then contain the following key elements: The renminbi would continue to be allowed to appreciate at a moderate but controlled pace against the dollar—say 5 to 8 percent a year. The scale of China's exchange market intervention would control the pace of renminbi appreciation. Coming on top of the 15 percent nominal appreciation already achieved between July 2005 and January 2008, this would produce a nontrivial cumulative appreciation vis-à-vis the dollar over the next few years—presumably enough to keep foreign criticism at bay. Several substitutes for larger exchange rate appreciation, such as reduced value-added tax (VAT) rebates and less favorable tax and tariff treatment for exporters, would continue to be employed to put upward pressure on export prices and/or to reduce the profitability of exporting. Also the central government would lean harder on both banks and local authorities not to finance or expand production in industries with clear excess capacity. More foreign buying trips could be arranged to publicize Chinese purchases of big-ticket US exports (e.g., Boeing aircraft). If China's global current account surplus and reserve accumulation prove more resistant to these measures than expected, restrictions on capital outflows can be liberalized somewhat further. The daily fluctuation band for the renminbi vis-à-vis the dollar, which was increased from 0.3 to 0.5 percent in May 2007, could also be increased to, say, 0.8 percent, so as to increase uncertainty for speculators betting on renminbi appreciation.

If all this is doable, what then are the objections to the stay-the-course option? The short answer is that renminbi undervaluation and China's external imbalance are much bigger than they were, say, four years ago, and the size and duration of the problem mean that small and gradual policy responses are not likely to be effective.[37]

Recall that in 2003, China's global current account surplus was about 3 percent of GDP, and the undervaluation of the renminbi was probably on

---

37. On the same day that China's new currency regime was announced, Goldstein and Lardy (2005b) argued that the size of the revaluation was likely way too small to achieve any of the authorities' objectives.

the order of 15 to 25 percent. At that point, it would probably have been possible to eliminate China's entire current account imbalance—albeit not also its capital account surplus—with a 15 percent step revaluation of the renminbi, without doing undue harm to the domestic economy; indeed, in 2003 we recommended (Goldstein and Lardy 2003b) such action as the first stage of what we called "two-stage currency reform," where the second stage entailed floating of the renminbi and a gradual lifting of capital account restrictions once China's financial sector was on a firmer footing. In 2007 China's global current account surplus was 11 percent of GDP, and renminbi undervaluation is much larger (conservatively, at least 30 to 40 percent). No longer can the exchange rate disequilibrium be eliminated in one step without a large contractionary impact on the domestic economy. And with such a large difference between the actual and equilibrium exchange rates, any "staged" approach to renminbi appreciation brings with it the challenge of coping with a "one-way bet" for speculators.

Consider several other features of the stay-the-course strategy.

First, tax and tariff substitutes for renminbi appreciation are not likely to have much impact. Reductions in the VAT rebate rate on exports cannot be expected to have a major effect on the export performance of firms because the magnitude of VAT rebates is small relative to the value of exports and, unlike appreciation, reducing rebate rates does nothing to make imported goods cheaper in China. In 2006, for example, VAT rebates on export goods were only 4.7 percent of the value of exports.[38] So if the government cancelled VAT rebates entirely, it would have an effect on the trade balance similar to an appreciation of the renminbi of slightly more than 2 percent. In practice, the scope of adjustment of VAT rebate rates is limited. For example, in the most comprehensive adjustment, which was announced in June and took effect July 1, 2007, the government eliminated rebates for 553 products and reduced the rate of rebate on another 2,268 products. But combined, these account for only 37 percent of all products.

The effect of adjustments in the export-processing regime likely will be even less significant than the adjustment of VAT rebate rates. On July 23, 2007 the authorities added 1,850 products to the "restricted list" for import processing. That means that starting August 1, firms importing parts and components to be assembled into exports could no longer import these items free of both import duties and VAT. Rather, firms now have to deposit with the government an amount equal to half of the import and VAT duties, with these amounts to be refunded when the related final goods are exported. The government estimated that this measure would increase costs to export-processing firms by RMB600 million (Shi Lu 2007). But this was extremely unlikely to dampen the growth of processed exports since

---

38. Total rebates were RMB428.49 billion, of which RMB61.3 billion was payment covering arrears. RMB367.19 billion was 4.7 percent of the value of exports in 2006.

it represents only 2 percent of the value of processed exports affected by the new restrictions and less than 0.1 percent of all processed exports.

Second, gradual appreciation of the renminbi vis-à-vis the US dollar may do little to produce much of an appreciation in China's real effective exchange rate, and it is the latter that matters for China's competitiveness and for engineering a reduction in China's global surplus via traditional relative-price channels.

Despite announcements at the time that China unveiled its new currency regime that henceforth the renminbi would be managed against a "basket" of major currencies (rather than the US dollar alone), studies show that the renminbi movements continue to be dominated by movements in the dollar (Frankel and Wei 2007). But if the US dollar declines further over the next several years, the renminbi will, as it has during the 2002–07 period, show much less appreciation in real effective terms. As noted earlier, whereas by January 2008 the renminbi has appreciated by 15 percent relative to the dollar since June 2005, the renminbi's has appreciated in real effective terms by only 8 percent. Betting against a dollar decline over the next few years seems a long shot. The global US current account deficit, while no longer growing as a ratio to US GDP, is expected to remain at 5 to 6 percent of GDP over the next few years (Cline 2007). Also, the weak US housing market and consensus projections of somewhat weaker GDP growth in 2008 suggest that relative interest rate movements are apt to be putting downward pressure on the dollar. If, say, the dollar declines on a real effective basis by 10 percent over the next two years, the real effective appreciation of the renminbi under a stay-the-course policy may be too small to make much of a dent in China's huge external surplus. If the dollar decline is more pronounced, this conclusion is reinforced.

Third, with US interest rates falling while Chinese rates are rising, the interest rate differential is widening in favor of renminbi-denominated assets, which—combined with a large gap between the actual and equilibrium values of the renminbi—is likely to lead in the period ahead to larger capital inflows. Small increases in the daily fluctuation band of the renminbi—or even marked differences in the monthly rate of renminbi appreciation—are not apt to offset this increasing incentive for capital inflows. Foreign investors who can make a good guess about the trend rate of appreciation will wait out short-term volatility. By the same token, even if restrictions on capital outflows are eased further, Chinese residents may reason that (with the renminbi expected to appreciate and with the Shanghai stock market outperforming many foreign markets over the past few years) this is not a good time to purchase foreign rather than domestic assets.

Fourth, if monthly intervention in the exchange market continues at anywhere near the $40 billion monthly rate in 2007, the sterilization task will become harder over time, and the burden placed on the banking system will grow. Recall that sterilization involves not only selling new sterilization bills/bonds to the banks to mop up much of the new reserve accumulation but also rolling over the existing stock of such instruments. Changing the mix among sterilization tools from bill/bond sales to increases in banks' reserve requirements does not really solve the problem because the low interest rate paid on reserves held at the central bank acts as a "tax" on the banks in much the same way as does the low interest rate on sterilization bills/bonds. As indicated earlier, this tax on banks due to sterilization operations is getting larger over time and is already a significant drain on their profitability. Banks' profitability (via interest rate margins) will also be squeezed over time by the increasing availability of alternatives to bank deposits and to bank loans for China's savers and borrowers. If bank profitability gets too low, more costly public-sector bailouts of the banks will be required.

Fifth, if exchange market intervention and sterilization continue at high levels, the Chinese authorities will continue to foster a monetary disequilibrium that will perpetuate the large external imbalance. As Mussa argues, the demand for base money is growing briskly in China, and the supply of base money has to grow briskly to accommodate that demand. But if the central bank's large-scale sterilization operations push the growth of net domestic assets to negative, then Chinese residents will reduce their expenditure and borrow money from abroad to satisfy the growing demand for base money—generating the very current account surplus and net capital inflow that the authorities claim they wish to reduce. To correct that monetary disequilibrium, the amount of sterilized, exchange market intervention has to be reduced. The relevant question is not whether sterilization (in isolation) can be continued indefinitely but rather whether large-scale sterilization can be continued at the same time that China is making significant progress in reducing its huge external imbalance.

Sixth, if the real exchange rate of the renminbi does not appreciate very much (i.e., the renminbi remains highly undervalued), it will be very difficult to reduce investment in tradable-goods industries with a tendency toward excess capacity since such industries will then have an export safety valve to dispose of their excess domestic production and to cushion what would otherwise be a steeper fall in their profits. And other (nonexchange rate) approaches to reducing capacity in excess supply industries do not seem to be making much headway. Anderson (2007c) notes that Chinese steel production is still outpacing domestic demand for steel by a wide margin. Trying to make real progress toward achieving domestic consumption-led economic growth, while there is a large undervaluation of the real exchange rate, is like pushing a very large boulder uphill.

And seventh, foreign pressure for China to move faster on renminbi appreciation appears to be building. In 2003 US Treasury Secretary John Snow could offer intensified bilateral negotiations and quiet diplomacy as a preferred approach to encouraging China to accelerate its currency reform. Similarly, in 2003–04 US senators contemplating the introduction of currency bills could be persuaded to hold their fire on the argument that China was on the verge of significant currency reform and that perhaps China's growing external surplus would prove temporary. In 2003 the Republicans held a majority in both the Senate and the House. Now, after three meetings of the SED, pleas for more patience are harder to sell because the deliverables on renminbi appreciation from the earlier approach have been modest. We are also not so far away from the 2008 US presidential election, in which states that have been most affected by competition from China (e.g., Ohio) could play a pivotal role in the outcome. Looking across the Atlantic, in 2003 the average value of the euro-dollar exchange rate was $1.13; today, the euro is above $1.40. If the euro area is not to suffer an excessive deterioration in its competitiveness, some other currencies will need to appreciate faster than the euro; the renminbi could be a leading candidate for that role. France also has a new president who has already expressed a keen interest in the external adjustment problem and has called specifically for a faster pace of renminbi appreciation. In Asia, as noted earlier, several of China's neighbors have permitted their own real exchange rates to appreciate significantly (20 percent or more on a trade-weighted basis) over the past four to five years; they may start asking, if we have already made our contribution to the global payments problem, why has not China done more? And perhaps the new managing director of the Fund, Dominique Strauss-Kahn, will reason that if he is to solve the Fund's identity crisis and establish some credibility for the Fund's new guidelines on exchange rate surveillance, he will not be able to avoid having the Fund label the renminbi as at least "fundamentally misaligned" if not "manipulated."

If the stay-the-course strategy does not look so promising, what is the relevant alternative? In our view, a bolder approach is called for that would permit China to catch up in correcting its very large external disequilibria, while still keeping a lid on domestic social pressures.[39] We label this the "three-stage approach" to currency reform. It would have the following broad outlines.

In stage one, to begin immediately, China would undertake a 15 percent revaluation/appreciation of the renminbi (from its existing level). This rise in the renminbi could be implemented either by a step revaluation or by allowing the exchange rate to appreciate by that amount in a relatively short period. The daily fluctuation limit on the renminbi with respect to the major currencies would also be increased to 1 or 1.5 percent. The Chinese authorities would accompany these exchange rate moves with an ex-

---

39. Prasad (2007, 3) also argues that now is the time for China to abandon its incremental reform approach in favor of something bolder: "One key principle…is to recognize that there are inherent limits to the incremental reform strategy that has worked well in the past. At a certain level of development and complexity of an economy, the connections among different reforms become difficult to ignore."

pansion and redirection of government expenditure aimed at existing weaknesses in China's social safety net (i.e., health, education, and pension systems). A package of trade adjustment assistance would be introduced to help cushion the impact of the initial renminbi revaluation on China's traditional (low-margin) export industries. Existing restrictions on capital outflows would be retained or liberalized only modestly. China would drop its insistence that the renminbi exchange rate is solely a matter of national sovereignty and would work with the IMF on the design and execution of the three-stage approach.

In stage two, the government would allow the renminbi to continue to float upward over the next several years, albeit at a gradual pace, say, 6 to 8 percent a year.[40] Limits on foreign ownership of China's banks would be reduced in an effort to improve credit allocation. Interest rate liberalization would continue. Debate within China would accelerate on greater central bank independence and on the merits of an inflation targeting approach to monetary policy (Goodfriend and Prasad 2006). Restrictions on capital inflows and outflows would continue to be liberalized but at a gradual pace.

Finally in stage three, say, four to six years down the road, intervention in the exchange market, along with sterilization operations, would be reduced still further, and the daily fluctuation limit on the renminbi would be dropped—so that the renminbi became essentially "floating." Monetary policy would continue to evolve toward an inflation targeting framework. Depending on how much progress had been made on bank reform, restrictions on capital flows could be liberalized much more substantially.

In our view, such a three-stage approach to renminbi reform would offer advantages over the stay-the-course option.

The immediate 15 percent revaluation/appreciation of the renminbi would represent a credible "down payment" on removing the large existing undervaluation of the renminbi. It would eliminate the need to play around with minor substitutes (e.g., reductions of VAT rebates for exporters) for exchange rate action. It would push the renminbi's real effective exchange rate in the right direction and provide some immediate offset in case of a further depreciation of the dollar. Since the initial revaluation would not be so large, and since it would be accompanied by both an expansion/redirection of government expenditures and introduction of a trade adjustment assistance program, the contractionary effects of revaluation on the economy—as well as income losses in traditional export industries—should be manageable, especially in view of China's relatively high growth rate. Increased expenditure on the social safety net would also reduce the need for such high precautionary saving on the part of households. The immediate 15 percent revaluation would also reduce

---

40. This pace of appreciation would have to be adjusted upward if China continued to achieve rapid productivity growth in export industries, a phenomenon discussed earlier.

the expected gain from speculating on the future appreciation of the renminbi, since the gap between the actual and equilibrium rates would be smaller than before. The immediate 15 percent "down payment," along with the agreement to work with the IMF in implementing this currency reform, should reduce foreign criticism of China's slow pace of reform—particularly in, but not limited to, the US Congress—and it should lessen the risk of protectionist trade policies being adopted at China's expense. The increase in the daily fluctuation limit for the renminbi—if utilized—would permit greater flexibility of the renminbi and provide some increased room for maneuver in the independence of monetary policy—maneuver that would also be enhanced by stopping well short of the elimination of existing restrictions on capital inflows. The greater independence of monetary policy would in turn allow the central bank to act more preemptively in its interest rate policy decisions.

The reduction in both exchange market intervention and sterilization operations in stages two and three would not only further push the real effective exchange rate of the renminbi in the right direction but also help to correct any monetary disequilibrium and reduce the strains on the banking sector. By liberalizing the capital outflow regime only slowly, there would be a degree of "insurance" against large-scale capital flight if a large, unexpected negative shock occurred during the currency reform process. The increase in foreign ownership limits on China's banks would provide a potential longer-term increase in bank profitability to help offset any transitional strains associated with remaining sterilization operations. Discussions of greater central bank independence and of the merits of an inflation targeting framework would anticipate the need for a new nominal anchor, as the fixity of China's exchange rate continued to decline.

Finally, in stage three, China should be close to eliminating any remaining undervaluation of the renminbi. It should also be closer to four of its longer-term goals: a truly market-determined exchange rate, an effective framework for independent monetary policy, a more open capital account, and a more harmonious relationship with its trading partners.

References

Adams, Timothy D. 2006. The IMF: Back to Basics. In *Reforming the IMF for the 21st Century*, ed., Edwin Truman. Washington: Institute for International Economics.

Ahearne, Alan, William Cline, Kyung Tae Lee, Yung Chul Park, Jean Pisani-Ferry, and John Williamson. 2007. *Global Imbalances: Time for Action*. Policy Briefs in International Economics 07-4 (March). Washington: Peterson Institute for International Economics.

Anderlini, Jamil. 2007. "China's Strong Earnings Growth Inflated by Stock Market Bull Run," *Financial Times*, August 28, 13.

Anderson, Jonathan. 2004. *China: Reminders on the RMB*. UBS Investment Research, Asian Economic Comment (November 5).

Anderson, Jonathan. 2006a. *The Complete RMB Handbook*, 4th ed. UBS Investment Research, Asian Economic Perspectives (September 16).

Anderson, Jonathan. 2006b. *The Sword Hanging over China's Banks*. UBS Investment Research, Asian Focus (December 15).

Anderson, Jonathan. 2007a. *The New China: Back to the Real World*. UBS Investment Research, Asian Economic Perspective (March 1).

Anderson, Jonathan. 2007b. *No Really, How Competitive Are China's Exports?* UBS Investment Research, Asian Focus (April 16).

Anderson, Jonathan. 2007c. *The Real Case for Revaluation*. UBS Investment Research, Asian Focus (July 13).

Anderson, Jonathan. 2007d. *Is China Export Led?* UBS Investment Research, Asian Focus (September 27).

Anderson, Jonathan. 2008. *Four Big Numbers*. UBS Investment Research, China Focus (January 15, 2008)

Bai Chong-En, Chang-Tai Hsieh, and Yingyi Qian. 2006. *The Return to Capital in China*. NBER Working Paper 12755 (December). Cambridge, MA: National Bureau of Economic Research.

Bergsten, C. Fred. 2005. "An Action Plan to Stop the Market Manipulators Now," *Financial Times*, March 14.

Bergsten, C. Fred. 2007. The Chinese Exchange Rate and the US Economy. Testimony before the Hearing on the Treasury Department's Report to Congress on International Economic and Exchange Rate Policy and the Strategic Economic Dialogue, Committee on Banking, Housing, and Urban Affairs, January 31. Washington.

Bernanke, Ben. 2006. The Chinese Economy: Progress and Challenges. Remarks at the Chinese Academy of Social Sciences, Beijing, December 15, 2006.

Bosworth, Barry. 2004. Valuing the RMB. Paper presented at the Tokyo Club Research Meeting, February.

Chinese Bank Regulatory Commission. 2007. *2006 Annual Report*. Available at www.cbrc.gov.cn (accessed on September 14, 2007).

Cheung, Yin-Wong, Menzie D. Chinn, and Eiji Fujii. 2007. *The Overvaluation of Renminbi Undervaluation*. NBER Working Paper 12850 (January). Cambridge, MA: National Bureau of Economic Research.

Cline, William. 2005. *The United States as a Debtor Nation*. Washington: Institute for International Economics.

Cline, William. 2007. Estimating Reference Exchange Rates. Paper presented at the workshop on policy to reduce global imbalances, sponsored by Bruegel, the Korea Institute for International Economic Policy, and the Peterson Institute for International Economics, Washington, February 8–9.

Cooper, Richard. 2005. *Living with Global Imbalances: A Contrarian View*. International Economics Policy Brief 05-3. Washington: Institute for International Economics.

Crockett, Andrew. 2007. The International Financial Architecture and Financial Stability. Dinner speech at the 50th anniversary celebration of the Bank of Ghana, August.

de Rato, Rodrigo. 2006. A Call for Cooperation: What the IMF and Its Members Can Do to Solve Global Economic Problems. Speech at the Peterson Institute for International Economics, Washington, April 20.

Dobson, Wendy, and Anil K. Kashyap. 2006. The Contradiction in China's Gradualist Banking Reforms. *Brookings Papers on Economic Activity* (Fall): 103–48.

Dodge, David. 2006. The Evolving International Monetary Order and the Need for an Evolving IMF. Speech at the Woodrow Wilson School, Princeton University, Princeton, NJ, March 30.

Dooley, Michael, David Folkerts-Landau, and Peter Garber. 2003. *An Essay on the Revived Bretton Woods System*. NBER Working Paper 9971 (September). Cambridge, MA: National Bureau of Economic Research.

Dunaway, Steven, and Xiangming Li. 2005. *Estimating China's Real Equilibrium Exchange Rate*. IMF Working Paper 05/202 (October). Washington: International Monetary Fund.

Dunaway, Steven, Lamin Leigh, and Xiangming Li. 2006. *How Robust Are Estimates of Equilibrium Real Exchange Rates for China?* IMF Working Paper 06/220 (October). Washington: International Monetary Fund.

Eichengreen, Barry. 2004. *Global Imbalances and the Lessons of Bretton Woods.* NBER Working Paper 10497 (May). Cambridge, MA: National Bureau of Economic Research.

Eichengreen, Barry. 2007. A Blueprint for IMF Reform: More than Just a Lender. *International Finance* 10, no. 2: 153–75.

El-Erian, Mohamed. 2007. "Foreign Capital Must Not Be Blocked," *Financial Times*, October 3.

Frankel, Jeffrey. 2006. On the Yuan: The Choice Between Adjustment Under a Fixed Exchange Rate and Adjustment Under a Flexible Exchange Rate. In *Understanding the Chinese Economy*, ed. Gerhard Illing. Munich: CESinfo Economic Studies.

Frankel, Jeffrey A., and Shang-Jin Wei. 2007. Assessing China's Exchange Rate Regime. *Economic Policy* 22, no. 51: 575–627.

Goldstein, Morris. 2004. *Adjusting China's Exchange Rate Policies.* Institute for International Economics Working Paper 04-1. Washington: Institute for International Economics.

Goldstein, Morris. 2006a. "Exchange Rates, Fair Play, and the 'Grand Bargain,'" *Financial Times*, April 21.

Goldstein, Morris. 2006b. Renminbi Controversies. *Cato Journal* 26, no. 2 (Spring/Summer).

Goldstein, Morris. 2006c. Currency Manipulation and Enforcing the Rules of the International Monetary System. In *Reforming the IMF for the 21st Century*, ed. Edwin Truman. Washington: Institute for International Economics.

Goldstein, Morris. 2007a. The IMF as Global Umpire for Exchange Rate Policies. In *C. Fred Bergsten and the World Economy*, ed. Michael Mussa. Washington: Peterson Institute for International Economics.

Goldstein, Morris. 2007b. *A (Lack of) Progress Report on China's Exchange Rate Policies.* Peterson Institute for International Economics Working Paper 07-5 (June). Washington: Peterson Institute for International Economics.

Goldstein, Morris, and Nicholas Lardy. 2003a. "A Modest Proposal for China's RMB," *Financial Times*, August 26.

Goldstein, Morris, and Nicholas Lardy. 2003b. "Two-Step Currency Reform for China," *Asian Wall Street Journal*, September 12.

Goldstein, Morris, and Nicholas Lardy. 2004. *What Kind of Landing for the Chinese Economy?* Policy Briefs in International Economics 04-7. Washington: Institute for International Economics.

Goldstein, Morris, and Nicholas Lardy. 2005a. *China's Role in the Revived Bretton Woods System: A Case of Mistaken Identity.* Institute for International Economics Working Paper 05-2. Washington: Institute for International Economics.

Goldstein, Morris, and Nicholas Lardy. 2005b. "China's Revaluation Shows Why Size Really Matters," *Financial Times*, July 22.

Goldstein, Morris, and Nicholas Lardy. 2006. China's Exchange Rate Dilemma. *American Economic Review* (May): 422–26.

Goldstein, Morris, and Michael Mussa. 2005. "The Fund Appears to Be Sleeping at the Wheel," *Financial Times*, October 3.

Goodfriend, Marvin, and Eswar Prasad. 2006. *A Framework for Independent Monetary Policy in China.* IMF Working Paper 06/11 (May). Washington: International Monetary Fund.

Green, Stephen. 2007a. This . . . is . . . Sparta!!! *Standard Chartered on the Ground—Asia* (April 12).

Green, Stephen. 2007b. China: Calling all PBoC FX Sterilization Geeks. *Standard Chartered On the Ground—Asia* (June 18).

Henning, C. Randall. 2007. *Congress, Treasury, and the Accountability of Exchange Rate Policy: How the 1988 Trade Act Should Be Reformed.* Peterson Institute for International Economics Working Paper 07-8. Washington: Peterson Institute for International Economics.

IEO (Independent Evaluation Office, International Monetary Fund). 2007. *An IEO Evaluation of the IMF's Exchange Rate Policy Advice, 1999–2005* (May). Washington: International Monetary Fund.

IMF (International Monetary Fund). 2004. *People's Republic of China: 2004 Article IV Consultation*. IMF Country Report 04/351 (November). Washington.

IMF (International Monetary Fund). 2006a. *People's Republic of China: 2006 Article IV Consultation*. IMF Country Report 06/394 (October). Washington.

IMF (International Monetary Fund). 2006b. *Methodology for CGER Exchange Rate Assessments* (November). Washington.

IMF (International Monetary Fund). 2007a. *Review of the 1977 Decision—Proposal for a New Decision* (May 22). Washington.

IMF (International Monetary Fund). 2007b. *IMF Surveillance—The 2007 Decision on Bilateral Surveillance* (June 21). Washington.

Ito, Takatoshi. 2004. The Yen and the Japanese Economy, 2004. In *Dollar Adjustment: How Far? Against What?* ed. C. Fred Bergsten and John Williamson. Washington: Institute for International Economics.

Keidel, Albert. 2005. *China's Currency: Not the Problem*. Policy Brief 39 (June). Washington: Carnegie Endowment for International Peace.

Keidel, Albert. 2007. *China's Financial Sector: Contributions to Growth and Downside Risks* (January 25). Washington: Carnegie Endowment for International Peace. Available at www.carnegieendowment.org (accessed on August 31, 2007).

King, Mervyn. 2006. Speech at the Indian Council for Research on International Economic Relations, New Delhi, India, February 20.

Kroeber, Arthur. 2007. The Incredible Shrinking FX Fund. *China Insight*, no. 41 (August 16). Dragonomics Research and Advisory.

Lachman, Desmond. 2007. "Complacency at the IMF," *Gazeta Mercantil*, October 3.

Lardy, Nicholas R. 1994. *China in the World Economy*. Washington: Institute for International Economics.

Lardy, Nicholas R. 2006. *China: Toward a Consumption-Driven Growth Path*. Policy Briefs in International Economics 06-6. Washington: Institute for International Economics.

Lardy, Nicholas R. 2007. China: Rebalancing Economic Growth. Available at www.chinabalancesheet.org.

Lee Kuan Yew. 2001. Interview with the *Wall Street Journal*, April 26.

Lee Hsien Loong. 2001. Speech at the Parliament, Singapore, May 16.

Ma Guonan, and Robert McCauley. 2007. *Do China's Capital Controls Still Bind? Implications for Monetary Autonomy and Capital Liberalization*. BIS Working Paper 233 (August). Bank for International Settlements. Available at www.bis.org.

McGregor, Richard. 2007. "China's Trade Surplus Overshadows Talks," *Financial Times*, May 11.

McKinnon, Ronald. 2007. Why China Should Keep Its Dollar Peg. *International Finance* 10, no. 1: 43–70.

Meade, James E. 1951. *The Balance of Payments*. London: Oxford University Press.

Morrison, Wayne, and Marc Labonte. 2007. *China's Currency: Economic Issues and Options for U.S. Trade Policy* (updated July 15). Washington: Congressional Research Service. Available at www.fas.org (accessed on September 17, 2007).

Mundell, Robert. 2004. China's Exchange Rate: The Case for the Status Quo. Paper presented at the International Monetary Fund seminar on the Foreign Exchange System, Dalian, China, May.

Mussa, Michael. 2005. Sustaining Global Growth While Reducing External Imbalances. In *The United States and the World Economy: Foreign Economic Policy for the Next Decade*, ed. C. Fred Bergsten and the Institute for International Economics. Washington: Institute for International Economics.

National Bureau of Statistics of China. 2007. *China Statistical Abstract 2007*. Beijing: China Statistics Press.

Obstfeld, Maurice, and Kenneth Rogoff. 2006. The Unsustainable US Current-Account Position Revisited. In *G-7 Current Account Imbalances: Sustainability and Adjustment*, ed. Richard Clarida. Chicago: University of Chicago Press.

Park, Yung Chul. 2007. Comments delivered at the conclusion of the workshop on policy to reduce global imbalances, sponsored by Bruegel, the Korea Institute for International Economic Policy, and the Peterson Institute for International Economics, Washington, February 8–9.

People's Bank of China. 2008. *China's Monetary Circulation Equilibrium in 2007* (January 11). Available at www.pbc.gov.cn (accessed on January 11, 2008).

People's Bank of China, Monetary Policy Analysis Small Group. 2007. Report on Implementation of Monetary Policy, Second Quarter 2007 (August 8). Available at www.pbc.gov.cn (accessed on August 8, 2007).

Podpiera, Richard. 2006. *Progress in China's Banking Sector Reform: Has Bank Behavior Changed?* IMF Working Paper 06/71 (March). Washington: International Monetary Fund.

Prasad, Eswar S. 2007. Is the Chinese Miracle Built to Last? Cornell University, Ithaca, NY. Photocopy.

Prasad, Eswar, Thomas Rumbaugh, and Qing Wang. 2005. *Putting the Cart Before the Horse? Capital Account Liberalization and Exchange Rate Flexibility in China.* IMF Policy Discussion Paper 05/1 (January). Washington: International Monetary Fund.

Preeg, Ernest. 2003. Exchange Rate Manipulation to Gain an Unfair Competitive Advantage. In *Dollar Overvaluation and the Global Economy*, ed. C. Fred Bergsten and John Williamson. Washington: Institute for International Economics.

Roach, Stephen. 2007. *Playing with Fire.* Morgan Stanley, Global Economic Forum (April 30).

Setser, Brad. 2007. Central Banks Came Close to Financing Almost All of the US Current-Account Deficit Over the Past Four Quarters. Brad Setser's Blog, Roubini Global Economics, New York, October 2. Available at www.rgemonitor.com/blog/setser.

Shi Lu. 2007. "New Policy on Processing Trade to Involve Exports Valued at $30 Billion," *China Economic News*, September 17, 8–9.

Shu, Chang, and Raymond Yip. 2006. Impact of Exchange Rate Movements on the Mainland Economy. *China Economic Issues* 3/06 (July). Hong Kong: Hong Kong Monetary Authority.

State Administration of Foreign Exchange, Balance of Payments Analysis Small Group. 2007. *Report on China's 2006 Balance of Payments* (May 10). Available at www.safe.gov.cn (accessed on May 10, 2007).

Summers, Lawrence H. 2004. The United States and the Global Adjustment Process. Third Annual Stavros S. Niarchos Lecture, Institute for International Economics, Washington, March 23.

Summers, Lawrence H. 2007. "Funds that Shake Capitalist Logic," *Financial Times*, July 29.

Truman, Edwin. 2005. *Postponing Global Adjustment: Analysis of the Pending Adjustment of Global Imbalances.* Institute for International Economics Working Paper 05-06. Washington: Institute for International Economics.

Truman, Edwin. 2007. *Sovereign Wealth Funds: The Need for Greater Transparency and Accountability.* Policy Briefs in International Economics 07-6. Washington: Peterson Institute for International Economics.

US Department of Labor, Bureau of Labor Statistics. 2007. Import/Export Price Indexes. Washington. Available at http://data.bls.gov (accessed on September 14, 2007).

US Treasury Department. 2005. *Report to the Congress on International Economic and Exchange Rate Policies* (May). Washington.

Williamson, John. 2003. The Renminbi Exchange Rate and the Global Monetary System. Lecture at the Central University of Finance and Economics, Beijing, October.

World Bank. 2007. *China Quarterly Update* (September). Washington. Available at http://siteresources.worldbank.org (accessed on September 12, 2007).

Yu Yongding. 2007a. Global Imbalances and China. *Australian Economic Review* 40, no. 1: 3–23.

Yu Yongding. 2007b. Ten Years after the Asian Financial Crisis: The Fragility and Strength of China's Financial System. *IDS Bulletin* 38, no. 4 (July).

Comment
China's Industrial Investment Boom and the Renminbi

JONATHAN ANDERSON

As a long-time fan of Morris Goldstein's and Nicholas Lardy's work, it is a pleasure to comment on their paper, a pleasure compounded by the fact that the authors have clearly done yet another excellent job. Indeed, I have yet to see anyone else succeed in laying out the terms of the "great renminbi exchange rate debate" so succinctly and even-handedly and in language accessible to the layman as well.

Needless to say, it makes the reviewer's job all the more difficult, essentially consigning one to pick at the remaining nits along the way. Luckily, at least two important issues are worthy of further commentary—issues I thought were not completely resolved in the paper itself and that also cut to the very heart of the China question.

In order to frame the questions correctly, it is helpful to summarize what is known about the Chinese external economy, so let us begin with a simple review of the facts at hand.

The Trade Balance

Over the past two decades, the mainland economy has nearly always recorded a surplus in manufacturing trade—but a relatively mild one. Between 1994 and 2004, the average trade surplus was more or less steady

Jonathan Anderson is managing director, Global Emerging-Markets Economist at UBS Investment Bank.

at 2 percent of GDP, hardly a matter for global attention or breathless commentary in the financial press. In the second half of 2004, however, things changed dramatically. By the end of the year, the surplus had risen above 3 percent of GDP. The average for 2005 was nearly 5 percent, rising to 7 percent in 2006 and an estimated 9 percent of GDP for 2007. China had never before seen such levels nor such a rapid increase.

Where did the sudden jump in the surplus come from? Clearly not from rising exports: Headline export growth fell gradually but steadily from 2003 through 2007, very much in line with the slowing momentum in China's neighboring economies. Rather, the main shock was a dramatic fall in import growth. In 2003 mainland imports increased by 35 percent in real terms, but by the first half of 2005, the growth rate had fallen to zero. While imports did recover somewhat over the past two years, that recovery has been anemic: around 10 percent real growth on average, far below the pace of export expansion.

Why were imports falling? Looking at the detailed statistics, the turn-around came almost completely from net trade in heavy industrial products: aluminum, machine tools, cement, key chemical products, and especially steel and steel products, which single-handedly account for at least one-quarter of the entire increase in China's trade balance.

Finally, why heavy industrial sectors? The answer lies in part in the intensive mainland investment boom of 2001–04, which resulted in a dramatic and historically unprecedented increase in the ratio of heavy industrial production to GDP between 2003 and 2006 and, in part, in the sharp slowdown in the pace of domestic construction demand in 2004–07 on the heels of macro tightening measures. As a result, by our estimates, Chinese heavy industrial producers have displaced imports (and in some cases taken over export markets as well) to the tune of 6 to 7 percent of GDP over the past four years. No other segment of the economy saw anything close to the same volatility; the capacity buildout in export-oriented light manufacturing and domestic services sectors was much more moderate, and demand trends in these areas were more stable.

In short, the story of China's trade surplus is to a large degree a story about heavy industry, with large swings in the supply-demand balance in a concentrated part of the economy.

Saving and Investment

Exactly the same is true in China's saving and investment behavior. As a macroeconomic identity, the dramatic rise in China's trade and current account balance is reflected in a rising gap between gross domestic savings and gross domestic investment—and once again, the mainland had never before seen anything close to the stunning increase in the gap over the past four years.

Where did the gap come from? Certainly not from falling investment: In fact, after a sustained rise in the beginning of the decade, China's investment/GDP ratio was broadly stable from 2003 to 2007. Instead, the culprit is rising savings. Based on official headline macro accounting figures, China's gross domestic saving rate was less than 40 percent of GDP in 2002; by 2006, only four years later, the saving rate had jumped to over 50 percent, a considerable feat for any economy and unprecedented in China.

Why the sudden rush of savings? The best work in this area comes from Bert Hofman and Louis Kuijs of the World Bank, whose latest research is also featured in this conference volume; their findings show that the household saving rate did not change at all as a share of GDP since the beginning of the decade, and the same is true for the estimated government saving rate. Instead, the entire 10-plus percentage-point increase in national savings as a share of the economy came from the corporate sector.

And not just anywhere in the corporate sector. We do not have complete data for earnings at the sectoral level, but the available figures for the industrial economy point to a dramatic upsurge in heavy industrial sectors—i.e., the same steel, machinery, and chemicals manufacturers who were responsible for the rise in the trade surplus. From only 40 percent of total ex-mining industrial profits at the beginning of the decade, heavy industries accounted for nearly 70 percent by the first three quarters of 2007.

Interestingly, this upsurge in gross earnings came at a time when average profit *margins* in these industries actually *fell*. How is this possible? Simple: As seen earlier, heavy industrial production *volumes* rose dramatically as a share of GDP—i.e., the increase in overall activity greatly outweighed the moderate decline in unit margins.

At the end of the day, the story is very much the same as it is for the trade surplus: large and concentrated capacity increases in heavy industry, which (against the backdrop of weaker domestic industrial demand) end up pushing out imported products to take over local market share, followed by an export surge in some cases. The resulting increase in the volume of gross domestic corporate earnings—offset by falling foreign corporate earnings due to the loss of export orders to China—essentially explains the sharply rising gap between saving and investment at home.

Expenditure Balances

Pause for a second and consider what this saving-investment gap means for the composition of total expenditure in the economy. Mathematically, if savings rise by 10 percent of GDP relative to investment, then net exports of goods and services increase by 10 percent of GDP as well—and domestic expenditure must fall by the same amount. If for some reason the investment share of the economy remains constant, then it must be the case that the consumption share declines by 10 percentage points.

Here is a thumbnail sketch of how the linkages have worked in China. Assume an economy growing at 8 percent year over year in real terms, with both consumption and investment growing at precisely the same pace—i.e., all domestic expenditure ratios are stable. Now assume that a big investment boom pushes overall growth to 10 percent year over year by increasing the investment share of the economy by two percentage points per year, with the trade balance initially unchanged. If real household income and consumption growth remains unchanged at 8 percent, then by definition the consumption share of GDP will fall by two percentage points per year.

Next, imagine that the pace of investment expenditure eventually subsides but is broadly offset by rising capacity creation from the earlier boom, which pushes up net exports by 2 percent of GDP per year. Again, the economy continues to grow at 10 percent—and again, if consumer incomes and spending are still growing at 8 percent, then the consumption share continues to fall by two percentage points per year.

A key assumption here is that households do not capture any increased income from the rise in domestic industrial capacity and corporate earnings, but in the Chinese context, where state firms generally do not pay dividends and there is also no clear mechanism to transfer their earnings back to the government "owners," this makes good sense to most observers.

Thus far, this is a very good description of what has actually happened in the mainland economy over the past five years—i.e., an initial sharp rise in the investment/GDP ratio, followed by a decline, which was more than offset by a rising net export balance, and a continued, sustained fall in consumer incomes and spending as a share of the economy.

But this does not necessarily reflect consumer "weakness," in the sense that the best available data show household incomes and consumption rising steadily at 8 percent per year or more in real terms. It could easily be argued that nothing changed for consumers in China—it is just that investment activity and then productive capacity exploded all around them, pushing up the level of GDP without giving them any stake in the additional growth.

And Now for the Fun Part

To sum up, so far I have examined the linkages between (1) the rise in the trade surplus, (2) the rise in trend growth, (3) the sharp increase in the saving-investment balance, and (4) the falling consumer share in the economy. As it turns out, the underlying driver of all these phenomena is the heavy industrial investment and capacity boom of the past five years. Without much exaggeration, if you can explain heavy industry, you can explain China.

And so far, I have not touched on anything remotely controversial. These are simply the starting facts, well recognized by most economists who look at the mainland.

This brings me to the "elephants in the room"—i.e., two remaining questions I have not yet addressed and which effectively hold the key to the entire debate. First, why did China have an industrial investment boom in the first place? And second, what does this have to do with the value of the renminbi?

With these questions we exit the realm of established facts and enter the world of conjecture and strong debate. There are at least three competing explanations (and likely many more) for what has been seen in China in recent years.

The first is rising competitiveness. In this view, China may not have had a strong trade surplus historically, but over the past five years the economy underwent a strong positive productivity shock, driven by improvements in infrastructure, technological capability, and human capital. For a given level of the real exchange rate, it became much more profitable to produce in higher value-added sectors, and the mainland began to rapidly move up the technology chain, taking over capital-intensive industries and displacing imports as it went.

The second is structural underpricing of capital. Here the main focus is artificially low real interest rates in China, which lead to artificially high investment in capital-intensive sectors, which in turn leads to displacement of imports and higher net exports—and in the context of a quasi-pegged exchange rate, the rising surpluses effectively prevent the central bank from raising interest rates due to fears of speculative pressures and increasing sterilization losses. This vicious circle feeds on itself as the domestic liquidity impact of ever-increasing foreign exchange intervention fuels the next round of capital investment.

The third is mistiming of the domestic cycle. The idea here is that the 2001–04 upturn was fueled primarily by a boom in housing and auto expenditure—i.e., very material- and infrastructure-intensive demand categories. Tight supply conditions and surging profits induced a strong investment reaction from machinery, steel, and other heavy industrial producers; however, by the time capacity came on line, the authorities had already tightened aggressively to prevent overheating in construction and auto lending. Domestic suppliers woke up with a significant excess capacity "hangover" and again displaced imports, shipped products abroad, and pushed up the trade surplus.

Does it matter which of these explanations is correct? From the viewpoint of currency dynamics and exchange rate policy, it matters very much indeed. In the first instance, China is undergoing a sharp structural depreciation of the productivity-adjusted real exchange rate and presumably needs both large and continuous renminbi strengthening for a good while to come in order to rebalance the economy. The second case has less to say about the level of the exchange rate per se; rather, the key is renminbi flexibility, which would remove the policy straitjacket on interest rate adjustment and domestic monetary tightening. And as for the third story, here the currency does not play any role at all in the initial supply shock, nor is it clear whether there are any implications for the exchange regime over the longer term; it is simply a matter of waiting for the market to clear away excess productive capacity.

Now, readers of Goldstein's and Lardy's previous work will know that Goldstein has been a strong proponent of the first explanation and that Lardy has written extensively on the second—and anyone who has looked at my own writing will know that I tend to favor the third case. So what better place than a comprehensive report on exchange rate issues coauthored by Goldstein and Lardy to tackle the evidence head on and try to reach some final conclusions?

After reading the paper, however, it does not feel as if we quite get there. The authors do spend a good bit of time on each point, but the discussion is rather more focused on outlining the debate as I did a few paragraphs ago and then restating findings from previous work. And at the risk of oversimplification, to the extent that Goldstein and Lardy do draw conclusions in the paper, they run as follows: (1) the rising current account surplus is by definition convincing evidence of structural productivity gains and therefore substantial long-term undervaluation, and (2) the large foreign exchange reserve accumulation and sterilization effort by the central bank are by definition signs of loss of control of domestic monetary policy. It should be clear from the earlier discussion that I would not necessarily agree a priori with either of those points.

There are of course obvious rejoinders to my mild complaints. This is, after all, a review paper and was never meant to provide final answers to the big questions of the day. Moreover, does it really matter anyway? Whatever the driving force, the fact that China has seen a high and sharply rising current account surplus over the past few years clearly means that the currency is undervalued in a near-term, workaday sense, and at least some real exchange rate appreciation is part of the policy prescription in all three of the cases I outlined above.

Fair enough indeed. But on the other hand, given the importance now ascribed to the renminbi exchange rate on the global stage—and nowhere is this more true than in the US policy circles at which this paper is aimed—and the very different implications for the magnitude and urgency of adjustment, it would be imperative to have more to go on in drawing conclusions at the end of the day.

A Final Diversion

Having gone through the above discussion, we are now ready to deal with one final issue. As it turns out, in addition to the "standard" questions about the renminbi exchange rate, Goldstein and Lardy also spend a surprising amount of time on a working model of the Chinese currency and monetary system that makes very little sense to me.

The basic outline is as follows. Practitioners familiar with central bank balance sheets will be aware that the outstanding stock of base or "high powered" money is equal by definition to the sum of net foreign assets (NFA) and net domestic assets (NDA) of the central bank, with the latter defined as total domestic claims less domestic non-base-money liabilities. Now, when China runs a large balance-of-payments surplus, the People's Bank of China (PBC) is forced to intervene in the foreign exchange market and buy up foreign exchange reserves in order to maintain the renminbi quasi-peg. If the PBC buys foreign exchange, it automatically creates new domestic liquidity as the offsetting portion of the transaction. So if we compare the central bank balance sheet before and after a large foreign exchange purchase, we would find that NFA has increased, with base-money liabilities rising by an equal amount, and that NDA is initially unchanged.

In the case of the mainland economy, the PBC has been unwilling to accept the enormous base-money expansion that these foreign exchange purchases would entail and as a result has been sterilizing liquidity through domestic debt issuance as well as other channels. By and large, these operations have led to a fall in base money on the central bank balance sheet and a rise in other liabilities—in other words, a drop in NDA.

Now, for anyone looking at this process from the outside, there are two possible explanations for what is going on. One is that the drop in NDA is an endogenous reaction to (or "caused by") the rise in NFA, and the other is just the reverse—i.e., that declining NDA is somehow causing the increase in NFA.

The first is what we might call the "balance-of-payments approach to the monetary accounts" and is the model that most working economists in China would use to analyze the effects of central bank policy: In the face of large external surpluses, the PBC uses sterilization policy to avoid a massive blowout in domestic base-money growth, but the surpluses themselves are the result of other factors that have little or nothing to do with the behavior of base money in a direct sense.

The latter, by implication, is called the "monetary approach to the balance of payments" and argues that conventional wisdom has it backwards: Actually, PBC sterilization is the main reason that the mainland has a trade surplus in the first place. This explanation, put forward by Michael Mussa (chapter 8 in this conference volume), suggests that by holding base-money growth below the rate of overall broad-money growth, the PBC is forcing Chinese consumers to curtail spending.

It is easy to see the temptations of this latter story, as it offers the economic equivalent of a "unified field theory," purporting to link exchange rate policy to both the rise of China's trade imbalance and the fall in consumer spending in one fell swoop. However, against the backdrop of mainland experience, it does not seem to hold up very well at all.

To begin with, Mussa's model hinges crucially on two key assumptions: that (1) households and firms hold a constant share of monetary balances in cash, and (2) banks have a constant base-money multiplier—i.e., that banks do not hold variable excess reserve balances as a share of deposits, neither of which is remotely true in practice. In fact, the ratio of cash to M2 has been both volatile and falling, on average, for the past two decades, and one of the reasons the ratio of base money to GDP could fall to 35 percent in 2005 from nearly 39 percent over the preceding decade without causing any trend slowdown in credit or broad-money growth is precisely that banks were stuffed with excessive reserve liquidity balances to begin with. Unfortunately, if these two assumptions are removed, the story breaks down completely—i.e., there is nothing left upon which to hang a "monetary approach" argument.

Nor have we seen any related signs of stress on balance sheets in China: Money market interest rates and long-term bond yields remained at rock-bottom levels from the beginning of the sterilization era in 2002 right through the end of 2006, and the mainland property and equity markets actually went through an unprecedented boom. This is hardly a picture of domestic agents scrambling to find funding in order to prop up their monetary holdings.

The biggest problem, however, is that the story does not fit the broader facts in China as laid out earlier on. Mussa identifies slowing consumer spending and rising household savings as the main drivers of the trade imbalance, but as seen above, the household saving ratio has not increased at all in the mainland. Instead, what really needs to be explained is the sharp rise in corporate savings together with the concomitant and equally sharp increase in domestic heavy industrial supply relative to demand, and the "monetary approach" is essentially helpless here (in fact, the model seems to predict a *fall* in corporate saving rates as Chinese firms borrow from abroad to prop up domestic activity in the face of a base-money crunch).

I would add as a final note that for Goldstein and Lardy's purposes, the story is downright redundant as well. If you conclude, as the authors have done both here and elsewhere, that the explosion in Chinese high value-added investment and subsequently in net high value-added trade is tied to a pegged/undervalued renminbi, then as discussed above you already have a "unified field theory" that explains the rise of the trade surplus, the increase in gross corporate saving, the falling household share of economic activity, and the sharply skewed sectoral growth pattern, all in terms of the exchange rate—and all without having to resort to problematic theories of monetary balance sheet adjustment in the process. In this light, it is all the more surprising that they chose to give the monetary approach arguments such prominence in their paper.

Comment
Renminbi Revaluation
and US Dollar Depreciation

FAN GANG

In addition to providing an excellent overview of all the issues in the debate on China's exchange rate regime and policies, Morris Goldstein and Nicholas Lardy make very strong and convincing arguments that the current gradual, small-step renminbi revaluation policy is costly for China for several reasons, among which are the following:

- growing protectionism against China's exports (or possible sanctions against it for alleged "manipulation" of its exchange rate) or the slowdown of the world economy caused by the global imbalances, both of which will make China gain less anyway from its undervalued currency;

- domestic overliquidity, which would lead to either overheating and inflation or asset bubbles, thus severely damaging China's long-term growth; and

- structural distortions caused by repressed interest rates and an undervalued currency, which may also lead to economic, financial, and social problems.

Fan Gang is director of the National Economic Research Institute, China Reform Foundation, and economics professor at Peking University, China.

Therefore, Goldstein and Lardy recommend faster revaluation and greater flexibility in the exchange rate regime for the sake of China's own interests.

Risks Associated with Different Approaches

China's monetary authority is aware of the costs and risks of quick and large renminbi revaluation, as China is facing increasing external trade frictions and domestic overheating. However, they might also be weighing the costs associated with the alternatives—i.e., the consequences of fast and large revaluation of the renminbi in a short period to meet the requirement of the US Congress and market speculators, say, a 30 percent renminbi revaluation in one year. The following may be some of their concerns.

First is job loss, which is the fundamental reason many political forces in China oppose large appreciation. There is a thing called "Chinese domestic politics." Compared with US domestic politics, which is very often used as an excuse for US foreign policies, Chinese domestic politics involves a much larger number of people, such as 300 million underemployed rural laborers, who earn about US$500 per year, and another 300 million immigrant workers, who earn about US$1,000 per year. Such domestic politics constrains policymakers from making a move when they are facing high pressure to create more jobs to ease social disparities.

But this is not the only problem. If the large appreciation were to solve the problem of China's external imbalance once and for all, the Chinese authorities would take the action. They would supplement it with financial subsidies to those who would suffer from the shocks caused by such currency revaluation. But the problem is that the Chinese authorities might not be sure that the problems would be solved that way. Jobs might be lost, but those lost jobs would not go to the United States but to countries such as Vietnam and Bangladesh, and the US current account deficit as a whole, or even the deficit with China, would remain unchanged. US politicians would be eased for a while but would still not be satisfied.

Meanwhile, more importantly, the US dollar has historically been falling against major world currencies, sharply in recent months, due to the subprime mortgage turmoil and other reasons. And it has been predicted to depreciate further no matter how much the renminbi appreciates.

So, given the expectation that the US current account deficit will remain unchanged and the US dollar will fall further, it seems rational for Chinese policymakers to believe that even if the renminbi were revalued by 30 percent today, the US Congress and market speculators might request another "jump" again very soon.

Even worse, between the large shocks (to the Chinese economy) caused by large revaluations, there would be greater speculation and greater capital movement, inward and outward, through various channels. China's immature and fragile financial system would not be able to bear those risks.

In summary, in the view of Chinese policymakers, the costs or risks associated with a quick revaluation are larger, and less predictable and manageable, than the costs associated with the current gradual approach, if their calculation goes beyond immediate consequences.

Equilibrium Exchange Rate?

The argument for quick revaluation of the renminbi is based on the assumption that there is a reasonably stable equilibrium exchange rate, which China should try to approach as soon as possible. But the problem here is that given the fast changes in the structure of the world economy and the recent turmoil in global financial markets, which is associated with global overliquidity with oversupplied US dollars, any exchange rate equilibrium for the renminbi may be very short-lived one way or another.

When it comes to their own interests, the Chinese take a long-term perspective rather than a short-term view. Today's China is different from Japan of the 1980s, with which many like to compare today's China. China is still a country with an per capita income of $2,000, and Japan was not a developing economy after World War II. While Japanese blue-collar workers earned a wage 80 percent that of their US counterparts in the 1980s, Chinese workers today earn 30 to 50 times less than what their US counterparts earn. China has a long way to go before it catches up. And during this long drive, China will face many risks and obstacles, which may require exchange rate adjustment one way or another. From this point of view, it may be wise for China to take small steps for any short term and avoid overshooting and large swings. It is also necessary to keep capital controls for a while to avoid being overexposed to risks in a highly volatile international financial market.

This does not mean that China should not go for a market system or financial-market liberalization with a free floating exchange rate regime in the long run. A developing country with very low bases needs to have different approaches to market-oriented transition. And hasty liberalization of the financial system and capital account when the whole domestic system (not only the financial but also all economic, legal, and political components) is still underdeveloped may lead to significant slowdown in both economic development and financial maturity, as shown by the Asia financial crisis of the late 1990s. Compared with Indonesia and Thailand, China is an even more complex, low-level developing economy with greater disparities and disorders. A gradual approach to currency revaluation may be more of "equilibrium" in terms of long-term economic development.

Manipulation and Surveillance

With the current account surplus up to 8 percent of GDP and increasing, China is now blamed as a country with "fundamental misalignment" in its exchange rate, even called a manipulator of its exchange rate.

First, it should be recognized that China's domestic structural problems have been contributing to the global imbalance. The most fundamental "misalignment" is actually its domestic saving and consumption imbalance, not the exchange rate disequilibrium. No matter how quick currency revaluation is, if the system repeatedly generates a saving rate up to 50 percent of GDP, the surplus will not be effectively reduced. Changing this situation requires reforming China's fiscal, financial, and social systems, as well as further economic development and employment generation.

In terms of exchange rate policy, it should also be recognized that it might be too late for China to give up the fixed exchange rate regime and go back to a more flexible exchange rate. As recently as 2003, the US government and the International Monetary Fund (IMF) applauded China for holding on to the fixed regime against market speculation for renminbi devaluation. China was benefiting from its policy of a stable exchange rate at that time too. So why have policymakers realized the need for change after so long?

However, how can one call a system moving away from a fixed regime (which has long been "compatible" with IMF rules) to managed floating as manipulation under the same IMF framework? Should it go back to the fixed regime to avoid being blamed for manipulation?

More importantly, it seems strange that the "surplus accumulator" is now blamed for manipulation, not the "deficit accumulator." According to banking theory and practice, loans create deposits (otherwise who would take the deposits?), debts create credits (people buy bonds only when bonds are issued), and deficits create surpluses, not the other way around! Why should one not ask the question, where are the US dollars or US dollar debt assets held by many countries as foreign exchange reserves coming from in the first place? Why is a money printer not "manipulating" but the ones who accept the money are?

One should not forget that, while globalization has proceeded in production and financial markets, the world does not yet have a global currency or a global central bank, and it has not had a gold standard since the Nixon Shock in 1970. As a result, we have currency asymmetry, or a monetary system in which some economically and financially stronger countries issue their own currencies, which serve as reserve currencies for others (who pay seigniorage, as they should).

In such an asymmetric system, when "private goods" (national currency) serve as public goods (international currency), the first problem one should be prepared to face is how to discipline money printing in order to avoid moral hazard. The reserve currency country could be tempted to print too much money for its own interests. It may not have an exchange rate policy per se; it simply does not need one because exchange with it is everyone else's problem. However, its fiscal and monetary policies all matter in determining how much money should be printed. And as the currency is used internationally, the risks from overliquidity will spread easily to all corners of the world and be shared by all nations that buy financial assets or hold reserve assets denominated in that currency (similar to what has happened in the current subprime mortgage crisis). Without an effective mechanism to prevent oversupply of reserve currency, there will be global overliquidity and repeated devaluation of the reserve currency.

Therefore, the IMF should first check US fiscal and monetary policies before checking whether developing countries are doing things (such as revaluation) to accommodate the falling US dollar. Unfortunately, just the opposite has happened because such surveillance of US policies does not exist, and the IMF was not created for that purpose in the first place. As a result, similar exchange rate problems have repeatedly arisen since the 1970s. Now it is the renminbi's turn.

We are in a typical, not unique, situation under the current global monetary arrangement: A country that does not fully, immediately, and quickly or "flexibly" accommodate US dollar depreciation may be blamed as a manipulator and be subjected to IMF surveillance.

Concluding Remarks

The Chinese currency should be revalued as China's productivity is increasing, and the country should improve its domestic economic structures so that the saving rate can be decreased in order to reduce the current account surplus. However, remember that the exchange rate involves at least two currencies, not one. The causes of the problem may also be on the other side of the equation. Finding out all causes of the problem may not mean that they are fixed soon, but at least it allows for a better understanding of the distribution of responsibility and the difficulties on both sides of the equation.

Global overliquidity and the repeated decline of the US dollar are part of a symptom of the profound cause of the ongoing global imbalance— i.e., the global monetary system itself, known as Bretton Woods II since 1970, the year that marked the abandonment of the gold standard in the global system. What has happened since is still to be fully understood. We are still searching for an agenda to improve global governance for more stable and balanced globalization.

References

Anderson, Jonathan. 2006. *The Complete RMB Handbook,* 4th ed. UBS Investment Research Asian Focus, September 16.

Fan, Gang. 2006. Currency Asymmetry, Global Imbalances, and Rethinking of the International Currency System. In *Global Imbalances and the US Debt Problem: Should Developing Countries Support the US Dollar?* ed., Jan Joost Teunissen and Age Akkerman. Forum on Debt and Development.

McKinnon, Ronald. 2005. *Exchange Rates under the East Asian Dollar Standard: Living with Conflicted Virtue.* Cambridge, MA: MIT Press. (Chinese translation, 2005; Japanese, forthcoming 2007).

McKinnon, Ronald. 2006. China's Exchange Rate Trap: Japan Redux. Paper prepared for the American Economic Association Meetings, Boston, January 7.

Mundell, Robert. 2004. China's Exchange Rate: The Case for the Status Quo. Paper presented at the International Monetary Fund seminar on the Foreign Exchange System, Dalian, China, May.

Prestowitz, Clyde. 2005. *Three Billion New Capitalists: The Great Shift of Wealth and Power to the East.* New York: Basic Books.

2

Monetary Policy Independence, the Currency Regime, and the Capital Account in China

ESWAR S. PRASAD

The Chinese economy has performed remarkably over the last two decades, with annual GDP growth averaging nearly 10 percent. The particular combination of macroeconomic and structural policies that has generated this growth has clearly worked well. But rapid growth can hide, and in some cases even exacerbate, a number of deeper problems. China's financial sector is in poor shape and has distorted domestic demand; the patterns of investment financing could lead to a resurgence of nonperforming loans (NPLs) in the future and, by fueling a buildup of excess capacity in some sectors, could generate deflationary risks in the medium term. In the short term, some pressures are becoming evident in other forms, such as asset price booms, particularly in equity markets.

The sustainability of growth, while an important concern, may not even be the key problem, as indirect and subtle costs in the current growth

Eswar S. Prasad is the Tolani Senior Professor of Trade Policy in the Department of Applied Economics and Management at Cornell University. Earlier versions of this chapter were presented at the American Enterprise Institute, the China Banking Regulatory Commission, the People's Bank of China, the China Center for Economic Research at Peking University, the European Bank for Reconstruction and Development, the Reserve Bank of India, and the Peterson Institute for International Economics. The author thanks Philip Levy, Justin Lin, Luo Ping, Li Ruogu, Andrew Sheng, and numerous other colleagues for useful discussions and comments. He is grateful to Sun Tao for help in obtaining some of the data used in this chapter. Rahul Anand provided able research assistance.

model deserve attention. Tight management of the exchange rate has been facilitated by financial repression and a relatively closed capital account. Among other things, this has meant very low real rates of return for households, which save a lot and have few investment opportunities other than domestic bank deposits. The policies have also curtailed financial sector development, leading to inefficient intermediation of domestic capital. Clearly, large welfare costs are associated with these constraints.

The growth strategy has also involved a number of policy distortions and constraints that have greatly reduced the room for policy maneuver if any large shocks hit the economy. Such shocks could come from internal sources, such as loss of confidence in the banking system or social instability generated by rising inequality. They could also arise from external sources, such as international capital-market crises, a collapse of external demand, US trade sanctions, or flaring tensions over Taiwan. Monetary policy is typically the first line of defense against such shocks, but constrained by maintaining a tightly managed exchange rate, it can at best play a very limited role for China. There appears to be room for fiscal maneuver because the explicit levels of the fiscal deficit and government debt are quite low, but these may be deceptive, as there are large contingent liabilities in the state-owned banking system and huge unfunded pension liabilities. The financial system is still dysfunctional in many ways and may not be deep or robust enough to withstand a significant shock.

What should China do to prepare itself to deal with shocks and make its growth more balanced and sustainable? The banking system should be made more robust and driven by market principles, and the financial system should be broadened to create both alternative sources of funding for firms and alternative investment opportunities for households and firms. The state-owned enterprise sector needs to be further corporatized by hardening budget constraints. There is a need for a better social safety net and a better system for delivery of social services.

Many of the reforms are interrelated and trying to implement them in isolation is not an effective way to proceed. Stable macroeconomic policies and a well-developed and efficient financial sector are essential ingredients for balanced and sustainable growth, but these two intermediate objectives would be helped by effective monetary policy and further capital account liberalization, which in turn require a flexible exchange rate. Ignoring these linkages—for instance, by trying to push forward with banking reforms while holding monetary policy hostage to an exchange rate objective—makes an already difficult reform process even harder. Similarly, financial repression has kept the real price of capital cheap and, along with subsidized energy and land prices, shifted production toward capital-intensive methods. This works at cross purposes with the authorities' goal of boosting employment growth and facilitating the transition of the rural unemployed and underemployed to employment in manufacturing and services.

Ultimately, the essence of the policy debate can be framed in terms of the pace and sequencing of reforms required to turn China's economic strengths into forces that allow the growth miracle to be sustained and reduce the risks of its being derailed by shocks.

Investment-Led Growth

One dimension of the Chinese growth story of particular relevance to the arguments in this chapter is the composition of growth. Investment in physical capital has been a major contributor to growth during this decade, in some recent years accounting for nearly two-thirds of nominal GDP growth. Private consumption, by contrast, has made a much smaller contribution to growth.[1] One consequence of the investment-heavy expansion has been relatively slow employment growth.[2] From 2000 to 2005, growth of total nonagricultural employment averaged only 3 percent per annum compared with average nonagricultural GDP growth of about 9.5 percent.

Why has investment growth been so strong? A substantial fraction of the investment in China has been financed by credit from state-owned banks offered at low interest rates. Cheap capital has played a big part in skewing the capital-labor ratio and holding down employment growth (Aziz 2006). Recent increases in the base lending rate have been far too small to raise the real price of capital to a meaningful level for an economy experiencing annual real growth of over 10 percent (figures 2.1a and 2.1b). Local governments provide subsidized land to encourage investment. And energy prices continue to be administered and made available to enterprises at prices below international levels.

Much of the recent investment has also been financed through retained earnings of profitable firms, which ought to be more defensible on the basis of the opportunity cost of alternative uses for those funds. However, even here the picture is not clear. Until very recently, profitable state enterprises were not required to pay dividends to the state. This suggests that investment may have been spurred by the minimal rates of return on bank deposits, which made even marginal investment projects seem in the money. The risk, of course, is that such high rates of investment in industries with favorable demand conditions may lead to a buildup of excess capacity in those industries, which could become evident in the event of adverse demand shocks (Goldstein and Lardy 2004).

National saving rates have been even higher than investment rates, as both household and corporate savings have risen in recent years. The uncertainties engendered by the transition to a market economy, the limited

---

1. For details on the composition of growth, see Aziz (2006) and Lardy (2006).

2. See Brooks (2004) for some detailed calculations.

Figure 2.1a   One-year base lending and deposit rates, 1989–2007

percent

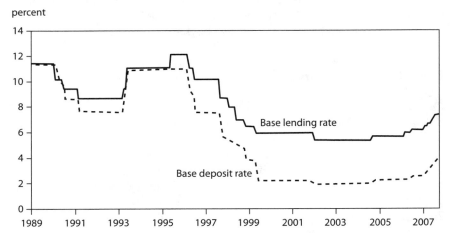

Note: Data are for January of years indicated.

Source: CEIC data.

Figure 2.1b   One-year real lending and deposit rates, 1998–2007

percent

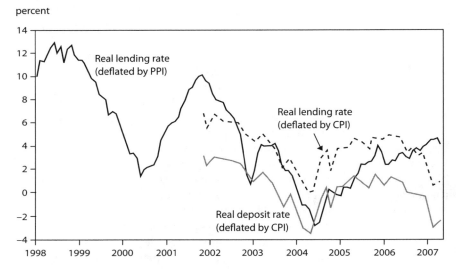

CPI = consumer price index
PPI = producer price index

Note: Real rates calculated by deflating the nominal rates by 12-month trailing CPI or PPI inflation. Data are for January of years indicated.

Sources: CEIC data and author's calculations.

availability of instruments to borrow against future income to finance purchases (e.g., major durable goods and housing), and the lack of international portfolio diversification opportunities have all contributed to high household savings (Chamon and Prasad 2007). Financial system repression has meant that there are few alternatives to funneling these savings into deposits in the state-owned banking system.

Households willingly hold bank deposits despite the weaknesses of the banking system because of the government's implicit deposit insurance. This provides abundant liquidity for banks to expand credit, which largely finances investment by state enterprises because of the distorted incentives that lenders face. As mentioned above, profitable state enterprises are not required to pay dividends, encouraging them to plow retained earnings (which are counted as enterprise savings) back into investment. Thus, the investment boom in recent years has been fueled by cheap credit and overoptimistic expectations of future demand growth in sectors that are doing well at present.

Macroeconomic Policies

China has had a relatively stable exchange rate against the US dollar since 1995. Since 2001 the exchange rate has been kept from appreciating only by massive intervention in the exchange market. Such intervention in tandem with sustained high export growth and a burgeoning current account surplus likely to hit 12 percent of GDP in 2007 (table 2.1), indicates a substantially undervalued currency. Figures 2.2a and 2.2b show that despite an appreciation of the renminbi against the dollar since June 2005, the real effective exchange rate of the renminbi is now below its recent peak in 2002, largely due to the dollar's depreciation against other major currencies.

Resisting pressures for exchange rate appreciation has fueled a surge in the accumulation of international reserves since 2001 (figure 2.3). Table 2.2 shows that, from 2001 to 2004, inflows of speculative capital in anticipation of eventual renminbi appreciation accounted for most of the pickup in the pace of reserve accumulation relative to the period from 1998 to 2000. During 2005–06, speculative inflows shrank, but the slack was more than taken up by a dramatic surge in the trade balance, which doubled the rate of reserve accumulation from 2001 to 2004. The inflows resulting from these factors have added to the liquidity in the banking system and further complicated the control of credit growth.

Why have these inflows not led to rampant inflation? The answer lies in the ability of the People's Bank of China (PBC) to sterilize these inflows. In most emerging market economies, such sterilization usually runs into limits quickly. Government bonds that are used to soak up liquidity have to offer increasingly higher yields to convince domestic economic agents to hold them, leading to ever-increasing costs to the budget.

Table 2.1 Balance of payments, 1997–2007 (billions of US dollars)

Item	1997	1998	1999	2000	2001	2002	2003	2004	2005	2006	2007
Gross international reserves	143.4	149.8	158.3	168.9	218.7	295.2	412.2	618.6	825.6	1,072.6	1,338.7
	(15.0)	(14.7)	(14.6)	(14.1)	(16.5)	(20.3)	(25.1)	(32.0)	(36.8)	(40.8)	n.a.
Change in international reserves	34.9	6.4	8.5	10.5	49.8	76.5	117.0	206.3	207.0	247.0	266.1
A. Current account balance	37.0	31.5	21.1	20.5	17.4	35.4	45.9	68.7	160.8	249.9	162.9
	(3.9)	(3.1)	(1.9)	(1.7)	(1.3)	(2.4)	(2.8)	(3.6)	(7.2)	(9.5)	n.a.
Merchandise trade balance	46.2	46.6	36.0	34.5	34.0	44.2	44.7	59.0	134.2	217.7	135.7
	(4.9)	(4.6)	(3.3)	(2.9)	(2.6)	(3.0)	(2.7)	(3.1)	(6.0)	(8.3)	n.a.
B. Capital account balance	21.0	–6.3	5.2	2.0	34.8	32.3	52.7	110.7	63.0	10.0	90.2
Net foreign direct investment (FDI)	41.7	41.1	37.0	37.5	37.4	46.8	47.2	53.1	67.8	60.3	51.0
C. Errors and omissions, net	–22.3	–18.7	–17.8	–11.9	–4.9	7.8	18.4	27.0	–16.8	–12.9	13.1
Memorandum items:											
Non-FDI capital account balance (including errors and omissions)	–42.9	–66.1	–49.6	–47.4	–7.4	–6.7	23.9	84.6	–21.6	–63.2	52.3
Nominal GDP	953	1,019	1,083	1,198	1,325	1,454	1,641	1,932	2,244	2,626	n.a.

n.a. = not available

Notes: Figures in parentheses are percent of GDP. Data for 2007 are end-June data. The non-FDI capital account balance is the capital account balance minus net FDI plus net errors and omissions.

Sources: CEIC data; International Monetary Fund, *International Financial Statistics*; author's calculations.

Figure 2.2a   Renminbi-US dollar exchange rate, 1996–2007

renminbi per US dollar

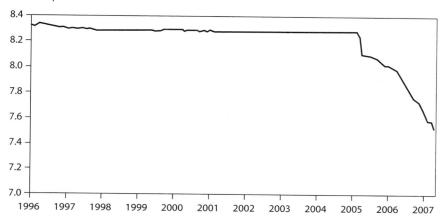

Source: International Monetary Fund, *International Financial Statistics.*

Figure 2.2b   Real and nominal effective exchange rates, 1996–2007

index (2000 = 100)

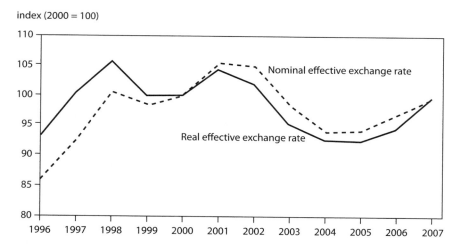

Note: Data for 2007 are for end-July.

Source: International Monetary Fund, *International Financial Statistics.*

However, in China, private saving rates, both household and corporate, continue to be very high; most of these savings invariably flow into the banking system, as there are few alternatives. This has made the banks flush with liquidity at a time when they are under pressure to hold down growth in credit. Banks also have an incentive to hold PBC bills rather

Figure 2.3   Foreign exchange reserves: Flows and stocks, 1995–2007

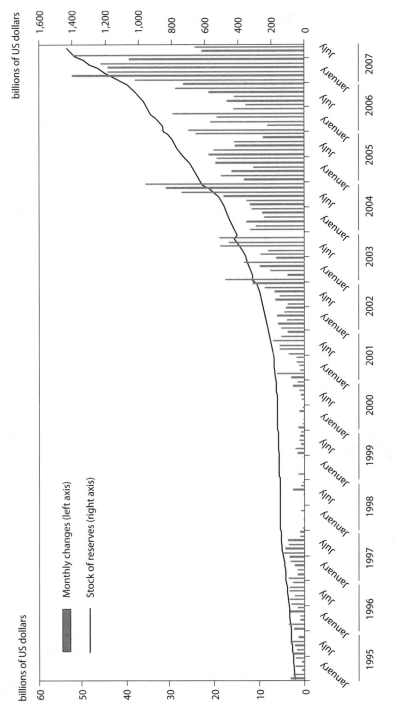

Sources: CEIC data and author's calculations.

Table 2.2   Decomposition of the recent reserve buildup
(billions of US dollars)

Item	Annual average 1998–2000 (1)	Annual average 2001–04 (2)	Annual average 2005–06 (3)	Change 2001–04 minus 1998–2000 (2)–(1)	Change 2005–06 minus 2001–04 (3)–(2)
Increase in foreign reserves	8.5	112.4	227.0	103.9	114.6
Current account balance	24.4	41.9	205.4	17.5	163.5
Capital account balance	0.3	57.7	36.5	57.4	−21.2
Net foreign direct investment (FDI)	38.5	46.1	64.1	7.6	17.9
Errors and omissions, net	−16.1	12.1	−14.9	28.2	−26.9
Non-FDI capital account balance (including errors and omissions)	−54.4	23.6	−42.4	78.0	−66.0

Notes: The non-FDI capital account balance is the capital account balance minus net FDI plus net errors and omissions.

Sources: CEIC data; International Monetary Fund, *International Financial Statistics*; author's calculations.

than increase their lending, as corporate lending, for instance, carries a capital requirement of 100 percent, whereas no capital needs to be put aside for lending to the government. Thus there is a great deal of demand for PBC bills even at relatively low interest rates. This means that, at the margin, sterilization is essentially a moneymaking operation for the PBC, abstracting from the effects of changes in the exchange rate. Figure 2.4 shows how the present configuration of interest rates in China and the United States generates this profit from the PBC's sterilization operations.

However, such a cost-benefit calculation can be deceptive. The lack of exchange rate flexibility not only reduces monetary policy independence but also hampers banking-sector reforms. The PBC's inability to use interest rates as a primary tool of monetary policy implies that credit growth has to be controlled by blunter and nonmarket-oriented tools, including targets or ceilings for credit growth as well as so-called nonprudential administrative measures, which effectively amount to moral suasion. This vitiates the process of banking reform by keeping banks' lending growth under the administrative guidance of the PBC rather than letting it be guided by market signals. The constraint has also perpetuated large efficiency costs due to provision of cheap credit to inefficient state enterprises (Dollar and Wei 2007). The incidence of these and other costs of banking system inefficiency are not obvious, but depositors may ultimately bear the burden in the form of low or negative real returns on their saving.[3]

---

3. In July 2007, the benchmark one-year deposit rate was raised to 3.33 percent and the tax rate on bank interest income was cut from 20 to 5 percent. The effective after-tax deposit rate is now 3.16 percent, which is still below the current rate of consumer price index inflation.

Figure 2.4   PBC bill rates versus US treasury yields

percent annualized

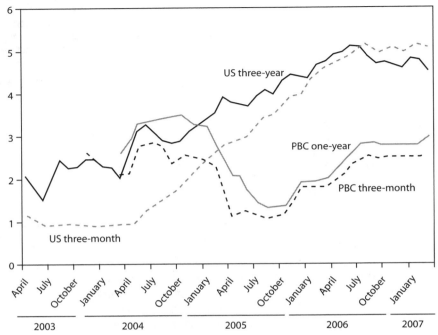

Sources: CEIC data; People's Bank of China (PBC); US Treasury.

The management of capital flows has been another crucial component of macroeconomic policy. Along with tax benefits and other incentives, extensive capital controls have been used to promote inward foreign direct investment while other forms of inflows, especially portfolio debt, have been discouraged (Prasad and Wei 2007). Capital controls have also been important in protecting the banking system from external competition by restricting the entry of foreign banks and making it harder to take capital out of the country. The limited development of debt and equity markets means that the state-owned banking system is effectively the only major game in town, for both borrowers and savers.

China's approach to exchange rate policy and capital account liberalization may indicate a desire to maintain stability on the domestic and external fronts, and the large stock of foreign exchange reserves resulting from these policies may insure against vulnerabilities arising from a weak banking system. But the policy distortions needed to maintain this approach could generate imbalances, impose potentially large welfare costs, and become a source of instability themselves.

Path to Reforms

It is not easy to isolate specific policies to deal with the particular problems identified above. The reform process appears to have reached a stage at which the traditional approach of undertaking incremental reforms in isolation from others may not work well any more.[4] Given the prominence of China's exchange rate regime in discussions about China-US bilateral relations as well as the issue of global current account imbalances, currency policy illustrates well the interconnectedness of various reforms.

What are the costs of an inflexible exchange rate? Figures 2.5a and 2.5b lay out some of the connections. The main point is that an inflexible exchange rate, while not the root cause of imbalances in the economy, requires a large set of distortionary policies to be maintained over long periods of time. Through multiple channels, these distortions hurt economic welfare and could, over time, shift the balance of risks in the economy. Flipping the argument around makes it easier to see why exchange rate flexibility matters for China. It is not necessarily because it will have a large or lasting direct impact on problems such as the US-China trade imbalance.[5] Rather, the case for a flexible exchange rate rests on a deeper set of policy priorities, with the ultimate objective being balanced and sustainable growth in the longer term.

An independent interest rate policy is a key tool for improving domestic macroeconomic management and promoting stable growth and low inflation. Monetary policy independence is, however, a mirage if the central bank is mandated to attain an exchange rate objective. Capital controls insulate monetary policy to some extent, but they are notoriously leaky and tend to become increasingly less effective over time.[6] Thus a flexible exchange rate is a prerequisite for an independent monetary policy. An independent interest rate policy is also a key input into financial sector reforms. Using interest rate policy rather than government directives to guide credit expansion is essential to encourage banks to become more robust financial institutions. Trying to foster the commercial orien-

---

4. See Blanchard and Giavazzi (2005) and Prasad and Rajan (2006) for more on this point.

5. While Chinese currency appreciation by itself may not affect global current account imbalances very much, it would be an important step toward resolving those imbalances, as other Asian economies may be emboldened to allow their currencies to appreciate if China made the first move.

6. A crude way of measuring net flows through unofficial channels is to look at the errors and payments category of the balance of payments. Prasad and Wei (2007) document that during periods of downward (depreciation) pressures on the renminbi—e.g., the Asian crisis period—errors and omissions were negative and large, suggesting significant capital flight. From 2003 to 2005, the errors and omissions turned into large positive numbers, reflecting speculative inflows in anticipation of renminbi appreciation. Gross unofficial flows could, of course, be much larger.

Figure 2.5a Lack of exchange rate flexibility complicates macro policy and reforms

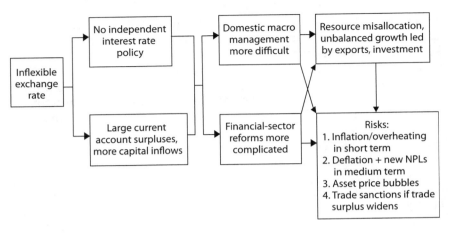

NPL = nonperforming loan

Figure 2.5b Making the right connections

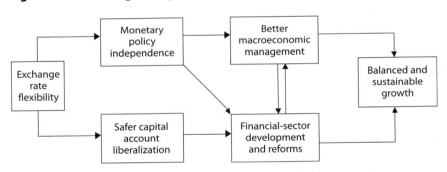

tation of the banking sector without monetary policy tools to guide credit and money growth vitiates banking reforms.

The argument that the financial system needs to be fully modernized before allowing currency flexibility therefore has the problem backward. Durable banking reforms are likely to be stymied if the PBC's ability to manage interest rates is constrained by the exchange rate objective. The PBC then has to revert to its old practice of telling state banks how much to lend and to whom, which hardly gives banks the right incentives to assess and price risk carefully in their loan portfolios. This makes banking reforms even more complicated than they already are.

Another requirement for broader financial development is a stable macroeconomic environment, for which—again—good macroeconomic policies, including effective monetary policy, are necessary. A lack of effective macroeconomic management could generate risks through the financial sector: Without room for maneuver on interest rates, liquidity flows into the economy could result in asset price bubbles, including in the real estate and stock markets. These markets could thus become vulnerable to sudden and unpredictable shifts in investor sentiment that send them tumbling at the slightest provocation, with broader ripple effects throughout the economy.

Opening the capital account to inflows and outflows could also be an important catalyst to developing the domestic financial sector (Kose et al. 2006). Inflows can bring in technical expertise in developing new financial instruments, creating and managing risk assessment systems, and improving corporate governance. The approach of using foreign strategic investors to improve the efficiency of domestic banks is a strategy that Chinese authorities see as useful in their overall reform effort. Allowing outflows would help increase efficiency by creating competition for the domestic banking system and limiting the captive source of funds—bank deposits—that now keep domestic banks flush with liquidity. However, opening the capital account ahead of introducing greater flexibility in the exchange rate could pose serious problems in the future (see Eichengreen 2004; Prasad, Rumbaugh, and Wang 2005; and Yu 2007).

Ultimately, stable macroeconomic policies and a well-developed and efficient financial sector are crucial ingredients for balanced and sustainable growth. Exchange rate policy is clearly not an end in itself; rather, as figure 2.5b shows, it is important in achieving deeper policy reforms and improving growth and welfare.

An Alternative Monetary Policy Framework

Instead of a tightly managed exchange rate, what could be a suitable alternative anchor for inflation expectations? Marvin Goodfriend and I have argued that China should adopt an explicit inflation objective—a long-run range for the inflation rate and an acknowledgement that low inflation is the priority for monetary policy—as a new anchor for monetary policy (Goodfriend and Prasad 2007). An inflation objective, coupled with exchange rate flexibility, would best stabilize domestic demand in response to internal and external macroeconomic shocks. More broadly, focusing on inflation stability is the best way for monetary policy to achieve financial stability and high employment growth. Over time, the inflation objective would provide a basis for currency flexibility. In short, exchange rate reform is a key component of an overall reform strategy that is in China's short- and long-term interests.

The time is right to make the switch, as economic growth is strong and headline inflation low. After the switch, the PBC could continue its current approach to monetary policy at an operational level, including setting targets for money and credit growth. The crucial difference would be to switch the strategic focus from the exchange rate to inflation, meaning that the currency could appreciate or depreciate in response to more fundamental economic forces, such as productivity growth. This framework would subsume monitoring of monetary aggregates such as M2 and private credit, but directly targeting these aggregates is increasingly inappropriate for an economy such as China's, which is undergoing rapid structural transformation and changes in its financial markets. A full-fledged inflation targeting regime could be a useful long-term goal, but the approach I have outlined above is more practical for the foreseeable future and should deliver most of the benefits of formal inflation targeting.

Two related points are worth noting. First, an independent interest rate policy requires a flexible exchange rate, not a one-off revaluation or a sequence of revaluations. A flexible exchange rate buffers some of the effects of interest rate changes, especially in offsetting the temptation for capital to flow in or out in response to such changes. A one-off revaluation can solve this problem temporarily but could create even more problems subsequently if interest rate actions in a different direction become necessary, or if investor sentiment and the pressures for capital inflows or outflows shift. Second, exchange rate flexibility should not be confused with full opening of the capital account. An open capital account would allow the currency to float freely and be determined by the market. But the exchange rate can be made flexible and the objective of monetary policy independence achieved even if the capital account is not fully open.

Chinese policymakers often express concern that, given the fragility of the domestic banking system, exchange rate flexibility could be disastrous. There are two possible factors behind this concern. One is that sharp changes in the value of the currency could destroy bank balance sheets. There is little evidence, however, that Chinese banks have large exposures to foreign currency assets or external liabilities denominated in renminbi that would hurt their balance sheets greatly if the renminbi were to appreciate in the short run.

A more serious concern is that outflows of capital could starve the domestic banking system of liquidity by allowing domestic savers to take their money abroad. This is where the difference between exchange rate flexibility and capital account liberalization becomes especially important. With even the moderately effective capital controls in place now, there is no reason why China could not allow for greater exchange rate flexibility. Even if a flexible exchange rate does not yield a true market equilibrium rate because capital flows are constrained, it can allow for an independent monetary policy. Also, such flexibility does not by itself generate channels for evading controls on capital flows. In short, as a reason for not moving more quickly toward a flexible exchange rate, banking system weaknesses constitute a red herring.

Conclusion

China has achieved remarkable economic progress in the last three decades, but a great deal of work remains to be done to make the economy resilient to large shocks, ensure the sustainability of its growth, and translate this growth into corresponding improvements in the economic welfare of its citizens. Now is a good time to implement some of these essential reforms.

External pressure can help in the reform process, but only if it is placed in the right context. The debate in the United States about the Chinese exchange rate regime has been distorted in some ways and made political rather than substantive by placing it in the narrow context of the US-China trade balance. There is an important strategic and educational element related to reframing the exchange rate issue in a broader context. This is where external pressure from the international community can be helpful, not by threatening China with sanctions but by reorienting the discussion to focus on the linkages between currency reform and other core reforms on which there is broad consensus within China (Prasad 2007a, 2007b).

Working with China in a collaborative rather than confrontational manner could also help Chinese authorities develop deadlines for achieving specific policy goals. Such intermediate steps could be guideposts for the reform process and help to break down internal resistance to reforms. Commitments that China made in the context of accession to the World Trade Organization have helped to galvanize internal reforms. In China as in any other country, some groups stand to lose disproportionately from certain reforms, even if those reforms may be hugely beneficial overall. This is precisely where external pressure, applied judiciously, can help to generate enough momentum to support the forces that are predisposed to undertaking reforms. By contrast, a confrontational approach could well prove counterproductive, bolstering the forces opposed to reform and allowing them to paint certain changes as detrimental to China and in the interests only of other countries.

Ultimately, as far as Chinese reforms are concerned, there is a set of shared interests among policymakers in China, the United States, and elsewhere. Deep and enduring reforms that promote sustained and balanced growth in China are in the best interests of both China and the world economy.

References

Aziz, Jahangir. 2006. *Rebalancing China's Economy: What Does Growth Theory Tell Us?* IMF Working Paper 06/291. Washington: International Monetary Fund.

Blanchard, Olivier, and Francesco Giavazzi. 2005. *Rebalancing Growth in China: A Three-Handed Approach.* MIT Department of Economics Working Paper 05/32. Boston, MA: Massachusetts Institute of Technology.

Brooks, Ray. 2004. Labor Market Performance and Prospects. In *China's Growth and Integration into the World Economy*, ed. Eswar Prasad. IMF Occasional Paper no. 232. Washington: International Monetary Fund.

Chamon, Marcos, and Eswar Prasad. 2007. *The Determinants of Household Savings in China*. IMF Working Paper (forthcoming). Washington: International Monetary Fund.

Dollar, David, and Shang-Jin Wei. 2007. *Das (Wasted) Kapital: Firm Ownership and Investment Efficiency in China*. IMF Working Paper 07/9. Washington: International Monetary Fund.

Eichengreen, Barry. 2004. *Chinese Currency Controversies*. CEPR Discussion Paper 4375. London: Center for Economic Policy Research.

Goldstein, Morris, and Nicholas R. Lardy. 2004. *What Kind of Landing for the Chinese Economy?* Policy Briefs in International Economics 04-7. Washington: Institute for International Economics.

Goodfriend, Marvin, and Eswar Prasad. 2007. A Framework for Independent Monetary Policy in China. *CESifo Economic Studies* 53, no. 1: 2–41.

Kose, M. Ayhan, Eswar Prasad, Kenneth Rogoff, and Shang-Jin Wei. 2006. *Financial Globalization: A Reappraisal*. IMF Working Paper 06/189. Washington: International Monetary Fund.

Lardy, Nicholas. 2006. *China: Toward a Consumption-Driven Growth Path*. Policy Briefs in International Economics 06-6. Washington: Peterson Institute for International Economics.

Prasad, Eswar. 2007a. Exchange Rate Flexibility in China: Why It Really Matters and How to Make Progress. Testimony at the Senate Finance Committee Hearing on Risks and Reform: The Role of Currency in the US-China Relationship, March 28, 2007. Available at http://prasad.aem.cornell.edu.

Prasad, Eswar. 2007b. Reform and Liberalization of China's Financial Sector. Testimony at the US House of Representatives Committee on Financial Services Hearing on US Interests in the Reform of China's Financial Sector, June 6, 2007. Available at http://prasad.aem.cornell.edu.

Prasad, Eswar, and Raghuram Rajan. 2006. Modernizing China's Growth Paradigm. *American Economic Review* 96, no. 2: 331–36.

Prasad, Eswar, Thomas Rumbaugh, and Qing Wang. 2005. Putting the Cart before the Horse? Capital Account Liberalization and Exchange Rate Flexibility in China. *China and the World Economy* 13, no. 4: 3–20.

Prasad, Eswar, and Shang-Jin Wei. 2007. China's Approach to Capital Inflows: Patterns and Possible Explanations. In *Capital Controls and Capital Flows in Emerging Economies: Policies, Practices, and Consequences*, ed. Sebastian Edwards. Chicago: University of Chicago Press.

Yu, Yongding. 2007. Ten Years after the Asian Financial Crisis: The Fragility and Strength of China's Financial System. Chinese Academy of Social Sciences, Beijing. Photocopy.

Comment
Some Bubbles in the Discussion
of the Chinese Exchange Rate Policy

SHANG-JIN WEI

The word "renminbi" (RMB) was essentially unknown to most Americans before 2003, but a search of an electronic database (NewsPlus/Factiva) of all news articles in the four largest newspapers—*New York Times, Wall Street Journal, Washington Post,* and *USA Today*—reveals explosive growth in interest in the Chinese exchange rate in recent years. Between January 1, 1980 and December 31, 1982 only four articles in the four newspapers combined mentioned the renminbi, RMB, or Chinese yuan. From 1990 to 1992 only 19 articles mentioned them; ten years later, from 2000 to 2002, the count increased to 33 articles, still a relatively low number. Between January 1, 2005 and October 18, 2007, however, no less than 231 articles mentioned the words. If the count of the news articles were an asset price, such a rapid rise could have sparked suspicion of bubbles. I would like to comment on some possible bubbles in the discussion of China's exchange rate policy.

Eswar Prasad has stressed the benefits of a move to a more flexible exchange rate for China in improving its macroeconomic management. Others have advocated the benefits of a more flexible Chinese renminbi in alleviating global imbalances. I would like to suggest that both benefits have been oversold a bit in policy circles. First, the role of a flexible exchange rate regime in facilitating current account adjustment may be

Shang-Jin Wei is professor of finance and economics and the N. T. Wang Professor of Chinese Business and Economy at Columbia University's Graduate School of Business.

vastly exaggerated. Second, the virtue of a flexible renminbi exchange rate regime in enhancing the effectiveness of China's macroeconomic stability may also be overrated.

Would a Flexible Exchange Rate Really Speed Up Current Account Adjustment?

The above question is relevant not only because a country's current account imbalance is the difference between its national savings and national investment, the large US current account deficit reflects its large saving deficit, and the US bilateral deficit with China is only part of its overall deficit with the rest of the world. All these are true. Beyond them, many economists and policy wonks take it as self-evident that a flexible exchange rate regime must deliver a faster current account adjustment. Many International Monetary Fund (IMF) statements also reflect this supposition. However, no systematic evidence supports it. I have taken to calling it a faith-based initiative, widely assumed to be true and actively peddled to countries as policy advice but with little solid supportive evidence.

In a systematic analysis of the issue, Menzie Chinn and I find absolutely no support in the data for the notion that countries on a de facto flexible exchange rate regime exhibit faster convergence of their current account to a long-run equilibrium (Chinn and Wei 2007). The finding holds when we control for trade and financial openness and when we separate large from small countries. The current account does tend to revert to its long-run steady state, as is clearly reflected in our empirical work. However, the speed of adjustment is not systematically related to the degree of flexibility of a country's nominal exchange rate regime.

Should we be surprised by this finding? Perhaps not. The current account responds to the real exchange rate, not the nominal exchange rate. If the real exchange rate adjustment does not depend very much on the nominal exchange rate regime, then neither does current account adjustment. Chinn and I therefore check whether the nature of a country's nominal exchange rate regime significantly affects the adjustment process of its real exchange rate. After looking at enough regressions, we conclude that the answer is no: Real exchange rate adjustment is not systematically related to how flexible a country's nominal exchange rate regime is. If anything, there is slight but not very robust evidence that less flexible nominal exchange rate regimes sometimes exhibit faster real exchange rate adjustment.

Just to be clear, if one could engineer a real appreciation of the renminbi, it could affect China's trade or current account balance. In a separate research project that I am conducting with Caroline Freund and Chang Hong, using China's bilateral trade data and separating processing from nonprocessing trade, we find evidence that bilateral trade volume clearly responds to changes in the level of bilateral real exchange rate, especially for nonprocessing trade (Freund, Hong, and Wei 2007). But a more flexible exchange rate does not promise a faster current account adjustment or resolution of global current account imbalances.

If China were to opt for a more flexible exchange rate regime today, its real exchange rate would most likely appreciate on impact. However, given China's still shaky financial sector and the credit crunch in advanced economies, it is certainly possible that the real exchange rate would depreciate the day after tomorrow. It is useful to recall that today's expectation of renminbi undervaluation is a relatively recent phenomenon, emerging in late 2003. As figure 2.C1 clearly shows, until October 2003, the market actually expected a renminbi depreciation, as measured by the nondeliverable forward rate (Frankel and Wei 2007). But the expectation shifted in late 2003 when US officialdom and scholars at prominent think tanks started to raise the volume of their calls for a renminbi revaluation.

The very high speed of China's foreign reserve accumulation really took off within the last four years, as figure 2.C2 shows. It may very well be responding to a shift in market expectations of renminbi movement, or at least the reserve accumulation and the exchange rate speculation feed on each other. However, if it took only four years for China's foreign exchange reserve to triple in value, it may take only another four years for it to lose 60 percent of its value once the exchange rate expectation starts to reverse itself. Economic history books are full of examples of seemingly sudden shifts in market sentiment. A tight credit market in developed countries, such as the one we are seeing today, has in the past engendered a reversal of global capital flows and a concomitant shift in the valuation of emerging market currencies.

Would a Flexible Regime Vastly Improve the Effectiveness of China's Macro Policies?

To appeal to China's self-interest, advocates of a more flexible exchange rate regime say it will greatly enhance the effectiveness of China's domestic macroeconomic policy. As the logic goes, a more flexible regime would free the domestic interest rate to be an instrument for domestic macroeconomic stability and may benefit other policy objectives as well, such as financial reform and addressing future shocks. I agree that a shift to a more flexible exchange rate regime is a net positive for China, but I would caution that the benefits of doing so for China should not be overrated.

First, China's current monetary policy still has room for maneuver. Fundamentally, China's capital controls, while leaky, are binding at the

Figure 2.C1 Spot and forward rates of renminbi-US dollar, 2003–07

exchange rate

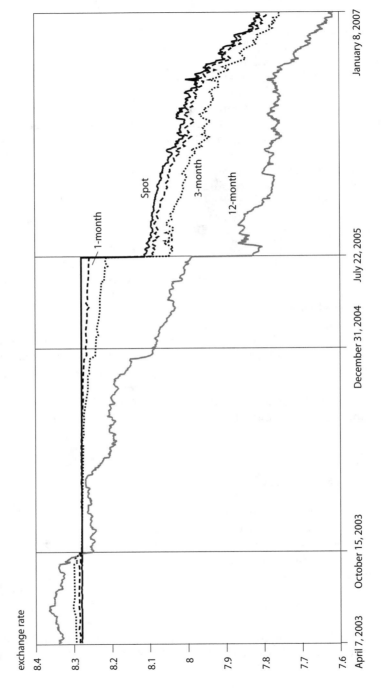

Source: Author's calculations based on the International Monetary Fund, *International Financial Statistics* and *World Economic Outlook* databases.

Figure 2.C2 China's current account and foreign exchange reserves, 1985–2006

percent of GDP

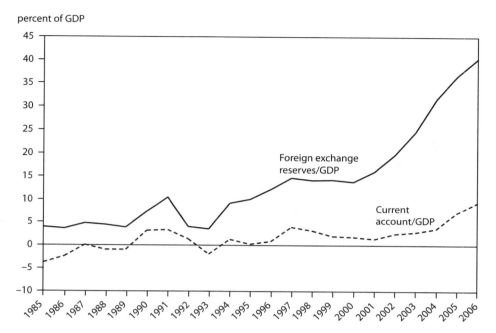

Source: Author's calculations based on the International Monetary Fund, *International Financial Statistics* and *World Economic Outlook* databases.

margin. The gap between lending and deposit rates can be widened and the required reserve ratio might also be raised if desired.

Second, China's fiscal policy also has room for maneuver. Many contingent liabilities should and may show up on the country's balance sheet, but state-owned firms collectively are making a profit that the government budget currently does not count. The state may require the firms to pay up more dividends to augment existing fiscal management tools. This provides a cushion for the use of the fiscal policy in managing macro economy.

Third, to the extent that the de facto dollar peg constrains the conduct of China's monetary policy, it may not be a bad policy. The most important goal of a good monetary policy is to maintain price stability. Beyond its role in promoting exports, the de facto peg to the US dollar has served China well as an anchor for the country's monetary policy. Once China switches to a substantially more flexible exchange rate regime, it will by definition lose this nominal anchor. One might prescribe an inflation-targeting framework, but one could question how faithfully China would follow such a framework.

Figure 2.C3 China's consumer price inflation, 1987–2006

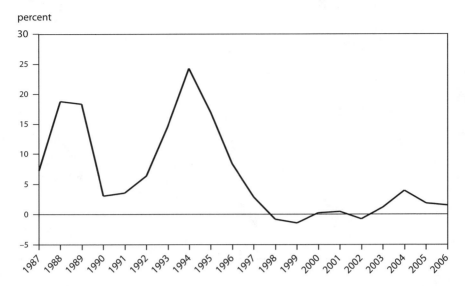

Source: Author's calculations based on the International Monetary Fund, *International Financial Statistics* and *World Economic Outlook* databases.

China's recent monetary history has clear bouts of double-digit inflation, as figure 2.C3 shows. Thus resisting political pressure to deviate from maintaining price stability is not necessarily a strong suit for the central bank. The current leadership at the central bank, Governor Zhou Xiaochuan and his deputies, happens to be superb. But leadership at the central bank could change (and there were indeed speculations of this kind recently), and a look at the recent history does not inspire absolute confidence that an inflation-targeting framework would be faithfully followed. A less stable domestic price is a risk that cannot easily be ruled out if and when the country shifts to a more flexible exchange rate regime.

Conclusion

I have stressed two points. First, empirical evidence does not support the notion that a flexible exchange rate regime would facilitate a faster current account adjustment. Second, the virtue of a flexible exchange rate regime in enhancing the effectiveness of China's macroeconomic policy may also be overrated.

I still think that the benefits of moving to a more flexible exchange rate regime likely outweigh the costs for China. However, China faces many challenges in its economy, including environmental degradation, rising income inequality, pervasive corruption, mining production safety, food production safety, and a constant threat of massive unemployment. In the grand scheme of things, in ranking the importance of all the reforms on the basis of a cost-to-benefit ratio, how much priority this particular reform—the shift of the exchange rate regime—should be given is a separate question.

References

Chinn, Menzie, and Shang-Jin Wei. 2007. Faith-Based Initiative: Do We Really Know that a Flexible Exchange Rate Regime Facilitates Current Account Adjustment? Unpublished working paper. University of Wisconsin, Madison, and Columbia University.

Frankel, Jeffrey, and Shang-Jin Wei. 2007. *Assessing China's Exchange Rate Regime*. NBER Working Paper 13100 (May). Cambridge, MA: National Bureau of Economic Research.

Freund, Caroline, Chang Hong, and Shang-Jin Wei. 2007. Bilateral Exchange Rates and Bilateral Trade Balance. Unpublished working paper. International Monetary Fund and Columbia University.

Comment
The Open Economy Trilemma:
An Alternative View from China's
Perspective

JIN ZHONGXIA

In my comments on Eswar Prasad's contribution to this volume, which covers issues that are important to both China and its major trading partners, I would like to begin with three observations. First, nobody is more concerned about the current imbalance than the Chinese authorities themselves. The government has placed the adjustment of imbalance at the highest priority this year. The difficulty is not in deciding whether the imbalance needs to be adjusted; it is in finding the best policy combination to accomplish it. Second, the degree of openness in China's capital account has been increasing over time, and as a result, the trade-off between exchange rate stability and the effectiveness of monetary policy may have become more relevant. Third, the renminbi's exchange rate in general has become more flexible in the past two years, and thus, there is more room for China's central bank to implement monetary policy more effectively.

Unanswered Questions

The so-called open economy trilemma (see Obstfeld and Taylor 1998), entailing the difficult decisions authorities make in determining exchange

Jin Zhongxia has been the chief representative of the Representative Office of the People's Bank of China for the Americas since June 2006.

Figure 2.C4   China's structural saving-investment imbalance, 1982–2006
(percent in current prices)

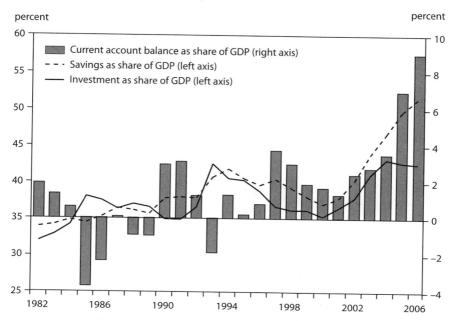

Source: National Statistics Bureau of China.

rate regimes, levels of capital mobility, and monetary policy effectiveness, is a useful analytical framework in general. However, some critical questions have not been answered—in particular, how effective the exchange rate policy could be in an economy with a structural imbalance between savings and investment. Figure 2.C4 shows the development in China's savings-investment imbalance in recent years. The corner solution implied by the trilemma (see figure 2.C5) is a theoretical answer (Yi and Tang 2001), but in reality, noncorner solutions could be more practical, especially for a developing country such as China (Jin 2007).

Exchange Rate: Stability Versus Flexibility

First, it is a demanding process to search for the appropriate degree of exchange rate flexibility or strike a balance between flexibility and stability. A number of factors must be considered. How flexible is flexible? What policy package can best adjust an imbalance? If the imbalance has not been significantly reduced in the short term, is it because the exchange rate is not flexible enough? Have the underlying structural issues been

Figure 2.C5 Open economy trilemma

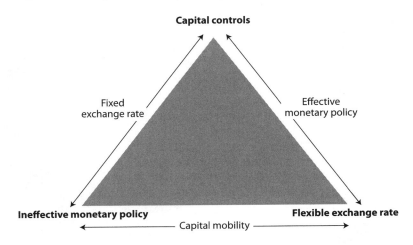

tackled with sufficient strength, or is the continued imbalance simply due to a time lag of the adopted policies?

Second, the actual currency regime in most economies lies between a fix and a free float (Reinhart and Rogoff 2002). The Fed has intervened in the foreign exchange market many times, in the late 1970s, 1980s, 1990s, and 2000. Even without direct intervention, the US dollar's exchange rate is not free from the effect of government intervention. The dollar has been subject to a strong influence of the federal funds rate, which in turn has been influenced heavily by monetary authorities aiming to achieve macroeconomic stability. Fortunately, nobody complains that the interest rate has been manipulated. Likewise, the International Monetary Fund (IMF) also gives its members the right to choose the currency regimes needed to achieve economic stability.

Monetary Policy Effectiveness: Beyond Currency Regime

The effectiveness of monetary policy is constrained by factors beyond currency regime. In China, the uncertainties in monetary transmission mechanisms, the rapid development of financial markets, and the technical difficulty in making the price index more reliable could affect the effectiveness of monetary policy. In addition, according to the Goldman Sachs Financial Conditions Index, though the Federal Reserve has tightened its policy stance by cumulatively raising the federal funds rate by 425 basis points between 2004 and 2007, real financial conditions have shown little sign of tightening if judged by higher stock prices, smaller term pre-

Figure 2.C6 Correlation between gap derived from interest rate parity and growth in foreign exchange reserves, 2001–07

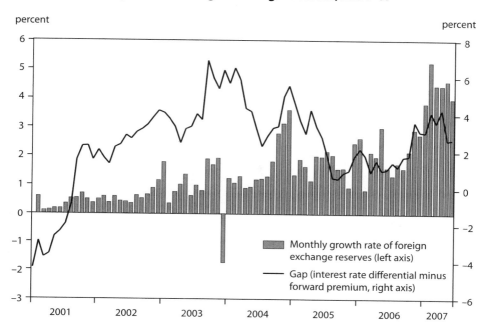

Sources: Bloomberg; People's Bank of China; author's calculations.

miums, and lower credit spreads (Hatzius 2007). Even when an economy chooses a very flexible currency regime, its monetary policy may not be as effective as expected.

Capital Account: Capital Mobility Is Increasing, but Management Matters

Capital mobility is increasing in China, but capital account management in both China and its major trading partners can greatly affect the exchange rate formation mechanism. On one hand, capital flow in China has become increasingly sensitive to changes in economic fundamentals. To illustrate, we can use an arbitrage indicator GAP (extent of deviation from interest rate parity) derived from interest rate parity, expecting that a rise or fall in the GAP leads to capital inflows or outflows and therefore changes in foreign exchange reserves. Figure 2.C6 shows that in China, since mid-2001, the correlation between the GAP and the growth rate of foreign exchange reserves has been quite obvious in many periods.

On the other hand, reforms of capital account management in China and the removal of investment protectionism abroad will help reduce the pressure of imbalance and potential excessive exchange rate fluctuation. Until very recently, China's foreign exchange management system had been biased toward encouraging capital inflow rather than outflow, which may have significantly exaggerated the renminbi's appreciation pressure. The recent surprise performance in the sale of a number of overseas portfolio investment funds under China's Qualified Domestic Institutional Investor (QDII) program has revealed great motivation in making overseas portfolio investments in household sector. In all cases, the subscription greatly exceeded the original quota in a single day. Without a more symmetric opening up of the capital account, it is unrealistic to estimate the equilibrium level of China's exchange rate.

Also, in spite of progress in financial globalization, restrictions in many countries on capital inflow and the lack of experience in overseas investment in China of both institutional and individual investors have been invisible obstacles to a market-based recycling of surplus. In developed countries, concerns about national security, sector monopoly, and interest groups could make many kinds of capital movement difficult. Both domestic and international factors have impeded the potential market-based recycling of surplus and could also have exaggerated the renminbi's appreciation pressure.

Two Additional Comments

First, the discussion of the open economy trilemma needs to include the trade-off between exchange rate flexibility and the effectiveness of fiscal or structural policy. In the case of perfect capital mobility, the trilemma shrinks to a dilemma, the Mundell-Fleming model (Mundell 1963, Fleming 1962), in which monetary policy is more effective under a flexible currency regime and fiscal policy is more effective under a stable currency regime. Therefore, there is also a trade-off between exchange rate flexibility and fiscal policy effectiveness. Given the structural nature of the imbalance in China, it is wise for the government to adopt various fiscal and structural measures to correct distortions. The more complete the structural reform is, the more effective the exchange rate adjustment will be, and the less demand there will be for excessive exchange rate movement. However, it may take time for the structural reform to become effective.

Second, and as a cautionary note, the real appreciation of the renminbi has been underestimated. IMF and Bank for International Settlements (BIS) statistics show that China's real effective exchange rate (REER) has been appreciating since early 2005 (see figure 2.C7). However, these REERs

Figure 2.C7 Renminbi real effective exchange rate, 1994–2007
(2000 = 100)

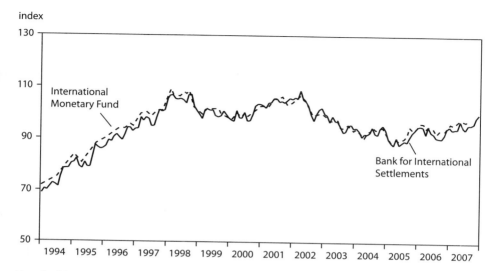

Note: Real (consumer price index–based), broad indices, monthly averages.

Sources: Bank for International Settlements; International Monetary Fund.

may have underestimated the renminbi's real appreciation due to their inability to measure accurately the price of tradable versus nontradable goods (Wickham 1993). They use a wholesale price index, producer price index, or sometimes a consumer price index (CPI) for tradable goods and a CPI for nontradable goods. As the CPI for China has a large portion of tradable goods, the resulting REER is more like a ratio of two general price levels between the home country and its major trading partners.

Figure 2.C8 decomposes China's CPI and shows their development since the end of 2000. Clearly, the prices of those typical nontradable goods, such as food and residence, have been rising remarkably, whereas the prices of typical tradable goods, such as clothing, transportation, and telecommunications, have been declining steadily. These diverging trends have become more significant since the end of 2003 and even more so since the beginning of this year.

Figure 2.C9 also shows a rapid increase in urban wage levels in recent years. All of the trends clearly indicate that the renminbi's real appreciation has been much more significant than conventional measurements suggested. The crucial implication is that there is no way for Chinese authorities to create a competitive advantage by choosing a specific currency regime, and they have no intention of doing so.

Figure 2.C8 Decomposition of China's consumer price index, 2001–07
(December 2000 = 100)

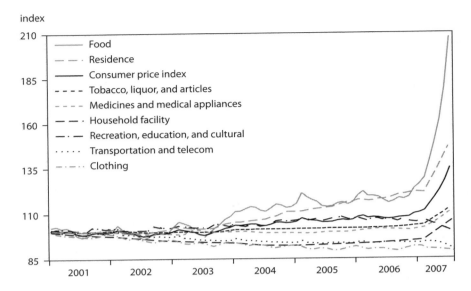

Source: CEIC data.

Figure 2.C9 Average annual urban wage in China, 2000–2006

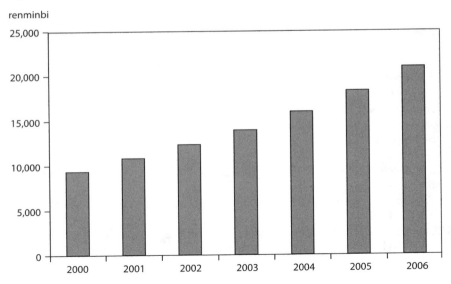

Source: National Statistics Bureau of China.

Conclusion

A practical policy package that follows a noncorner solution to the open economy trilemma may have a higher chance of being successful. Measures may include

- a reasonably flexible exchange rate, which may make a monetary policy more effective;

- a more active and well-targeted fiscal policy, which will help to reduce distortion in the taxation system unduly biased toward the tradable sector, absorb excess liquidity, and allow more active spending on infrastructure, social security, and environmental protection;

- a deepening of financial reform, which could channel savings into investment, including overseas investment, more efficiently;

- a more symmetric capital account management and rapid build-up of expertise in overseas investment (through international cooperation if necessary), which could facilitate surplus recycling into the international financial market; and

- a constructive international environment, including a trustworthy IMF not unduly influenced by parties with stakes in multilateral disputes. Such an environment can better understand the noncorner solution of the imbalance and facilitate the adoption of a package of policies rather than advocating a single tool; this will help to achieve a win-win solution for both China and its economic partners.

References

Fleming, J. M. 1962. Domestic Financial Policies under Fixed and under Flexible Exchange Rates. *IMF Staff Papers* 9: 369–79. Washington: International Monetary Fund.

Hatzius, Jan. 2007. Financial Conditions: The Fed's Your Friend. Goldman Sachs US Economics Research Group, March 2.

Jin, Zhongxia. 2007. The Open-Economy Trilemma and the Chinese Reality. *China Finance* [*Zhong Guo Jin Rong*] 11: 87–88.

Mundell, Robert A. 1963. Capital Mobility and Stabilization Policy under Fixed and Flexible Exchange Rates. *Canadian Journal of Economics and Political Science* 29, no. 4 (November): 475–85.

Obstfeld, Maurice. 1998. The Global Capital Market: Benefactor or Menace? *The Journal of Economic Perspectives* 12, no. 12 (Autumn): 9–30.

Obstfeld, Maurice, and Alan M. Taylor. 1998. The Great Depression as a Watershed: International Capital Mobility over the Long Run. In *The Defining Moment: The Great Depression and the American Economy in the Twentieth Century*, ed. Michael D. Bordo, Claudia D. Goldin, and Eugene N. White. Chicago: University of Chicago Press.

Reinhart, Carmen, and Kenneth Rogoff. 2002. *The Modern History of Exchange Rate Arrangements: A Re-Interpretation.* NBER Working Paper 8963. Cambridge, MA: National Bureau of Economic Research.

Wickham, Peter. 1993. *A Cautionary Note on the Use of Exchange Rate Indicators.* Papers on Policy Analysis and Assessment no. 93/5 (March 17). Washington: International Monetary Fund.

Yi, Gang, and Xuan Tang. 2001. A Theoretical Foundation of the Corner Solution of Currency Regime. *Financial Research* [*Jin Rong Yan Jiu*] 8.

3

Rebalancing China's Growth

BERT HOFMAN and LOUIS KUIJS

The sustainability of China's growth has moved center stage. After three decades of exceptionally rapid growth, the sustainability of this growth in terms of the environment, social stability, and even GDP growth itself is being widely debated. As a harmonious society—one of the proclaimed goals of China's leadership—aims for more equitable and environmentally sustainable growth, the quality and efficiency of growth are now as important as its speed.[1]

This chapter argues that more sustainable growth requires greater reliance on services and less on industry, more reliance on factor productivity growth and less on capital accumulation, and more reliance on domestic demand and less on net exports. It reviews China's growth experience over the past 30 years, identifies key imbalances in China's growth pattern, and provides two policy scenarios for China's future, one illustrating the consequences of continued growth along past trends and the other spelling out the implications of a set of policies that would rebalance the economy in the direction of meeting the goals of a harmonious society.

Bert Hofman is the World Bank's country director for the Philippines. Louis Kuijs has been a senior economist at the World Bank's China office in Beijing since September 2004. This chapter draws on World Bank (2007a) and He and Kuijs (2007). It reflects the authors' personal opinions and should not be attributed to the organizations they work for or to the executive directors or member countries of the World Bank. The authors would like to thank the editors of this volume for their extensive input to this chapter and Professors Barry Bosworth and Kenneth Rogoff for excellent comments.

1. Premier Wen Jiabao in his *Report on the Work of Government* to the 2007 National People's Congress announced that China would move from rapid and efficient growth to efficient and rapid growth, emphasizing efficient growth.

Table 3.1 Explaining China's growth, 1978–2005
(average annual increase, percent)

Source	1978–93	1993–2005
GDP growth	9.7	9.6
Total employment growth	2.5	1.1
Labor productivity growth	7.0	8.4
From TFP growth	3.3	2.8
Of which: From reallocation of labor		
between sectors	1.3	1.1
From increasing human capital	0.5	0.2
From increasing capital/labor ratio	3.2	5.3
Memorandum item:		
Investment/GDP ratio (period average, percent)	29.9	36.8

TFP = total factor productivity

Note: Methodology as in Kuijs and Wang (2006) but adjusted to identify the contribution of human capital and using revised GDP data. Assuming Cobb-Douglas technology and a capital-output ratio of 2.4 in 1978 (as in Wang and Yao 2002, Chow 1993, and Hu and Khan 1996), depreciation of 5 percent per year (as in Wang and Yao 2002), and an elasticity of output with respect to labor of 0.5, as in Wang and Yao (2002), and broadly the average of the range. The update presented in this table further separates out an estimate of the contribution of human capital accumulation, using Barro and Lee (2000) data and an assumption of the rate of return to education of 10 percent.

Source: He and Kuijs (2007).

China's Past Growth Performance

China's growth over the last 30 years is in a league of its own. Since the 1978 reforms, annual GDP growth has averaged more than 9.5 percent. This rapid growth has lifted hundreds of millions of people out of poverty. The poverty rate, measured as $1 a day of purchasing power parity (PPP) consumption, fell from over 60 percent of the population in the early 1980s to 10.3 percent in 2004 (Ravallion and Chen 2004, World Bank 2006), lifting some 500 million people out of poverty over that period. However, not everyone has benefited equally from growth, and income inequality has risen after an initial decline in the early years of reform that focused on rural reforms. China's Gini coefficient[2] increased from 0.25 in the mid-1980s to more than 0.45 today.

Using a growth accounting framework, China's growth can be decomposed into contributions of employment, capital, human capital, and total factor productivity (TFP) growth. The estimates in table 3.1 show that the contribution of capital accumulation to GDP growth was significantly

---

2. The Gini coefficient is used as a measure of inequality in income or wealth distribution. 0 corresponds to perfect equality and 1 to perfect inequality.

larger in the period 1993–2005 than it was in 1978–93, reflecting rapid growth in investment over the last decade. Meanwhile, TFP growth declined after the first period, and its contribution to GDP per employee dropped from almost 50 percent in 1978–93 to about a third in 1993–2005.[3] The contribution of capital accumulation to labor productivity growth increased to 5.3 percentage points in 1993–2005, a very high figure compared with other countries. High capital accumulation explains more than two-thirds of the difference in labor productivity growth between China and other countries or regions. With overall employment growth slowing, the contribution of labor growth has been modest, especially over the last decade. Human capital's contribution to growth is also modest. China started its reforms with an already fairly high level of human capital—measured as the number of years of schooling in the working population—but progress since then has been unremarkable. The recent sharp increase in tertiary school attendance is likely to change that in the future.

An important feature of China's growth is that much of GDP growth since the early 1990s has come from rapid growth of industrial production. Industrial value added increased, on average, 12.6 percent per year during 1990 and 2006, and the share of industry in GDP rose from 42 percent in 1990 to almost 49 percent in 2006 in current prices, among the highest for any country since the 1960s.[4] In 2003–06, industry contributed 60 percent of total GDP growth, compared with 6 percent by agriculture and 34 percent by the services sector. Industrial growth has largely been in the form of higher labor productivity, much of it in the form of rising within-firm productivity.

China's Unbalanced Growth

China's record growth performance has come at a price. The current growth pattern relies heavily on manufacturing, investment, and external demand. The accompanying large and growing current account surpluses have become an issue in the international arena, whereas domestically, the accumulation of international foreign exchange reserves is not only becoming increasingly a macroeconomic issue but also signifies a suboptimal allocation of resources from China's point of view. China's reliance on manufacturing, especially heavy industry, has become a growing burden on the environment and made the country increasingly dependent on imported energy resources. Finally, China's rapid growth has been asso-

---

3. They suggest the difference may be because of a different assumption for the elasticity of output with respect to capital.

4. In fact, the increase would have been larger but for declining relative prices of industry. In constant 1995 prices, the share of industry in GDP rose from 37 percent in 1990 to 53.5 percent in 2006.

Table 3.2   Savings, investment, and current account in China
(percent of GDP)

Item	1996	2000	2002	2004	2006
Gross domestic savings	40.7	36.9	37.6	43	50.6
Households	20.1	14.8	16.3	15.4	15.3
Enterprises	15.6	15.3	14.4	19.8	28.3
Government	5.0	6.8	6.9	7.8	7.0
Gross capital formation	40.4	35.1	37.9	43.3	44.9
Net factor income plus net transfers	−1.2	−0.7	−0.1	1.0	1.0
Gross national savings (above the line)	39.5	36.1	37.4	44	51.6
Discrepancy	1.8	0.7	2.9	2.8	2.8
Gross national savings (below the line)	41.3	36.8	40.3	46.8	54.4
Current account	0.8	1.7	2.4	3.6	9.5

Sources: National Bureau of Statistics of China; authors' estimates.

ciated with rising income inequality, which has become a key issue in the political debate in China. Addressing the imbalances in China's growth has become the main driver of the policy agenda as included in the 11th Five Year Plan.

China's Macroeconomic Imbalances

By definition, the current account surplus of a country equals the surplus of savings over investment. China's traditionally high saving rates have risen even further in recent decades. Investment rose with savings, but less rapidly, and as a result, China's current account surplus has boomed. Contrary to popular thinking, the recent increase in savings did not come from households: Household savings at around 30 percent of disposable income is high but no higher than the savings of other rapidly growing Asian countries. The bulk of the increase has come from enterprises, the savings of which, calculated as retained earnings plus depreciation charges, have boomed in the last decade (table 3.2).

China's high and rising savings combined with its managed capital account has been a main driver of the country's capital-intensive, industry-led growth. This growth pattern has served the country well in many respects. High saving and investment, combined with respectable rates of technological progress, mean that China's production capacity grew rapidly. In recent years, potential GDP growth, or the capacity to produce, has increased in line with actual GDP growth to over 10 percent per year. This means that the economy can grow rapidly without running into the problems that emerging markets often run into, such as high inflation, large current account deficits, and bottlenecks in the real economy.

Table 3.3   Growth patterns on past trends (percent)

Source	1993–2005	On past trends			
		2005–15	2015–25	2025–35	2035–45
GDP growth[a]	9.6	8.3	6.7	5.6	4.6
Total employment growth	1.1	0.1	–0.5	–0.9	–1.1
Labor productivity growth	8.4	8.1	7.2	6.6	5.7
From TFP growth	2.8	2.5	2.2	1.9	1.6
From higher capital/labor ratio	5.3	5.3	4.7	4.4	3.8
From higher human capital	0.2	0.3	0.3	0.3	0.3
Investment/GDP ratio (period average, percent)	37	44	49	55	60
Share of industry in GDP (end of period)	49	50	50	51	n.a.
Share of employment in agriculture (end of period)	45	38	36	33	n.a.
Urbanization rate (end of period)	43	50	52	55	n.a.
Urban-rural income disparity (end of period)[b]	3.8	4	4.4	4.6	n.a.

n.a. = not applicable
TFP = total factor productivity

a. Potential GDP growth. In 2005–07, actual GDP growth is assumed to differ from potential GDP growth. From 2008 onward, actual growth is assumed to equal potential.
b. 2002 prices.

Sources: National Bureau of Statistics of China; authors' estimates.

At the same time, China's growth pattern has its macroeconomic downsides. First, it may not be possible to finance the current capital-intensive mode of growth in the long run. Over time, economic growth has increasingly relied on capital accumulation and less from employment and TFP growth. If China's rapid growth continues in its current mode, the investment rate will need to increase to 50 to 60 percent of GDP in the decades ahead (table 3.3), which will be difficult to finance given the pressures for savings to fall, including from demographics. Moreover, investment as such does not contribute to a population's standard of living.

A second macroeconomic downside is that this pattern of growth has created fewer urban jobs than a more labor-intensive pattern and has in the process increased urban-rural inequality. Industry creates fewer urban jobs than services, and in 1993–2005, six-sevenths of the growth in industry has come from increased labor productivity instead of new employment, with industrial employment growing 1.6 percent per year in 1993–2005, compared with value-added growth of 11.2 percent.

Third—and most central to the US debate about China—a significant part of China's growth stems from increasing production of manufactured goods with a tendency to boost current account surpluses. Although demand and supply in China's economy are growing broadly in line with each other, a significant share of the demand comes from abroad, not from Chinese households and businesses. Under such an investment-heavy, export-oriented pattern of growth, production in China increasingly outstrips domestic demand. From an external perspective, accelerating manufacturing production means continued strong export expansion, whereas import growth has been more subdued, partly because of increased import substitution. As a result, the current account surplus is rising steadily: Having reached 9.5 percent of GDP in 2006, it has become the key source of China's impressive balance-of-payments surpluses. As the People's Bank of China buys the associated foreign exchange, it needs to sterilize the purchases by issuing central bank paper, which creates tensions and risks in its balance sheet, keeps domestic interest rates low, and has started to feed a rapid rise in asset prices. A large difference between production and domestic demand in China can contribute to global imbalances and trigger trade tension, which could over time undermine other countries' willingness to further open up, and thus reduce growth prospects for China to grow.

Environmental Strains

China's heavy reliance on industry for growth has put increasing strains on the environment.

- The energy intensity (energy use per unit of output) is some 4 to 6 times that of advanced countries, measured in current dollars. China's high share of industry in the economy, which is 4 or more times those of advanced countries, largely explains this discrepancy, but even at the level of industry it is still some 1.5 to 2 times higher than it is in advanced economies.[5] The changing pattern of energy use has resulted in steeply rising consumption of fuels and increasing imports of petroleum (Berrah et al. 2007). Reliance on coal for 71 percent of the total energy consumed and the rapid spread of motorization has intensified air pollution and contributed to greenhouse gas emissions.

- Although the average pollution index for China's cities has improved in the past decade, poor air quality is still a very visible issue in China, and costly, especially in large cities: 16 of the 20 cities with the worst air pollution in the world are in China, and according to the State Environmental Protection Agency (SEPA), two-thirds of China's urban

---

5. If measured in PPP in contrast, China uses as much energy per output as the United States.

population breathes air of substandard quality. Particle matter, SO_2, NO_x, and other pollutants are, according to the World Health Organization, the cause of 250,000 premature deaths each year. A recent study by SEPA and the World Bank (2007b) estimates that the health costs of air pollution amount to 3.8 percent of GDP. In addition, one-third of China's landmass regularly experiences acid rain according to SEPA, causing an estimated damage of some $13 billion, or 1 percent of (2003) GDP per year.

- Water is becoming increasingly scarce relative to the nation's requirements. The country has only one-third of the world average in water availability and low efficiency of water usage: China used 537 cubic meters of water to produce RMB10,000 of output, four times the world average (World Bank 2007a). In individual industries, water usage is 5 to 10 times that of advanced countries. The use of recycled water in industry reached barely 50 percent, compared with 75 to 80 percent in advanced economies.

Thus, despite China's remarkable progress, it still has a long way to go to make its growth more environmentally sustainable. The route ahead is likely to be more difficult, as the relatively easy gains that were achieved by moving away from the inefficiencies of central planning have been realized already. Arguably, as China grows richer, the demand for higher environmental standards will also grow, requiring the country to balance the apparently conflicting goals of economic growth and the environment.

China's environmental issues also have a global dimension: The International Energy Agency estimates that the country will become the largest greenhouse gas emitter in the world by the end of the decade; some say the country already is.[6]

Rising Income Inequality

The current growth pattern has contributed to growing inequality. Accumulation of capital in urban industry has led to starkly widening productivity differences, which in turn have led to large income inequalities. With an estimated Gini coefficient of more than 0.45, China is now less equal than the United States and Russia and, given current trends, is akin to Latin American countries in income inequality.

China's rising inequality resulted in part from the country's development strategy. Heavy investment in manufacturing created jobs for only a limited number of people, and urbanization and decline in low-productivity agricultural unemployment have been less than one would expect based on China's growth and level of income. China's coastal

---

6. Data are from the World Bank, *World Development Indicators 2007*, and authors' estimates.

development strategy increased interprovincial inequalities, whereas the country's household registration system hampered rural citizens in competition for higher-paying urban jobs.[7] And China's heavy reliance on investment and manufacturing meant that urban formal-sector jobs rapidly became more productive, and wages rose in line. As a result, agricultural incomes increasingly lagged behind average income per capita, contributing to inequality. More recently, intraurban and intrarural inequality has risen as well.

Future Consequences of the Current Growth Pattern

Based on current trends, China's three imbalances—investment- and industry-driven growth, environmental strains, and income inequality—are likely to worsen. To illustrate this, we develop a growth scenario that broadly incorporates the features of past growth and extrapolates this to the year 2035. The scenario is developed with the use of the computable general equilibrium (CGE) model for the Chinese economy from the Development Research Center (DRC).[8]

In the past-trend scenario, growth remains largely investment-led and driven by industry. Thus it has high savings and high investment, with corporate savings playing an important role while household savings also remains high. Patterns of employment growth and TFP are expected to continue as they have in recent decades, that is, employment grows somewhat slower than the working age population and TFP edges downward over time. This scenario is calibrated as follows. Employment is projected using demographic projections. Using a Cobb-Douglas production function, we calculate how much investment is necessary to reach a target rate of growth of GDP, assuming some moderation of TFP growth over time. The target rate of GDP growth is over 8 percent from 2005 to 2015 and under 7 percent from 2015 to 2025 (table 3.3).

The DRC's CGE model suggests that with a policy setting on past trends, the share of industry in GDP ("secondary industry") would increase another 3.5 percentage points between 2005 and 2035. The share of services ("tertiary industry") would also increase by around 5.5 percentage points in this period, but the tertiary sector would remain smaller than the secondary sector through 2035. The calibration mentioned above requires an investment-to-GDP ratio of almost 50 percent, on average, from 2015 to 2025 and a higher percentage later. In this scenario, we assume that

---

7. China's household registration system, or *hukou*, has been in place since the 1950s. The system tied most citizens to their place of birth, as health care, education, social security, housing, and previously food grain were only available in a citizen's locality of registration.

8. For a detailed description of the model, see He and Kuijs (2007).

the policies that affect saving and investment patterns remain unchanged. Consistent with that, we find broadly extrapolated sectoral patterns of saving and investment. In particular, with unchanged policies affecting industry and services, dividends, the labor market, and the financial sector, enterprise investment increases further over time in an increasingly industry- and enterprise–led economy, with the increase matched by higher enterprise saving.[9] With unchanged policies on health, education, and the social safety net, household saving also continues to rise. In all, in line with recent patterns, the current account surplus remains high despite high and increasing investment.

In our industry-led scenario, energy and resource intensity would continue to be high, and pollution and emissions would continue to rise rapidly. Limited urban job creation would further accentuate urban-rural income disparity and overall inequality. Such a scenario would see only moderate urban employment growth and a moderate labor flow out of agriculture, leaving a relatively large share of people employed in agriculture. In 2035, 33 percent of total employment would still be in agriculture, a high share for a country with a per capita income projected at $10,000 in 2035 (in 2000 international prices). Consequently, urbanization would continue, but at a modest rate, reaching around 55 percent in 2035. The productivity gap between agriculture and the rest of the economy would rise from an already high 6 to over 8 times by 2025. The rural-urban income disparity would remain high, with urban per capita incomes 4.6 times higher than rural ones (in constant prices) in 2035, compared with 3.8 times in 2006.[10] Income inequality as measured by the Gini coefficient rises further, from 0.46 in 2005 to 0.48 in 2035.

The model suggests that it will be increasingly difficult for China to continue with its current pattern of growth, economically, environmentally, socially, and internationally. China's government is fully aware of these constraints and is seeking to change China's pattern of growth. The current 11th Five Year Plan has this new growth pattern as an explicit goal. The harmonious society is seeking still rapid but more equitable and sustainable economic growth. A host of measures and policies to achieve this have been announced, and explicit targets on pollution and energy use have been set in the plan and are being used to hold local government officials accountable for results. The questions are whether such goals are feasible and whether government has the tools to turn around current growth trends. China's past attempts to change the pattern of growth,

---

9. In the sectorally disaggregated saving-investment projections, we assume that household investment and government investment are constant as a share of GDP. Much of enterprise investment is saved by the enterprise sector, in line with recent patterns.

10. The urban-rural real income disparity is smaller than the productivity disparity because of factors including nonagricultural income of rural people.

while modestly successful, have largely relied on administrative means. These means may not work effectively in China's highly decentralized environment, where local governments face stark conflicts among the emerging objectives of growth, environmental sustainability, and equity.

An Alternative Growth Strategy for China

Rebalancing the economy and striving for a harmonious society have now firmly become key economic policy objectives in China. As presented at the National People's Congress in March, the government's 2007 work programs indicated that, while rapid economic growth remains important, the government aims to improve the quality of economic growth, rebalance the growth pattern, and strive toward a harmonious society. The government would like to change China's growth to be less intensive in resources and capital, cleaner, more knowledge driven, and more equally distributed. On the macroeconomic side, the government would like to change the composition of demand to rely more on consumption and less on exports and investment and reduce the external surplus.[11]

Broadly, five types of policies would help rebalancing. In many of these areas, policy plans or proposals are in the pipeline. That does not guarantee that they will be introduced soon, as it is difficult to implement policies with short-term costs to certain segments of the population. The types of policies we use to illustrate a rebalancing scenario are:

- several macroeconomic measures—largely fiscal—to stimulate domestic consumption, reduce saving, and stimulate the services sector;

- several price and tax measures to help rebalancing by readjusting the relative attractiveness of manufacturing production (tradables) over producing services (nontradables);

- relaxed restrictions on the movement of labor and land transactions to facilitate rural-urban migration and mitigate rural poverty. The fiscal system could be improved to provide host cities with more incentives to deliver social services to incoming migrants;

- institutional reforms to give local decision makers stronger incentives and better tools to pursue rebalancing. Central here is the performance evaluation of local officials. The recent measure to include land revenues in the local government budget, rather than as part of the extrabudgetary funds managed by the land bureau, could improve the governance of these funds and reduce the incentive to pursue a land-intensive development pattern; and

---

11. These objectives are quantified by anticipative benchmarks in Special Column 2 of the 11th Five Year Plan.

- policies to help upgrade the production structure and promote the so-called knowledge economy, including well-targeted government support for research and development and improving access to financing (e.g., venture capital) for innovators.

The above policy reforms have been modeled with the DRC's CGE model. The second scenario, with rebalanced policies as discussed above, has more growth coming from services and less from industry (table 3.4). The contribution of the secondary sector to GDP declines by over 10 percentage points through 2035, while that of the service sector increases by 20 percentage points. On the expenditure side, more growth comes from consumption and less from investment and exports. In this scenario, continued rapid growth would require significantly less capital accumulation. However, the rebalanced policies allow for higher TFP growth, with much of the improvement coming from greater reallocation of labor, largely from rural to urban. Thus the scenario has higher TFP growth from reallocation of labor, by about 0.6 to 0.8 percentage points, than the "on past trends" scenario, which is the broadly the same as the difference in nonhuman capital–related TFP growth between the two scenarios. A more employment-friendly setting also allows for somewhat higher overall employment growth: It is assumed that in this scenario employment grows in line with growth in the working-age population. This means that, even though saving and investment are significantly lower in this scenario, GDP growth is the same.[12] As a result, it is more balanced in three aspects.

First, saving and investment decline significantly over time because of policy reform. Saving and investment are significantly lower than in the "on past trends" scenario, with the investment-to-GDP ratio averaging a more sustainable 35 and 32 percent in the periods 2015–25 and 2025–35, respectively, compared with over 44 percent and almost 50 percent in the "on past trends" scenario over the same periods.[13] This lower overall investment-to-GDP ratio is more consistent with prospective long-term trends in demographics and saving. As for sectoral patterns of saving, with policy reforms affecting the industry-services trade-off, dividends, the labor market, and the financial sector, enterprise saving is lower in a less capital-intensive, less industry-based economy.[14] Reforms in health,

---

12. However, with a vintage-type capital stock, less new investment means less embodied technological progress. This may be of particular importance for environmental standards.

13. Specifics about the long-term saving and investment projections and the estimated impact of policy reforms are discussed in Kuijs (2006).

14. In the sectorally disaggregated saving-investment projections, we assume that household and government investment are constant as a share of GDP. Much of enterprise investment is saved by the enterprise sector, in line with recent patterns.

Table 3.4 Growth patterns in two scenarios (percent)

Source	On past trends				With rebalanced policies			
	2005–15	2015–25	2025–35	2035–45	2005–15	2015–25	2025–35	2035–45
GDP growth[a]	8.3	6.7	5.6	4.6	8.3	6.7	5.6	4.6
Total employment growth	0.1	–0.5	–0.9	–1.1	0.5	–0.1	–0.5	–0.7
Labor productivity growth	8.1	7.2	6.6	5.7	7.7	6.8	6.2	5.3
From TFP growth	2.5	2.2	1.9	1.6	3.1	2.8	2.5	2.2
From higher capital/labor ratio	5.3	4.7	4.4	3.8	4.0	3.5	3.2	2.6
From higher human capital	0.3	0.3	0.3	0.3	0.5	0.4	0.4	0.4
Investment/GDP ratio (period average, percent)	44	49	55	60	35	31	29	26
Share of industry in GDP (end of period)	50	50	51	n.a.	44	40	37	n.a.
Share of employment in agriculture (end of period)	38	36	33	n.a.	29	18	12	n.a.
Urbanization rate (end of period)	50	52	55	n.a.	59	68	72	n.a.
Urban-rural income disparity (end of period)[b]	4.0	4.4	4.6	n.a.	3.2	2.8	2.8	n.a.

n.a. = not applicable
TFP = total factor productivity

a. Potential GDP growth. In 2005–07, actual GDP growth is assumed to differ from potential GDP growth. From 2008 onward, actual growth is assumed to equal potential.
b. 2002 prices.

Sources: National Bureau of Statistics of China; authors' estimates.

education, and the social safety net allow household saving to decline as a share of GDP. In all, the current account surplus gradually declines over time as a share of GDP.

Second, China uses fewer primary commodities and less energy and produces less pollution. This is because it has less industry and, within industry, less heavy and dirty industry, in large part because of better pricing of energy, commodities, and environmental degradation. The difference in structure within these broader sectors is also quite interesting: In the rebalanced scenario, significantly less heavy industry and construction but more education, science, and technology.

Third, the economy creates more urban employment and, as a result, more rural-urban migration, higher rural productivity and incomes, and less urban-rural inequality. Urbanization rises to 72 percent in 2035 compared with about 55 percent on past trends. At the same time, more urbanization stimulates the services industry, including through the spending patterns of urban residents.[15] Combined, these factors mean more urban employment growth and more transfer of labor out of agriculture. The share of employment in agriculture in this scenario falls to 12 percent in 2035.[16] As a result, labor productivity in agriculture rises much faster, supporting higher incomes there. The decrease in the productivity gap between agriculture and the other sectors underlies lower urban-rural income inequality. The ratio of urban over rural per capita income declines to 2.7 in 2035, while the Gini coefficient decreases to 0.38 in 2035.

Conclusion

China's rapid growth faces macroeconomic, environmental, and social challenges that have their origin in its pattern of growth. Using simulations with a CGE model, this chapter has shown that, on current trends, current account surpluses, environmental stress, and inequality are likely to remain a feature of China's growth. A policy package that reduces savings, better prices capital and environmental damage, and allows for more labor movement is likely to produce better outcomes on all three counts. The exchange rate plays a minor role in this package, and an adjustment would mainly serve to limit expectations for an exchange rate appreciation and accompanying foreign capital inflows.

---

15. Urban residents spend 8 percentage points more of their income on services than do rural residents.

16. This may seem fast. However, it is not exceptional compared with experiences in other southeast Asian countries. South Korea witnessed a similar pace, from 50 percent in 1973 to 10 percent in 2001. Malaysia decreased its agricultural employment from 37 percent in 1980 to 18.4 percent in 2001.

References

Barro, Robert J., and Jong-Wha Lee. 2000. *International Data on Educational Attainment: Updates and Implications*. CID Working Paper 42 (April). Cambridge MA: Center for International Development, Harvard University. Available at www.cid.harvard.edu.

Berrah, Noureddine, Fei Fang, Roland Priddle, and Leiping Wang. 2007. *Sustainable Energy in China: The Closing Window of Opportunity*. Washington: World Bank, Development Research Center of China, and Energy Sector Management Assistance Programme.

Chow, Gregory. 1993. How and Why China Succeeded in her Economic Reform. *China Economic Review* 4, no. 2: 117–28.

He, Jianwu, and Louis Kuijs. 2007. *Rebalancing China's Economy—Modeling a Policy Package*. World Bank China Research Paper 7. Beijing: World Bank (September).

Hu, Zuliu, and Moshin Khan. 1996. *Why is China Growing so Fast?* IMF Working Paper 96/75 (July). Washington: International Monetary Fund.

Kuijs, Louis. 2006. *How Would China's Saving and Investment Evolve?* World Bank Policy Research Working Paper 3958. Washington: World Bank.

Kuijs, Louis, and Tao Wang. 2006. China's Pattern of Growth, Moving to Sustainability and Reducing Inequality. *China and the World Economy* 14, no. 1 (January): 1–14.

Ravallion, Martin, and Shaohua Chen. 2004. *China's Uneven Progress in Poverty Alleviation*. Policy Research Working Paper Series 3408. Washington: World Bank.

Wang, Yan, and Yudong Yao. 2002. Sources of China's Economic Growth 1952–1999: Incorporating Human Capital Accumulation. *China Economic Review* 14, no. 1: 32–52.

World Bank. 2006. *Where Is the Wealth of Nations: Measuring Capital for the 21st Century*. Washington.

World Bank. 2007a. *China: Towards a Resource Saving Society*. Country Economic Memorandum for China (forthcoming). Washington.

World Bank. 2007b. *Cost of Pollution in China: Economic Estimates of Physical Damages*. Washington: Environment and Social Unit, East Asia Region, World Bank. Available at http://siteresources.worldbank.org.

Comment
Approaches to Rebalancing
China's Growth

KENNETH ROGOFF

China's breathtaking economic growth continues to astonish the world. As Hofman and Kuijs illustrate, China is rapidly moving into a league all its own in the modern annals of growth, equaling and surpassing the peak years of the Korean and Japanese miracles despite being an order of magnitude larger. How long can China's growth be sustained?

The Hofman and Kuijs paper is useful particularly in its first part, in which the authors starkly illustrate the unsustainability of China's current trajectory. Table 3.1, which decomposes Chinese growth into productivity improvements, capital deepening, and labor reallocation, is particularly important. The basic message is that, although productivity growth continues to play a significant role, it accounts for only one-third of China's growth from 1993 to 2005 versus 50 percent from 1978 to 1992. The estimated total factor productivity growth of 2.8 percent for the 1993–2005 period is still quite respectable and probably double that of the likely US rate for the next decade. But considering how far China still lags behind the United States in income today, China will have to sustain ever-higher rates of capital deepening to keep closing the gap at the rapid pace of recent years.

Kenneth Rogoff has been a professor of economics at Harvard University since September 1999 and the Thomas D. Cabot Professor of Public Policy there since January 2004. The author is grateful to Andrew Feltenstein for helpful discussions.

Another important fact the authors emphasize is the importance of rising enterprise saving in China's phenomenally high saving rate. Household saving, at roughly 25 percent of disposable income, is actually fairly normal in Asia. But the corporate sector has been enjoying phenomenal profits, with wages falling sharply as a share of GDP down to less than 40 percent. Low wages combined with high profit rates are at the heart of China's sharply growing income inequality, perhaps even more so than in the developed world. The authors show that by standard measures (the Gini coefficient), China's income inequality is surpassing that of the United States and heading toward Latin American levels. Income inequality is exacerbated by the very low returns suffered by China's savers in financial markets, despite the country's high rate of growth. Financial repression constitutes an enormous tax on China's poor, who can expect to earn roughly 2.5 percent on their savings accounts in a country growing at 10 to 11 percent per year. That said, most estimates suggest that China's inequality is not yet as extreme as Latin America's though it has surpassed the United States. The environment section of the paper shows that China contains 16 of the world's 20 most-polluted cities but observes that in many cities, objective measures of pollution have not been getting worse. The problem, of course, is that urbanization is sprawling into the countryside, bringing pollution with it.

The paper's presentation of the above facts is excellent. The model-based exercises in the second section of the paper, however, have some interesting ideas but lack sufficient transparency to make them terribly convincing. The authors use a computable general equilibrium (CGE) model, a nomenclature that no longer makes sense; with today's easy access to computer simulation methods, virtually all macroeconomists use them to calibrate their models, so the phrase "computable general equilibrium model" no longer has any meaningful information or distinction. Each model must be judged on its own merits, and unfortunately, the details of the model used here are to be found in other papers.

The first empirical exercise the authors conduct looks to be simply an extrapolation of current trends or something quite similar. It should be thought of as China's trajectory based on unchanged policies. Even assuming a fall in China's growth to 8 percent for the next decade and 7 percent thereafter, China will have to invest 60 percent of its GDP to keep up the pace of growth. Even for China, which has averaged investment of 37 percent of GDP over the past decade, this looks nearly impossible. Decreasing returns to capital eventually have to set in, even with China's still vast unemployed-labor pool. Presumably, such a trajectory would eventually force China to shift from being a net saver to a huge net borrower, not to mention the pollution implications. If this scenario were realized, one piece of good news would be that China's trade balance surplus would likely evaporate. China would need to borrow massively even to maintain a far more modest level of consumption than it currently enjoys. It might even need to borrow from the International Monetary Fund some day.

The second empirical exercise is supposed to be loosely grounded in an alternative growth strategy that does all sorts of wonderful things, such as "advancing the knowledge economy," introducing reforms to give local officials better incentives, and fixing the tax system. How the authors manage to calibrate these wonderful things within their modest empirical model is hard to fathom. I do not know what to make of the calibration, although the numbers the authors crank out seem to be much more satisfactory than the extrapolation exercise. The authors talk about better pricing of energy. Does this mean relaxing price controls? This is very hard to handle in any CGE model I know of; it would be interesting to hear more discussion of what was actually done. How the authors can argue that exchange rate adjustment is not important, when their model does not seem to have any meaningful monetary or financial sector, is also unclear.[1]

Turning Hofman and Kuijs's analysis on its head, one might note that, to dispense with exchange rate adjustment, China needs to perform policy reform miracles on numerous fronts, and fairly quickly given the political obstacles. The exercise is interesting and the authors have earned the right to speculate given their excellent facts section. But the window dressing of their CGE model does not seem to bring any great light beyond the authors' own expert judgments.

Hofman and Kuijs have written a very useful paper, and I learned a lot from it, but the final section on what China ought to do to make its growth sustainable would be better treated as a speculative flourish rather than a centerpiece.

References

Feltenstein, Andrew, Celine Rochon, and Maral Shamloo. 2007. *High Growth and Low Consumption in East Asia: How to Improve Welfare while Avoiding Financial Failures.* IMF Working Paper 07/278. Washington: International Monetary Fund.
Lipschitz, Leslie, Celine Rochon, and Genevieve Verdier. 2007. *Blessings in Disguise: Surplus Labor and Excess Saving in China.* Washington: International Monetary Fund (November).

---

1. Applying a model with rational expectations and learning to China, Feltenstein, Rochon, and Shamloo (2007) show that current growth trends lead to excessive foreign direct investment as well as increasing domestic investment. The resulting unanticipated fall in the return to capital causes bank failures, higher interest rates, and yet more bank failures. The investment boom collapses and growth declines. This happens after about nine years in a discrete time simulation. Another approach to the same set of issues, with similar results, is Lipschitz, Rochon, and Verdier (2007).

Comment
Domestic Imbalances
and Data Ambiguities

BARRY BOSWORTH

Bert Hofman and Louis Kuijs's paper summarizes recent research at the World Bank on the economic imbalances that have emerged in China in recent years and simulations of potential policy responses. The imbalances are very evident on the external side in the form of a rapidly rising current account surplus, which is likely to reach 12 percent of GDP in 2007 and even higher in 2008. However, the imbalances are also evident in the domestic economy in the form of a rapidly growing gap between domestic saving and investment. World Bank researchers have contributed significantly to efforts to measure the extent of the saving-investment imbalance within China as a counterpart to the more obvious worsening of the country's external imbalance.

Two major themes emerge from the paper. First, as foreigners have focused on China's large external surplus, less attention has been paid to the large domestic surplus of saving over investment that Hofman and Kuijs argue is the driving force behind the trade imbalances. The authors assert that the aggregate saving surplus is due largely to rapid increases is enterprise saving and that the shares of household and government saving in income have been stable or declining in recent years. Second, the solution to the imbalance is a series of reforms aimed at stimulating domestic

Barry Bosworth is a senior fellow in the Economic Studies Program (the Robert V. Roosa Chair in International Economics) at the Brookings Institution, where he has been a senior fellow since 1979 and served as a research associate from 1971 to 1977.

demand. The authors outline a package of policy reforms and provide some results from a simulation model.

To begin, I would like to emphasize both how recent the emergence of the imbalances has been and how unexpected their magnitudes are. Despite the common characterization of China as an example of export-led growth, exports were a stable or declining share of GDP between the adoption of the fixed exchange rate in 1994 and World Trade Organization (WTO) membership at the end of 2001, and current account surpluses were consistently small, seldom exceeding 2 percent of GDP. Predictably, China's export and import growth both accelerated after joining the WTO, but again there was little change in the current account balance. The external imbalance emerged only after 2005, when exports continued to grow rapidly while imports slowed and stabilized as a share of GDP. This is particularly surprising in that we can identify no significant change in the exchange rate that would account for this pattern. On a trade-weighted basis, China's real exchange rate has remained relatively constant or even appreciated slightly, while the dollar has experienced significant depreciation. The explanation for the break in the correlation of the two countries' exchange rates is that China's trade is oriented toward Asia while the United States has a larger trade relationship with countries outside of the region, for which the decline in the dollar's value has been most dramatic. Some commentators question the continued surge of China's exports, arguing that it might reflect overinvoicing as enterprises use the trade channel to move funds into China in anticipation of revaluation. Others focus on the slowing of import growth, suggesting that it results from an emphasis on import substitution from surging domestic production capacity in the areas of capital goods and basic metals.

The changes in the domestic saving-investment balance raise equivalent questions. Apparently, national saving has suddenly come to exceed domestic investment by a stunning 12 percent of GDP. Many have noted the small role of consumption growth in domestic demand, but without good data we are unsure of the reason. The authors' emphasis on enterprise saving suggests that a significant part of the problem is that only a small portion of the growth in aggregate income is being passed through to households. This contrasts with the more common explanation that, without a social safety net, households save an unusually large portion of their income because of fears of illness or old age. Rather than focusing only on creating a Western-style social safety net, the authors also propose a set of measures designed to force the enterprises to pay out a larger portion of their profits. There are conflicting estimates of the appropriate distribution of Chinese saving between enterprises and households, yet the issues would seem fundamental to adopting appropriate remedial measures.[1]

---

1. See a recent paper by Marcos Chamon and Eswar Prasad (2007) for a contrary perspective on the relative roles of enterprises and households.

The emphasis on enterprise saving suggests a possible role for foreign invested enterprises, the exports and profits of which have increased rapidly in recent years. With expectations of exchange rate appreciation, they have a strong incentive to retain their profits in renminbi. Finally, it is very difficult to fully integrate the evidence of external and internal imbalances because of a very large statistical discrepancy in the accounting relations among saving, investment, and the current account.

It is easy for foreigners to focus on the exchange rate as a central feature of an expenditure-switching policy to reduce the imbalances, but China must also be concerned about adjustments on the domestic side, given the risk that exchange rate changes alone could precipitate a recession. A considerable degree of uncertainty and conflicting interpretations of the data remain, yet recent changes have left China with an unusual degree of exposure to developments in both the United States and the global economy. The authors draw greater attention to the domestic side of the imbalance and need for policies to stimulate domestic demand. However, if the origins of the problem are on the domestic side, I am surprised at the speed with which they have spilled over into the external sector with no slowing of domestic economic activity.

Finally, as a background to their rebalancing scenario, the authors use a growth-accounting framework to assess the opportunities for sustained growth in future years. Their view is that GDP growth will continue at a high rate over the next two decades, averaging 7 to 8 percent annually, compared with a rate just short of 10 percent from 1993 to 2005 (I prefer to ignore the projections to 2035). While China still has a large reserve of underemployed labor and much room for a continued pattern of productivity catch-up, the projection is inconsistent with past patterns, in which the growth of high-performing economies inevitably slowed over time. However, China has already become a truly exceptional case, and there is no firm basis other than probability for predicting a significant slowdown. Certainly, I would argue that one can discern no significant evidence of an impending slowdown in the available data. Instead, the greatest threat to China's future growth is the imbalances, both internal and external, that have developed since 2005. China is now exposed to and dependent upon continued expansion of the global economy in ways that it was not in the past. This may not bode well for China, as it appears the long-predicted correction of the US external deficit and overvalued dollar has now begun.

Hofman and Kuijs contribute to the literature in directing attention to the domestic side of the economic imbalances that have developed within China's economy since 2005. The global discussion of China's role in the global economy has often focused too narrowly on exchange rate issues. It is unfortunate, however, that the ambiguities of the data have left us so uncertain about the causes of the growing gap between domestic demand and supply. The suddenness of its emergence and its size are disconcerting.

Reference

Chamon, Marcos, and Eswar Prasad. 2007. *The Determinants of Household Savings in China.* IMF Working Paper (forthcoming). Washington: International Monetary Fund.

4

Estimates of the Equilibrium Exchange Rate of the Renminbi: Is There a Consensus and, If Not, Why Not?

WILLIAM R. CLINE and JOHN WILLIAMSON

Is there a consensus on what the equilibrium exchange rate of the renminbi is? If not, why not? The answer to the first of the two questions is clearly no. The 18 studies summarized in table 4.1 reveal that the literature offers widely differing answers, even sticking to post-2000 estimates and even when one recognizes—as not everyone has done—that an effective exchange rate is a totally different creature from a bilateral dollar exchange rate and that one should expect estimates of undervaluation on each concept to be quite different.[1]

However, of all 18 studies, only one (Wang 2004) tries to argue that the renminbi might be overvalued. Moreover, the average estimates indicate substantial undervaluation. The simple average of the 14 estimates of the correction needed in the real effective exchange rate (REER) is a 19 percent appreciation; the corresponding simple average of the 16 estimates

William R. Cline is a senior fellow jointly at the Center for Global Development and the Peterson Institute for International Economics. John Williamson, senior fellow at the Peterson Institute, has been associated with the Institute since 1981.

1. Moreover, several leading economists wish (or wished before July 21, 2005) to maintain an unchanged bilateral dollar exchange rate and therefore presumably do not regard it as meaningful to speak of misalignments, including Robert Mundell (2004); Ronald I. McKinnon (2007); and Michael Dooley, David Folkerts-Landau, and Peter Garber (2003).

for the bilateral rate against the dollar is an appreciation of 40 percent.[2] The undervaluation shows signs of growing worse over time, as the average real effective appreciation needed rises from 17 percent in studies using data from the period 2000–2004 to 26 percent in those using data from 2005–07 (table 4.1).[3] Thus, although most of this paper concerns the answer to the second question, the source of differences among the estimates, dispersion of the individual results should not divert policy attention away from the forest to the trees.[4]

We first review the methodological issues associated with the three main measurement approaches: purchasing power parity (PPP), behavioral equilibrium exchange rate (BEER), and fundamental equilibrium exchange rate (FEER)—as well as the concepts of multilateral (real effective) and bilateral misalignment.[5] We then examine the results of each of the studies considered, grouped by each of the three approaches. We conclude with an overview of the estimates and the reasons for the differences among them.

Approaches and Methodological Issues

Purchasing Power Parity

One ancient if not very well-respected approach to identifying equilibrium exchange rates is to find the exchange rate that would lead to PPP. The *Economist*'s Big Mac Index falls squarely into this category, even though the price index used to establish PPP contains only one good. Much more meaningful are the several estimates based on a so-called enhanced-PPP approach, which starts from the strong empirical regularity linking per capita income with the REER. It has been rationalized by Bela Balassa (1964) and Paul Samuelson (1964), who suggest that the productivity rise

---

2. The extreme Big Mac estimate of a needed appreciation of 138 percent is omitted from this average because a simple PPP approach is widely regarded as inappropriate.

3. The corresponding drop in the bilateral correction from 42 to 38 percent is misleading because none of the enhanced-PPP studies is for the latter period, and it is this approach that systematically produces the highest estimates of undervaluation.

4. Thus, we fundamentally disagree with Dunaway, Leigh, and Li (2006) and Cheung, Chinn, and Fujii (2007) that the variations are so wide as to preclude drawing policy implications.

5. Throughout this paper we measure REER in the normal way, as the price of a nation's output relative to the trade-weighted price of other nations' outputs, typically deflated over time by consumer price indices. The Salter-Swan-Scandinavian-Chicago-Latin American alternative definition, as the ratio of the domestic price of tradables to the domestic price of nontradables, corresponds to this measure so long as the price of tradables moves 1:1 with the exchange rate and the price of nontradables is unaffected by the exchange rate.

Table 4.1   Estimates of renminbi appreciation needed to eliminate undervaluation (percent)

Study	Year	REER range	Bilateral dollar rate range	Approach
Anderson (2006)	2006	—	18 to 25	FEER
Bénassy-Quéré et al. (2004)	2001	16	41 to 44	BEER
Bénassy-Quéré et al. (2006)	2004	31 to 45	30 to 59	BEER
Big Mac	2007	—	138	PPP-S
Bosworth (2004)	2004	—	67	PPP-E
Cheung, Chinn, and Fujii (2007)	2007	—	≈100	PPP-E
Cline (2005)	2005	21	45	FEER
Cline (2007)	2007	11 to 18	34 to 39	FEER
Coudert and Couharde (2005)	2003		41 to 50	PPP-E
	2002		18	BEER
	2002–03	23 to 30	44 to 54	FEER
Frankel (2006)	2000		56	PPP-E
Funke and Rahn (2005)	2002	3 to 6	12 to 14	BEER
Goldstein (2004)	2004	15 to 30	—	FEER
Goldstein and Lardy (2006)	2004	20 to 35	—	FEER
Goldstein and Lardy (chapter 1)	2007	30 to 55	—	FEER
Jeong and Mazier (2003)	2000	29	67	FEER
MacDonald and Dias (2007)	2007	8 to 42	—	BEER
Stolper and Fuentes (2007)	2007[a]	—	7	BEER
	2007[b]		15	FEER
Wang (2004)	2003	5	—	BEER
		0 to 5		FEER
		0 to –5		FEER
Wren-Lewis (2004)	2003	—	19 to 22	FEER
Average	All	19	40[c]	
Average A	2000–2004	17	42[c]	
Average B	2005–07	26	38[c]	

BEER = behavioral equilibrium exchange rate
FEER = fundamental equilibrium exchange rate
PPP = purchasing power parity
REER = real equilibrium exchange rate
-S = simple
-E = enhanced

a. Goldman Sachs dynamic equilibrium exchange rate (GSDEER) model.
b. Elasticities model.
c. Excluding Big Mac.

associated with development is concentrated primarily in tradables. The consequence is that the ratio of the market exchange rate to the PPP exchange rate is well below unity for low-income countries and eventually rises to approximately unity at the per capita income levels of rich coun-

Figure 4.1   Ratio of market exchange rate to PPP exchange rate and real per capita income

market exchange rate/PPP exchange rate

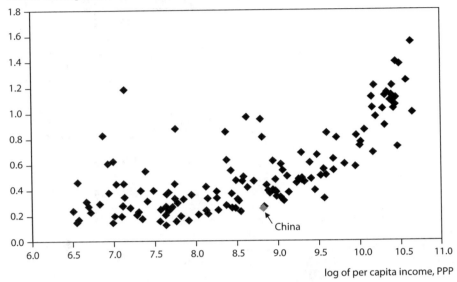

PPP = purchasing power parity

Source: World Bank (2007b).

tries, as figure 4.1 illustrates.[6] Undervaluation or overvaluation is defined as the percentage by which a country's exchange rate diverges from the regression line linking per capita income and the real exchange rate (RER).[7] It is possible for the regression line to take account of other variables beyond real per capita income that may systematically influence RERs, such as net foreign assets or the terms of trade. In this case, enhancement of the PPP approach goes well beyond including a Balassa-Samuelson effect and incorporates variables that often feature in the BEER approach, such as productivity growth and net foreign assets.

---

6. Data are for 2005 for 138 countries with population exceeding 1 million (World Bank 2007b).

7. Note that this relationship is also used by Rodrik (2007) and Bhalla (2007) to identify undervaluation. Both authors argue that undervaluation can contribute to growth, Rodrik because of the need to offset purported greater contracting difficulties in the tradable sector and Bhalla more simply in a neomercantilist sense that does not take account of pressures on inflation that would result from chronic current account surpluses (Meade's "internal imbalance").

We are skeptical of the enhanced-PPP approach in general and its application to China in particular. One major limitation is that, by definition, the US dollar can never be overvalued or undervalued: It is the numeraire for PPP exchange rate equal to market rate. This is a gaping hole for an analytical approach considering that the US current account deficit currently absorbs the vast bulk of the combined surpluses of the rest of the world. More generally, ample historical experience—including that of China today—shows that the deviation of the PPP/market exchange rate ratio (PPP/er) from the international norm can be a wholly misleading guide as to whether a country has a current account surplus or deficit, let alone whether the balance is a meaningfully sustainable equilibrium.

For China, it is well known that until recently, the available price surveys were much less reliable than those for most countries (Cooper 2005, Heston 2001, Lardy 1994). It is also well known that China was an extreme outlier, with low domestic prices. The presumption was thus that China's prices were measured unreliably, at below actual levels. If so, then the percentage shortfall of x from the actual level would not only impute an undervaluation of x percent, but also overstate the real per capita income on the horizontal axis, thereby making the seeming shortfall from the international line even greater and registering an undervaluation greater than x percent. Indeed, after the conference that led to this volume, the World Bank released its 2007 PPP estimates in its International Comparison Program. China participated in the survey for the first time ever and India for the first time since 1985. The new estimates sharply reduced the ratio of the PPP exchange rate to the market rate for both countries. For China, the ratio fell from 3.3 to 2.4; for India, it fell from 5 to 3 (World Bank 2007a, 2007b).

Figure 4.2 illustrates the problems with interpreting divergence from adjusted PPP as a guide to exchange rate policy. The figure shows the PPP/er on the left vertical axis and the current account surplus as a percent of GDP on the right vertical axis.[8] When the PPP/er measure is higher, the currency is asserted to be more undervalued. The first panel, for Japan, shows a reasonably clear correlation between this measure of the degree of exchange rate undervaluation and the current account. Such direct comparisons can be made for Japan because it is now at about the same per capita income as the United States and so does not require Balassa-Samuelson adjustment. Thus, from 1995 to 2006 the PPP/er ratio has risen from 0.54 to 0.95; over the same period the current account surplus has risen from 2.1 to 3.9 percent of GDP.

However, the PPP metric seriously misjudges even Japan's misalignment because the level for the entire period suggests that the yen was con-

---

8. Data are from the IMF *World Economic Outlook* database. The PPP/er ratio is the ratio of GDP in dollars at PPP to nominal dollar GDP at the current exchange rate.

**Figure 4.2   Ratio of PPP exchange rate to market exchange rate (PPP/er)
              and current account balance**

a. Japan, 1984–2006

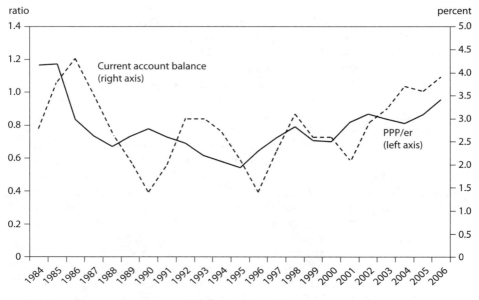

b. China, 1988–2006

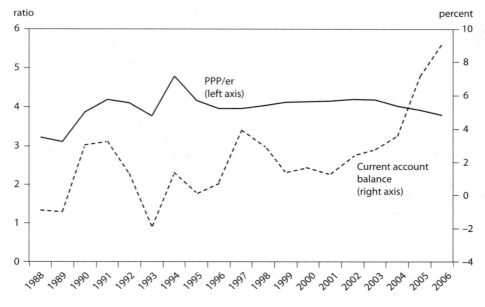

Source: IMF (2007).

tinuously overvalued rather than undervalued: For 1986 and all years thereafter, the ratio of the PPP exchange rate to the actual exchange rate is below unity. If we take 2 percent of GDP as a more appropriate current account equilibrium range for Japan than 4 percent, then the equilibrium PPP rate for Japan implied by the figure is only about 0.6. That is, the international basket of goods and services can cost about 50 percent more in Japan than in the United States with external equilibrium still being maintained. Thus the Japan example suggests that the PPP approach may be useful to examine trends but not to identify over- or undervaluation at a point in time.

The PPP approach is even less consistent with the current account outcome for China. The current account surplus soared from 1 percent of GDP in 1994–96 to 9 percent in 2006, when the PPP-gauged undervaluation registered a small reduction. This rough comparison does not incorporate a Balassa-Samuelson adjustment, but such an adjustment would merely accentuate the conclusion.

Behavioral Equilibrium Exchange Rate

A BEER aims to estimate the index level to which the market exchange rate might be expected to revert in the medium or long run, given an absence of shocks.[9] Unlike the enhanced-PPP approach, which deals in direct price comparisons for internationally comparable baskets of goods, the BEER deals with indexes over time of domestic versus international prices and exchange rates. It implicitly assumes that the currency was, on average, in equilibrium over the period for which the estimation was made, which means that it is only possible to use the BEER to determine whether a currency is under- or overvalued compared with its own past averages, not on an absolute basis.

To determine whether a currency is under- or overvalued, the analysis typically examines the departure of the country's observed REER at the latest date available from the equation-predicted BEER, but this method is only as good as the assumption of an equilibrium average real exchange rate over the sample period. The BEER is typically specified as a function of productivity (or, what amounts to the same thing, of relative productivity in the tradable and nontradable goods sectors); net foreign assets (NFA); openness (high protection implies a limited need for exports to balance the current account and therefore allows an uncompetitive currency); and sometimes the level and/or composition of government expenditure. It may also be specified as a function of the average current account balance, or of variables (e.g., demographic) that are thought to influence the average current account balance. Other variables are occasionally added.

---

9. The BEER approach was introduced by Clark and MacDonald (1998).

BEERs are the basis on which estimates of equilibrium real exchange rates (ERERs) are usually calculated.[10]

A problem with some BEER estimates is that they are calculated from a regression for a single country rather than from cross-country experience. Such studies are surely incapable of examining whether a country's policy intervention is or is not making the country's currency over- or undervalued. Suppose a country persistently intervenes to keep its currency from appreciating while accumulating ever-rising reserves. By most definitions, the country's currency will be increasingly undervalued. But if a regression is run for this country alone, comparing today's exchange rate against an earlier exchange rate using such variables as NFA, the premise that the country must have been in equilibrium for the full period, on average, will force a negligible coefficient on NFA. Meanwhile, a larger coefficient estimated from cross-country data would diagnose increasing undervaluation.

Fundamental Equilibrium Exchange Rate

The third approach is the FEER, or macroeconomic balance, concept of equilibrium. One of the present authors (Williamson 1983) introduced this concept into academic analysis. The International Monetary Fund (IMF) has widely employed it, including as the basis for the first and third approaches to estimating equilibrium exchange rates described in IMF (2006). The basic idea is to search for a set of exchange rates that will simultaneously achieve internal and external balance in every country (Meade 1951). Internal balance is defined as noninflationary full employment or whatever is judged to be the optimal pressure of demand. In an era when long-run Phillips curves are widely believed to be vertical—except, perhaps, at minimal inflation rates—there is not much room for arguing about levels of internal balance. External balance is far more controversial. Everyone agrees that a current account balance has to be sustainable to be called external balance, but it is easy to argue that this criterion does not pin down values uniquely. Many authors have argued that it has to be a normative concept, and that is certainly one interpretation.[11]

Traditionally, the assumption has been that the current account target should be either a moderate deficit—1 to 3 percent of GDP—or at most a

---

10. They also provide the basis for the second of the IMF calculations of exchange rate equilibria (IMF 2006).

11. It was presumably an attempt to escape from a normative definition of external balance that led the IMF to introduce its third concept of equilibrium exchange rates, which defines these as the set that would achieve current account outcomes that would keep ratios of NFA to GDP unchanged.

modest surplus for most developing countries and a surplus for rich countries, on the grounds that capital should be expected to flow from the latter to the former. Beyond identifying the target current account, two additional elements are key to estimating under- or overvaluation. First, it is necessary to determine how much of the present current account divergence from the target is strictly cyclical and transitory, a step that turns out to be critical for China.

Second, it is necessary to know the appropriate price elasticities and pass-through ratios for exports and imports to calculate how much the exchange rate would need to move to close the gap between the cyclically adjusted actual and target current account balances. For China, an important consideration in judging trade elasticities is the relatively large share of imported intermediates used to produce exports. Even after accounting for this influence, China's current account should be expected to show relatively high response to the real exchange rate in light of its large share of trade in GDP.[12]

Bilateral Versus Multilateral Misalignment

Whichever of the three approaches is used, it is important to recognize the difference between estimates of bilateral undervaluation against the US dollar and multilateral undervaluation of the currency on a trade-weighted real effective basis. The central point in this regard is that the relationship between them is contingent: The degree of difference will depend on whether there is a generalized realignment of other currencies against the dollar or instead a correction by China alone. In the extreme case of revaluation solely by China, the two measures are identical. In the more policy-relevant context, in which much of Asia—including Japan, Malaysia, Singapore, Taiwan, and arguably Philippines, India, and Thailand—probably would also tend to revalue if China were to do so, the bilateral appreciation against the dollar will be considerably larger than the real effective appreciation.

---

12. Without special treatment for component imports used in exports, Cline (2005) estimates that a 1 percent rise in the real exchange rate should be expected to reduce China's current account balance by 0.3 percent of GDP. Exports of goods and services were 40 percent of GDP and imports 32 percent in 2006. Perhaps 40 percent of imports are for intermediates used in exports, so half of imports are reexportable components and half are final goods. Suppose the price elasticity is unity for exports and for final-good imports. With unitary elasticity, appreciation will leave the renminbi value of final-good imports unchanged. The other half of imports will decline linearly with exports. So a 1 percent real appreciation will reduce exports by 1 percent or 0.4 percent of GDP, while reducing component imports by 1 percent or 0.16 percent of GDP, placing the overall result at 0.24 percent of GDP reduction in the current account.

Review of Estimates

PPP-Based Studies

The only simple direct PPP comparison is the *Economist's* Big Mac Index.[13] Specifically, we have included the latest calculation found on the internet at the time of writing, which suggested an undervaluation of 58 percent in mid-2007.[14] Correspondingly, it would require a rise of 138 percent in the renminbi against the US dollar to place the cost of a Big Mac at the same price in dollars in the two countries.[15]

The first enhanced-PPP study in table 4.1 is Bosworth (2004), prepared for the Tokyo Club. Most of it is devoted to expounding the principles involved in calculating misalignments, but when the author mentions figures, he points out that, while a simple PPP comparison would suggest that the renminbi's value would need to quadruple, the standard Balassa-Samuelson analysis implies that this would be excessive. Accounting for per capita income, the renminbi is still undervalued, but only by an estimated 40 percent, indicating that a revaluation of 67 percent would be needed to eliminate undervaluation. However, Bosworth (2004) notes the fragility of this approach and points out that the departure from the PPP line is "even larger for India, a country whose exchange rate has attracted little claim of being undervalued" (p. 11).

Coudert and Couharde (2005) have entries in all three approaches. Their enhanced-PPP estimate places Chinese undervaluation between 41 percent and just over 50 percent, depending on whether they omit certain countries from the regression.

Frankel (2006) primarily discusses the merits of various exchange rate regimes for China but also utilizes the enhanced-PPP approach; on that basis, Frankel estimates that the renminbi was about 36 percent undervalued relative to the dollar in 2000 (i.e., a revaluation of 56 percent would be required to eliminate undervaluation). Frankel also finds, however, that the undervaluation was almost identical to this amount in 1990 (at 34 percent). The unchanged degree of undervaluation in the face of far higher current account surpluses in recent years raises further doubts about the reliability of the enhanced-PPP approach in general.

---

13. This section should be read in light of the sharp downward revision of China's ratio of PPP to market exchange rate in the 2007 World Bank International Comparison Program results released after the conference at which this paper was presented. That ratio was only 2.4 to 1, about half the ratio in the Cheung et al. (2007) study considered below. Broadly, the implied errors in measurement in past studies suggest that the entire set of enhanced-PPP studies for China is unreliable and that these studies should be reestimated using the new survey results.

14. *Economist*, July 5, 2007.

15. For an undervaluation of x percent, the appreciation needed for correction is 100 $([1/(1 - .01x] -1)$.

The most recent enhanced-PPP study for China is that of Cheung, Chinn, and Fujii (2007). They estimate their model using annual data over 1975–2004 and have by far the largest country sample (132 countries). The equation for price level relative to US price level is estimated on a joint time series/cross-section basis, and a correction for serial correlation is introduced. The renminbi is estimated to be undervalued by about 50 percent in various alternative specifications, implying a needed revaluation of about 100 percent. However, the authors then argue that there is no evidence of undervaluation because the results lie within two standard errors of zero.

We suspect that the authors have conducted the wrong test. The relevant standard deviation is not that for the observations (i.e., the square root of the sum of squared residuals—but instead the standard deviation of the regression line itself, based on the standard errors of the parameter estimates. These are actually estimated quite tightly: The standard error is only 8 percent of the constant coefficient and 2 percent of the coefficient on the log of relative income. The central regression line states that China's ratio of actual to PPP exchange rate should be 0.481, at China's relative PPP per capita income. Dropping the line by two standard deviations of the regression estimates places the lower corridor at 0.449 at the same relative income. In contrast, China's actual PPP/er ratio is only 0.21, far below two standard deviations of the regression estimate.[16] So although we consider the enhanced-PPP approach to be fragile and less reliable than the BEER and FEER alternatives, we do not consider the statistical inference by Cheung, Chinn, and Fujii to provide a sound basis for rejecting the approach.

The simple average for the needed real appreciation bilaterally against the dollar in the four enhanced-PPP approaches in table 4.1 is 67 percent, considerably above the average of the other approaches. Even after enhancement for the Balassa-Samuelson effect, then, the PPP approach appears to give high estimates for the amount of correction needed. This may reflect a bias introduced by an understatement of the price of an internationally comparable basket of goods in China, as suggested above.

BEER Estimates

BEER estimates can differ because of differences in independent variables, estimation periods, country samples, and estimating techniques. All of the BEER studies include the productivity variable, and all except

---

16. The regression estimate is $z = -.134$ (.011) $+ 0.299$ (.006) $\ln(y^*/y^*_u)$, where z is the logarithm of the ratio of the market to the PPP exchange rate, standard errors are in parentheses, and the final term is the logarithm of China's PPP per capita income relative to that of the United States (which turns out to be –2). The lower corridor for two standard deviations of the regression coefficients would turn this equation into $z = -.156 + 0.311 \ln(y^*/y^*_u)$. Taking the corresponding exponents yields the text estimates.

one (MacDonald and Dias 2007) include net foreign assets. It turns out, however, that the crucial distinction in this set of studies is whether the model is estimated using an international panel approach or instead uses data solely for China.

The two BEER studies in table 4.1 by Agnes Bénassy-Quéré and her coauthors (Bénassy-Quéré et al. 2004; Bénassy-Quéré, Lahrèche-Révil, and Mignon 2006) aimed to estimate the equilibrium exchange rate of the renminbi in the context of simultaneously estimating the equilibrium exchange rates of all the currencies of Group of 20 countries. Bénassy-Quéré et al. (2004) estimate the real effective appreciation needed to eliminate undervaluation at 16 percent and the corresponding bilateral rise of the renminbi against the dollar at about 40 percent.

The second study, Bénassy-Quéré et al. (2006), estimated using quarterly data from 1980 to 2004 for 15 countries, pays special attention to how much impact the treatment of the residual countries has on the estimate of misalignment. Unfortunately, this impact seems to be considerable. In one treatment, they consider the 15 major currencies as though they were the whole world, while in the other, they add a rest of the world sector. The effective misalignment of the renminbi is then calculated to vary between 31 and 45 percent, depending on which of the treatments is used, while the corresponding implied revaluation against the dollar varies from 30 to 59 percent.[17]

For their entry in the BEER approach, Coudert and Couharde (2005) apply a panel-data estimation of the Balassa-Samuelson effect in 21 emerging markets from the first quarter of 1980 to the fourth quarter of 2002. The dependent variable is a real exchange rate index against the dollar. The authors obtain an estimate that China was substantially less misaligned (18 percent undervalued in 2002) than identified in their enhanced-PPP test. They discuss why there is no noticeable Balassa-Samuelson effect at work in China from the first quarter of 1998 to the fourth quarter of 2004, for which they have data, but do not note the obvious candidate: that China's exchange rate policy thwarted adjustment.

Funke and Rahn (2005), like others, start off by noting that the renminbi appears to be highly undervalued on a PPP comparison and that a substantial undervaluation remains after adjusting for the Balassa-Samuelson effect. However, they quickly move on to calculate a BEER and a permanent equilibrium exchange rate, which is a BEER with the independent variables set at their permanent values. They estimated their model on quarterly data for China alone, from the first quarter of 1985 to the fourth quarter of 2002; however, when they discovered a break in the series, they estimated their final model only from the first quarter of 1994 to the

---

17. The authors use a higher index for more units of domestic currency per unit of foreign currency, so the estimates they cite for undervaluation are equivalent to percent revaluation implied.

fourth quarter of 2002. They find that the renminbi was undervalued by only 3 to 6 percent in 2002 on a real effective basis and by 11 to 12 percent bilaterally against the dollar.

The paper by MacDonald and Dias (2007) was presented to the February 2007 workshop at the Peterson Institute on what would be necessary to reduce the global imbalances. The paper aimed to estimate a BEER model and use it to predict which exchange rate changes would be consistent with the three patterns of global current account outcomes. In addition to including the standard productivity variable, but omitting the usual net foreign assets, MacDonald and Dias also included the trade balance (though its coefficient was small), the terms of trade, and the real interest rate, the last of which was insignificant, which is not surprising as real interest rates are now more of a world than a national variable. They calculate changes in the effective exchange rate rather than the dollar rate and again get a wide range, from 8 to 30 percent undervaluation. As the target current account outcomes were suggested by the organizers of the workshop at which the paper was originally presented, the authors should not be held accountable for this wide range of estimates.[18]

Stolper and Fuentes (2007) of Goldman Sachs also presented their paper at the same workshop. They made the point that the implicit implication of the finding of no dollar overvaluation in the Goldman Sachs dynamic equilibrium exchange rate (GSDEER) model is that the US deficit would asymptotically approach a sustainable level at the current exchange rate of the dollar. Hence any renminbi adjustment would permit a depreciation of other currencies, such as the euro, against the dollar. Introducing terms of trade into their model did, however, point to a modest renminbi undervaluation of about 7 percent against the dollar.

Wang (2004) includes a section on determinants of the medium-run path of the real exchange rate in her chapter of an IMF study of the Chinese economy. She estimates an ERER model for China alone using annual data over the period 1980–2003. Her variables include productivity changes, NFA, and openness. She finds that the estimated equilibrium exchange rate was only about 5 percent more than the actual exchange rate in 2003 and concludes that any undervaluation was small.

The salient difference in the BEER group results is between those studies that use international panel data and those that use only Chinese data. The former tend to find much larger estimates of the degree of undervaluation, whereas the latter find only small estimates. In the China-only studies, Wang's finding implies that undervaluation was only about 5 percent greater in 2003 than the average across the estimation period (1980–2003). Even that is surprising, as everyone agrees that the renminbi was severely overvalued in the early 1980s.

---

18. In a subsequent letter to the *Economist* (July 14, 2007), the senior author gave a BEER estimate of renminbi undervaluation of 30 percent.

Similarly, the Funke and Rahn finding that undervaluation was modest in 2003 should really be read as a finding that it was only modestly larger than it was over the period 1994–2003 as a whole. What one concludes from BEER models therefore depends critically on whether one uses them to evaluate the path of the real exchange rate over time based on movements that would have been expected from international experience of response to changes in productivity, NFA, and other explanatory variables, or whether one relies exclusively on Chinese experience.

FEER Estimates

The first FEER study listed is that of Anderson (2006), who estimates that the Chinese current account balance was artificially boosted in 2006 by factors such as excess heavy industrial capacity and that the cyclically adjusted current account surplus stood at 5 percent of GDP. The underlying foreign direct investment (FDI) inflow is estimated as 1 percent of GDP, giving a target adjustment of 6 percent of GDP. Applying a model with export elasticities of 0.5 and an import elasticity of 0.8, Anderson estimated that this adjustment would require a revaluation of 18 to 25 percent (undervaluation of 15 to 20 percent). This is subsequently interpreted as appreciation against the dollar in the same range, implying that Anderson does not anticipate that other countries would appreciate against the dollar in response to a renminbi appreciation.

The assumption that the surplus has cyclical causes is crucial because in 2006 the actual current account surplus was 9 percent of GDP, so the target adjustment would widen to about 10 percent of GDP if one did not believe that a cyclical component to the surplus would naturally unwind without currency appreciation. In view of the still larger prospective surplus in 2007—on the order of 11 percent of GDP—it seems difficult to give much weight to the notion that a large portion of the surplus will naturally reverse as the cycle runs its course.[19]

The next two studies in the FEER school are by one of the authors of the present paper (Cline 2005, 2007). The first of these, Cline (2005), studies the optimal way to achieve a target adjustment of the US current account to reduce it to 3 percent of US GDP by 2010. It assumes that, as part of a multilateral adjustment process, the current account surpluses of China and other countries would decline by 40 percent—for China, from 4.2 percent of GDP in 2004 to 2.5 percent in 2010. Cline calculated that this adjustment would require an effective renminbi appreciation of 8 percent from the 2002 level and 21 percent from the March 2005 level, with a corresponding bilateral appreciation of 45 percent against the dollar from the

---

19. Goldstein and Lardy (in chapter 1) estimate the 2007 outcome at 11 percent of GDP.

latter base. Cline is like Bénassy-Quéré et al. in estimating simultaneously a set of exchange rates for all of the major economies. His second study, Cline (2007), which was presented at the workshop mentioned earlier, accepts the IMF projection that China's current account is on track for a surplus of 6.3 percent of GDP in 2011 following present trends. Cline interpreted the three objectives he was given by the workshop organizers as being to seek what would be necessary to reduce the current account surplus, first, to 1.7 percent of GDP; second, to zero; and third, to transform the surplus into a deficit of 1.4 percent of GDP. In this study, he estimated the needed remaining appreciation of the renminbi to be in a range of 11 to 18 percent from its 2006 level in real effective terms and 34 to 39 percent against the dollar.

Coudert and Couharde (2005) complete their study with a FEER-type estimate of undervaluation. They do not state explicitly what outcome they expect given present trends, but their calculations are intended to illuminate the revaluation of the renminbi that would be needed, first, to induce a current account deficit of 1.5 percent of GDP, and second, to induce a current account deficit of 2.8 percent of GDP. They obtain corresponding estimates of 23 and 30 percent, respectively, for undervaluation of the effective exchange rate and 44 and 54 percent, respectively, for the dollar rate.

Goldstein (2004) uses the underlying balance approach to estimate a FEER for the renminbi. He takes a net capital inflow of 1.5 percent of GDP as normal, and therefore assumes that China should target a current account deficit of that size. He estimates that China had a normal current account surplus of 2.5 percent of GDP, implying the need for an adjustment of 4 percent of GDP. He states that a "small, bare-bones, elasticity-based trade model" (that was nonetheless sufficiently sophisticated to recognize that the answer needs to reflect China's important role in processing intermediate goods for assembly) implied a need for a renminbi appreciation in the upper half of a 15 to 30 percent range (Goldstein 2004, 201). Goldstein appears to have been thinking of an effective appreciation of that size, though this is not explicit. He also presents an analysis based on the need for global payments adjustment, in which he argues rather informally that the Chinese adjustment just advocated would be consistent with the needs of the global economy.

Goldstein and Lardy (2006) adopt a similar approach, though with a little more history behind them. They argue that the underlying Chinese current account surplus in 2005 was in the range of 5 to 7 percent of GDP (against their predicted 2005 actual outcome of 7 to 9 percent, which reflected somewhat slower domestic growth and some real appreciation in 2005). The bare-bones elasticity model now gave them answers in the upper part of a 20 to 40 percent range. Although this may seem a rather modest response to an increase of at least 2.5 percent of GDP in the need for adjustment, the final figure is consistent with the elasticities and current account response suggested in the first section of the present paper.[20] A footnote in Goldstein and Lardy (2006) gives a range of 20 to 35 percent effective undervaluation, taking a broad view across several methodologies: This is stated in table 4.1 of the present paper as their estimate. However, Goldstein and Lardy (2006) are quite unambiguous in speaking of an undervaluation of the effective rate.

Goldstein and Lardy (in chapter 1) raise their previous estimate of needed appreciation to eliminate undervaluation to a range of 30 to 55 percent. Once again their framework is the elasticity approach. They place the range for the parameter relating real exchange rate change to current account change at 2 to 3.5 percent of GDP adjustment for a 10 percent real exchange rate change. This range results from applying the parameter range to an 11 percent current account surplus for 2007 and, by implication, assumes that no part of the surplus is cyclical and likely to decline without a change in the exchange rate.

Jeong and Mazier (2003) also aim to calculate FEERs in a model comprising China, Japan, Korea, the United States, Euroland, and the rest of the world. They estimate the influence of various variables (e.g., FDI, demographics, and income) on the current account balance for industrial countries and emerging markets separately, then estimate from those variables the equilibrium current account for each country in the model. Internal balance is estimated by the Organization for Economic Cooperation and Development approach—or, in the case of China, by a Hodrick-Prescott filter.[21] Like Coudert and Couharde, Jeong and Mazier do not state explicitly a figure for the underlying current account surplus but calculate what would be necessary to induce a deficit of 1 to 1.5 percent of GDP. The exchange rate that would reconcile internal and external balance is compared graphically with actual exchange rates. The graphs (Jeong and Mazier 2003, 1177) indicate that by 2000, the final year in the estimates, the actual REER was 22 percent below the equilibrium level, indicating 29 percent needed appreciation, and the bilateral rate against the dollar was correspondingly undervalued by 40 percent, indicating a 67 percent needed appreciation.

In addition to a BEER model, Stolper and Fuentes (2007) estimate a supplementary elasticities (i.e., FEER) model. The results suggest that the US dollar needs to decline by about 15 percent; China would be expected to play a proportionate part.

---

20. The Goldstein-Lardy implicit parameter of 0.25 percent of GDP reduction in current account surplus for a 1 percent rise in the real exchange rate is virtually the same as suggested in note 13 above.

21. The first measures capacity by connecting cyclical peaks in output over time; the second generates a smooth nonlinear representation of the time series.

Exploring the macroeconomic balance approach to supplement her BEER approach, Wang (2004) estimates the underlying Chinese current account balance as a surplus of 2.1 percent of GDP and contrasts it with, first, a target surplus of 3.1 percent of GDP, which she estimates as appropriate based on savings and investment, and second, a surplus of 1 percent of GDP, which would stabilize the NFA to GDP ratio at its 2001 level. These targets would require a small depreciation or a small appreciation, respectively, of the effective rate of the renminbi (these conclusions are interpreted as changes of 0 to 5 percent in table 4.1).

The last study listed in table 4.1 is that of Simon Wren-Lewis (2004), which employs a FEER-like approach: He uses a global model that calculates the bilateral exchange rates that would produce target current account outcomes in equilibrium and undertakes a special extension to estimate renminbi values consistent with various current balance adjustments. Wren-Lewis estimates that China had an underlying current account surplus equal to 3.4 percent of GDP in 2002. To reduce this to a 1 percent surplus would have required a bilateral appreciation against the dollar of 19 percent. Eliminating the surplus entirely would have required a 22 percent appreciation.

It should be emphasized that most of the above estimates were calculated between 2000 and 2005, when China's current account surplus averaged 3.2 percent of GDP. With a surplus almost four times this large in 2007, the magnitude of undervaluation appears to be larger today. It should also be stressed that the studies that attribute a large part of China's surplus to temporary cyclical factors raise special questions. It seems increasingly implausible that China's underlying current account surplus after removing cyclical factors is only 2.1 percent of GDP (Wang 2004) or 5 percent (Anderson 2006; Goldstein and Lardy's low alternative), and thus, that the great bulk of today's much larger surplus can be expected to disappear naturally without exchange rate appreciation as the business cycle runs its course.

Probably the major source of discrepancies among the FEER estimates is the studies' assumptions about how large a change in the current account of the balance of payments should be targeted. A key source of diverging adjustment targets is differences in identifying whether the present level of the current account represents a longer-term trend or is temporarily exaggerated. After that come different assumptions about the price elasticities of demand, including assumptions about the import content of exports.

Most of the FEER estimates suggest a widespread judgment that an appropriate target for China is a current account outcome that is not enormously different from a balanced current account. The biggest surplus is one of Wang's targets, rationalized by China's high saving propensity. The next largest is one of Cline's targets, which resulted from a desire to treat all surplus countries equally rather than a belief that it is in China's national interest to export real resources.[22]

Wang's view implicitly assumes that world welfare is maximized by allowing countries that wish to save in excess of the level of investment that is efficient at the world interest rate to do so and export the resulting savings as a current account surplus. The counterargument is that such a view assumes, first, that a national government's decision should be accepted uncritically as the judge of what is in the social interest of its citizens, and second, that there is no problem of world consistency of current account objectives that needs to be dealt with.

Regarding the first point, there are still about a hundred million desperately poor people in China, who save a lot partly because much of the saving is corporate and is not their decision at all and partly because they are afraid of the future because of the lack of a safety net. The international community should take their interests into account even if China's government ignores them. If one holds such a view, then a current account close to balance seems to be a more natural target than is a large surplus. China's policy should aim to reduce the saving rate, as indeed it does, at least in theory. We do not attempt to deal with the second problem here.

Another obvious source of differences in FEER estimates lies in differing assumptions about trade elasticities.[23] Anderson (2006) uses an export elasticity of 0.5—which he asserts is probably too high—and an import elasticity of 0.8. Cline (2005, 2007) assumes that all price elasticities, both of exports and imports, are of unity. Coudert and Couharde (2005) take their elasticities from the NiGEM model, in which all elasticities satisfy the Marshall-Lerner condition (though in the case of the United States they only just satisfy it) and vary from 0.50 to 1.19 for the export price elasticity and from 0.41 to 0.95 for the import price elasticity. Neither Goldstein (2004) nor Goldstein and Lardy (2006) state their assumed elasticities but do state that they are conventional. Jeong and Mazier (2003) also take their elasticities from other models with specifications similar to their own, and compare the estimated elasticities from different models. Wren-Lewis (2004) uses export price elasticities of 2 and import price elasticities of 0.5.

---

22. His largest deficit target is one suggested by Williamson and a coauthor, in a period when it was widely held that developing countries ought to be importing real resources and there was little concern about having a competitive exchange rate.

23. One study not included here that investigates the impact of variations in the trade elasticities is that of Dunaway, Leigh, and Li (2006). Their estimates of the impact of increased export and import elasticities from 1 to 1.5 are interdependent with those of the current account adjustment to be accomplished: If this is only 1 percent of GDP, lower elasticities would increase undervaluation by about 4 percent, whereas with a gap of 3 percent of GDP, the impact on undervaluation would be about 13 percent. The difference is substantial.

Figure 4.3   Real renminbi appreciation needed to eliminate undervaluation

a. Enhanced PPP (bilateral against dollar)

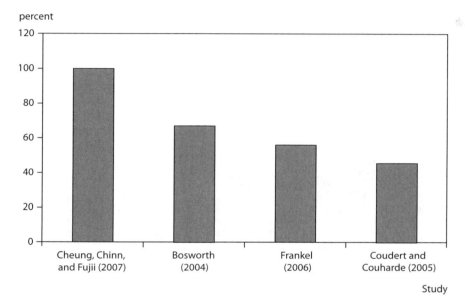

(figure continues next page)

Conclusion

Figure 4.3 summarizes the estimates in table 4.1, which are grouped by each of the three approaches above, showing multilateral and bilateral estimates separately.[24] For studies showing a range, the figure shows the midpoint. The studies are ordered by descending magnitude of estimated misalignment within each approach. It is evident that the largest undervaluations are found in the enhanced-PPP estimates.[25] The simple average for the four enhanced-PPP studies is a needed real appreciation against the dollar of 67 percent for the renminbi, whereas the simple averages for bilateral real appreciations given by the BEER and FEER approaches are smaller, at 25 and 36 percent, respectively. The simple averages for the multilateral real revaluations in the BEER and FEER approaches are even more moderate, at 18 and 20 percent, respectively. Also, as figure 4.3 shows, there is considerably more agreement among the enhanced-PPP

---

24. None of the enhanced-PPP estimates include multilateral realignment, so all are treated as bilateral.

25. The Big Mac simple PPP is excluded as conceptually flawed.

Figure 4.3 Real renminbi appreciation needed to eliminate undervaluation *(continued)*

b. Behavioral equilibrium exchange rate (BEER) and fundamental equilibrium exchange rate (FEER)

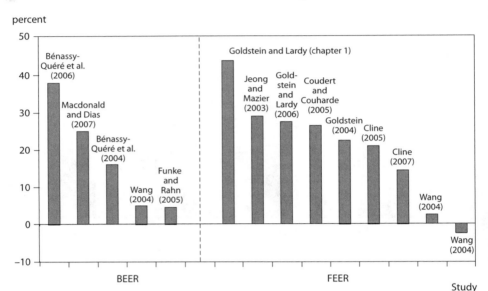

Real effective exchange rate

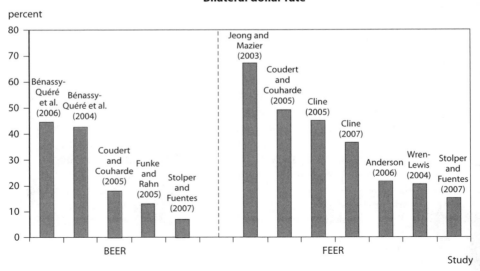

Bilateral dollar rate

Source: Table 4.1

estimates than among the BEER estimates. The FEER estimates also show more agreement than do the BEER estimates if the two outliers proposed by Wang (2004) are excluded.

It seems highly likely that the enhanced-PPP estimates overstate the needed degree of appreciation for China. New World Bank estimates that became available subsequent to this conference, based on International Comparison Program surveys that for the first time directly included China, sharply reduce the ratio of the PPP exchange rate to the market rate, confirming suspicions that the ratio had been exaggerated by erroneous estimation of China's price level and broadly superseding the PPP studies surveyed here. More generally, although the approach relies on a robust empirical generalization about the ratio of the PPP exchange rate to the market rate, it does not estimate what one is conceptually seeking to measure. Even using only the data available before the 2007 World Bank results, the enhanced-PPP approach shows chronic undervaluation for China going back a quarter century, whereas policy concerns about undervaluation have escalated only in recent years.

Among the BEER approaches, the two based purely on Chinese data (Funke and Rahn 2005, Wang 2004) suggest a much smaller undervaluation, but intervention to prevent appreciation may have made them misleading. BEER approaches that use cross-sectional panel data show a much larger degree of undervaluation, similar to that suggested by the FEER approach. The average in figure 4.3 excluding China-only estimates is a 23 percent needed appreciation in the real effective multilateral rate, and 32 percent bilaterally, against the dollar. Thus, under the BEER approach, the renminbi seems to be substantially undervalued by normal international standards.

Attempts to measure a FEER assume that one is seeking a normative measure of undervaluation. FEERs depend primarily on the target current account that is fed into them as an objective. The view that China should aim for a large current account surplus because it has a high saving rate is acknowledged, but it is argued that a normative exercise should not automatically accept the government-stated social objective but should ask whether phenomena such as China's high saving rate are calculated to maximize social welfare. When this is done, an objective in the vicinity of zero surplus—similar to the objectives of most of the FEER exercises— seems reasonable. Among the FEER estimates, we consider the Wang (2004) calculations seriously understated because they assume that China's cyclically adjusted current account surplus is running at only 2 percent of GDP rather than the actual 9 percent in 2006 and 12 percent in 2007. Excluding these two estimates, the average for the FEER estimates in figure 4.3 is a needed appreciation of 27 percent in the REER, close to the international BEER estimates, and 36 percent in the bilateral exchange rate.

Because of its underlying fragility and likely bias in past Chinese price comparison estimates, we consider the estimates in the enhanced-PPP school to be unreliable. In contrast, the BEER estimates using cross-country data and the FEER estimates using plausible cyclical components of the current account surplus arrive at the same range of renminbi undervaluation, with about 25 percent real effective appreciation needed to remove undervaluation in both sets of estimates.

Methodologically, we prefer the FEER approach because the necessary assumption of average equilibrium over the estimation period makes even the internationally based BEER approach less reliable. Within the FEER school of estimates, the main need seems to be to work toward agreement on, first, how much of China's current account surplus is underlying and how much is temporary, and second, what magnitude of surplus (if any) makes sense over the medium term. On the latter issue, it is highly likely that most analysts, as well as the Chinese authorities themselves, would agree that the medium-term current account surplus should not be anywhere near double digits as a percentage of GDP. The needed correction is thus at a minimum several percentage points of GDP.

Finally, it should be reiterated that most of the studies surveyed in this chapter were conducted using the lower earlier levels of the current account. If there have been structural changes toward a current account surplus, the needed real effective appreciation could be larger than the roughly 25 percent real effective range suggested by the international-BEER and most of the FEER studies. For example, using the parameter suggested both here and in Goldstein and Lardy (chapter 1) that a 10 percent real exchange rate change with supporting expansion of internal demand leads to a change of about 2.5 percent of GDP in the current account, complete elimination of the 2007 surplus could require as much as a 43 percent real effective appreciation. However, it seems likely that a significant part of the surplus is cyclical. In particular, application of the same parameter to the effective real depreciation of the renminbi in recent years cannot explain the full surge in the surplus.

The IMF and the Bank for International Settlements place the real effective depreciation of the currency from 2002 to 2006 at 8 percent, deflated by consumer prices. The decline reflects the renminbi riding the dollar down. If one adopts the Goldstein-Lardy argument of additional productivity influences and places the relative price change for China's exports from 2002 to 2006 at zero (rather than the cumulative consumer price inflation of 8 percent) over these four years, then real effective depreciation would have been about 16 percent. But applying the parameter above would then have implied a rise of the surplus by 4 percent of GDP, not 9 percent of GDP (the increase from 2003 to 2007).

Anderson (2006) suggests that excess capacity in heavy industry following unusually large investment spurred atypical exports in 2005 and after, indicating one possible source of temporary exaggeration of the surplus this year. As a consequence, whereas some of the studies surveyed in this study using data before 2004 may have understated the extent of exchange rate correction needed by 2007, applying a FEER approach to the full magnitude of the 2007 surplus rather than an adjusted estimate would likely overstate the correction needed.

References

Anderson, Jonathan. 2006. *The Complete RMB Handbook*, 4th ed. Hong Kong: UBS.

Balassa, Bela. 1964. The Purchasing Power Parity Doctrine: A Reappraisal. *Journal of Political Economy* 72: 584–96.

Bénassy-Quéré, Agnès, Pascale Duran-Vigneron, Amina Lahrèche-Révil, and Valérie Mignon. 2004. Burden Sharing and Exchange Rate Misalignments Within the Group of Twenty. In *Dollar Adjustment: How Far? Against What?* ed. C. Fred Bergsten and John Williamson. Washington: Institute for International Economics.

Bénassy-Quéré, Agnès, Amina Lahrèche-Révil, and Valérie Mignon. 2006. *World Consistent Equilibrium Exchange Rates*. CEPII Working Paper 2006-20. Paris: Centre D'Etudes Prospectives et D'Informations Internationales.

Bhalla, Surjit S. 2007. There Are No Growth Miracles. Paper presented to a seminar at the International Monetary Fund, Washington.

Bosworth, Barry. 2004. Valuing the Renminbi. Paper presented to the annual conference of the Tokyo Club, February 9–10.

Cheung, Yin-Wong, Menzie D. Chinn, and Eiji Fujii. 2007. *The Overvaluation of Renminbi Undervaluation*. NBER Working Paper 12850. Cambridge, MA: National Bureau of Economic Research.

Clark, Peter, and Ronald MacDonald. 1998. *Exchange Rates and Economic Fundamentals: A Methodological Comparison of BEERs and FEERs*. IMF Working Paper 98/67. Washington: International Monetary Fund.

Cline, William R. 2005. *The United States as a Debtor Nation*. Washington: Institute for International Economics and Center for Global Development.

Cline, William R. 2007. Estimating Reference Exchange Rates. Paper presented to a workshop on policy to reduce global imbalances, sponsored by Bruegel, the Korea Institute for Economic Policy, and the Peterson Institute for International Economics, Washington, February 8–9.

Cooper, Richard. 2005. *Whither China?* JCER Bulletin, September. Tokyo: Japan Center for Economic Research.

Coudert, Virginie, and Cécile Couharde. 2005. *Real Equilibrium Exchange Rates in China*. CEPII Working Paper 2005-01. Paris: Centre D'Etudes Prospectives et D'Informations Internationales.

Dooley, Michael, David Folkerts-Landau, and Peter Garber. 2003. *An Essay on the Revived Bretton Woods System*. NBER Working Paper 9971. Cambridge, MA: National Bureau of Economic Research.

Dunaway, Steven, Lamin Leigh, and Xiangming Li. 2006. *How Robust Are Estimates of Equilibrium Real Exchange Rates: The Case of China*. IMF Working Paper 06/220. Washington: International Monetary Fund.

Dunaway, Steven, and Xiangming Li. 2005. *Estimating China's "Equilibrium" Real Exchange Rate*. IMF Working Paper 05/202. Washington: International Monetary Fund.

Frankel, Jeffrey. 2006. On the Yuan: The Choice between Adjustment under a Fixed Exchange Rate and Adjustment under a Flexible Rate. *CESifo Economic Studies* 52, no. 2 (June): 246–75.

Funke, Michael, and Jörg Rahn. 2005. Just How Undervalued is the Chinese Renminbi? *The World Economy* 28, no. 4 (April): 465–89.

Goldstein, Morris. 2004. Adjusting China's Exchange Rate Policies. Paper presented at the International Monetary Fund Seminar on the Foreign Exchange System, Dalian, China, May 26–27.

Goldstein, Morris, and Nicholas Lardy. 2006. China's Exchange Rate Policy Dilemma. *American Economic Review* 96, no. 2 (May): 422–26.

IMF (International Monetary Fund). 2006. *Methodology for CGER Exchange Rate Assessments.* Washington.

IMF (International Monetary Fund). 2007. *World Economic Outlook* database (October). Washington.

Heston, Alan. 2001. Treatment of China in PWT6. University of Pennsylvania, Philadelphia. Available at pwt.econ.upenn.edu (accessed on January 18, 2008).

Jeong, Se-Eun, and Jacques Mazier. 2003. Exchange Rate Regimes and Equilibrium Exchange Rates in East Asia. *Revue économique* 54, no. 5 (September): 1161–82.

Lardy, Nicholas R. 1994. *China in the World Economy.* Washington: Institute for International Economics.

MacDonald, Ronald, and Preethike Dias. 2007. BEER Estimates and Target Current Account Imbalances. Paper presented to a workshop on policy to reduce global imbalances, sponsored by Bruegel, the Korea Institute for Economic Policy, and the Peterson Institute for International Economics, Washington, February 8–9.

McKinnon, Ronald I. 2007. Why China Should Keep its Exchange Rate Pegged to the Dollar: A Historical Perspective from Japan. *International Finance,* March.

Meade, James E. 1951. *The Balance of Payments.* Oxford: Oxford University Press.

Mundell, Robert A. 2004. China's Exchange Rate: The Case for the Status Quo. Paper presented at the International Monetary Fund Seminar on the Foreign Exchange System, Dalian, China, May 26–27.

Nurkse, Ragnar. 1945. *Conditions of International Monetary Equilibrium.* Princeton Essays in International Finance 4. Princeton, NJ: International Finance Section, Princeton University.

Rodrik, Dani. 2007. The Real Exchange Rate and Economic Growth: Theory and Evidence. Harvard University. Photocopy.

Samuelson, Paul A. 1964. Theoretical Notes on Trade Problems. *Review of Economics and Statistics* 46: 145–54.

Stolper, Thomas, and Monica Fuentes. 2007. GSDEER and Trade Elasticities. Paper presented to a workshop on policy to reduce global imbalances, sponsored by Bruegel, the Korea Institute for Economic Policy, and the Peterson Institute for International Economics, Washington, February 8–9.

Wang, Tao. 2004. Exchange Rate Dynamics. In *China's Growth and Integration into the World Economy: Prospects and Challenges,* ed. E. Prasad. IMF Occasional Paper 232. Washington: International Monetary Fund.

Williamson, John. 1983. *The Exchange Rate System.* Washington: Institute for International Economics.

World Bank. 2007a. The 2005 International Comparison Program: Preliminary Results. Available at www.worldbank.org (accessed on December 18, 2007).

World Bank. 2007b. *World Development Indicators.* Washington: World Bank.

Wren-Lewis, Simon. 2004. The Needed Changes in Bilateral Exchange Rates. In *Dollar Adjustment: How Far? Against What?* ed. C. Fred Bergsten and John Williamson. Washington: Institute for International Economics.

Comment
Equilibrium Exchange Rate
of the Renminbi

JEFFREY A. FRANKEL

William Cline and John Williamson have performed a timely and useful service in providing a well-executed survey of recent estimates of the proper value of the renminbi. The literature is by now large enough to merit a survey, and the topic remains one of the hottest policy questions of international finance in recent years. The width of the range of estimates is an appropriate subject of consideration in its own right: The failure of experts to come to even a rough consensus on whether a currency is undervalued or overvalued calls into question giving the International Monetary Fund (IMF) or the US Treasury legal mandates to assess the correct value and to levy penalties if corrections by the erring government are not forthcoming.

A Technical Point

At the risk of sounding too professorial, I begin with a technical point. Table 4.1 and the rest of the Cline-Williamson paper generally report the percentage appreciation needed to eliminate undervaluation, as distinct from percentage undervaluation. I feel strongly that all of these numbers ought to be converted to logs. I understand fully that saying the word

Jeffrey A. Frankel is James W. Harpel Professor of Capital Formation and Growth at Harvard University's Kennedy School of Government.

"logarithm" in a congressional hearing will probably clear the room faster than an anthrax scare. But in academic papers we do it in logs. My judgment is the Peterson Institute should do it in logs as well. My recommended phrasing is "the percentage undervaluation of the renminbi is estimated at X percent," followed by the word "logarithmically," either in parentheses or in a footnote.

Even judged purely from the standpoint of user-friendliness to nonspecialists, my recommended phrasing is likely to be less confusing than the repeated practice of reporting two numbers, one for percentage undervaluation (say, 50 percent) and another for required appreciation to return to equilibrium (100 percent), which causes the uninitiated reader to wonder why on earth the two numbers are not the same. For example, the authors correctly report both my estimates that the renminbi was 36 percent undervalued relative to the average normal Balassa-Samuelson relationship and that a 56 percent revaluation would be required to reverse it. Citing both numbers seems potentially confusing to noneconomists. Better to emphasize the single log number, as I do (45 percent), which represents both the percentage undervaluation and the percentage appreciation that would be needed hypothetically to reach long-run equilibrium. The authors' choice of reporting percentages can also make the numbers sound large (e.g., "100 percent" rather than "50 percent").

Approach 1: Purchasing Power Parity (PPP)–Enhanced by Balassa-Samuelson

Cline and Williamson label the first category of techniques for estimating the value of the renminbi as the enhanced-PPP approach, which computes absolute PPP for individual countries relative to the Balassa-Samuelson line, that is, relative to the usual relationship under which the real exchange rate, on average, rises with the level of productivity or real income—across countries but also across time. The authors are skeptical of the enhanced-PPP approach. Some of their concerns are justified, but not all.

One place where Cline and Williamson have a good point is that many of the calculations of overvaluation, including my own, have been made relative to the dollar. But this approach neglects the possibility that the dollar itself is over- or undervalued. It is better to calculate the overvaluation of the renminbi relative to a weighted basket rather than relative to the dollar alone. But nothing in the enhanced-PPP approach prevents this.

Another place where I agree with them is in their judgment that the most recent enhanced-PPP study by Cheung, Chinn, and Fujii (2007), though otherwise excellent, does not use the most appropriate standard errors and thereby conveys less confidence in their own estimates than is merited. The Balassa-Samuelson relationship itself is highly significant statistically, and so it is appropriate to conclude that large deviations from it are significant.[1] China may not quite make it into the 5 percent of currencies most out of line by the Balassa-Samuelson criterion, as the Cheung, Chinn, and Fuji application of a 95 percent confidence criterion apparently requires, but this should not preclude us from saying that the calculation shows that it is undervalued.

Most important, Cline and Williamson question the reliability of the Chinese price data in the Penn World Tables (PWT), which are the basis for the absolute-PPP calculations, specifically suggesting a downward bias (Keidel 1994, Summers and Heston 1991). They make an excellent point that such measurement errors, to the extent they are important, distort not only the variable measured on the vertical axis of the Balassa-Samuelson relationship but also the real income or productivity measure on the horizontal axis. The possibility that the PWT data were subject to measurement error, and that this might be especially true of the data for China because of a paucity of genuine within-country data, has long been evident. In the past, little information has been available on why the measurement errors for China should be strongly biased in a particular direction, as the authors assert.[2]

Several weeks after the Peterson Institute conference that led to this volume, however, the authors were proven spectacularly right when the Asian Development Bank (2007) and the International Bank for Reconstruction and Development (IBRD 2007) released the preliminary results of a new study of absolute PPP. This study, under the International Comparison Program (ICP), used much more extensive data, in particular for China, than had previously been available. According to the new numbers, which pertain to 2005, China's price level is 42 percent of the US price level. This is far less of an undervaluation against the dollar. The new numbers also show China's real income per capita to be 9.8 percent of the US level. Using estimated Balassa-Samuelson coefficients from either Rogoff (1996) or Frankel (2006)—0.37 or 0.38—this implies that the appropriate long-run equilibrium real exchange value for the renminbi is 42

---

1. I say as much in my own comment on the paper by Cheung, Chinn, and Fujii (Frankel 2008).

2. I was not particularly persuaded, for example, by an argument of the authors that seems to be circular: "It is also well known that China is an extreme outlier, with low domestic prices. The presumption is thus that China's prices have been measured unreliably at below actual levels." Perhaps we should grant Cline and Williamson extra credibility on this claim in that it runs counter to the claims of their colleagues at the Peterson Institute that the renminbi is undervalued. See C. Fred Bergsten, Testimony before the Hearing on US-China Economic Relations Revisited, Committee on Finance, United States Senate, March 29, 2006; Morris Goldstein, "China's Exchange Rate Regime," Testimony before the Subcommittee on Domestic and International Monetary Policy, Trade, and Technology, Committee on Financial Services, US House of Representatives, October 1, 2003; Morris Goldstein and Nicholas Lardy, "Two-Stage Currency Reform for China," *Wall Street Journal*, September 12, 2003. See also Goldstein (2004) and Goldstein and Lardy (2005).

percent of the US price level.[3] In other words, by these calculations, the renminbi is exactly where it should be vis-à-vis the dollar.

Three qualifications are necessary, each suggesting some remaining undervaluation. First, as Cline and Williamson point out, there is no guarantee that the dollar is not itself overvalued or undervalued. By the PPP criterion, it is probably by now undervalued globally, particularly when one includes the depreciation of 2007, which would imply that the renminbi is too.[4] Second, because the new ICP numbers on prices and real incomes are both more up-to-date and more reliable than those previously available, it makes sense to reestimate the Balassa-Samuelson estimation. Arvind Subramanian has done this, and he computes that the renminbi is still 15 percent below where it ought to be. Third, the price data for China might not account sufficiently for the effect of lower prices in rural districts, which would again imply that the renminbi is more undervalued than the latest numbers suggest. Certainly, however, the new ICP numbers imply that the renminbi is far less undervalued under the extended-PPP approach than we had previously thought.

I am less convinced by the authors' remaining two critiques of the enhanced-PPP approach.[5] They say (chapter 4, 135), "There is ample historical experience (including that of China today) to show that the deviation of the PPP/market exchange rate ratio (PPP/er) from the international norm can be a wholly misleading guide as to whether the country has a current account surplus or deficit. . . ." I cannot think of anyone who claims that this ratio is a reliable guide to whether a country is in surplus or deficit, so I do not see how it can be misleading. The authors point out that China established large trade surpluses only in the last five years, whereas the renminbi has been "undervalued" on the enhanced-PPP basis for a lot longer: "The enhanced-PPP approach seems to show chronic undervaluation for China going back a quarter century, whereas policy concerns about undervaluation have escalated only in recent years" (chapter 4, 151). I hope we are not going to use as the economic criterion for over-

---

3. To say that Chinese income is 9.8 percent of US income is to say that there is a gap of 2.32 in log terms. Multiply by 0.37 or 0.38 to get the estimate that the price level gap should be 0.87 in log terms—i.e., that the Chinese price level should be 42 percent of the US price level.

4. Relative to developing Asia, Chinese prices are an estimated 3 percent above average, according to the Asian Development Bank (2007). China's income is 14 percent above the average for developing Asia, which implies that its prices should be 5 percent above the Asian average. By this calculation the renminbi is undervalued by a mere 2 percent relative to the Asian average.

5. It may sound like I have just agreed with three out of five of the authors' critiques of enhanced-PPP as a methodology. But the third point was merely a critique of the numbers available before 2007. Now that we have the new absolute-PPP numbers from the ICP, the enhanced-PPP approach is more useful.

valuation whichever country politicians choose in any particular decade as the scapegoat for US deficits or other escalating policy concerns.

The most natural explanation for China's large trade surplus is that this has been a period in which previously high trade barriers between China and the rest of the world have come down, most conspicuously as China has joined the World Trade Organization and the West has dropped barriers including the Multi-Fiber Arrangement and the earlier quasi-sanctions that the United States arrayed against China, such as the annual dangling of renewal of most favored nation or normalized trading relations status. The combination of tumbling barriers and a substantial pre-existing cost advantage explains the rapid increase in China's trade balance. An equally important part of the story is China's extraordinarily high saving rate.

The authors' example of Japan perhaps gives one more genuine cause for worry (especially figure 4.2). How can Japan have consistently run such large current account surpluses in recent decades even though its currency has been greatly overvalued—more so in 1995 than in 1985 or today—relative to the Balassa-Samuelson relationship? One possible answer is that the Balassa-Samuelson relationship applies more strongly to Japan than to other countries: The rate of growth of productivity in traded goods and the rate of increase in the relative price of nontraded goods have both been higher in Japan over the postwar period than would typically be implied by its rate of growth of real income. Still, their point is a good one.

The authors' fifth criticism of the enhanced-PPP approach is that it is not suited to normative statements. The public wants an estimate of how much China should revalue, preferably right now. I certainly did not intend for my estimate of a 45 percent undervaluation relative to the Balassa-Samuelson relationship to be interpreted as a statement that the currency should be revalued by anything like that in a short period. I moved closer to a normative argument with the following logic. According to my estimates, from one decade to the next, the typical country closed almost exactly one-half of its deviation from the Balassa-Samuelson relationship. That alone would be sufficient to produce an estimate that the renminbi would appreciate at 22 percent over the next ten years, or 2.2 percent per year.

But in addition, we expect China to continue to experience higher productivity growth than its trading partners. Assuming that China's growth continues on the order of 6 percent greater than US growth, the standard Balassa-Samuelson effect, which is a movement along the curve rather than to the curve, would require adding another 2.3 percent of real appreciation per year, or 0.38 times the relative growth rate. The total is a predicted rate of real appreciation of 4½ percent per year. My prescriptive conclusion was that it would be better to take this real appreciation in the form of nominal appreciation rather than build in an inflationary bias (above the world rate) of this magnitude.[6] These numbers now need to be substantially revised in light of the new price numbers released in December 2007 by the International Comparison Program of the World Bank.

Approach 2: Exchange Rate Equations

Cline and Williamson next look at behavioral equilibrium exchange rates (BEER). I agree with their identification of the shortcomings of these approaches, in the present context, which is that they can only deliver a statement about the valuation of a given currency today relative to its own past history. As with the simpler relative-PPP calculations, one needs to be able to assert that there was a particular year when a currency was in equilibrium, or else assert that it was in equilibrium, on average, during the sample period.[7] I do not think this approach will work for China because the hypothesis—my hypothesis, anyway—is that the renminbi may have been undervalued for a long time, at least as long as the period for which it has had the semblance of a market economy.[8] Particularly for the study that allows a break at the time of the Chinese devaluation (unification) in 1994, I do not see how one can presume that the post-1994 period was properly valued on average. The hypothesis under consideration is that the currency has been undervalued throughout this period. One cannot test a hypothesis by means of an assumption that rules out the hypothesis a priori.

MacDonald and Dias (2007) do not get a significant effect on the real interest rate. I am surprised to read the authors explain this on the grounds that "this is not surprising since real interest rates are now more a world rather than a national variable" (chapter 4, 143). It is very clear in theory and practice that even if capital mobility is perfect and domestic and foreign assets are perfect substitutes, it only implies uncovered interest parity, not real interest parity. As a result, the real interest differential should be an important determinant of countries' exchange rates, as it is in Dornbusch overshooting.[9] In the case of China, I agree that the lack of an effect

---

6. As McKinnon (2006) and McKinnon and Schnabl (2003) have emphasized repeatedly, to build in a trend of real appreciation of 4½ percent per year is eventually to build in real interest rates 4½ percent below world levels, which is not desirable. For this reason, I would favor an abrupt nominal revaluation of, perhaps, 10 percent in the first year.

7. "This is only as good as the assumption of an equilibrium average real exchange rate over the sample period" (chapter 4, 137).

8. I would like to hear the authors elaborate on their statement that "everyone agrees that the renminbi was severely overvalued in the early 1980s" (chapter 4, 143). I suspect that it depends on one's definition of overvaluation.

9. See Dornbusch (1976) and Frankel (1979). A recent example for a financially open emerging-market currency is Frankel (2007).

is not surprising but for the opposite reason: China retains important capital controls and domestic interest rates are not yet fully market determined. In other words, financial liberalization has been too little, not too much, to see this effect show up. That said, I share the authors' bottom line that "the necessary assumption of average equilibrium over the estimation period makes even the internationally based BEER approach less reliable" (chapter 4, 152).

Approach 3: Fundamental Equilibrium Exchange Rates (FEERs)

The third approach is FEER, which is, of course, the authors' own preference. Although John Williamson has made us familiar with this approach over the years, their definition somehow still surprises me (chapter 4, 138): "The basic idea is to search for a set of exchange rates that will simultaneously achieve internal and external balance in every country (Meade 1951)." But I would have thought it a basic proposition, of Meade in particular, that exchange rates are not in themselves sufficient to achieve simultaneously internal and external balance. The Tinbergen-Meade principle is that if one has N policy goals, one must have at least N independent policy instruments. Because countries have goals for both internal and external balance, they need a second policy instrument in addition to the exchange rate: in Harry Johnson's classic terminology, an expenditure-reducing instrument, such as monetary or fiscal policy. Perhaps Cline and Williamson dismiss the internal balance consideration because, as they state (chapter 4, 138), "In an era when long-run Phillips curves are widely believed to be vertical . . . there is not much room for arguing about levels of internal balance." If so, I disagree. They seem to think that agreeing on where the desirable point of external balance lies is the main issue of difficulty. I believe that deciding where internal balance lies is at least as difficult as deciding where external balance lies.

Admittedly, there is also a wide range of disagreement about external balance. On the one hand, Dooley, Folkerts-Landau, and Garber (2004, 2007) believe that China is deliberately keeping its currency undervalued as part of an intelligent development strategy. Some of my colleagues believe that other countries should do the same (e.g., Rodrik 2007), while others have said that it makes perfect sense for the United States to run a current account surplus due to its comparative advantage as the world's banker (e.g., Caballero, Farhi, and Gourinchas 2006). In other words, one view is that external balance for China implies a trade surplus. On the other hand, as the authors point out, the traditional view is that a poor country with a low capital-to-labor ratio—or a country that is rapidly and successfully developing—ought to be importing net capital inflows from abroad, which means running a trade deficit. My own view is somewhere in between. The choice is arbitrary, but zero surplus or deficit is perhaps as good a number as any (under the Polonius principle, "neither a borrower nor a lender be").

The question of external balance is indeed hard to settle convincingly, but so is the internal balance question. The difficulty in choosing optimal targets for either external or internal balance in a way that convinces a majority of reasonable economists is the prime reason why I have long felt that there are limits to the practical usefulness of the FEER approach developed by my beloved friends at the Peterson Institute. Indeed, it is part of why there are limits to the practical usefulness of any attempt to say what the correct values of most currencies are. I see the renminbi as a rare exception, in that almost all of the different criteria that one might apply, even if one limits the list to those from the perspective of domestic Chinese interests, happen to have pointed toward the same direction in recent years.

Cline and Williamson indirectly address the issue of internal balance when they talk about cyclically adjusted trade balances. But the issue requires much more discussion. First, one must be explicit about the distinction between the appropriate exchange rate conditional on current spending and the appropriate exchange rate conditional on an assumed change in spending policy that would permit the restoration of internal and external balance simultaneously. This would make a huge difference in some contexts, such as that of the United States. My view is that the dollar is not necessarily overvalued currently if one takes the current trajectory of budget deficits and low national saving as given—quite relevant in that the George W. Bush administration has been unwavering in its commitment to tax cuts despite the resultant deficits. However, the dollar is clearly at too high a level if the standard of comparison is what would be appropriate if one were free to adjust fiscal policy and other settings as part of an overall package of orderly adjustment.[10]

Second, although it is much less clear that China's spending policies have tended too far in one direction or the other over the last couple decades than is the case with the Unites States—China was suffering from deflation in 2001—I believe that China has crossed the internal balance line in the past few years, and is now on the "excess demand" side. The Chinese private saving rate is extremely high, and I agree with Cline and Williamson that one should not presume that this is necessarily optimal. But its investment level is also very high. A growth rate in excess of 11 percent, the reaching of chokepoints and bottlenecks, rising inflation—particularly in food and raw material inputs—and a bubble in the Shanghai stock market all point to excess demand rather than excess supply.

Thus if one cyclically adjusted China's trade surplus, it would look even larger than it does today. The authors do not even seem to consider this

---

10. This position is the same that I had in 1983–84 (see the *Economic Report of the President 1984*) and should not be an unfamiliar one—e.g., it is consistent with that of Paul Krugman in an old debate with Ron McKinnon.

Figure 4.C1 Choosing policy settings to attain internal and external balance

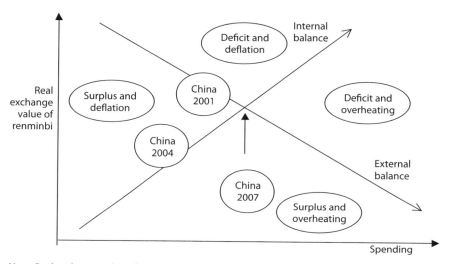

Note: Real exchange value of renminbi is defined, for example, as the relative price of nontraded goods ($P_{NTG}/\$P_{TG}$).

possibility; instead, they cite others' estimates as to how much cyclical adjustment would reduce China's trade surplus ("... it is necessary to determine how much of the present current account divergence from target is strictly cyclical and transitory, a step that turns out to be critical for China" [chapter 4, 139]. Apparently, Jonathan Anderson believes there is excess heavy industrial capacity, and many others as well are cited implicitly as presuming that China is on the excess supply side of internal balance. The authors themselves agree. This seems to me out of date.) Thus even if one accepts the methodology that implicitly assumes that spending policies are adjusted at the same time as the exchange rate, one will get very different numbers for the recommended revaluation depending on one's estimates of the needed adjustment in spending policies.

Apparently, Cline and Williamson feel that the range of possibilities runs roughly between the areas that I have labeled China2001 and China2004 in figure 4.C1. In that case, when trying to decide which exchange rate change would restore external balance, it makes a huge difference, first, whether one thinks of the question as predicated on the current level of spending. At China2004 it would imply an appreciation, but at China2001 it might not. Furthermore, if one assumes that an appropriate change in spending policy is part of the adjustment process, then China2001 would actually imply a devaluation, but China2004 would imply a small revaluation, whereas China2007 would imply a substantially larger revaluation. My own view is that China over the last four years has crossed over to the vicinity of the area I have labeled China2007. If so, then only a revaluation is needed, roughly speaking, to return to both external and internal balance.[11] But most of the time, the answer depends on whether or not one takes internal balance as given.

References

Asian Development Bank. 2007. *2005 International Comparison Program in Asia and the Pacific* (December).

Balassa, Bela. 1964. The Purchasing Power Parity Doctrine: A Reappraisal. *Journal of Political Economy* 72: 584–96.

Caballero, Ricardo, Emmanuael Farhi, and Pierre-Olivier Gourinchas. 2006. *An Equilibrium Model of Global Imbalances and Low Interest Rates.* MIT Economic Department Working Paper 06/02. Cambridge, MA: Massachusetts Institute of Technology.

Cheung, Yin-Wong, Menzie Chinn, and Eiji Fujii. 2007. China's Current Account and Exchange Rate. Paper presented at a conference on China's growing role in world trade, sponsored by the National Bureau of Economic Research, Chatham, MA, August 27.

Dooley, Michael, David Folkerts-Landau, and Peter Garber. 2004. The Revived Bretton Woods System. *International Journal of Finance & Economics* 9, no. 4 (November): 307–13.

Dooley, Michael, David Folkerts-Landau, and Peter Garber. 2007. Direct Investment, Rising Real Wages, and the Absorption of Excess Labor in the Periphery. In *G7 Current Account Imbalances: Sustainability and Adjustment,* ed. Richard Clarida. Chicago: University of Chicago Press.

Dornbusch, Rudiger. 1976. Expectations and Exchange Rate Dynamics. *Journal of Political Economy* 84, no. 6 (December): 1161–76.

Frankel, Jeffrey. 1979. On the Mark: A Theory of Floating Exchange Rates Based on Real Interest Differentials. *American Economic Review* 69, no. 4 (September): 601–22.

Frankel, Jeffrey. 2006. On the Yuan: The Choice between Adjustment under a Fixed Exchange Rate and Adjustment under a Flexible Rate. *CESifo Economic Studies* 52, no. 2 (June): 246–75.

Frankel, Jeffrey. 2007. On the Rand: Determinants of the South African Exchange Rate. *South African Journal of Economics* 75, no. 3 (September): 425–41.

Frankel, Jeffrey. 2008. Comment on "China's Current Account and Exchange Rate," by Yin-Wong Cheung, Menzie Chinn, and Eiji Fujii. Paper presented at a conference on China's growing role in world trade, sponsored by the National Bureau of Economic Research, Chatham, MA, August 27.

Goldstein, Morris. 2004. *Adjusting China's Exchange Rate Policies.* Working Paper 04-1. Washington: Institute for International Economics.

Goldstein, Morris, and Nicholas Lardy. 2005. *China's Role in the Revived Bretton Woods System: A Case of Mistaken Identity.* Working Paper 05-2. Washington: Peterson Institute for International Economics.

IBRD (International Bank for Reconstruction and Development). 2007. *2005 International Comparison Program: Preliminary Results.* Washington (December).

---

11. I certainly do not mean to imply that revaluation of the currency is the only policy change China should make. Rather, appreciation should be part of a broad strategy of more fully developing the domestic economy—e.g., health care and other services, retirement plans, social safety nets, infrastructure, and environmental protection. My point is only that it is not clear to me that a large overall monetary and fiscal expansion should be part of the package.

Keidel, Albert. 1994. *China GNP Per Capita*. Report 13580-CHA. East Asia and Pacific Regional Office, International Bank for Reconstruction and Development. Washington: World Bank.

MacDonald, Ronald, and Preethike Dias. 2007. BEER Estimates and Target Current Account Imbalances. Paper presented to a workshop on policy to reduce global imbalances, sponsored by Bruegel, the Korea Institute for Economic Policy, and the Peterson Institute for International Economics, Washington, February 8–9.

McKinnon, Ronald. 2006. Comment in Response to "Request for Public Comments on the Report to Congress on International and Exchange Rate Policies." Stanford University. Photocopy (April).

McKinnon, Ronald, and Gunther Schnabl. 2003. The East Asian Dollar Standard, Fear of Floating, and Original Sin. Stanford University. Photocopy (September).

Meade, James E. 1951. *The Balance of Payments*. Oxford: Oxford University Press.

Rodrik, Dani. 2007. The Real Exchange Rate and Growth: Theory and Evidence. Kennedy School of Government, Harvard University. Photocopy (August).

Rogoff, Kenneth. 1996. The Purchasing Power Parity Puzzle. *Journal of Economic Literature* 34, no. 2 (June): 647–68.

Summers, Robert, and Alan Heston. 1991. The Penn World Table (Mark5): An Expanded Set of International Comparisons, 1950–1988. *Quarterly Journal of Economics* 106, no. 2 (May): 327–68.

Comment
Toward a Balanced Approach

SIMON JOHNSON

Bill Cline and John Williamson have produced a comprehensive and clear survey of methods used to assess China's exchange rate. It is no surprise to find, once again, that the Peterson Institute is at the forefront of exchange rate analysis and, in this key analytical and policy context, providing sensible and compelling assessments of the various methods used to determine whether and to what extent China's exchange rate is undervalued.

It is also most useful to be reminded that, while no one method always and everywhere dominates in thinking about exchange rate values, a balanced approach using two or three reasonable methods can move us a long way in the right direction. We may not be able to set a precise numerical value for misalignment, but we can find a range of plausible estimates.

I expect that the Cline and Williamson paper will be highly influential, particularly as academia, the private sector, and officials start seriously rethinking exchange rate valuation more generally. There is already a renaissance in substantive research in this area—with real and immediate policy impact—and a user's guide to what is already available and what remains to be done is most helpful.

I strongly encourage Cline and Williamson to package their insights here, together with their other broad and high-impact work on this topic, into an easy-to-use analytical tool to help a wide range of users think through the key concepts. I would also make three fairly modest sugges-

Simon Johnson is economic counselor and director of the Research Department at the International Monetary Fund.

tions as the authors further develop the Peterson Institute's influential thinking on exchange rates.

First, Cline and Williamson could be a bit more forthright in their judgments regarding the advantages and disadvantages of each method. There is plenty of content and nuance in the authors' assessments, but I was hoping for some bluntness as well, ideally even a letter grade ranking the implementation in various approaches.

In particular, while purchasing power parity (PPP)–based methods have their attractions in some contexts, they are most dubious when applied to China precisely because until December 2007, there were no real comparable price data for China. Currently, we have actual survey-based price data, but these should presumably also be handled with caution, as they are quite new. In addition, the theoretical link from the PPP approach to external stability needs much more elaboration if it is to stand shoulder to shoulder with methods that have much stronger analytical underpinnings. Hopefully, the authors can reassess the existing PPP studies covered in their paper to determine how the results change on the basis of this new data. It would also be most interesting to learn how the authors think the PPP revision affects the more general appeal of the approach to exchange rates for both China and India, the data for which were also largely revised in the World Bank's price data.

Second, I am slightly surprised that the authors focus so much on studies of China's exchange rate that look only at that single country's rate, rather than at the full multilateral system of exchange rates. Exchange rates are relative values, and if one country is undervalued, then intuitively, other countries must be overvalued; that is, the system must balance overall. It thus seems entirely reasonable that any method should be able to assess not only China's exchange rate but all exchange rates on an even methodological playing field. Methods can reasonably be assessed in terms of how they give answers across all major trading countries. This is not as hard as it sounds, as including 30 or 40 countries covers most of world trade. I would further suggest that the authors put rather less weight on studies or methods that do not explicitly add up multilaterally. Also, it is generally less useful to focus on the bilateral dollar rate rather than on the real effective exchange rate. The authors do both, but I fear that an unsophisticated or selective reader may need more guidance— and the Peterson Institute is usually at the forefront of such guidance.

Third, I am disappointed that the authors did not include the International Monetary Fund's exchange rate methodology in their assessment. Its approach is in the public domain, and almost all of the data are also readily available (Lee, Milesi-Ferretti, and Ricci 2008). Particularly, as other official organizations develop exchange rate methodologies, it would be helpful and productive to have the authors' independent views on the comparative strengths and weaknesses of all available official methods vis-à-vis those covered in their paper. Even if official point estimates are not published, which may often be the case, the methods are and should be subject to outside review and comment.

Overall, I fully agree with the authors' main idea that there is value in looking at varieties of both behavioral and current account–based approaches to the exchange rate. The behavior of net foreign assets can also be extremely informative regarding whether external payments are in something approaching equilibrium. A balanced approach, of the kind the authors prefer, is an excellent way to progress.

We have to become more discerning and honest about the methodological and data limitations of certain approaches and papers. The economics profession, leading journalists, and the broader economics-informed public very much look to the Peterson Institute to continue its leadership role on this issue.

Reference

Lee, Jaewoo, Gian-Maria Milesi-Ferretti, and Luca Ricci. 2008 (forthcoming). *Methodology for CGER Exchange Rate Assessments.* IMF Occasional Paper. Washington: International Monetary Fund.

5

The Management of China's International Reserves: China and a Sovereign Wealth Fund Scoreboard

EDWIN M. TRUMAN

China's international reserves as of the end of September 2007 were $1.4 trillion, or close to 50 percent of GDP, virtually all of which were in foreign exchange. In 1992, China's foreign exchange reserves were $19.4 billion, or 4 percent of GDP. They crossed the $100 billion line in 1996, the $200 billion line in 2001, and the $500 billion line in 2004.[1] At the end of 2006, China's foreign exchange reserves were $1.1 trillion (figure 5.1).

In 2003, the People's Bank of China (PBC) established the Central Huijin Investment Company, a type of sovereign wealth fund (SWF), with $67.5 billion of its foreign exchange reserves to recapitalize four state-owned banks. On September 29, 2007, Chinese authorities established the China Investment Corporation (CIC). It absorbed the Central Huijin Investment Company and China Jianyin Investment Limited and has initial capital of $200 billion.

Edwin M. Truman, senior fellow at the Peterson Institute since 2001, was assistant secretary of the Treasury for international affairs (1998–2000). Doug Dowson provided tenacious assistance in the research underlying this paper as well as dedication to preparing the presentation of the results. In revising the original paper, the author benefited from the comments of and subsequent interchanges with Mohamed El-Erian and Brad Setser.

1. China's foreign exchange reserves reached 10 percent of GDP in 1995, 20 percent of GDP in 2003, and 30 percent of GDP one year later.

Figure 5.1 China's foreign exchange reserves, 1992–2006

percent of GDP

billions of US dollars

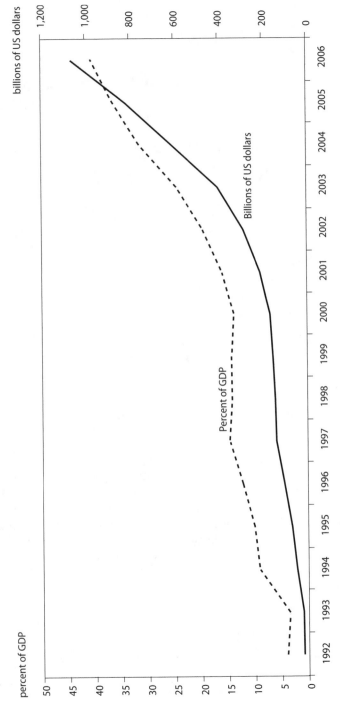

Billions of US dollars

Percent of GDP

Source: China State Administration of Foreign Exchange.

Table 5.1 Foreign exchange reserves and current account balances

Country	Foreign exchange reserves				Current account/GDP[b] 2002–06 (percent)
	End of year, 2006 (billions of US dollars)	Change, 2001–06 (percent)	Share of GDP, 2006 (percent)	Reserves/GDP[a] 2002–06 (percent)	
China[s]	1,066	403	41	8.6	5.5
Japan	875	126	20	2.2	3.5
Russia[sr]	295	807	30	8.4	9.7
Taiwan	266	118	75	8.9	7.1
Korea[sr]	238	133	27	3.9	1.9
India	170	276	19	3.7	−0.3
Singapore[sr]	136	81	103	11.3	22.5
Hong Kong	133	20	70	2.6	9.9
Brazil	86	139	8	1.4	1.0
Malaysia[s]	82	185	54	8.9	13.3
Algeria[s]	78	333	68	14.0	17.2
Norway[s]	56	153	17	2.6	14.3
United Arab Emirates[s]	28	98	16	2.4	12.3
Kuwait[s]	12	32	13	0.9	32.9
Qatar[s]	5	346	10	2.4	20.0

r = reserves include sovereign wealth fund in whole or in part
s = has one or more sovereign wealth funds

a. Sum of changes in reserves as a ratio to sum of total output.
b. Sum of current account balances as a ratio to sum of total output.

The major issue addressed in this paper is the future accountability and transparency of the CIC. I present the results of research on 32 SWF of 28 countries by scoring them on their structure, governance, transparency and accountability, and behavior. The Central Huijin Investment Company scores substantially below average for all the funds. Given the actual and potential size of the new CIC and China's growing importance in the international financial system, Chinese authorities should seek to place the CIC at the top of the league of SWF. They should work with other countries to establish a set of best practices for all SWF, using the scoreboard presented in this paper as a point of departure.

China is not the only country with large foreign exchange reserves. Table 5.1 lists the countries with the ten largest holdings of foreign exchange reserves as of the end of 2006 along with the holdings of five other countries with large SWF.[2] China's foreign exchange reserves now exceed 40 percent

---

2. SWF for these purposes are (normally) separate pools of (generally) international assets owned and managed (directly or indirectly) by government to achieve various economic objectives, such as macroeconomic stabilization or contributing to a process of saving and

of GDP; at least four other countries can claim the same distinction. China also has not experienced the largest percentage increase in reserves since 2001, as Russia has recorded a larger increase from a lower base.

Finally, China is not the only country for which a rapid rise in reserves since 2001 has been associated with large cumulative current account surpluses. However, for the majority of the 11 countries listed in the table with average surpluses over the past five years of more than 5 percent of GDP (last column), those surpluses were associated with substantial earnings from natural resource–based exports. In addition, China had significant capital account surpluses during this period, as indicated by the difference between the figures for each country in the last two columns of the table. China shared that distinction with Taiwan, Korea, India, and Brazil. For the four countries listed at the bottom of the table, large current account surpluses were on balance recycled via net capital outflows that were not recorded as increases in reserves but at least partly involved governments and their SWF.[3]

The literature on the demand for and appropriate level of international reserves dates back to the 1960s (Frankel and Jovanovic 1981, Hamada and Ueda 1977, Heller 1966, Heller and Knight 1978). With the 175 percent increase in foreign exchange reserve holdings from 2001 to May 2007 by all countries and the 230 percent increase over that period in holdings excluding traditional industrial countries, the literature has experienced a resurgence (Flood and Marion 2002, Jeanne 2007, Jeanne and Rancière 2006). Rules of thumb have been developed for determining the adequacy of reserves. They are expressed in terms of months of imports of goods and services; a ratio of reserves to short-term debt immediately coming due or in total, to the total external debt of a government or country, or to external obligations; a ratio to GDP or to some measure of the money supply; or combinations of the above.

Theoretical and empirical analyses also have sought to explain the behavior of countries that build up their reserves and to determine the appropriate cutoff for excess reserves (Aizenman 2007; Aizenman and Lee

---

intergenerational wealth transfer. In its September 2007 *Global Financial Stability Report*, the International Monetary Fund (IMF 2007b) provides a taxonomy of SWF and discusses some of the fiscal issues that they raise, but the report fails to identify or address any of the major issues that SWF raise for the international financial system; see Truman (2007). Conspicuously missing from the list in table 5.1 is Saudi Arabia, even though as of August 2007 the Saudi Arabian Monetary Agency reporting holdings of $27.0 billion in foreign exchange reserves, $205.7 billion of other international securities on its balance sheet, and $51.3 billion in holdings on behalf of other government entities that are not on its balance sheet. The IMF (2007b) includes Saudi Arabia as an example of a country with an SWF despite its apparent lack of such a formal structure.

3. Those countries also have substantially lower official reserves as a ratio to GDP than does China. For the last five countries listed in the table, their foreign exchange reserves plus SWF amount to at least 100 percent of GDP.

2005; Aizenman, Lee, and Rhee 2004; Aizenman and Marion 2003; Garcia and Soto 2006; IMF 2003; Jeanne 2007). My reading of the literature is that there is no consensus about the optimal level of foreign exchange reserves. It thus follows that there is no consensus about the level at which foreign exchange reserves become excessive. One simple explanation for these results is that, as countries have added to their international reserves and it is assumed that these decisions are rational within the context of the models employed, more reserves are found to be better: As in flipping coins, there is always a small probability that the bank will be broken or that reserves considered to be more than adequate prove in the end not to be sufficient.

A more prosaic explanation is that, for most countries, the level of reserves is a by-product of other economic and financial policies, in effect the residual. This explanation, in my view, better characterizes what has happened in China. China's exchange rate policy has failed to adjust to changes in China's development progress, with the result that it has turned mercantilist, as is discussed in other papers in this volume.

Slightly more than a decade ago, before the outbreak of the Asian financial crises, Governor Dai Xianglong of the PBC used the steady accumulation of China's foreign exchange reserves as one of his prominent talking points to demonstrate that China deserved a place in the first rank of nations. When China's reserves passed the $100 billion mark in 1996, he cited this fact in conversations with officials in the Federal Reserve and—showing a lack of appreciation of the independence of central banks—US Treasury officials to justify why China should be given a seat on the board of the Bank of International Settlements, to which his successor, Governor Zhou Xiaochuan, was elected in 2006 in his personal capacity.

As China developed an ever-wider current account surplus after 2001 and its surplus on the nonreserve financial account continued, at least until 2006, it became clear that the continued accumulation of China's foreign exchange reserves was intimately connected with its exchange rate policy interacting with a rapidly expanding current account surplus as well as with capital inflows responding to the incentives created by its exchange rate policy. As a practical matter, despite Chinese authorities' various efforts to disguise the accumulation of foreign exchange reserves by creating special purpose vehicles and to manipulate controls on capital outflows to promote recycling through the private sector, China is destined to continue to rack up huge annual increases in foreign exchange reserves as long as one can reasonably project.[4] With reserves including its SWF easily in excess of $1.5 trillion by the end of 2007, even a modest an-

---

4. Recognizing this reality in no way detracts from the view that the continued accumulation of foreign exchange reserves by China and other countries should be used to test their intent in increasing the flexibility of their currencies. It does suggest that the analysis, at least in part, should be conducted net of earnings on existing reserves, which not only add to the existing stock but also boost the current account surplus.

nual return of 5 percent implies an annual increase in reserves of $75 billion, more than the stock of foreign exchange reserves of all but 11 countries at the end of 2006.

Some authors, such as Caballero, Farhi, and Gourinchas (2007) and Mendoza, Quadrini, and Ríos-Rull (2007), attempt to explain the accumulation of foreign exchange reserves by countries such as China in terms of the weaknesses of their domestic financial systems and the strength of financial systems and the rule of law in other countries through which saving in the first group of countries is intermediated. These analyses are built on a flimsy empirical base and fail to distinguish between actions by the private sector and the public sector.

Dooley, Folkerts-Landau, and Garber (2007), in their writings on Bretton Woods II, are more imaginative. They implicitly assume that the government of China knows better than its citizens how to manage China's financial investments. For them, the government is the only relevant actor and its aim is to provide collateral in the form of foreign exchange reserves for foreign direct investment in China. However, in my view, these are rationalizations, not explanations; none pass the test of common sense.[5]

Nevertheless, a few countries, such as Chile and Mexico (see Jadresic 2007, Ortiz 2007) have examined the optimal level of their foreign exchange reserves, implementing policies to limit their accumulation as a result. As described in Bakker (2007) and Bakker and van Herpt (2007), a number of European countries have taken steps to reduce their foreign exchange reserve holdings or to hedge them into local currency. In doing so, they are responding to the exchange risk associated with such holdings as well as to dual pressures, first, by their fiscal authorities to increase the return on foreign exchange holdings, and second, on central banks managing those holdings to limit the asymmetric risks involved. In many cases, the central bank absorbs capital losses at the same time that it is mandated to pass on positive returns to its fiscal authorities.

---

5. The facts on which the Bretton Woods II boys base their analysis are essentially nonexistent. In recent years, external financing has accounted for less than 5 percent of fixed investment in China; the figures are similar for other Asian countries. All the US government asset seizures they cite were motivated by political rather than private financial considerations (the use of the Iranian assets to pay off non-American commercial or personal noncommercial claims are exceptions that prove the rule, as they were driven by US domestic politics). Countries are slowly diversifying away from the US dollar; based on IMF Currency Composition of Official Foreign Exchange Reserves (COFER) data, the dollar's value share in the reserves of developing countries declined by 10.5 percentage points from the end of 2001 to the end of 2006, and the quantity share declined by 4.6 percentage points. The Bretton Woods II system in Asia today, as a explanation of exchange rate policies, consists of greater China, Malaysia, and Singapore because the Korean won, the Thai baht, the Indonesian rupiah, and the Philippine peso have appreciated substantially. For the won, baht, and rupiah, the real effective appreciation since the dollar's peak in February 2002 through August 2007 was larger than that of the euro.

A slightly more pragmatic view of international reserves distinguishes between those held for liquidity purposes and those held as longer-term investments. Often the tranche of longer-term investments is split between the reserve holdings of the monetary authorities—the central bank or finance ministry—and reserves held in an SWF or the equivalent.[6] This strand of the literature recognizes, at the level of the government of a country, the continuum of purposes in holding international assets ranging from managing exchange rates and meeting short-term external financial obligations to investing for the long term. Working out the associated arrangements in practice is more difficult because foreign exchange reserves are normally held on the books of the central bank, at least in developing countries, while it is more rational that policies governing longer-term investments are set by the government and associated returns and losses accrue to the fiscal authorities.[7]

For the governments of countries such as China, with their huge hoards of foreign exchange reserves, the basic question is what to do with the reserves once they are there. One approach is to limit their further accumulation, net of earnings on the existing stock, by adopting a currency policy directed at appreciation and flexibility supported by macroeconomic and microeconomic policies that are in turn directed at maintaining sustainable growth and price stability. This is a major theme of other papers presented in this volume.

A second approach, in particular for a developing country such as China, where the accumulation of foreign exchange reserves does not reflect the conversion of wealth from nonrenewable resources underground into wealth in financial assets above ground, is to try to use the foreign exchange reserves for domestic development purposes. This approach is understandable but problematic. If China is to use its foreign exchange reserves to finance domestic investment or government expenditures, it must not only halt the gross and net accumulation of reserves but also reverse the accumulation of reserves to repatriate the principal into domestic financial resources. The former requires economic and financial policies to be recalibrated; the latter requires their reversal.

China has implemented the indirect use of foreign exchange reserves to support domestic policies, and India is in the process of doing so.[8] In the

---

6. As noted in appendix table 5.A1, the latter distinction is not always made in practice.

7. In Canada, Japan, and the United Kingdom, the great bulk of foreign exchange reserve holdings are on the books of the finance ministry rather than the central bank. In the United States, they are split essentially evenly between the Federal Reserve and the exchange stabilization fund of the US Treasury.

8. Several years ago, Montek Ahluwalia, deputy chairman of India's Planning Commission, raised the issue of how India's growing foreign exchange reserves could be used in a noninflationary way to finance domestic expenditures. Press reports suggested that the idea would be to borrow abroad against India's foreign exchange reserves to finance investment

Chinese case, an amount of foreign exchange reserves estimated at $67.5 billion has been used since 2003 to fund the Central Huijin Investment Company, which in turn helped to fund the recapitalization of four major government-owned banks and financial institutions. The new CIC has absorbed the Central Huijin Investment Company and is expected to make similar investments in the Agricultural Bank of China and the China Development Bank. Thus, about two-thirds of the initial $200 billion in CIC investments nominally will be domestic.[9]

China's approach to using foreign exchange reserves is problematic, first, because it is unclear where the exchange risk lies. Second, excepting the limiting case in which the banks involved have foreign currency–denominated liabilities that they otherwise cannot hedge, for the capital injections to be useful to the banks, they have to be converted into domestic currency. To the extent that the Central Huijin Investment Company has absorbed exchange risk and the banks converted the foreign currency into domestic currency, the foreign exchange is returned to the books of the PBC. The general public does not know what has happened. This situation illustrates a fundamental issue in managing large official holdings of cross-border assets: the importance of transparency. Diverting resources from an SWF for domestic investment purposes without a high degree of transparency and accountability also creates opportunities for corruption.

A third approach is to use the accumulated foreign exchange holdings to meet China's external economic or political objectives. China may make loans to African countries,[10] or Chinese government-owned banks or cor-

---

in domestic infrastructure. However, to do so without recalibrating its macroeconomic policies in the direction of current account deficits, India would have to convert the foreign exchange into domestic currency, which either expands the money supply and lowers interest rates or requires the central bank to purchase foreign exchange with domestic currency and sterilize the monetary effects through sales of government debt. In effect, infrastructure investment has been financed by an increase in government debt in the hands of the public. Nevertheless, the government of India has continued to pursue some variant of the idea; see Committee on Infrastructure Financing (2007). Indian Finance Minister Palaniappan Chidambaram explained at the Peterson Institute on September 25, 2007 that foreign exchange reserves would be used to finance the import content of infrastructure investments in India. However, there is little difference between the government buying foreign exchange to finance imports from the central bank and buying it in the private market, as long as the central bank pegs the exchange rate.

9. Even though the investments will be domestic, given that they are financed out of foreign exchange, the underlying international assets either have to be sold in the market or managed by someone. China is not the only country with an SWF that invests domestically as well as internationally. Singapore's Temasek Holdings, Russia's Stabilization Fund, the Alaska Permanent Fund, and Alberta Heritage Savings Trust Fund, among others, do so as well.

10. Such an operation could take the form of recycling: The government or a government-owned entity could make a loan to a foreign borrower denominated in foreign currency and purchase the foreign currency from the central bank (directly or indirectly through the market) to fund the loan.

porations may directly invest in foreign countries. Such investments might be funded indirectly out of foreign exchange reserves or through an SWF or the equivalent to which the foreign exchange has been effectively transferred.[11] The investments may be for economic or political purposes, illustrating an additional ambiguity as well as an issue for the Chinese government vis-à-vis its own citizens and vis-à-vis the international community.

Fundamentally, the preferable approach to managing excess foreign exchange reserves is to try to apply strict economic and financial criteria and to maximize their return over a relevant horizon, subject to whatever constraints may be imposed for risk management purposes.[12] As Lawrence H. Summers (2006, 2007) has argued with his characteristic force and eloquence, to do anything else amounts to financial malpractice.[13] More concretely, he has pointed out that for a country like China, a difference of 100 basis points on average over time on its holdings of cross-border financial assets, with foreign exchange reserves at 50 percent of GDP by the end of 2007, amounts to half a percentage point of GDP per year. Such calculations apply regardless of whether the cross-border assets are held in the central bank as foreign exchange reserves, are held in an SWF or the equivalent, or are held in some looser structure on the books of some government agency. However, sovereign wealth funds may be second-best arrangements to the use of the private sector. Recall that, in general, governments are not skilled investors. They are not good at picking winners. Government-owned banks tend not to be the most profitable. Recently, I was told by Anusha Chari of the University of Michigan that her preliminary research suggests that recent mergers and acquisitions by Chinese corporations, many of which are government-owned or government-controlled, under perform other cross-border mergers and acquisitions.

Thus, China faces major issues in managing its foreign exchange reserves. It is the elephant in the room of the international financial system not only because of its exchange rate policies and outsized current account surplus but also because of its large official holdings of foreign assets. As far as is known, China has the largest stock of cross-border as-sets

---

11. See the previous footnote. According to published reports, China's new SWF, the CIC, also involved multiple contortions in connection with allocating exchange risk when foreign exchange was transferred from the PBC. Students of the independence of central banks were amused in that mobilizing some of the domestic resources to fund the CIC, the government of China evaded the spirit but not the letter of its law by "selling" RMB600 billion in bonds to the state-owned Agricultural Bank of China. The PBC, in turn, made an "open market purchase" of those bonds in effect to fund the purchase of foreign exchange from the PBC to provide the initial resources for the CIC.

12. In narrow financial terms, the return to be maximized should be calculated net of the cost of any liabilities associated with the external assets.

13. See also Lawrence H. Summers, "Funds that Shake Capitalist Logic," *Financial Times*, July 29, 2007.

controlled by a government.[14] This fact alone means that the Chinese government's management of cross-border assets potentially raises major issues not only for China and its citizens but also for the international financial system. China is being, will be, and should be held to the highest standard of accountability and transparency in this area. The Chinese authorities may not like this fact, but as a citizen and former official of the country long characterized as the elephant in the room of the international financial system, my advice is to get used to it.

On the other hand, diversification of China's cross-border assets away from US dollar assets and short-term assets issued by the US and other governments is appropriate and inevitable. It is part of a pattern of financial globalization that has generally positive, as well as occasional negative, implications for the international financial, system and the global economy. Therefore, for the rest of the world, my advice is to get used to it!

The potential issues raised by China's management of its international assets including those of the CIC are the following:

1. concern that its investment policies will be motivated by political or economic power considerations, producing protectionist reactions in other countries;
2. concern that in implementing its investment policies, it may provoke a reaction of financial protectionism *even if* that reaction is *not* justified;
3. concern that implementing its investment policies contributes otherwise to uncertainty and turmoil in financial markets;
4. to the extent that intermediary financial institutions are used to execute its investment policies, concern that conflicts of interest may arise with respect to those intermediaries;
5. concern about the domestic political fallout from its international investment decisions; and
6. domestic concern that the mismanagement of China's external wealth is wasteful and adversely affects the country's economic, financial, and political stability.

Many of the above concerns are hypothetical at this stage. The concerns do not apply uniquely to China and its new sovereign wealth fund, the CIC. Such funds have been around for decades. There is considerable evidence that the last concern about the squandering of international assets is something about which countries should worry. On the third risk, most experienced observers with whom I have spoken, for example, Mohamed El-Erian in his comments on this paper, do not see SWF posing a threat to financial-market stability on the basis of the past behavior of the owners

---

14. It is possible that the United Arab Emirates has larger holdings, but we cannot confirm this from published information. Estimates suggest that its holdings are less than two-thirds of China's approximately $1.5 trillion.

and managers of these funds. Nevertheless, such assurances may not be sufficient to satisfy politicians or the general public in countries receiving investments by foreign governments.

For China, because of the potential size and scope of the CIC's operations, each of these six concerns should be central for the authorities. The rest of the world will hold them responsible for its actions to a greater degree than it would a country with much smaller holdings of cross-border assets.

How might this responsibility be established and monitored? Most governmental organizations promulgate laws, guidelines, and standards as the basis for establishing their accountability and use transparency to demonstrate that they have lived up to their commitments.

In Truman (2007) I advocated the establishment of a standard or set of best practices for governmental cross-border investments in general and SWF in particular. For SWF, the set of best practices would cover four categories: structure, governance, transparency and accountability, and behavior. In my research, I have developed a scoreboard for 32 SWF in 28 countries, including 25 different elements grouped in these four categories.[15] The construction of the scoreboard and the detailed results for each SWF appear in the appendix.

Table 5.2 summarizes the preliminary results of the exercise based on systematic publicly available information about SWF.[16] Out of a possible maximum of 25 points, the highest score is 24 points recorded for New Zealand's Superannuation Fund, followed closely at 23 points for Norway's Government Pension Fund–Global.[17] The Abu Dhabi Investment Authority (ADIA) and Abu Dhabi Investment Corporation (ADIC) in the United Arab Emirates post the lowest score, at 0.5 points. The average is 10.27 points. Six of the 10 largest SWF (see table 5.1) score at or below the average, including two of the three largest funds near the bottom of the table.[18]

---

15. As a point of reference, we also scored the California Public Employees' Retirement System (CalPERS), which scores slightly lower than Norway's SWF at 21.75, the same score as Timor-Leste's Petroleum Fund.

16. The results summarized in table 5.2 are preliminary in two respects. First, we are in the process of scoring additional SWF, or their equivalent. Second, we have received comments on the results presented in table 5.2 that will change some of the scoring and we are collecting additional information that may change some of the scoring. For example, additional information about Mexico's Oil Income Stabilization Fund would significantly boost our score for that SWF shown in table 5.2. See also the next footnote.

17. Norway's SWF has not strictly followed its rules on using earnings from its SWF, does not provide the currency breakdown of its investments, and is not subject to a fully independent audit. Subsequent to our preparation of table 5.2, we learned that information on the currency composition of the investments of Norway's SWF is available annually, which would boost it into a tie. To our knowledge, New Zealand's SWF does not have a formal guideline governing the speed of adjustment in its portfolio.

18. One of the two is the Government of Singapore's Investment Corporation. At the same time, Singapore's Temasek Holdings scores considerably above the average.

Table 5.2 Summary scoreboard for sovereign wealth funds

Country	Fund	Structure	Governance	Transparency and accountability	Behavior	Total
New Zealand	Superannuation Fund	8.00	4.00	12.00	0.00	24.00
Norway	Government Pension Fund–Global	7.50	4.00	10.50	1.00	23.00
Timor-Leste	Petroleum Fund	8.00	2.00	11.75	0.00	21.75
Canada	Alberta Heritage Savings Trust Fund	7.50	3.00	9.00	0.00	19.50
United States	Alaska Permanent Fund	7.50	2.00	8.50	0.00	18.00
Australia	Future Fund	8.00	2.00	7.00	0.00	17.00
Azerbaijan	State Oil Fund of the Republic of Azerbaijan	5.00	2.00	9.50	0.00	16.50
Chile	Economic and Social Stabilization Fund	7.00	2.00	6.50	0.00	15.50
Botswana	Pula Fund	5.50	2.00	7.00	0.00	14.50
Kazakhstan	National Oil Fund	6.00	2.00	6.50	0.00	14.50
Singapore	Temasek Holdings	4.00	1.50	8.00	0.00	13.50
São Tomé and Principe	National Oil Account	8.00	2.00	2.25	0.00	12.25
Trinidad and Tobago	Heritage and Stabilization Fund	6.50	2.00	3.75	0.00	12.25
Kuwait	Kuwait Investment Authority	6.00	3.00	3.00	0.00	12.00
Malaysia	Khazanah Nasional	4.00	1.50	4.00	0.00	9.50
Russia	Stabilization Fund of the Russian Federation	4.00	2.00	3.50	0.00	9.50
Korea	Korea Investment Corporation	6.00	2.00	1.00	0.00	9.00
Kiribati	Revenue Equalization Reserve Fund	5.00	2.00	0.50	0.00	7.50
Mexico	Oil Income Stabilization Fund	5.00	0.00	2.00	0.00	7.00
China	Central Huijin Investment Company	5.50	0.00	0.50	0.00	6.00
Venezuela	National Development Fund	1.50	0.50	4.00	0.00	6.00
Iran	Oil Stabilization Fund	4.00	1.00	0.50	0.00	5.50
Venezuela	Macroeconomic Stabilization Fund	3.00	0.50	2.00	0.00	5.50
Oman	State General Reserve Fund	3.00	0.00	2.00	0.00	5.00
Sudan	Oil Revenue Stabilization Account	4.00	0.00	1.00	0.00	5.00
Algeria	Revenue Regulation Fund	3.00	1.00	0.50	0.00	4.50
United Arab Emirates	Istithmar	3.00	0.50	0.25	0.00	3.75
United Arab Emirates	Mubadala Development Company	3.00	0.50	0.00	0.00	3.50
Brunei	Brunei Investment Agency	1.00	0.50	1.00	0.00	2.50
Singapore	Government of Singapore Investment Corporation	1.50	0.00	0.75	0.00	2.25
Qatar	Qatar Investment Authority	2.00	0.00	0.00	0.00	2.00
United Arab Emirates	Abu Dhabi Investment Authority and Corporation	0.50	0.00	0.00	0.00	0.50
Total possible points		**8.00**	**4.00**	**12.00**	**1.00**	**25.00**
Average number of points		4.80	1.42	4.02	0.03	10.27
United States	California Public Employees' Retirement System	8.00	3.00	10.25	0.50	21.75

As table 5.2 shows, the 32 funds fall into five groups of five to eight funds each. The first and third groups could be further subdivided. In the first three categories—structure, governance, and transparency and accountability—scores within the categories are correlated with overall scores. On balance, the scores are higher (relative to the potential maximum) in the structure category and lower in the governance and transparency and accountability categories. However, in the last category, the variance of the scores is the largest.

Before discussing the relevance of the scoring exercise to China, three points of qualification are in order. First, the objective in presenting the scoreboard is to offer an illustrative benchmark that could be used in designing a set of best practices. Second, the scoreboard is based on public information that we accessed principally using the Internet, as is appropriate today. To be useful in establishing accountability and transparency, information should be public, but we may not have accessed all the information available and necessarily applied judgment in some of our interpretations.[19] Third, any benchmark provides a basis for countries to assess their own practices and performance. Countries in different circumstances may conclude that particular elements are irrelevant to their situations, but even so, the benchmark stands as a reference point to justify such decisions.

China's Central Huijin Investment Company receives an overall score of 6.0, the same as Venezuela's National Development Fund. Both are well below the average.

To date, there is not enough public information about the CIC to provide a score for that entity, but based on what we know to date, it is not in the first two groups. The CIC's economic objective is unclear. "The purpose is to realize a maximization of long-term investment returns within an acceptable risk range," CIC chairman Lou Jiwei is reported in the press to have said, though Lou's characterization is hardly operational, in particular given the context in which two-thirds of the CIC's initial investment is to be domestic. One would want to know how the recipient banks are going to deploy the foreign currency assets they receive as well as what return the CIC will receive on its investments in those banks. More broadly, what is the CIC's strategy for its other investments?

The CIC appears to have a detailed governance structure, but how it will operate and relate to the actual managers of the investments remains to be clarified. Will it primarily make direct investments, as with China Jianyin Investment Limited's stake in Blackstone (discussed below), or will it largely invest in marketable instruments, such as bonds and equities? Will it follow guidelines for corporate responsibility to the extent that it holds voting shares or stakes? What assurances are there of domestic or international accountability and transparency? Will the CIC publish re-

---

19. See footnote 16.

ports on its size and operations? Will it be subject to a published independent audit?

Why should any of these questions be important to the sovereign Chinese authorities? First, as noted earlier, because of the potential size of the CIC and the actual size of the country's foreign exchange reserves, the reality is that China's investments, including by government-owned or government-controlled financial and nonfinancial entities, are the target of principal concern to the international financial system. Therefore, China will be held to the highest standard in the operation of its SWF as well as in its other investment activities, whether or not the authorities embrace that standard. China is sovereign within its own borders, but in the international financial context, in its investment policies as well as its exchange rate policies, China's sovereignty is constrained because other countries' interests are involved.

Second, Chinese authorities should embrace some standard to increase the accountability of its own SWF to domestic and international critics. It follows that, in their own interests, Chinese authorities should lead the way in developing the standard to be applied.[20]

Third, unless China leads in setting and adhering to such a standard and can demonstrate that it is a good international financial citizen, it risks protectionist reactions that limit its investments in other countries nominally seeking to defend their national security interests but in fact seeking to protect narrow national commercial interests.

Fourth, it is well known that there have been controversies in China already about official financial investments, such as the Chinese investment in Blackstone through China Jianyin Investment Limited, which has been transferred to the CIC. The value of that investment has declined substantially since it was first made, generating controversy and criticism within China. Presumably, the investment was part of an overall strategy that is expected to generate higher long-term returns than investments in short-dated US treasury instruments, but there is increased risk and the potential for losses, at least on paper and in the short run. This goes with the territory, but a clear investment strategy would help to blunt such criticism.

Another controversy surrounds investments by Temasek Holdings, one of Singapore's SWF, in Chinese banks at share prices substantially discounted relative to prices paid in their initial public offerings. These transactions involved the sale of strategic stakes, and often, other foreign institutions also purchased stakes on similar terms; nevertheless, the transactions have been criticized as sweetheart deals smacking of crony capitalism.

---

20. At the same time, Chinese authorities should embrace greater transparency in managing their international reserves more broadly, as advocated in Truman and Wong (2006).

As Chinese authorities roll out the structure, governance, transparency, and ground rules for the CIC, they have good reason to think hard about the above issues due to the actual and potential size of the CIC, general anxiety around the world about anything that concerns China's economic expansion, and the reality that China is subject to multiple suspicions about its political and strategic objectives. These suspicions derive from the fact that the scope for true private enterprise grounded on the rule of law is still minimal in China, and the country is associated with economic espionage and the proliferation of strategic technologies (Graham and Marchick 2006).

Along with other countries with large SWF or their equivalent, China should take the lead in developing a set of best practices for SWF operation. I offer my scoreboard exercise as a point of departure. Such an approach will facilitate the smooth management of China's outsized foreign exchange reserves, respecting the interests of China as well as those of the global financial system.

References

Aizenman, Joshua. 2007. *Large Hoarding of International Reserves and the Emerging Global Economic Architecture.* NBER Working Paper 13277 (July). Cambridge, MA: National Bureau of Economic Research.

Aizenman, Joshua, and Jaewoo Lee. 2005. *International Reserves: Precautionary vs. Mercantilist Views: Theory and Evidence.* IMF Working Paper 05/198. Washington: International Monetary Fund.

Aizenman, Joshua, Yeonho Lee, and Yeongseop Rhee. 2004. *International Reserves Management and Capital Mobility in a Volatile World: Policy Considerations and a Case Study of Korea.* NBER Working Paper 10534. Cambridge, MA: National Bureau of Economic Research.

Aizenman, Joshua, and Nancy Marion. 2003. The High Demand for International Reserves in the Far East: What Is Going On? *Journal of the Japanese and International Economies* 17, no 3: 370–400.

Bakker, Age. 2007. Reserve Management in the Eurosystem: From Liquidity to Return. In *Sovereign Wealth Management*, ed. Jennifer Johnson-Calari and Malan Rietveld. London: Central Banking Publications.

Bakker, Age, and Ingmar van Herpt. 2007. Central Bank Reserve Management: Trends and Issues. In *Central Bank Reserve Management: New Trends, from Liquidity to Return*, ed. Age F. P. Bakker and Ingmar R. Y. van Herpt. Cheltenham, UK: Edward Elgar.

Caballero, Ricardo J., Emmanuel Farhi, and Pierre-Olivier Gourinchas. 2007. An Equilibrium Model of Global Imbalances and Low Interest Rates. Paper presented at the Bank of Korea International Conference 2007, Seoul, Korea, June 18–19.

Committee on Infrastructure Financing. 2007. Report of the Committee on Infrastructure Financing. New Delhi, India (May).

Dooley, Michael, David Folkerts-Landau, and Peter Garber. 2007. *The Two Crises of International Economics.* Deutsche Bank.

Flood, Robert, and Nancy Marion. 2002. Holding International Reserves in an Era of High Capital Mobility. In *Brookings Trade Forum 2001*, ed. Susan M. Collins and Dani Rodrik. Washington: Brookings Institution.

Frenkel, Jacob A., and Boyan Jovanovic. 1981. Optimal International Reserves: A Stochastic Framework. *Economic Journal* 91, no. 362: 507–14.

García, Pablo, and Claudio Soto. 2006. Large Hoardings of International Reserves: Are They Worth It? In *External Vulnerability and Preventive Policies*, ed. Ricardo Caballero, César Calderón, and Luis Felipe Céspedes. Santiago, Chile: Central Bank of Chile.

Graham, Edward M., and David M. Marchick. 2006. *US National Security and Foreign Direct Investment*. Washington: Peterson Institute for International Economics.

Hamada, Koichi, and Kazuo Ueda. 1977. Random Walks and the Theory of Optimal International Reserves. *Economic Journal* 87, no. 848: 722–42.

Heller, H. Robert. 1966. Optimal International Reserves. *Economic Journal* 76, no. 302: 296–311.

Heller, H. Robert, and Malcolm Knight. 1978. Reserve-Currency Preferences of Central Banks. *Essays in International Finance* 131. Princeton, NJ: International Finance Section, Princeton University.

IMF (International Monetary Fund). 2003. Issues in Reserve Adequacy and Management. In *World Economic Outlook* (September). Washington.

IMF (International Monetary Fund). 2007a. *The Role of Fiscal Institutions in Managing the Oil Revenue Boom* (March 5). Washington.

IMF (International Monetary Fund). 2007b. Sovereign Wealth Funds. Annex 1.2 in *Global Financial Stability Report* (September). Washington.

Jadresic, Esteban. 2007. The Cost-Benefit Approach to Reserve Adequacy: The Case of Chile. In *Central Bank Reserve Management: New Trends, from Liquidity to Return*, ed. Age F. P. Bakker and Ingmar R. Y. van Herpt. Cheltenham, UK: Edward Elgar.

Jeanne, Olivier. 2007. International Reserves in Emerging Market Countries: Too Much of a Good Thing? *Brookings Papers on Economic Activity* 2007, no. 1: 1–79.

Jeanne, Olivier, and Romain Rancière. 2006. *The Optimal Level of International Reserves for Emerging Market Countries: Formulas and Applications*. IMF Working Paper 06/229. Washington: International Monetary Fund.

Mendoza, Enrique G., Vincenzo Quadrini, and José-Víctor Ríos-Rull. 2007. Financial Integration, Financial Deepness, and Global Imbalances. Paper presented at the Bank of Korea International Conference 2007, Seoul, Korea, June 18–19.

Ortiz, Guillermo. 2007. A Coordinated Strategy for Assets and Liabilities: The Mexican Perspective. In *Sovereign Wealth Management*, ed. Jennifer Johnson-Calari and Malan Rietveld. London: Central Banking Publications.

Summers, Lawrence H. 2006. Reflections on Global Current Account Imbalances and Emerging Markets Reserve Accumulation. L. K. Jha Memorial Lecture, Reserve Bank of India, Mumbai (March 24).

Summers, Lawrence H. 2007. Opportunities in an Era of Large and Growing Official Wealth. In *Sovereign Wealth Management*, ed. Jennifer Johnson-Calari and Malan Rietveld. London: Central Banking Publications.

Truman, Edwin M. 2007. *Sovereign Wealth Funds: The Need for Greater Transparency and Accountability*. Policy Briefs in International Economics 07-6 (August). Washington: Peterson Institute for International Economics.

Truman, Edwin M., and Anna Wong. 2006. *The Case for an International Reserve Diversification Standard*. Working Paper 06-2. Washington: Peterson Institute for International Economics.

Appendix 5A
A Scoreboard for Sovereign Wealth Funds

Sovereign wealth funds (SWF) or their near equivalents come in many forms with a variety of objectives in countries with a range of governmental structures. Consequently, comparing them is difficult. Nevertheless, it is possible to outline a core set of elements that are substantially relevant for all such entities, whether the objective is short-term macroeconomic stabilization, wealth transfer across generations, or a combination of objectives, the last of which is usually the case. Using these elements, one can then create a scoreboard to evaluate each individual SWF on the extent to which its structure and operation embrace these elements.

This appendix presents the scoreboard that I have constructed with the assistance of Doug Dowson. It covers four basic categories: structure, governance, transparency and accountability, and behavior. Within each category, we pose a set of yes-or-no questions, for a total of 25 questions. For two of the categories, we group the questions into subcategories.

For each question, if the answer is an unqualified yes, we score it as a 1. If the answer is no, we score it as a 0. However, for many elements, we allow for partial scores of 0.25, 0.50, and 0.75, indicated by (p) in the descriptions below. For each of our 25 questions, the answer is yes for at least one SWF.

We evaluate 32 SWF in 28 countries (table 5.A1), as well as the California Public Employees' Retirement System (CalPERS) as a reference point.[21]

In collecting the answers to our questions, we looked for sources of systematic and continuously available public information. For some of our facts, we relied on independent published reports, such as those of the International Monetary Fund (IMF) or World Bank. However, in general, we required that the SWF produce an ongoing flow of systematic information. Consequently, for some SWF, more is known about them than is reflected in our scoring, but the information is anecdotal and occasional rather than systematic and regular. In our view, it is not sufficient that an individual SWF provide information in ad hoc interviews with the press, as the Government of Singapore Investment Corporation and the Abu Dhabi Investment Authority have done. We have tried to be rigorous and

---

21. In our evaluation of SWF, we include the funds of two subnational units, the Alberta (Canada) Heritage Savings Trust Fund and Alaska (United States) Permanent Fund. We might have included Wyoming's similar fund. We also include two national pension funds, New Zealand's Superannuation Fund and Australia's Future Fund. We might have included the national pension funds of a number of other countries, such as Ireland. We do not classify Norway's Government Pension Fund–Global as a pension fund, despite the appearance of that phrase in its title, because at present, earnings from the fund are used to finance Norway's general budget. For pension funds such as CalPERS, established by law and generally subject to restrictions under such a law, it is somewhat easier for the SWF to record a high score.

Table 5.A1　Sovereign wealth funds

Country	Fund	Year established	Current size[a] (billions of US dollars)
United Arab Emirates			522 to 897[e]
	Abu Dhabi Investment Authority and Corporation	1976	(500 to 875[e])
	Istithmar (Dubai)	2003	(12[e])
	Mubadala Development Company (Abu Dhabi)	2002	(10[e])
Singapore			208 to 438[er]
	Government of Singapore Investment Corporation	1981	(100 to 330[er])
	Temasek Holdings[b]	1974	(108)
Norway	Government Pension Fund–Global	1990	329
Kuwait	Kuwait Investment Authority	1953	213
Russia	Stabilization Fund of the Russian Federation	2004	148[r]
China	Central Huijin Investment Company[b]	2003	68[e]
Qatar	Qatar Investment Authority	2005	50[e]
Australia	Future Fund[b]	2006	49
Algeria	Revenue Regulation Fund	2000	43
United States	Alaska Permanent Fund[b]	1976	40
Brunei	Brunei Investment Agency	1983	35[e]
Korea	Korea Investment Corporation	2005	20[r]
Kazakhstan	National Oil Fund	2000	19
Malaysia	Khazanah Nasional[b]	1993	18
Canada	Alberta Heritage Savings Trust Fund[b]	1976	15
Venezuela			16
	National Development Fund[c]	2005	(15)
	Macroeconomic Stabilization Fund	1998	(1)
Chile	Economic and Social Stabilization Fund	2006	10
New Zealand	Superannuation Fund[b]	2001	10
Oman	State General Reserve Fund	1980	10[e]
Iran	Oil Stabilization Fund	2000	9[e]
Botswana	Pula Fund	1997	6
Mexico	Oil Income Stabilization Fund	2000	3
Azerbaijan	State Oil Fund of the Republic of Azerbaijan	2000	2
Trinidad and Tobago	Heritage and Stabilization Fund	2007	1
Timor-Leste	Petroleum Fund	2005	1
Kiribati	Revenue Equalization Reserve Fund	1956	< 1[e]
São Tomé and Príncipe	National Oil Account	2004	< 1
Sudan	Oil Revenue Stabilization Account	2002	< 1
Total[d]			2,148

e = estimate
r = some or all assets are included in reserves

a. Data are from the end of 2006 or the most recent date available.
b. A portion of the holdings is in domestic assets.
c. A portion of these holdings is intended for domestic investment.
d. Total uses the midpoint of the range of estimates.

systematic in our evaluation of each entity, but some degree of subjectivity necessarily is present in our procedure.

The four categories in our scoreboard are listed below with subcategories where relevant. The 25 questions are stated with explanatory comments on some of them. Table 5.A2 provides the scores of the 32 funds on each element as well as subtotals for each category and the overall score for each SWF that is also in table 5.2.

Structure (8)[22]

1. Is the SWF's **objective** clearly communicated? (p: 28)[23]

Fiscal Treatment (4)[24]

Fiscal treatment is central to an SWF's role in the macroeconomic stability of a country. This involves several components, including how an SWF receives its funding, how the government may employ the SWF's principal and earnings, and whether the government actually follows the procedures it has established. As detailed in IMF (2007a), basic principles of good public finance aim at limiting procyclical influences on fiscal policy. It follows that the SWF should not be used as a second budget, should be integrated with the overall budget of the government, and that the government should not explicitly or implicitly borrow against resources building up in the SWF. In addition, clear rules and principles help to limit the potential scope for corruption in using the SWF for foreign or domestic purposes.

2. Is the **source** of the SWF's **funding** clearly specified? (p: 25.5)
3. Is the nature of the subsequent **use** of the principal and earnings in the fund clearly stated? (p: 16)
4. Are these elements of fiscal treatment **integrated with** the **budget**? (p: 17.5) In some cases, the integration is looser than in others. For this element, as well as the element that follows, some recently created SWF do not have an established record of compliance. In those cases, we gave the SWF full credit.

---

22. The number in parentheses indicates the number of elements included in the category as well as the maximum number of points that can be recorded for each SWF in the category.

23. The number in parentheses, for some elements preceded by a "p," indicates the total number of points out of 32 (the number of funds) recorded in this category. In other words, the number summarizes the score of the SWF as a group on each element. The figure is also at the bottom of each column in table 5.A2. A "p" indicates the potential for partial scores.

24. The number in parentheses indicate the number of elements included in the subcategory as well as the maximum number of points that can be recorded for each SWF in the subcategory.

Table 5.A2 Scoreboard for sovereign wealth funds

Country	Fund	Objective	Fiscal Treatment			Guidelines followed	Structure			Subtotal
			Source of funding	Use of fund	Integrated with budget		Investment strategy	Changing the structure	Separate from international reserves	
Algeria	Revenue Regulation Fund	1.00	1.00	0.00	0.00	0.00	0.00	0.00	1.00	3.00
Australia	Future Fund	1.00	1.00	1.00	1.00	1.00	1.00	1.00	1.00	8.00
Azerbaijan	State Oil Fund of the Republic of Azerbaijan	1.00	1.00	0.50	0.50	0.00	1.00	0.00	1.00	5.00
Botswana	Pula Fund	1.00	0.50	1.00	1.00	1.00	0.00	1.00	0.00	5.50
Brunei	Brunei Investment Agency	1.00	0.00	0.00	0.00	0.00	0.00	0.00	0.00	1.00
Canada	Alberta Heritage Savings Trust Fund	1.00	1.00	1.00	1.00	0.50	1.00	1.00	1.00	7.50
Chile	Economic and Social Stabilization Fund	1.00	1.00	1.00	0.50	1.00	0.50	1.00	1.00	7.00
China	Central Huijin Investment Company	0.50	1.00	1.00	1.00	1.00	0.00	0.00	1.00	5.50
Iran	Oil Stabilization Fund	1.00	1.00	1.00	0.00	0.00	0.00	0.00	1.00	4.00
Kazakhstan	National Oil Fund	1.00	1.00	1.00	0.50	0.00	1.00	0.50	1.00	6.00
Kiribati	Revenue Equalization Reserve Fund	1.00	1.00	1.00	1.00	0.00	0.00	1.00	0.00	5.00
Korea	Korea Investment Corporation	1.00	1.00	0.00	1.00	1.00	0.00	1.00	1.00	6.00
Kuwait	Kuwait Investment Authority	1.00	1.00	0.00	1.00	0.00	1.00	1.00	1.00	6.00
Malaysia	Khazanah Nasional	0.50	1.00	0.00	0.00	1.00	0.50	0.00	1.00	4.00
Mexico	Oil Income Stabilization Fund	1.00	1.00	0.50	1.00	0.00	0.50	0.00	1.00	5.00
New Zealand	Superannuation Fund	1.00	1.00	1.00	1.00	1.00	1.00	1.00	1.00	8.00
Norway	Government Pension Fund–Global	1.00	1.00	1.00	1.00	0.50	1.00	1.00	1.00	7.50
Oman	State General Reserve Fund	0.50	0.50	0.50	0.50	0.00	0.00	0.00	1.00	3.00
Qatar	Qatar Investment Authority	0.50	0.50	0.00	0.00	0.00	0.00	0.00	1.00	2.00
Russia	Stabilization Fund of the Russian Federation	1.00	1.00	0.00	1.00	1.00	0.00	0.00	0.00	4.00
São Tomé and Principe	National Oil Account	1.00	1.00	1.00	1.00	1.00	1.00	1.00	1.00	8.00
Singapore	Government of Singapore Investment Corporation	1.00	0.50	0.00	0.00	0.00	0.00	0.00	0.00	1.50
Singapore	Temasek Holdings	1.00	1.00	0.00	0.00	0.00	1.00	0.00	1.00	4.00
Sudan	Oil Revenue Stabilization Account	0.50	1.00	0.50	0.00	0.00	1.00	0.00	1.00	4.00
Timor-Leste	Petroleum Fund	1.00	1.00	1.00	1.00	1.00	1.00	1.00	1.00	8.00
Trinidad and Tobago	Heritage and Stabilization Fund	1.00	1.00	1.00	0.50	1.00	1.00	0.00	1.00	6.50
United Arab Emirates	Abu Dhabi Investment Authority and Corporation	0.00	0.00	0.00	0.00	0.00	0.50	0.00	0.00	0.50
United Arab Emirates	Istithmar	1.00	0.50	0.00	0.00	0.00	0.50	0.00	1.00	3.00
United Arab Emirates	Mubadala Development Company	1.00	0.00	0.00	0.00	0.00	1.00	0.00	1.00	3.00
United States	Alaska Permanent Fund	1.00	1.00	1.00	1.00	1.00	1.00	0.50	1.00	7.50
Venezuela	Macroeconomic Stabilization Fund	1.00	1.00	0.00	0.00	0.00	0.00	0.00	1.00	3.00
Venezuela	National Development Fund	0.50	1.00	0.00	0.00	0.00	0.00	0.00	1.00	1.50
Total[a]		28.00	25.50	16.00	17.50	13.00	16.50	12.00	25.00	4.80
United States	California Public Employees' Retirement System	1.00	1.00	1.00	1.00	1.00	1.00	1.00	1.00	8.00

a. For each category, the value under subtotal represents the average for all funds.

Table 5.A2 Scoreboard for sovereign wealth funds (continued)

Country	Fund	Governance					Transparency and accountability				
							Reports		Investments		
		Role of government	Role of manager	Guidelines for corporate responsibility	Ethical guidelines	Subtotal	Annual report	Quarterly report	Size of fund	Returns	Types
Algeria	Revenue Regulation Fund	0.00	1.00	0.00	0.00	1.00	0.00	0.00	0.50	0.00	0.00
Australia	Future Fund	1.00	1.00	0.00	0.00	2.00	1.00	0.00	1.00	1.00	1.00
Azerbaijan	State Oil Fund of the Republic of Azerbaijan	1.00	1.00	0.00	0.00	2.00	1.00	1.00	1.00	1.00	1.00
Botswana	Pula Fund	1.00	1.00	0.00	0.00	2.00	1.00	1.00	1.00	1.00	1.00
Brunei	Brunei Investment Agency	0.00	0.50	0.00	0.00	0.50	0.00	0.00	0.00	0.00	0.00
Canada	Alberta Heritage Savings Trust Fund	1.00	1.00	1.00	0.00	3.00	1.00	1.00	1.00	0.00	0.00
Chile	Economic and Social Stabilization Fund	1.00	1.00	0.00	0.00	2.00	1.00	1.00	1.00	1.00	1.00
China	Central Huijin Investment Company	0.00	0.00	0.00	0.00	0.00	0.00	0.00	0.00	0.00	0.50
Iran	Oil Stabilization Fund	0.00	1.00	0.00	0.00	1.00	0.00	0.00	0.50	0.00	0.00
Kazakhstan	National Oil Fund	1.00	1.00	0.00	0.00	2.00	0.50	0.50	1.00	1.00	0.50
Kiribati	Revenue Equalization Reserve Fund	1.00	1.00	0.00	0.00	2.00	0.00	0.00	0.50	0.00	0.50
Korea	Korea Investment Corporation	1.00	1.00	0.00	0.00	2.00	0.00	0.00	1.00	0.00	0.00
Kuwait	Kuwait Investment Authority	1.00	1.00	0.00	1.00	3.00	0.00	0.00	0.50	0.00	0.00
Malaysia	Khazanah Nasional	0.50	1.00	0.00	0.00	1.50	0.50	0.00	1.00	0.00	0.50
Mexico	Oil Income Stabilization Fund	0.00	0.00	0.00	0.00	0.00	0.00	0.00	1.00	0.00	0.00
New Zealand	Superannuation Fund	0.00	1.00	1.00	1.00	4.00	1.00	1.00	1.00	1.00	1.00
Norway	Government Pension Fund–Global	1.00	1.00	1.00	1.00	4.00	1.00	1.00	1.00	1.00	1.00
Oman	State General Reserve Fund	0.00	0.00	0.00	0.00	0.00	0.00	0.00	0.00	0.00	0.00
Qatar	Qatar Investment Authority	0.00	0.00	0.00	0.00	0.00	0.00	0.00	0.00	0.00	0.00
Russia	Stabilization Fund of the Russian Federation	1.00	1.00	0.00	0.00	2.00	0.00	0.00	1.00	0.00	1.00
São Tomé and Principe	National Oil Account	1.00	1.00	0.00	0.00	2.00	0.00	0.00	0.00	0.00	0.25
Singapore	Government of Singapore Investment Corporation	0.00	0.00	0.00	0.00	0.00	0.00	0.00	0.25	0.00	0.50
Singapore	Temasek Holdings	0.00	1.00	0.50	0.00	1.50	1.00	0.00	1.00	1.00	0.50
Sudan	Oil Revenue Stabilization Account	0.00	1.00	0.00	0.00	0.00	1.00	0.00	1.00	1.00	0.00
Timor-Leste	Petroleum Fund	1.00	1.00	0.00	0.00	2.00	1.00	1.00	1.00	1.00	1.00
Trinidad and Tobago	Heritage and Stabilization Fund	1.00	1.00	0.00	0.00	2.00	0.50	0.00	1.00	0.00	0.00
United Arab Emirates	Abu Dhabi Investment Authority and Corporation	0.00	0.00	0.00	0.00	0.00	0.00	0.00	0.00	0.00	0.00
United Arab Emirates	Istithmar	0.00	0.50	0.00	0.00	0.50	0.00	0.00	0.25	0.00	0.00
United Arab Emirates	Mubadala Development Company	0.00	0.50	0.00	0.00	0.50	0.00	0.00	0.00	0.00	0.00
United States	Alaska Permanent Fund	1.00	1.00	0.00	0.00	2.00	1.00	1.00	1.00	1.00	1.00
Venezuela	Macroeconomic Stabilization Fund	0.00	0.50	0.00	0.00	0.50	0.25	0.25	1.00	0.00	0.50
Venezuela	National Development Fund	0.00	0.50	0.00	0.00	0.50	1.00	0.50	1.00	0.00	0.00
Total[a]		16.50	22.50	3.50	3.00	1.42	13.25	9.25	21.50	10.00	13.50
United States	California Public Employees' Retirement System	1.00	1.00	1.00	0.00	3.00	1.00	1.00	1.00	1.00	1.00

a. For each category, the value under subtotal represents the average for all funds.

Table 5.A2. Scoreboard for sovereign wealth funds *(continued)*

Country	Fund	Investments: Location	Specific	Currency composition	Man-dates	Audit: Regular	Published	Inde-pendent	Sub-total	Behavior: Speed of adjustment	Grand total
Algeria	Revenue Regulation Fund	0.00	0.00	0.00	0.00	0.00	0.00	0.00	0.50	0.00	4.50
Australia	Future Fund	0.00	0.00	0.00	0.00	1.00	1.00	1.00	7.00	0.00	17.00
Azerbaijan	State Oil Fund of the Republic of Azerbaijan	0.50	0.00	1.00	0.00	1.00	1.00	1.00	9.50	0.00	16.50
Botswana	Pula Fund	0.00	0.00	0.00	0.00	1.00	0.00	1.00	7.00	0.00	14.50
Brunei	Brunei Investment Agency	0.00	0.00	0.00	0.00	1.00	0.00	0.00	1.00	0.00	2.50
Canada	Alberta Heritage Savings Trust Fund	1.00	0.00	0.00	0.00	1.00	1.00	1.00	9.00	0.00	19.50
Chile	Economic and Social Stabilization Fund	0.50	0.00	1.00	0.00	1.00	0.00	0.00	6.50	0.00	15.50
China	Central Huijin Investment Company	0.00	0.00	0.00	1.00	0.00	0.00	0.00	0.50	0.00	6.00
Iran	Oil Stabilization Fund	0.00	0.00	0.00	0.00	0.00	0.00	0.00	0.50	0.00	5.50
Kazakhstan	National Oil Fund	0.00	0.00	0.50	0.50	1.00	0.00	1.00	6.50	0.00	14.50
Kiribati	Revenue Equalization Reserve Fund	0.00	0.00	0.00	0.00	0.00	0.00	0.00	0.50	0.00	7.50
Korea	Korea Investment Corporation	0.00	0.00	0.00	0.00	0.00	0.00	0.00	1.00	0.00	9.00
Kuwait	Kuwait Investment Authority	0.00	0.00	0.00	0.00	1.00	0.00	1.00	3.00	0.00	12.00
Malaysia	Khazanah Nasional	1.00	0.00	0.00	0.00	1.00	0.00	0.00	4.00	0.00	9.50
Mexico	Oil Income Stabilization Fund	0.00	0.00	1.00	0.00	1.00	0.00	0.00	2.00	0.00	7.00
New Zealand	Superannuation Fund	1.00	1.00	1.00	1.00	1.00	1.00	1.00	12.00	0.00	24.00
Norway	Government Pension Fund–Global	1.00	1.00	0.00	1.00	1.00	1.00	0.50	10.50	1.00	23.00
Oman	State General Reserve Fund	0.00	0.00	0.00	0.00	1.00	0.00	1.00	2.00	0.00	5.00
Qatar	Qatar Investment Authority	0.00	0.00	0.00	0.00	0.00	0.00	0.00	0.00	0.00	2.00
Russia	Stabilization Fund of the Russian Federation	0.50	0.00	1.00	0.00	0.00	0.00	0.00	3.50	0.00	9.50
São Tomé and Príncipe	National Oil Account	0.00	0.00	0.00	0.00	0.00	0.00	1.00	2.25	0.00	12.25
Singapore	Government of Singapore Investment Corporation	0.00	0.00	0.00	0.00	1.00	0.00	1.00	0.75	0.00	2.25
Singapore	Temasek Holdings	1.00	0.50	0.00	0.00	1.00	1.00	1.00	8.00	0.00	13.50
Sudan	Oil Revenue Stabilization Account	0.00	0.00	0.00	0.00	0.00	1.00	0.00	1.00	0.00	5.00
Timor-Leste	Petroleum Fund	1.00	1.00	1.00	0.75	1.00	1.00	1.00	11.75	0.00	21.75
Trinidad and Tobago	Heritage and Stabilization Fund	0.00	0.00	0.00	0.25	1.00	0.00	1.00	3.75	0.00	12.25
United Arab Emirates	Abu Dhabi Investment Authority and Corporation	0.00	0.00	0.00	0.00	0.00	0.00	0.00	0.00	0.00	0.50
United Arab Emirates	Istithmar	0.00	0.00	0.00	0.00	0.00	0.00	0.00	0.25	0.00	3.75
United Arab Emirates	Mubadala Development Company	0.00	0.00	0.00	0.00	0.00	0.00	0.00	0.00	0.00	3.50
United States	Alaska Permanent Fund	0.50	0.00	1.00	0.00	1.00	0.00	1.00	8.50	0.00	18.00
Venezuela	Macroeconomic Stabilization Fund	0.00	0.00	0.00	0.00	0.00	0.00	0.00	2.00	0.00	5.50
Venezuela	National Development Fund	0.00	0.00	0.00	0.00	1.00	0.00	0.50	4.00	0.00	6.00
Total[a]		8.00	3.50	7.50	4.50	17.00	7.00	14.00	4.00	1.00	10.27
United States	California Public Employees' Retirement System	0.25	0.00	1.00	1.00	1.00	0.00	1.00	10.25	0.50	21.75

a. For each category, the value under subtotal represents the average for all funds.

5. Are the **guidelines** for fiscal treatment generally **followed** without frequent adjustment? (p: 13)

Other Structural Elements (3)

6. Is the overall **investment strategy** clearly communicated? (p: 16.5)
7. Is the procedure for **changing the structure** clear? (p: 12) When an SWF has been established by law, the procedure for changing many elements of the structure is clearer than when the SWF has not been established by law.
8. Is the SWF **separate from** the country's **international reserves**? (25) A lack of separation between the SWF and international reserves creates ambiguity about the investment objectives of the SWF as well as about the management of the government's international reserves.

Governance (4)

9. Is the **role of the government** in setting the investment strategy of the SWF clearly established? (p: 16.5)
10. Is the **role of the manager** in executing the investment strategy clearly established? (p: 22.5)
11. Does the SWF have in place, and publicly available, **guidelines for corporate responsibility** that it follows? (p: 3.5)
12. Does the SWF have **ethical guidelines** that it follows? (3) It reasonably could be argued that an SWF's objectives should be merely to implement its investment strategy and maximize financial returns subject to whatever risk management constraints have been established. In this case, its ethical guidelines would involve ignoring ethical considerations, but we would still score such an SWF as a 1. However, in some cases, the SWF may implicitly limit its investments in certain instruments, entities, activities, or countries without a clearly articulated set of guidelines. In the absence of any information on this point, an SWF receives a 0 in our scoring.

Transparency and Accountability (12)

Accountability is the principal objective of the scoreboard exercise and any set of best practices for SWF. Transparency is a key means of establishing accountability.

Reports (2)

Any SWF that does not provide some sort of regular public report on its activities does not score many points in this subcategory or for the category as a whole.

13. Does the SWF provide at least an **annual report** on its activities and results? (p: 13.25) If there is an annual report but it contains little or no information on the SWF's activities, we give it a score of more than 0 but less than 1. We also give partial credit (0.25) for an unpublished report to a parliament.

14. Does the SWF provide **quarterly reports** on its activities? (p: 9.25) As with element 13, we allow for a partial score. We acknowledge that views differ on the desirability of quarterly financial reporting. Some argue that it promotes too much focus on short-term returns. In our view, the principal argument for quarterly reporting rests on transparency. The entity should be able to withstand the influence of excessive short-term emphasis given that it is not subject to the disciplines of the market.

Investments (7)

15. Do regular reports on the investments by the SWF include the **size of the fund**? (p: 21.5) If an SWF states that it is at least of a certain size, we give partial credit (0.25).

16. Do regular reports on the investments by the SWF include information on the **returns** it earns? (10) In a number of cases, reports indicate an overall increase in the size of the fund without distinguishing between adding new resources and earnings on resources previously incorporated in the fund. This practice receives no credit. Some reports on returns may provide an overall figure, perhaps translated into domestic currency, as well as additional detail, which one might think deserves extra credit, but we do not give extra credit.

17. Do regular reports on the investments by the SWF include information on the **types** of investments? (p: 13.25) Specifying what sectors and in which instruments. A general description receives only partial credit.

18. Do regular reports on the investments by the SWF include information on the geographic **location** of investments? (p: 8) A listing of broad regions of the world receives only partial credit.

19. Do regular reports on the investments by the SWF include information on **specific** investments? (p: 3.5) Which instruments, countries, and companies? In some cases, the SWF only reports the investments it considers to be significant. This receives partial credit.

20. Do regular reports on the investments by the SWF include information on the **currency composition** of investments? (p: 7.5) Partial credit is given when an SWF provides information on broad groups of currencies.

21. Are the holders of investment **mandates** identified? (p: 4.5) By disclosing the holders of individual investment mandates, both in the

country and outside the country, the public can check on the records, quality, and reliability of those intermediaries. Such disclosure also limits the scope for sweetheart arrangements and corruption. To receive full credit, a SWF must publish the names of each holder of a mandate. If it merely states that it grants mandates, we give it no credit.

Audits (3)

Regular audits, preferably independent as well as published, are a central element of accountability. For this reason, we have assigned a maximum of three points to this subcategory.

22. Is the SWF subjected to a **regular audit**? (p: 17)
23. Is the audit **published**? (7)
24. Is the audit **independent**? (p: 14) In some cases, SWF are subjected to regular published audits, but the auditing is internal to the SWF in whole or in part, which takes away some of the objectivity and receives a partial deduction.

Behavior (1)

We include only one element in this category. One could imagine several other elements that might be included, such as whether the SWF engages in short sales or derivatives, which many SWF with moderately active investment strategies do in part and also disclose. In addition, it might be desirable if the SWF consulted with the country of location for any large investment or disinvestments, or with the country of issue of the currency involved. An initial version of our scoreboard included such an element, but because we could not find an SWF that followed such a practice, we dropped it from our scoring exercise.

25. Does the SWF indicate the nature and **speed of adjustment** in its portfolio? (p: 1) This is done only by the Norwegian Government Pension Fund-Global, as far as we have determined. That fund's declared policy is to use new inflows to adjust its portfolio in light of market changes that move its existing portfolio away from its benchmarks; in other words, it follows a policy of portfolio rebalancing. CalPERs states that it seeks to invest efficiently, bearing in mind the impact of management and transaction costs on the return on its assets. We gave it partial credit.

Comment
Toward a Better Understanding
of Sovereign Wealth Funds

MOHAMED A. EL-ERIAN

My objective is to comment on Edwin Truman's paper, which deals with the management of China's reserves and, more generally, the growing systemic role of sovereign wealth funds (SWF).

At the outset, I would like to thank him for his thoughtful work on SWF, not only in this paper but also in his August 2007 policy brief (Truman 2007). While I have some questions about the methodology that he uses in the paper, his work is helping to bring some rationality to a topic that, until now, has been overly dominated by incomplete analysis, ill-defined concepts of national security and reciprocity, and monster-like characterizations of motives pertaining to political, military, and/or mercantilist aspects.

The importance of more thoughtful and well-researched analyses of the SWF phenomenon cannot be overemphasized. After all, the phenomenon is part of a broader realignment of the global economy that, if well managed, can be part of an orderly solution to current national and international imbalances—a solution that can alleviate the growing risk of global financial dislocations while preserving the prospects for continued robust global growth.

This comment reflects the perspective of a market participant who, first, is involved on a daily basis in market segments in which SWF have a pres-

Mohamed A. El-Erian is co-chief executive officer and co-chief investment officer of Pacific Investment Management Co. (Pimco).

ence, and second, has spent time thinking and writing about the SWF phenomenon, including in the context of the secular and quarterly themes that anchor various investment strategies.[1] The comment starts by summarizing the key points in Truman's paper. It then discusses the methodology that the paper uses to score SWF, asking why some of the scores conflict so strongly with the likely perceptions of a large number of market participants who have interacted with some of the SWF for long periods. It then shifts from what is covered in the paper to some elements that could be considered in designing the future research agenda on SWF, focusing mainly on how best to formulate and implement a strategy that can successfully enhance the governance and institutional robustness of the SWF complex in general while also recognizing its important systemic role.

Summary of the Main Points

In summarizing the paper's main points, let me start with the three main areas in which there is likely to be complete agreement.

First, the paper points to the tremendous increase in the level and rate of accumulation of China's international reserves—a phenomenon that is also well documented in Morris Goldstein and Nicholas Lardy's overview paper for this conference (see chapter 1). Second, it rightly argues that the reserve accumulation has not been an end in itself, but rather a by-product of other economic and financial policies, not only in China but elsewhere. Finally, the paper suggests that, while the literature is far from precise on the topic, it is fair to say that China's reserves now exceed what would be deemed reasonable for balance-of-payments purposes, particularly in light of the country's current economic parameters, including its set of capital controls. These considerations lead the paper to argue, correctly, that the policy issue for China and other emerging economies relates not just to flows but to the stock of international reserve holdings: Once they are there, the paper asks, what does a country's government do with them? It then argues that "China is being, will be, and should be held to the highest standard of accountability and transparency in this area" (Truman 2007).

In this context, the paper seeks to demonstrate that China falls short of expectations when judged by an SWF scoreboard that captures structure, governance, transparency and accountability, and behavior. Several other SWF are shown to score poorly as well, generalizing the paper's argument to the SWF complex as a whole.

---

1. See, for example, El-Erian (2007) and Mohamed A. El-Erian, "Foreign Capital Must Not Be Blocked," *Financial Times*, October 3, 2007.

Some Methodological Considerations

Let us now turn to the methodology used in the paper, focusing mainly on why the paper's scoreboard results in poor assessments of several SWF that, for many funds, conflicts with the perceptions of market participants who interact with them.

Why Are SWF Special?

It is highly likely that if the paper's methodology were applied to the most rapidly growing investment vehicles in the private sector—namely, hedge funds and private equity—the scores would be as low if not lower than those for the SWF complex. Also, because of these alternative private-sector vehicles' higher leverage and shorter investment horizons compared with SWF, the potential systemic effects emanating from them are greater. Yet the serious regulatory debate is still quite a distance away from the set of best practices and standards that Truman suggests through his paper and earlier policy brief.

Simon Johnson, economic counselor and director of the Research Department at the International Monetary Fund, touches on the issue of hedge funds in one of his recent writings. As he notes, "The consensus so far is that while hedge funds deserve considerably greater scrutiny, there are advantages for the allocation of global capital flows if this sector continues to have a relatively light direct regulatory burden" (Johnson 2007). Interestingly, those in markets with significant capital exposure to these vehicles—that is, institutional investors—are still happy to judge the vehicles by their output (i.e., risk-adjusted investment returns) rather than their strict adherence to elements such as those in the paper's scoreboard.

Such an initial comparison of hedge funds and private equity firms and SWF does not, of course, account for a notable difference in their structures. Hedge funds and private equity firms are owned and controlled by the private sector, whereas SWF have governments behind them. As such, SWF are inevitably subject to higher scrutiny lest their investment decisions be hijacked by noncommercial considerations pertaining to political, military, and mercantilist drivers.

Interestingly, the issue that dominates the public debate is not whether SWF will produce superior investment returns and, in the process, benefit current and future generations and enhance international capital flow efficiency and market completion. There was less public concern among observers when the investments of China's and Russia's excess reserves were even more highly concentrated than they are now (i.e., an even greater concentration in holdings of US government and agency bonds), which, virtually by definition, was inefficient from a return and risk perspective.

In the past, concerns about the impact of noncommercial investments by foreign governments have been handled by imposing the appropriate screening mechanisms in the recipient countries. Such mechanisms are visible in the United States (e.g., the work of the Committee on Foreign Investment in the United States [CFIUS]) and have been used successfully to block investments in what are deemed to be sensitive areas from a national security perspective. In the current debate, however, they seem to be viewed as necessary but insufficient. One argument in support of this is the risk that the absence of adequate safeguards at the level of the SWF—as opposed to that of the recipient country—will end up feeding general protectionist pressures into the global economy. The specific risk is a proliferation of capital account protectionism and negative externalities in the form of further delays in completing the next stages of trade liberalization.

There could well be merit in concerns about protectionism given what else is happening in industrial economies and particularly in the United States. The political calendar is approaching a cyclical peak with upcoming presidential and congressional elections, the debate about financial-sector instability has been fueled by the sudden liquidity stops and market turmoil that started last summer, and the economy is facing headwinds on account of its weakening housing sector and employment outlook.

The multilateral framework of international finance is also under pressure and, accordingly, cannot be expected to act as a credible circuit breaker in preventing protectionist pressures from rising. The legitimacy and effectiveness of the multilateral institutions are being questioned openly and widely, as is the underlying architecture, which is viewed as increasingly obsolete.[2] Moreover, given the current configuration of influences on global growth, trade, price formation, and capital flows, the Group of Seven process is viewed increasingly as outmoded and unproductive because it excludes key emerging economies that have systemic importance. That said, a credible substitute has yet to emerge. Accordingly, the argument for SWF to commit to higher standards relates in large part to deficiencies in the international economy as a whole. To use a sports analogy, to play defense in limiting their sensitivity to collateral damage, SWF need to play offense, particularly regarding specific aspects of disclosure and transparency.

The agenda here is not open ended; it need not encompass every element of SWF operations, as some have suggested. Rather, the emphasis should be on three aspects: first, the governance structure and, in particular, the extent to which political ownership is appropriately separated from operational issues and subject to the required level of checks and balances; second, the investment process, including the robustness of the approaches that underpin asset allocation and the related choice of in-

---

2. See, for example, the discussion in Truman (2006).

vestment vehicles; and third, risk management, including the ability to set appropriate risk limits, monitor them, and implement the required reaction function.

Limitations of the Scoreboard Approach

The paper's scoreboard exercise results in some highly counterintuitive outcomes with respect to long-established SWF, the behavior patterns of which have been repeatedly observed by market participants. I would postulate that the vast majority of experienced market participants would be shocked to see the low scores that the paper assigns to some SWF—including the Abu Dhabi Investment Authority (ADIA), Singapore's Government Investment Corporation (GIC), and the Kuwait Investment Authority (KIA)—whose behavior, investment savvy, and systemic impact have been observable for long periods of time. It also runs counter to the way that some of the newer SWF, including the Dubai entities and the Qatar Investment Authority (QIA), have approached their recent investments.

If the underlying concern relates to the impact of SWF on global stability, funds such as those mentioned above have simply not behaved in a manner that their low scores might suggest. If anything, the recent deployment of their patient capital has been a highly stabilizing influence on a global economy that has been increasingly sensitive to balance-sheet excesses and extreme financial alchemy in industrial countries. The catalyst to and aftermath of the liquidity dislocations and market turmoil that started this summer are yet another example of this duality.

The paper's attribution of low scores to several SWF does not reflect their activities, behavior, or temperament, nor is it due to how they have interacted with the realities of the marketplace. Rather, it reflects the paper's limited access to information. Understandably, the paper uses publicly available information to compile the rankings and is explicit about it. The rather puzzling outcome likely indicates how little information is disseminated by SWF as a group, and the approach would probably yield similar outcomes were it applied to hedge funds, private equity firms, or the proprietary desk activities of major Wall Street banks. Given the scope and recommendations of the paper, I would suggest that further work seek to expand the information set. Pending this, the paper's findings speak more to data limitations than to a genuine assessment of SWF.

Strategy for Productively Engaging SWF

Let me now turn to a strategic issue that would benefit from greater attention in the work plan on SWF: how best to engage SWF and encourage them to make progress, as appropriate, on issues pertaining to governance, investment process, and risk management.

In the vast majority of cases, history suggests that the approach of debtors lecturing to creditors is not very effective. It does not help that such lecturing materially intensified after some of the newer SWF, including those of China, sensibly decided to gradually diversify hitherto excessively concentrated reserve holdings. It is also inconvenient that such lecturing comes on the heels of the disruptions of the summer of 2007. After all, the systemic shock originated in the most sophisticated financial system in the world, involved the migration of activities outside the purview of adequate oversight, and led to disruptions at the very heart of the market system in industrial countries, in terms of segments (i.e., interbank, commercial paper, and money markets) and market parameters (e.g., valuations, price discovery, and visibility).

The risk is that, no matter how sensible the proposals may be, they will fall on deaf ears because of the strategy deployed to advocate them. This consideration is additionally important because it is reinforced by another hypothesis: Ill-conceived pressure could not only be ineffective but also be harmful to the long-term welfare of the global economy.

One possibility is that ill-conceived pressure ends up inhibiting the asset diversification process that SWF are and should be embarking on. The result would be a set of market mispricings and distortions, including in US fixed income. We already know how these can contribute to interest rate conundrums, overly subdued market volatility, and excessively tight credit spreads. The result could well be another phase of overproduction and overconsumption of risk assets in the most sophisticated financial system, subsequently requiring a costly clean-up process.

Another possibility is that China and other SWF could adopt an approach that heavily outsources its reserves management to private-sector institutions in the hedge fund space. While such private vehicles theoretically come under the domain of industrial country oversight, they involve a significant degree of limitations on information dissemination. Transparency thus would still be lacking, and a host of other considerations would arise, including whether these vehicles would efficiently deal with size.

Bottom Line

Where does all of the above leave us? The debate on China and other SWF should start from the hypothesis that it is in the interest of the global economy to have excess reserves managed in a diversified and commercially oriented manner. The resulting flow of capital—across geographical, product, and risk boundaries—can help sustain economic growth in the context of a process of adjustment necessitated by large global imbalances, overstretched US consumers, and a need for emerging economies to gradually shift to greater emphasis on the domestic components of aggregate demand.

Against this background, the analyses of how SWF behave, including their systemic impact, should be based on a comprehensive set of data. It should include an assessment of how long-standing SWF have actually operated in many different market environments, which would help to refine what tends to be an overly broad set of recommendations to China and other SWF. The outcomes would be targeted improvements in governance, investment process, and risk management, as opposed to an excessively expansive approach that has little chance of gaining traction and may even be counterproductive. That said, for such an effort to have a greater chance of being effective, it is best pursued in the context of a holistic approach that would be well advised to address the legitimate deficiencies in the international system—including questions of representation in multilateral forums—that penalize countries such as China.

References

El-Erian, Mohamed A. 2007. Asset-Liability Management in Emerging Economies. In *Sovereign Wealth Management,* ed. Jennifer Johnson-Calari and Malan Rietveld. London: Central Banking Publications.

Johnson, Simon. 2007. The Rise of Sovereign Wealth Funds. *Finance and Development* 44, no. 3 (September): 56–57.

Truman, Edwin M., ed. 2006. *Reforming the IMF for the 21st Century.* Washington: Institute for International Economics.

Truman, Edwin M. 2007. *Sovereign Wealth Funds: The Need for Greater Transparency and Accountability.* Policy Briefs in International Economics 07-6 (August). Washington: Peterson Institute for International Economics.

Comment
Impact of China Investment Corporation on the Management of China's Foreign Assets

BRAD SETSER

My comments focus on my comparative advantage: China's external portfolio, the composition of Chinese demand for US financial assets, and the potential impact of the creation of the China Investment Corporation (CIC) on China's portfolio. I cannot match Edwin M. Truman's experience in central banking and successfully leading an international effort to increase central bank transparency. I also cannot match Mohamed El-Erian's experience in managing large portfolios, whether Harvard University's portfolio or a large portfolio of emerging-economy bonds.

These comments more complement Truman's paper than critique it. My only real criticism is that the paper's subtitle downplays the scope of Truman's argument: Rather than being called "China and a Sovereign Wealth Fund Scoreboard," it should be titled "How China's Proposed Investment Corporation—And Many Other Funds—Fall Short of the Truman Standard for Transparent Sovereign Wealth Management." I share Truman's belief that the expansion of sovereign wealth funds (SWF) calls for an increase in their transparency. Citizens of countries with large assets should be able to assess how their money is being invested. More transparency

Brad Setser is a fellow at the Greenberg Center for Geoeconomic Studies at the Council on Foreign Relations.

would help address US and European concerns about SWF by, among other things, allowing independent observers to assess whether SWF portfolios are consistent with the funds' stated objectives.

Truman's paper both defines a standard for SWF transparency and names and shames institutions that fall short of this standard. In doing so, Truman moved faster than the Group of Seven or the International Monetary Fund (IMF), and no doubt his work will shape their subsequent efforts. In the 1990s, from inside the Federal Reserve and US Treasury, Truman led a global effort to dramatically increase central bank transparency, including standards for the transparent and timely disclosure of central bank reserves. My own work tracking global reserves has benefited immensely from that effort. I can only hope Truman experiences the same success at the Peterson Institute that he experienced in government.

El-Erian argues forcefully that many of the institutions that score poorly on the Truman standard for transparency, notably the Abu Dhabi Investment Authority and Singapore's Government Investment Corporation, are among the most well-respected global fund managers. In his view, these institutions pose little risk to systemic stability, as market participants know their track record and understand their investment processes. Their low level of public disclosure—and low scores on Truman's matrix—do not, in El-Erian's view, correlate with risk to the integrity of the global financial system.

El-Erian may be correct, but growing public attention to SWF suggests that it is no longer sufficient for their activities to be known and understood by market insiders while remaining indecipherable to the broader public. China's new investment fund is a case in point. Even if the CIC receives only a modest share of the ongoing increase in China's foreign asset growth and its purchases of US equities only modestly diversify China's overall portfolio, it could easily generate far larger portfolio inflows than any existing oil-investment fund could.

Transparency alone will not address all US or European concerns. Some stem from the sheer size of Chinese foreign asset growth and general discomfort with the notion that states, and not private investors, are influencing the allocation of capital, both globally and in the US economy. But more transparency could allow sovereign funds to establish a public track record that will, over time, reduce many of the concerns associated with the rapid rise in their assets.

My remaining comments can be divided into three sections. The first section reviews the pace of China's reserve growth and the available data on the composition of its foreign assets. China currently has a large and concentrated bet on a relatively narrow segment of the US fixed-income market. The case for including equities in the set of securities that China holds in its foreign portfolio is compelling.

The second section argues that the current pace of Chinese asset growth—counting reserves that have been farmed out to the banks for management—is now so rapid that even a fairly modest shift in Chinese demand toward equities could dramatically affect US markets. Assuming that around 70 percent of Chinese flows go to the United States, if only one-quarter of China's total new flows are directed toward equities, then total Chinese flows would be far larger than estimated purchases of US equities by any of the large Gulf SWF. Indeed, total Chinese demand could top the combined impact of the existing oil funds and come close to current (net) private purchases of US portfolio equity.

The third section highlights a set of specific issues raised by the CIC:

- the likelihood that the current governance structure of the CIC will magnify rather than reduce global concerns about the politicization of Chinese investment decisions—a particular concern for a government with large domestic investments in manufacturing companies that compete globally;

- the need for coordination with the People's Bank of China (PBC) to assure that the CIC's portfolio allocation does not work against the PBC's efforts to support China's existing link to the dollar;

- the CIC's high cost of funding and the risk that the desire to avoid losses from renminbi appreciation will result in excessive risk taking; and

- the case for investing the CIC's funds in assets that are not correlated with China's own growth—and the risk that the CIC will instead buy a portfolio the performance of which is tightly correlated with China's own economic performance.

China's Foreign Assets

China accounts for roughly one-third of global reserve growth over the four quarters between mid-2006 and mid-2007 (figure 5.C1). The pace of increase in China's reserves is unprecedented: After adjustments are made to account for the rise in the dollar value of China's reserves due to the rise in the euro and pound, China added about $125 billion to its reserves in the first and second quarters of 2007. If that pace of growth is sustained for the entire year, China's total reserves will rise by $500 billion. That is more than twice the largest annual increase in Japan's reserves. The creation of the CIC combined with pressure on Chinese state banks and state firms to hold more reserves may slow formal reserve in the second half of 2007; reserve growth in the third quarter was only around $80 billion after adjusting for valuation gains. However, the total increase in China's foreign assets will unquestionably be exceptionally strong (figure 5.C2).

Figure 5.C1   Distribution of global reserve growth, rolling four-quarter sums, 2000–2007

billions of US dollars

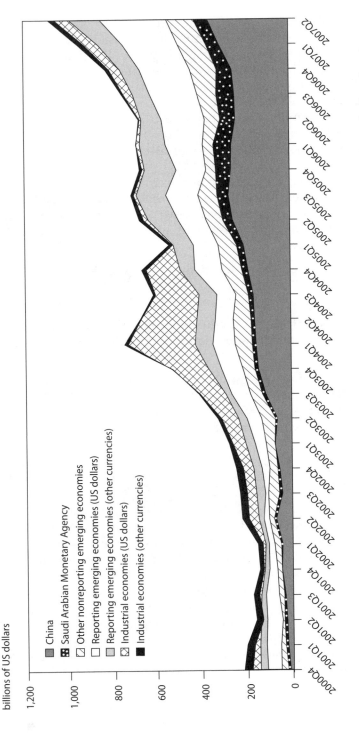

■ China
■ Saudi Arabian Monetary Agency
☐ Other nonreporting emerging economies
☐ Reporting emerging economies (US dollars)
☐ Reporting emerging economies (other currencies)
☐ Industrial economies (US dollars)
☐ Industrial economies (other currencies)

Sources: International Monetary Fund COFER database; national data (China and Saudi Arabia); author's estimates (for valuation effects/valuation-adjusted growth).

Figure 5.C2 China's reserve growth, rolling 12-month sum, valuation adjusted, 2000–2007

billions of US dollars

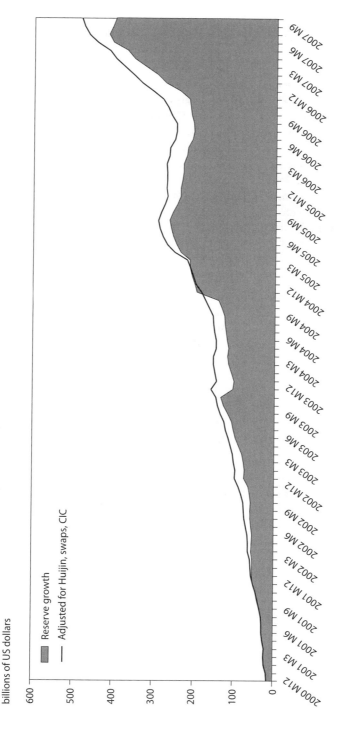

Reserve growth
Adjusted for Huijin, swaps, CIC

CIC = China Investment Corporation

Sources: China State Administration of Foreign Exchange (Chinese reserves); People's Bank of China (banking data); author's estimates (for the China Investment Corporation, valuation effects).

The increase in China's dollar holdings, assuming a constant 70 percent portfolio share, should top $350 billion and could approach $400 billion. Keeping the dollar share of China's portfolio constant would require that China disproportionately hold its new reserves in dollars to offset the increase in the euro value of its existing reserves. Dollar-asset growth of $350 billion to $400 billion over the course of 2007 would be equal to about one-half of the financing the United States needs to sustain a $750 billion to $800 billion current account deficit.[1] Never before in the postwar period has the world's largest economy depended so much on financing from another country's government.

China's foreign exchange reserves currently make up the vast majority of China's foreign assets. China's foreign reserves totaled $1.066 trillion at the end of 2006, about 65 percent of all Chinese foreign assets reported in China's net international investment position. They are on track to rise to above $1.4 trillion by the end of 2007 (figure 5.C3). However, the formal foreign exchange reserves are not the only existing pools of foreign funds controlled by China's state. Three other pools are important:

■ the assets of Central Huijin ($67.5 billion), the PBC's bank recapitalization vehicle. The PBC transferred $67.5 billion in foreign exchange reserves to Huijin in 2003 and 2005, receiving a claim on Huijin in exchange. Those reserves were then injected into three of the four large state commercial banks as part of their recapitalization, with Central Huijin receiving equity in the banks. The banks were required to hold these assets abroad, though they reportedly also received forward contracts hedging their balance sheets from renminbi appreciation and assumed responsibility for investing the funds. The CIC bought Central Huijin's domestic assets in September 2007.

■ the foreign assets of Chinese domestic financial institutions. Ning Ma and Roy Ramos of Goldman Sachs (Ma and Ramos 2007) report that the five banks with the largest foreign securities holdings held $209 billion in debt securities at the end of 2006, $159 billion in dollars. The balance of payments data indicate that Chinese nonreserve holdings of foreign debt increased by $109 billion in 2006, rising from $117 billion to $226 billion. This total likely includes the foreign exchange that the banks received from the Huijin recapitalization. But most of the 2006 increase seems to have been financed through various swaps with the PBC, which reported that the banks' foreign currency liabilities from the "sale and purchase of foreign exchange" rose by $73 billion in 2006,

---

1. The United States also relies on net capital inflows to finance its purchases of foreign assets. Assuming that gross bank flows can be netted out, the United States will need to attract around $1.3 trillion—around 10 percent of its GDP—in net inflows to finance both a large current account deficit and rising purchases of foreign assets.

Figure 5.C3 Adjusted reserves versus known US holdings, 2000–2007

billions of US dollars

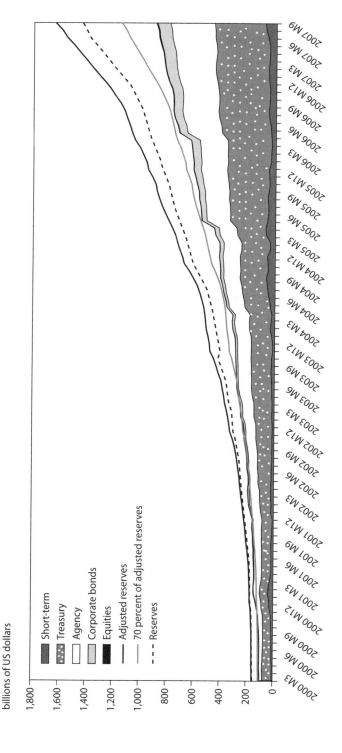

CIC = China Investment Corporation

Note: Adjustments include other foreign exchange liabilities, foreign exchange purchases and sales, and CIC.

Sources: China State Administration of Foreign Exchange (Chinese reserves); People's Bank of China (banking data); US Treasury (international capital data and annual survey of foreign portfolio investment in the United States); author's estimates.

reaching $123 billion by the end of the year.[2] Judging from the state commercial banks' disclosed holdings of subprime debt, this pool of money has been managed more aggressively than have China's reserves.[3] There are strong signs that the banks have resumed the accumulation of foreign exchange in the third quarter.

■ foreign direct investment (FDI) by state-owned Chinese firms. Outward FDI totaled $82 billion at the end of 2006.

China's reserves have been invested more aggressively than the reserves of some other countries. Chinese holdings of so-called mortgage-backed securities, backed in fact by a guarantee from a US government-sponsored enterprise like Fannie Mae (Agency MBS), are particularly large. The pace of increase in the sheer size of China's reserves—from mid-2006 to mid-2007, China added roughly $400 billion to its reserves after adjusting for valuation gains—at least partly explains why China has been more aggressive than some other central banks. From mid-2006 to mid-2007, the stock of outstanding treasury bonds, net of the increase in the Federal Reserve's holdings, was only $120 billion. The stock of outstanding agencies—the debt that the agencies issue to finance their own mortgage portfolio—increased by $25 billion. The stock of Agency MBS, by contrast, increased by $400 billion.[4]

China's large purchases of treasuries and agencies almost certainly have reduced equilibrium interest rates in the US bond market. Warnock and Warnock (2005) have examined the overall impact of foreign flows on US Treasury rates. Their analysis suggests that the 7 percent of US GDP inflow from foreign investors into US bonds of all kinds from May 2004 to May 2005 reduced US treasury benchmark yields by 150 basis points. If, as seems likely, China is on track to buy between $350 billion and $400 billion in US bonds in 2007, or about 3 percent of US GDP, Chinese demand alone would be reducing US interest rates by around 60 basis points.

Warnock and Warnock (2006) estimated that central bank demand for treasuries and agencies between May 2004 and May 2005 reduced Treasury yields by 90 basis points and had an impact of more like 120 basis

---

2. According to PBC data, Chinese banks' foreign currency–denominated portfolio investment rose by $57 billion over 2006. It is unclear if these data include investments financed by the proceeds of the Chinese state banks offshore IPOs (initial public offerings).

3. McCormack (2007); Ma and Ramos (2007); State Administration of Foreign Exchange, China's international investment position, 2006, available at www.safe.gov.cn.

4. Data from the Federal Reserve's flow of funds. The total stock of treasuries and agencies is far larger—$4.1 trillion of treasuries and $2.7 trillion of the agencies' own issues. However, central banks are already rumored to hold very large shares of certain parts of the treasury market, as they tend not to hold treasury inflation-protected securities or long bonds and are underweight bills. The stock of available Agency MBS is comparable to the stock of outstanding treasuries—$3.8 trillion—and until recently was growing far faster.

points in early 2004, when strong Japanese intervention pushed total official inflows up toward 4 percent of US GDP.[5] Assuming that Chinese inflows are now close to 3 percent of GDP, Chinese purchases could be depressing US interest rates by as much as 90 basis points. Not all these flows show up in the recent US data, but this is not a major concern: The change in Chinese holdings in the annual survey is typically much larger than the increase in holdings implied by summing up the monthly Treasury international capital flow data. The last survey captured China's holdings in mid-June 2006. The next survey will likely revise estimated Chinese flows up significantly (figure 5.C4).

China is holding far more liquid dollar-denominated assets than it needs to meet any plausible liquidity need. It is overweight in relatively safe US assets. Its holdings of safe US treasury and agency bonds will likely top $1 trillion at the end of 2007, a sum equaling close to 35 percent of China's GDP. Conversely, China is underweight in currencies other than the dollar and risk assets. Chinese holdings of US corporate debt, including asset-backed securities, have increased rapidly since 2005. However, they still are a relatively small share of China's total portfolio. Chinese holdings of portfolio equity are negligible. Chinese investment in foreign equity, both portfolio equity and FDI, are also small relative to foreign equity investment in China.

It is reasonable for China to want to hold a more balanced portfolio, both to obtain higher returns than would be possible holding only safe liquid assets and to minimize the concentration of China's portfolio. However, this can only happen if China's government diversifies its portfolio, whether by changing the assets it holds directly or by handing more funds to outside asset managers to invest in a wider range of assets. At current exchange rates, the only actor consistently willing to accumulate foreign assets is China's government, as private investors naturally prefer holding appreciating renminbi to depreciating dollars. Chinese firms, including state firms, generally only add to their dollar or euro portfolios if required to do so by China's government, or if offered a government guarantee against exchange rate losses.

CIC's Demand for US Equities Is Potentially Large Relative to Existing Flows

Spreading China's investment broadly across a broad range of asset classes would tend to minimize its impact on any specific market. However, the impact of spreading the impact of large Chinese purchases across a range of markets could be offset, as the impact of Chinese demand on smaller,

---

5. Frey and Moec (2005) also found that the approximately $300 billion in central bank purchases of treasuries reduced Treasury yields by 115 to 125 basis points in 2004; others have found a smaller impact.

Figure 5.C4 China's purchases of US debt versus adjusted foreign exchange reserve growth, 2001–07

billions of US dollars

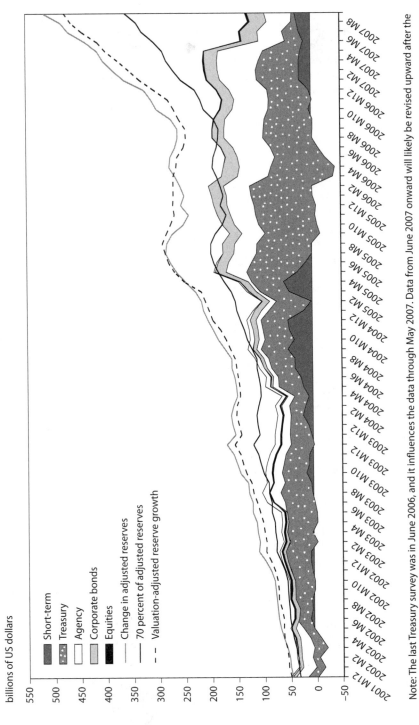

Note: The last Treasury survey was in June 2006, and it influences the data through May 2007. Data from June 2007 onward will likely be revised upward after the next survey.

Sources: China State Administration of Foreign Exchange (Chinese reserves); People's Bank of China (banking data); US Treasury (international capital data and annual survey of foreign portfolio investment in the United States); author's estimates.

less liquid markets may be larger than the impact of Chinese demand on larger markets.

Formal studies of the impact of official purchases on the equity market have not been done, largely because official purchases have been negligible until recently. A bit of ballpark math suggests that the CIC quickly could become the largest single source of official demand for US equities and that Chinese purchases could be comparable in size to private investors' net demand for US equities ($150 billion to $200 billion annually). However, efforts to assess the scale of China's prospective purchases are hampered by uncertainty about the scale of future Chinese demand for equities and the scale of current purchases of equities from SWF.

The CIC used most of its initial $80 billion allocation to buy the assets of central Huijin from the PBC, effectively shifting $67 billion of the total foreign exchange purchased by the CIC back to the central bank. The CIC has indicated that a large fraction of its remaining $120 billion in funds will be used to recapitalize the Agricultural Bank of China and the China Development Bank, effectively handing another $60 billion to 70 billion of foreign exchange over to the banks to manage. If past patterns hold, most of the funds that the banks receive will be invested in corporate bonds. Only about one-third of the CIC's initial $200 billion allocation is likely to be invested in global equities.

Over time, though, the CIC could receive additional funds from the ongoing increase in China's foreign assets. Assuming that the CIC receives $50 billion each quarter from investments abroad and places 80 percent of that inflow into global equities, it will have roughly $40 billion a quarter, or $160 billion a year, to invest in equities. As the CIC is managing only a fraction of China's total foreign assets, it has little need to hold a large share of its portfolio in safe assets. China's ongoing desire to manage its exchange rate relative to the US dollar likely implies that China will need to invest a large share of the incremental increase in its assets in US dollars. Bernhard Eschweiler of JPMorgan argues that "countries that shadow the dollar have to hold their reserves in dollars."[6] If, like the PBC, the CIC puts around 70 percent of its assets into US dollars, it could soon be buying roughly $30 billion a quarter in US equities, or $120 billion a year. In the aggregate, though, China would continue to buy far more bonds than equities (figure 5.C5), and its overall portfolio would remain weighted toward bonds (figure 5.C6).

This is a significant sum relative to current foreign demand for US equities. It is only a bit smaller than total foreign purchases of US equities in 2006 ($150 billion)[7] and over half the peak recent four-quarter total of

---

6. Berhard Eschweiler, "Don't Blame the Central Banks for the Falling Dollar," *Financial Times*, December 4, 2007.

7. Foreign demand for US equity picked up in early 2007. Total demand between mid-2006 and mid-2007 reached $200 billion.

Figure 5.C5   CIC changes the composition of flows, 2001–10

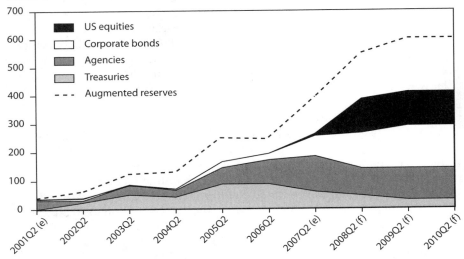

billions of US dollars

CIC = China Investment Corporation
(e) = estimate
(f) = forecast

Sources: China State Administration of Foreign Exchange and People's Bank of China (Chinese data); US Treasury (international capital data and annual survey of foreign portfolio investment in the United States); author's estimates.

$200 billion in the second quarter of 2007 ($200 billion). It is far larger than recorded official purchases of US equities ($6 billion in 2006, net outflows in the four quarters through the second quarter). However, the US data unquestionably understates current official demand, as it does not capture the money that various sovereign funds and central banks have farmed out to outside portfolio managers.

The IMF's data on inflows into official funds offers another and hopefully more accurate way to estimate sovereign purchases of US equities. According to IMF (2007), the world's governments transferred about $130 billion to their investment funds in 2006. Norway accounts for $50 billion of this increase; the oil funds in the Middle East account for most of the rest. Norway's fund is quite transparent, so we know that only $3 billion of the $50 billion in new funds handed over to Norway's fund was invested in US equities, as the rise in the equity markets led Norway to direct its purchases toward the bond market to meet its portfolio targets. If both the bond and equity market increased in value at the same pace, Norway would, after increasing its equity target from 40 to 60 percent of

Figure 5.C6 Projected Chinese holdings of US assets, 2000–2010

billions of US dollars

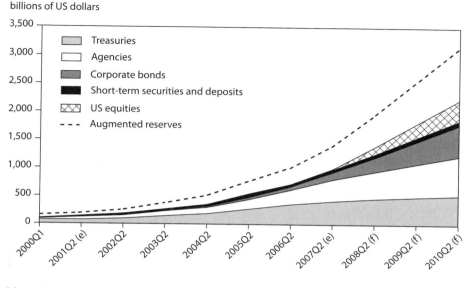

(e) = estimate
(f) = forecast

Sources: China State Administration of Foreign Exchange and People's Bank of China (Chinese data); US Treasury (international capital data and annual survey of foreign portfolio investment in the United States); author's estimates.

its portfolio, put about 17 percent of the annual increase in its assets into US equities.

Setting the Saudis aside, the major Gulf funds likely received an inflow of around $80 billion from their oil revenue. Some of this inflow was used to purchase bonds and some was invested outside the United States, as several Gulf funds seem to be in the process of diversifying their holdings. It is unlikely that more than $20 billion—roughly 25 percent of the new inflow into the big Gulf funds—went to purchase US equities or to outside fund managers who made unleveraged bets on the US equity market. The Gulf funds also invest in both hedge funds and private equity funds as so-called alternatives, and both private equity funds and hedge funds make leveraged bets on the equity market. As much as $20 billion from the Gulf funds might have been invested in hedge funds and private equity funds, and a large share of this likely would have been invested in the US market.

Finally, the Saudis added about $60 billion to the foreign assets of the Saudi Arabian Monetary Agency, which is widely believed to hold most of its assets in dollars and has been estimated to have up to 25 percent of its portfolio in equities. On the assumption that it holds 80 percent of its assets in dollars and is not bound by a strict portfolio share target that forces it to buy fewer equities, it might have put around 20 percent of the $60 billion increase in its overall holdings ($12 billion) into US equities. Singapore's Government Investment Corporation (GIC) also buys US equities, but the magnitude of the new GIC flows is likely to be relatively small.

This estimate suggests that the official sector bought around $35 billion of US equity in 2006 and by contributing to private equity funds, indirectly supported a much larger indirect bid. That total likely increased in 2007 as more central banks added equities to their portfolio and the sizes of the Gulf funds swelled. Nonetheless, there is little doubt that even a relatively modest reallocation of China's portfolio away from bonds[8] would still produce large equity inflows in relation to existing official purchases (figure 5.C7).

CIC's Challenges

Setting Singapore's GIC aside, the large existing SWF have emerged from small, wealthy oil-exporting economies and generally countries that are part of a security alliance with the United States. As China is neither small nor wealthy, neither an energy exporter nor a US ally, its SWF consequently raises a different set of issues than do the funds from transparent Norway, the small oil-exporting city-states of the Gulf, or for that matter, even Russia's new investment fund. Russia's fund seems to be modeled on Norway's transparent fund, not the less transparent funds from Singapore and the Gulf.

China's economy already produces goods that compete directly with US and European products.[9] That much of this production is done either by US and European firms or by subcontractors working for US and European firms has minimized commercial tension. However, China's development policy envisions that Chinese firms, including state-owned firms, will move up the value-added ladder and emerge as global players in many sectors. Most small oil-exporting economies, by contrast, lack the industrial base to compete with US or European production. As a result, CIC purchases of direct stakes in US or European manufacturing firms likely will receive far more scrutiny than comparable investments from oil-exporting economies. These concerns flow both ways: Chinese state

---

8. In my scenario, China invests only $160 billion of its $500 billion to $600 billion in foreign-asset growth in equities and does not reallocate any of its existing holdings.

9. The interest of US domestic oil producers and the Gulf states are generally aligned, as both benefit from higher oil prices. Certainly, US firms would like additional opportunities to help produce oil in countries that grant their national oil company a monopoly on local production.

Figure 5.C7 Estimated CIC and oil fund US equity purchases versus recorded private flows, rolling four-quarter sums, 2000–2008

billions of US dollars

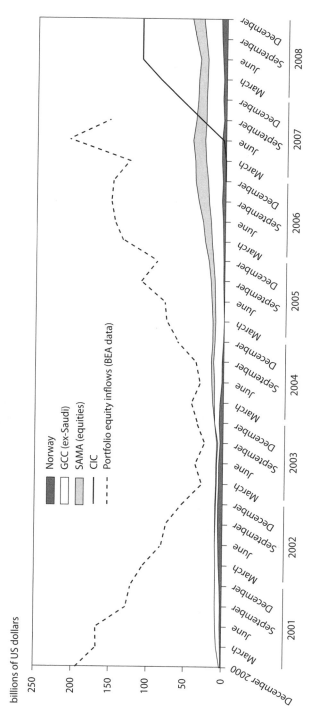

Legend:
- Norway
- GCC (ex-Saudi)
- SAMA (equities)
- CIC
- Portfolio equity inflows (BEA data)

BEA = Bureau of Economic Analysis
CIC = China Investment Corporation
GCC = Gulf Cooperation Council
SAMA = Saudi Arabian Monetary Agency

Sources: US Bureau of Economic Analysis; national data (Norway and Saudi Arabia); International Monetary Fund (Article IV reports for the GCC countries); author's estimates (CIC).

firms are also unlikely to welcome Chinese government investment in US firms that compete with them.

The governance structure of the CIC seems certain to magnify concerns. The CIC reports directly to the state council. Representatives of the parts of the Chinese bureaucracy that are tied to the state sector, including the Commerce Ministry and the National Development and Reform Commission, are represented on its board. Its mandate includes managing the state's large strategic stakes in China's main banks and making strategic investments to facilitate the outward expansion of Chinese firms. The CIC recently bought into China Rail's Hong Kong listing, helping it raise funds offshore. Housing a set of strategic investments in large state banks and state firms under the same roof as China's investment in US and European equities inevitably will generate concerns that strategic goals, and not only returns, are motivating its investment decisions.

China is also likely to face difficulties increasing its exposure to emerging Asian economies. Most Asian economies either have current account surpluses or are already attracting more private inflows than they need to finance their existing deficits. Most are already intervening heavily to limit upward pressure on their currencies. Additional inflows from China would either push other Asian currencies up or result in additional intervention by other Asian central banks. Neither development would be welcome. The Bank of Thailand and Reserve Bank of India were severely criticized for allowing their currencies to appreciate against the renminbi earlier in 2007, putting pressure on both countries' export sectors. Both banks are currently intervening heavily to keep their respective currencies from appreciating, and clearly would not want to help the CIC diversify at their expense. Any decision to invest in the assets of countries that are likely to request to be excluded from China's portfolio would be intrinsically political.

Even with a governance structure that insulated its investment decisions from noncommercial considerations, the CIC would still face a daunting set of challenges. These include

- *coordination with the central bank.* If the CIC adopts an asset allocation that has a lower dollar share than China's existing portfolio, the growth of the CIC portfolio will increase China's net sales of dollars. Such sales could put additional downward pressure on the dollar, and in turn, push the renminbi down against a range of currencies, so long as the renminbi is managed primarily against the dollar. A weaker renminbi would not help to reduce inflationary pressures and could prompt additional hot money inflows into China. The net result might well be that China's total dollar accumulation does not slow, as CIC diversification would be offset by stronger net inflows and faster overall official asset growth. Alternatively, the State Administration of Foreign Exchange (SAFE) could increase its dollar allocation to create space for the CIC to hold fewer dollars. In either case, some coordination between the CIC, PBC, and SAFE is necessary.

- *CIC's high effective cost of funds and risk of losses.* The Ministry of Finance has financed the CIC by selling long-term renminbi-denominated bonds that yield between 4 and 5 percent to the PBC and to the state banks. This is unlikely to be a true market rate, as it is unlikely that the banks would voluntarily buy large quantities of long-term bonds yielding around 4.5 percent when the PBC is raising short-term rates. The renminbi's expected appreciation in the forward market has been around 6 percent against the dollar. It rose above 9 percent in November 2007 before falling back to around 8 percent against the dollar, a bit less against the euro. If the market's expectation for the renminbi is correct, then the CIC needs to obtain dollar returns of over 12 percent just to break even. Even if the expected pace of appreciation falls to 6 percent, China still needs returns of around 10 percent. This requires taking substantial risks. Rather than seeking a positive return in renminbi, the CIC should aim for a return somewhat above the return SAFE achieves on its less risky portfolio. That implies losses in renminbi terms, however, which may be a hard sell for a fund marketed as way to increase China's return on its foreign assets.

- *a portfolio highly correlated with China's economic growth.* Michael Pettis (2008) of Beijing University has argued that the CIC should hold assets that are negatively correlated with China's own economic performance. However, it now looks likely that the CIC's portfolio will include assets that are highly correlated with China's growth. A Chinese slump would increase bank nonperforming loans and cut into bank profit margins, reducing the market value of the CIC's large stake in China's state banks. If the CIC also invests in resource companies, it will end up holding another asset the financial value of which would fall in the event of a slump. Rather than holdings assets that would increase in value when China slows, the CIC is likely to hold assets that fall in value.

Conclusion: Transparency Can Help

The challenges facing the CIC are daunting. The CIC has a much broader mandate than the typical oil investment fund, one that includes managing the government's stake in China's large banks and helping Chinese firms expand abroad. The CIC has to borrow in an appreciating currency to buy assets denominated in depreciating currencies. The enormous scale of China's foreign asset growth implies that the CIC will inevitably affect the internal dynamics of any market it invests in. The CIC will not immediately be the world's largest SWF, but it could easily generate the largest flows. Norway currently invests $50 billion a year. The large Gulf funds collectively invest less than $100 billion a year.

Transparency will not eliminate concerns about the CIC's impact on global markets or fears that the CIC's investments are motivated by noncommercial goals. But the absence of transparency is certain to increase such concerns. Truman's paper has done the world a tremendous service by creating a baseline for evaluating the level of transparency of different funds. Long-established and widely respected funds with low scores should consider dramatically increasing their transparency. Likewise, Chinese policymakers should not emulate the poor example set by some existing large funds, but rather aim to create a fund that is as transparent as the world's most transparent funds.

References

Frey, Laure, and Gilles Moec. 2005. US Long-Term Yields and Forex Interventions by Foreign Central Banks. *Banque de France Bulletin Digest* 137 (May): 19–32.

IMF (International Monetary Fund). 2007. *World Economic Outlook*, statistical appendix (September). Washington.

Ma, Ning and Roy Ramos. 2007. *China: Banks*. Goldman Sachs Investment Research (August 2). Hong Kong: Goldman Sachs.

McCormack, James. 2007. *China's External Assets*. Fitch Ratings (March 20).

Pettis, Michael. 2008. *China Financial Markets* (January 23). www.piaohaoreport.sampasite.com/blog.

Warnock, Francis E., and Veronica Cacdac Warnock. 2005. *International Capital Flows and U.S. Interest Rates*. International Finance Discussion Papers 840 (September). Washington: Board of Governors of the Federal Reserve System.

Warnock, Francis E., and Veronica Cacdac Warnock. 2006. *International Capital Flows and U.S. Interest Rates*. NBER Working paper 12560. Cambridge, MA: National Bureau of Economic Research.

6

The US Congress
and the Chinese Renminbi

GARY CLYDE HUFBAUER and CLAIRE BRUNEL

In September 2003 Senators Charles Schumer (D-NY) and Lindsey Graham (R-SC) introduced the first congressional bill (S 1586) targeting the value of the renminbi, then RMB8.28 to the dollar. Schumer and Graham's blunt remedy would have authorized a 27.5 percent US duty on all merchandise imports from China, if negotiations did not succeed in revaluing the renminbi. The 27.5 percent figure represented Schumer and Graham's arithmetic average of two private estimates (40 and 15 percent undervaluation).

Since September 2003, senators and representatives, both Republicans and Democrats, have largely come to agree that something ought to be done about China's currency. Some three dozen new congressional bills with various sponsors have been floated to challenge Chinese commercial practices, and bills introduced since January 2005 have focused increasingly on the currency value.[1] Figures 6.1 through 6.3 portray the real effective exchange rate (REER), reserve accumulation figures, and bilateral trade statistics that fuel congressional discontent with China. There is little difference of opinion in Congress about the objective: sharp appreciation of the renminbi.[2] Rather, congressional differences center on which

Gary Clyde Hufbauer resumed his position at the Peterson Institute as Reginald Jones Senior Fellow in 1998. Previously he was the Marcus Wallenberg Professor of International Financial Diplomacy at Georgetown University and served in the US Treasury Department from 1974 to 1980. Claire Brunel is a research assistant at the Peterson Institute.

1. For a listing of bills through the mid-2006, see Hufbauer, Wong, and Sheth (2006).

2. The leading candidates for the Democratic presidential nomination are all in accord.

Figure 6.1   Real effective exchange rate of the renminbi, 2000–2007

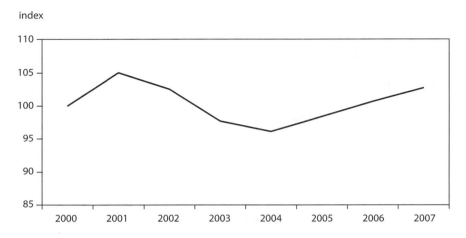

index

Note: Higher number means renminbi appreciation. 2007 estimate is based on data from the first half of 2007.

Source: JPMorgan.

levers should be applied to move Beijing, which legislators should claim patrimony for the law that emerges, and which congressional committees should oversee subsequent developments.

While none of the proposed legislation has yet reached the desk of President George W. Bush, the White House has certainly taken notice. Treasury Secretaries John Snow and Henry Paulson have valiantly tried to persuade Beijing that exchange rate flexibility is in China's own interest as well as the interest of the United States and the world economy. In response, Chinese authorities introduced a very constrained float in July 2005, and slightly widened the permitted daily fluctuation in May 2007. The net result of China's moves is that the renminbi is now 7.49 to the dollar, an appreciation of 9.4 percent since September 2003. However, because the dollar has declined against most other currencies, in trade-weighted terms, the renminbi has appreciated only 6.2 percent since September 2003. By whatever metric the change in the renminbi is calculated, the extent of appreciation falls far short of congressional aspirations.

The predictable result was a fresh crop of congressional proposals in 2007,[3] of which three are prominent: the Senate Finance Committee bill (S 1607) sponsored by Max Baucus (D-MT), Charles Grassley (R-IA), Gra-

---

3. For a comprehensive list of all China-related legislation introduced in the first session of the 110th Congress as of December 14, 2007, see US-China Business Council, "110th Congress, First Session, Legislation Related to China," available at www.uschina.org (accessed December 18, 2007).

Figure 6.2   China's foreign exchange reserves, 2000–2007

billions of dollars

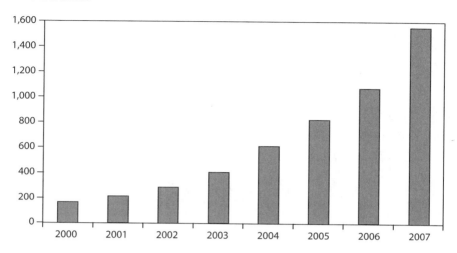

Note: 2007 estimate is based on data from the first half of 2007.

Source: People's Bank of China, online statistics.

ham, Schumer, and others; the Senate Banking Committee bill (S 1677) sponsored by Christopher Dodd (D-CT) and Richard Shelby (R-AL); and a House of Representatives bill (HR 2942) sponsored by Timothy Ryan (D-OH) and Duncan Hunter (R-CA).

If jurisdictional disputes can be settled—a big if—then the House and Senate may approve some amalgam of these bills before the 110th Congress adjourns its first session in December 2007. The Treasury report on currency, which by law should have been presented to Congress on October 15, 2007, was delayed, possibly until after the December 2007 US-China Strategic Economic Dialogue (SED). The new International Monetary Fund (IMF) managing director, Dominique Strauss-Kahn, who took office on November 1, 2007, will inevitably be drawn into the currency debate. Congress may well take advantage of the shift in leadership at the Fund and the December SED meetings to assert its own views. The House is likely to move first, as the Senate is locked in a jurisdictional struggle between its banking and finance committees. Congressional sponsors will attempt to draft veto-proof legislation enacted by two-thirds majorities in both the House and Senate.

Table 6.1 summarizes the details of the three referenced bills. Essentially, the bills have five moving parts. First, while they differ in covering a wider or narrower range of currency practices, all the bills eliminate "intent" in determining whether or not a currency is manipulated or mis-

Figure 6.3   US-China bilateral merchandise trade, 2000–2007

billions of dollars

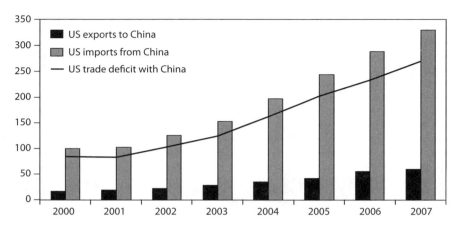

Note: 2007 estimate is based on data from the first half of 2007. US bilateral trade figures differ significantly from those published by China.

Source: US Census Bureau.

aligned.[4] Second, they instruct the Commerce and Treasury departments to invoke unilateral and multilateral trade remedies if China does not revalue. Third, they instruct the Treasury to present a more forceful case in the IMF. Fourth, they enunciate various deadlines for action, ranging up to 360 days. Fifth, some of the bills allow a presidential waiver. For the purposes of this short review, we discuss four important questions:

- Will the process of congressional enactment and subsequent implementation be a helpful lever to persuade Beijing to revalue the renminbi?

- What will come from engaging the World Trade Organization (WTO) in exchange rate questions, either directly through a General Agreement on Tariffs and Trade (GATT) Article XV(4) frustration case or through an Agreement on Subsidies and Countervailing Measures (ASCM) prohibited subsidy case, or indirectly through US countervailing and antidumping (AD) duty cases?

---

4. In its June 2007 semiannual currency report, Treasury suddenly added an "intent" test to determine whether a currency is manipulated and found that no intent could be ascribed to China (these reports are mandated by legislation enacted in 1988). Before 2007, Treasury drew upon a shifting basket of touchstones to determine manipulation. See Henning (2007).

Table 6.1 Three leading congressional bills on China's currency

Item	Ryan-Hunter (House): Currency Reform for Fair Trade Act of 2007 (HR 2942)	Schumer-Grassley-Graham-Baucus (Senate Finance): Currency Exchange Rate Oversight Reform Act of 2007 (S 1607)	Dodd-Shelby (Senate Banking): Currency Reform and Financial Market Access Act of 2007 (S 1677)
Overview	<ul><li>Many countries intervene in currency markets leading to misaligned currencies; e.g., the renminbi is undervalued by 40 percent or more.</li><li>Undervaluation, regardless of intent, acts as an export subsidy and a nontariff barrier against imports; a misaligned exchange rate should be defined as a countervailable subsidy, for both market and nonmarket economies (NME).</li></ul>	<ul><li>Replace the term "manipulation," and its connotation of intent with "fundamentally misaligned," which could result either from government policy or from market forces.</li><li>Revise US antidumping law so that the export price is adjusted to account for undervaluation, thereby augmenting the penalty duty.</li></ul>	<ul><li>"Manipulation" is an unfair trade practice, and strategic dialogue with China has not worked.</li><li>Currency manipulators need to be identified and addressed, with no regard to intent.</li><li>The United States should promote market access for financial firms in China.</li></ul>
Procedures	<ul><li>Treasury should consult with the Federal Reserve and the newly formed Advisory Committee on International Exchange Rate Policy and submit a report to Congress twice a year identifying misaligned currencies and engage in bilateral negotiations with those countries.</li><li>In the case of "fundamental and actionable misalignment," the Treasury should seek the support of the IMF and other countries; the United States should oppose any change of rules at the IMF that would benefit a misaligned country; it should oppose multilateral bank financing and Overseas Private Investment Corporation (OPIC)</li></ul>	<ul><li>Treasury should consult with the Federal Reserve and the new Advisory Committee on International Exchange Rate Policy to identify "fundamentally misaligned" currencies twice a year and consult with those governments.</li><li>If misalignment is driven by explicit government policy, then Treasury must designate that currency for "priority action;" consult with that country; seek advice and support from the IMF and other countries; and oppose any IMF rule change that would benefit that country.</li><li>If there is no result in 180 days, the United States should stop all federal purchases of</li></ul>	<ul><li>Treasury should submit a plan of action to Congress within 30 days of finding manipulation and engage in bilateral and multilateral negotiations.</li><li>Treasury must seek IMF consultation with the country and use its IMF voting power against this country if necessary.</li><li>If there is no result after nine months, the Treasury has the authority to file a WTO Article XV (4) case.</li><li>Congress can originate a joint resolution of disapproval when Treasury does not cite manipulation.</li></ul>

(table continues next page)

Table 6.1   Three leading congressional bills on China's currency *(continued)*

Item	Ryan-Hunter (House): Currency Reform for Fair Trade Act of 2007 (HR 2942)	Schumer-Grassley-Graham-Baucus (Senate Finance): Currency Exchange Rate Oversight Reform Act of 2007 (S 1607)	Dodd-Shelby (Senate Banking): Currency Reform and Financial Market Access Act of 2007 (S 1677)
	loans to companies in that country; and the United States should take misalignment into account for NME status and antidumping cases. ■ If there is no result in 360 days, the United States should initiate a WTO dispute settlement case and consider remedial intervention.	that country's goods and services; reflect the undervalued exchange rate in antidumping duties; request the IMF to consult with the misaligned country; and oppose multilateral bank financing and OPIC loans to US companies operating in that country. ■ If there is no result in 360 days, the United States should initiate a WTO dispute settlement case and consider remedial intervention.	
Waiver	■ None	■ Presidential waiver if the actions in the bill can have damaging consequences for vital economic or security interests. ■ Congress can override the waiver through a joint resolution of the House and Senate.	■ Presidential waiver if the actions in the bill can have damaging consequences for vital economic or security interests.
Definitions	■ Fundamental and actionable misalignment: "the situation in which an exporting country's prevailing real effective exchange rate is undervalued relative to the exporting country's equilibrium real effective exchange rate and the secretary of Treasury determines that	■ Fundamentally misaligned: "significant and sustained undervaluation of the prevailing real effective exchange rate, adjusted for cyclical and transitory factors, from its medium-term equilibrium level." ■ Fundamentally misaligned currency for priority action: "if the country that issues	■ Manipulator: A country that has "a material global current account surplus and has significant bilateral trade surpluses with the US and has engaged in prolonged one-way intervention in the currency markets."

the policy is engaging in protracted large-scale intervention in one direction in the currency exchange market, accompanied by partial or full sterilization; engaging in prolonged official or quasi-official accumulation of foreign assets for balance of payments purposes; introducing or substantially modifying for balance of payment purposes a restriction on, or incentive for, the inflow or outflow of capital that is inconsistent with the goal of achieving full currency convertibility; or pursuing any other policy or action that, in the view of the Secretary, warrants designation for priority action."

(i) the amount of the undervaluation exceeds 5 percent and has consistently exceeded 5 percent on average in the 18-month period preceding the date of the calculation; and

(ii) the undervaluation is a result of protracted, large-scale intervention in the currency exchange markets; excessive reserve accumulation; restrictions on or incentives for the inflow or outflow of capital that is inconsistent with the goal of achieving currency convertibility; or any other policy or action by the country that issues the currency."

Special committees

- Creation of an Advisory Committee on International Exchange Rate Policy—consisting of 7 members (3 Senate appointees, 3 House appointees, and 1 presidential appointee)—to advise the secretary of Treasury, Congress, and president on international exchange rate matters. The committee can submit a report disagreeing with the Treasury.

- Creation of an Advisory Committee on International Exchange Rate Policy—consisting of 9 members (8 Senate Finance and Banking Committees appointees and 1 presidential appointee)—to advise the secretary of Treasury, Congress, and president on international exchange rate matters.

WTO compliance

- GATT Article XV(4) would take WTO into IMF turf; exchange rate needs to "frustrate" another GATT article for Article XV(4) to apply; the WTO would probably look to the IMF to declare "manipulation."
- For Agreement on Subsidies and Countervailing Measures (ASCM): Need to prove financial contribution from the government to a specific enterprise or industry (as well as other tests).

- What are the consequences of legislation that gives Congress a larger oversight role over exchange rate questions at the expense of the Treasury and the Federal Reserve?

- What are the chances of mirror legislation abroad that might, in the future, target the dollar as an undervalued currency?

Legislation as a Lever?

By contrast with earlier drafts, the current bills deliberately stretch out the period for China to revalue before consequences are felt. Since WTO litigation and IMF deliberations could easily take a year or more, the bills contemplate an action horizon of two to four years. Moreover, the Senate bills allow the president to invoke a national interest waiver—subject to congressional override in the finance committee bill—thereby holding out the possibility for China to escape any penalties. In short, the bills are akin to turning the screw rather than slamming the hammer. Congress, however, will keep a watchful eye while the screw is turned: Designated congressional committees, chiefly the Senate and House finance and banking committees, will closely monitor the administration's actions, the value of the renminbi, and the path of China's bilateral and multilateral trade balances.

On July 31, 2007 Secretary Paulson, joined by Commerce Secretary Carlos Gutierrez and United States Trade Representative (USTR) Ambassador Susan Schwab, speaking in Beijing, declared that new legislation would jeopardize their efforts to persuade China to move quickly toward a market-determined exchange rate.[5] Moreover, congressional bills have attracted sharp criticism from prominent economists—including Nobel laureates—and respected columnists, such as Nicholas Kristof of the *New York Times*.[6] But administration opposition and ill-considered comparisons to the Smoot-Hawley tariff are not likely to derail the congressional locomotive.

A crucial question in the fall of 2007 is whether the prospect of legislation will persuade Beijing either to accelerate its appreciation of the renminbi or to allow more flexibility. As a stand-alone measure, a new US law might have little effect. Powerful forces within China stoutly oppose revaluation, particularly export industries that operate on thin profit margins and discount the offsetting effect that appreciation would exert on the prices they must pay for imported inputs. Wu Xiaoling, former deputy governor of the People's Bank of China (PBC), explained that an appreci-

---

5. Mark Drajem, "Paulson Calls China Currency Legislation the 'Wrong Approach,'" Bloomberg, July 31, 2007.

6. Pat Toomey, "Economists Against Protectionism," *Wall Street Journal*, August 1, 2007; Nicholas Kristof, "The New Democratic Scapegoat," *New York Times*, July 26, 2007, A18.

ation of the renminbi would not decrease the dependence of the Chinese economy on exports and that internal restructuring is indispensable to boost consumption and move smoothly toward more flexibility.[7]

But prospective US legislation is not a stand-alone measure. Any new law looks likely to be enacted at a time when multilateral forces are gathering to confront China. Rodrigo de Rato, erstwhile IMF managing director, set in motion a review of the 1977 guidelines to Fund Article IV that was concluded in June 2007. The review proposed a more assertive IMF posture toward the renminbi. New managing director Strauss-Kahn will likely amplify de Rato's initiative. President Nicolas Sarkozy of France has added a fresh European voice to calls for revaluation.[8] Other European leaders, noting the rapid appreciation of the euro against the dollar and the possibility that the euro will top $1.50, will likely become more eager for Asian currencies to absorb part of the global adjustment burden. The next US president seems certain to accede to the thrust of congressional complaints, especially as both Republicans and Democrats are prominent sponsors of new legislation. Finally, the textile, clothing, and steel industries can be counted on to push the currency bills (Cooney 2007).

Taking a page from scholarship on economic sanctions to achieve political goals, the evidence suggests that multilateral pressure is somewhat more likely than unilateral pressure to change the target country's policies in a desired direction (Hufbauer et al. 2007). It seems possible that China, faced with a growing coalition, will accelerate the path of renminbi flexibility and appreciation, in hopes of softening the final bill and preventing the nascent US-EU alliance's crystallization into a solid front.

Engaging the WTO?

A theme among several bills is to engage the WTO in the currency dispute, directly or indirectly. The direct approach has two prongs: a US case brought to the WTO under GATT Article XV(4), alleging that China's undervalued renminbi "frustrates the intent of the provisions of [the GATT]" and a US case brought to the WTO under Article 3 of the ASCM, alleging that the undervalued renminbi amounts to a "prohibited [export] subsidy."

The indirect approach would characterize the undervalued renminbi as a subsidy for purposes of the US countervailing duty (CVD) law or would use the "corrected" value of the renminbi to calculate the margin in an AD case. Under the CVD and AD remedies, an affected US industry could bring a case to the US Department of Commerce on the subsidy determi-

---

7. "A Warning on Chinese Currency," *Washington Trade Daily*, October 22, 2007.

8. George Parker and Mark Schieritz, "Sarkozy Pushing for Tougher Line on China," *Financial Times*, July 23, 2007, 2.

nation and to the International Trade Commission on the injury determination; an affirmative finding by both agencies would lead to the imposition of a CVD or AD duty on imported Chinese merchandise, calculated to reflect the extent of renminbi undervaluation. Thereafter, China could mount challenges in both US courts and the WTO.

Elsewhere, my colleagues and I have written that the United States would face an uphill battle, in legal terms, in bringing a GATT Article XV(4) case (Hufbauer, Wong, and Sheth 2006, 17–20). Certainly one can argue that prolonged undervaluation of a major currency threatens the world trading system. But a GATT Article XV(4) case faces a fundamental obstacle: When the Bretton Woods institutions were founded, exchange rate issues were assigned to the IMF and trade questions to the GATT. While each institution intrudes to some degree into the business of the other, the intrusions are at the margins, not the core. If the WTO were to declare that China's exchange rate practices violate the GATT without a prior but contemporaneous IMF determination that the renminbi's value threatens the world trading system, a considerable part of the Fund's mandate would migrate from Washington to Geneva. That prospect would prompt a collective gasp of horror in finance ministries and central banks worldwide.

To be sure, in October 2006 the Fund declared in its staff report concerning Article IV consultations with China that the renminbi is undervalued.[9] But this was a staff report, not a direct pronouncement of the managing director or the executive board. Moreover, the Fund staff did not allege that the currency is "manipulated," the legal term for an offensive practice under Article IV. Nor did the Fund staff use language that would put China in the dock for upsetting world trade. If senior Fund officials are prepared to criticize China in plain language, mere anticipation of such criticism, combined with pressure from the European Union and the United States, would likely foster a new exchange rate regime by Beijing.

---

9. The report states that ". . . since the previous peak in the renminbi's real effective value in early 2002, the currency has depreciated, while such factors as a substantial net foreign asset accumulation and a sharp rise in China's productivity relative to partner countries over the period since 2001 would be expected to have contributed to a real appreciation of the currency. . . . It is especially difficult to pinpoint a change in fundamental determinants [of savings behavior] that would explain the doubling of the [current account] surplus in relation to GDP in 2005 and that would suggest that the surplus at its present level could be considered to be a new 'normal' level of the savings-investment balance for China. In addition, gross official reserves have risen from $219 billion in 2001 to $930 billion at end-May 2006. . . . All of these developments point to the currency as being undervalued and that this undervaluation has increased further since last year's Article IV consultation." (IMF 2006). In October 2007, the Group of Seven (G-7) countries released the following statement: "We welcome China's decision to increase the flexibility of its currency, but in view of its rising current account surplus and domestic inflation, we stress its need to allow an accelerated appreciation of its effective exchange rate." See "Text of G-7 Communiqué," *MarketWatch*, October 19, 2007. Again, this language from the G-7 (not the IMF) does not amount to an explicit condemnation of China for bad behavior.

If China did not move, the IMF's lead members might collectively devise a financial solution to prompt good behavior without resorting to WTO-authorized trade measures. Only as a last resort, in our opinion, would the Fund give a green light to the WTO to authorize trade sanctions.

Other more technical weaknesses of the hypothetical GATT Article XV(4) case can be pointed out,[10] but in any event, debating the pros and cons of a case could easily occupy the WTO's dispute settlement mechanism for two years or longer. We are left with the conclusion that an Article XV(4) case can best be justified as a lever to prompt more forceful action by the IMF, if only to preserve its turf, and as one means of focusing Beijing's attention on the currency question.

Congressional legislation also contemplates a US case in the WTO characterizing the undervalued renminbi as a "prohibited [export] subsidy," citing Article 3 of the ASCM. For the United States, this case would entail another uphill legal battle. First, to be characterized as a subsidy under the ASCM, a public measure must entail a "financial contribution" from the government (ASCM Article 1.1). One can argue that an undervalued exchange rate extends a financial contribution to exporters and imposes a financial penalty on importers. But public budgets have seldom if ever characterized changes in the exchange rate as a form of public revenue or expenditure. If trade negotiators had meant to ignore budget conventions and characterize an undervalued exchange rate as a subsidy, they would have said so in the ASCM or predecessor agreements as far back as the 1960s.

Second, to be actionable under either the WTO or national CVD laws, a subsidy must be "specific" as defined in ASCM Article 2. The basic idea is that the public financial contribution should confer a benefit on an enterprise, industry, or group of enterprises and industries. Changes in exchange rates and interest rates would seem to be the opposite of specific policies, as they rank among the broadest measures that a government can employ to influence the economy.

Considering just the tests of financial contribution and specificity,[11] a strong policy argument can be made that the ASCM never intended to intrude on the Fund's mandate as the arbiter of exchange rates. However, as with a WTO case under GATT Article XV(4), a WTO case under ASCM Article 3 might focus Beijing's attention on the tensions that an undervalued renminbi fosters, even if the case does not rest on the strongest legal foundation.

---

10. These are explored in Hufbauer, Wong, and Sheth (2006). Besides these technical difficulties, it should be remembered that every undervalued currency implies that some other currency is overvalued. China might respond to a US Article XV(4) case against the renminbi with its own Article XV(4) case against the dollar.

11. Other tests of a more technical nature need to be met for a practice to be designated as a prohibited export subsidy. See Hufbauer, Wong, and Sheth (2006, 20–24).

Congressional legislation might also authorize penalty duties against an undervalued renminbi in the context of US CVD and AD determinations. Compared with a WTO case, national CVD and AD cases would alter the sequence between legal argument and commercial penalty. In the WTO, even in a winning case, legal arguments can easily take three years before a countermeasure is authorized against the respondent country. In a national CVD or AD case, however, after six months of legal argument, penalty duties are often applied. In practical terms, the burden is on the exporter to disprove the allegation of unfair trade practices. The exporting country (China) could contest penalty duties in US courts, and if it prevailed, the duties collected would be refunded; in the meantime, however, US imports of the affected merchandise would certainly be reduced, perhaps sharply.

China could also challenge a CVD or AD determination in the WTO. Against a CVD determination, China could cite the ASCM tests of financial contribution and specificity. Against an AD determination, China could argue the absence of authority in the GATT Agreement on the Implementation of Article IV for calculating the dumping margin using a corrected exchange rate; China could also argue the absence of precedent in prior antidumping cases. To us, it appears that the legal arguments against AD penalties are weaker than the arguments against other trade penalties we have reviewed. Still, China might eventually prevail, but WTO relief is not retroactive: Penalty duties collected in the meantime—perhaps two or three years' worth—would never be refunded.

We are left to conclude that trade remedy measures, sought in the WTO or under US laws, can best be justified as levers to prompt more forceful IMF action and focus Beijing's attention on the currency question.

Giving a Larger Voice to Congress?

Apart from whatever influence congressional legislation might exert on the Chinese renminbi in the contemporary debate, another consequence is that Congress—more specifically, the Senate and House finance and banking committees—would establish a claim for more and larger chairs at the exchange rate table. In the Ryan-Hunter and Senate Finance Committee bills, this claim is reinforced by the proposed establishment of a new Advisory Committee on International Exchange Rate Policy, with several members designated by the Senate or House. The congressional assertion of a larger role in exchange rate matters can be seen as part of the enduring contest between the president and the Congress over their respective powers in the arena of foreign affairs. President Bush is clearly on the defensive in terms of war powers and trade agreements, and currency relations could be added to the list.

The different congressional bills also reflect a power struggle within the Senate regarding which committee should have jurisdiction over the currency issue. The discord is reflected in definitions of offensive undervaluation that should elicit action—specifically, the distinction between manipulated and misaligned currencies. Manipulation, with its emphasis on one-way central bank intervention and its antecedents in IMF Article IV, would more clearly confer jurisdiction to the Senate Banking Committee.

On the other hand, "misalignment," with its emphasis on trade consequences, would confer at least some oversight authority to the Senate Finance Committee. Misalignment is a broader concept, as it encompasses undervaluation resulting from market forces as well as central bank intervention, thus potentially sweeping in the Japanese yen and other Asian currencies as well as the Chinese renminbi.[12] The auto industry and Michigan congressmen strongly support the misaligned currency concept because of the role that Japanese auto firms play in the US market.[13]

The clear losers from giving congressional committees more and larger chairs at the exchange rate table would be the Treasury and the Federal Reserve, which for decades have enjoyed almost exclusive authority over exchange rate questions, usually exercised behind closed doors.[14] In legislative specifics, the Senate Banking Committee bill would guide Treasury's hand in dealing with the IMF and would constrain Treasury's latitude in composing its semiannual exchange rate report to Congress. The Senate Finance Committee bill would give the USTR a role in bringing cases to the WTO and the Commerce Department a second-string role after the Treasury in determining the extent of undervaluation in CVD and AD cases. Both provisions would erode Treasury's primacy within the administration and would confer oversight responsibilities to the congressional finance and banking committees (Henning 2007).

---

12. At around 107 yen to the dollar (January 23, 2007), the yen is arguably misaligned, as Japan continues to run huge current account surpluses. However, because the Japanese authorities have not intervened in the exchange market for the past three years, it is hard to say the yen is manipulated; yen undervaluation largely reflects the eagerness of Japanese households and firms to earn higher returns by placing their capital abroad.

13. In an interesting twist, while the Senate Finance bill headlines the term misalignment, when defining priority action countries, the bill reverts to the concept of manipulation, namely countries that are "engaging in protracted large-scale intervention in one direction in the currency market." Perhaps the drafters understand that other countries could say that the dollar is misaligned, as the value is far from a rate that would be consistent with a current account deficit under 3 percent of GDP. By creating a priority action category, they may hope to avoid scrutiny of the dollar if other countries enact mirror legislation.

14. Mandated in 1988, the semiannual Treasury currency reports represent the first significant congressional intrusion into the secretive realm of Treasury and Federal Reserve diblierations. See Henning (2007).

Those with long memories will hear an echo from earlier episodes when Congress shifted responsibility for trade negotiations from the State Department to the USTR in 1963 and responsibility for administering the US CVD and AD laws from Treasury to the Commerce Department in 1979. The earlier events reflected congressional dissatisfaction with the commercial vigor of the State Department as a negotiator and the Treasury Department as an enforcer. At the same time, both changes enlarged Congressional oversight.

From the perspective of a smoothly functioning international system, more and larger congressional chairs at the exchange rate table will raise questions. The beauty of the post-Smithsonian system is that a small number of finance ministers and central bankers, sometimes joined by senior Fund officials, can quickly respond to exchange rate crises. If the enlarged congressional voice is only heard in exceptional circumstances and does not impede crisis management, it would be hard to criticize the new arrangement.

On the other hand, if congressional committees use their seats at the exchange rate table to pressure foreign countries over collateral grievances—bilateral trade balances, investment regimes, labor rights, carbon emissions, and the like—they could severely disrupt the international system. On present evidence, there is no indication of such tendencies. Moreover, if four congressional committees—Senate Finance, House Ways and Means, Senate Banking, and House Banking—collectively share the congressional seat, it seems less likely that collateral grievances will intrude on deliberations.

Mirror Legislation Abroad?

When Congress enacts legislation affecting foreign commerce, it often overlooks the likelihood that its handiwork will be mirrored abroad in ways that do not favor US economic interests. Secretary Paulson has warned against a global cycle of protectionist legislation at a time of growing US exports. The most memorable and regrettable experience was the Smoot-Hawley Tariff Act of 1930, but other ricochet examples can be cited: CVD and AD penalties, Buy America provisions, cabotage limits on maritime and air traffic, and agricultural import quotas to reinforce domestic farm subsidies. If Congress enacts legislation that guides the administration's hand, ultimately leading to penalty trade measures, it seems likely that the European Union, China, and perhaps Japan will fashion their own exchange rate laws that might, at some future date, target trade remedies against an undervalued dollar. After all, if the United States eventually balances its prolonged run of current account deficits and capital account surpluses with a prolonged run of opposite signs, important trading partners will likely consider the US dollar undervalued.

How should the possibility of mirror legislation be factored into the congressional debate? One recommendation, not likely to gain traction on Capitol Hill, is simply to set aside trade measures that would penalize an undervalued exchange rate and instead concentrate new legislation entirely on IMF deliberations. A more plausible recommendation is to limit trade measures to situations in which four criteria are met: the country is a major commercial power, the foreign currency is manipulated through persistent one-way official intervention as determined by the Fund; the country is running large current account surpluses on a global basis, and the country's official reserves substantially exceed an adequate level for prudential purposes.

References

Cooney, Stephen. 2007. *Steel: Price and Policy Issues*. CRS Report for Congress RL32333. Washington: Congressional Research Service (August 30).

Henning, C. Randall. 2007. *Congress, Treasury, and the Accountability of Exchange Rate Policy: How the 1988 Trade Act Should Be Reformed*. Working Paper 07-8 (September). Washington: Peterson Institute for International Economics.

Hufbauer, Gary Clyde, Yee Wong, and Ketki Sheth. 2006. *US-China Trade Disputes: Rising Tide, Rising Stakes*. POLICY ANALYSES IN INTERNATIONAL ECONOMICS 78 (August). Washington: Institute for International Economics.

Hufbauer, Gary Clyde, Jeffrey J. Schott, Kimberly Ann Elliott, and Barbara Oegg. 2007. *Economic Sanctions Reconsidered*, 3d ed. Washington: Peterson Institute for International Economics.

IMF (International Monetary Fund). 2006. *People's Republic of China: 2006 Article IV Consultation—Staff Report; Staff Statement; and Public Information Notice on the Executive Board Discussion*. IMF Country Report 06/394. Washington.

Comment
The Politics of Trade Frictions

STEPHEN S. ROACH

China is the scapegoat du jour for all that ails the American middle class. At least that is the conclusion that can be drawn from spending any time these days in Washington. Unfortunately, the US body politic has long had a penchant for such scapegoating when it comes to trade policy. Remember the Japan bashing of the late 1980s? And just three years ago there was an outcry over India, as it became a lightning rod for concerns about the new threat of white-collar offshoring. Meanwhile, the Doha Round is dead, bilateral free trade agreements are going nowhere, Congress has allowed fast-track presidential negotiating authority to lapse, and opinion polls show an American public with a serious distaste for trade liberalization and globalization.

The politics of congressional-led China bashing fit into the current inflammatory climate all too neatly. While there is always a certain amount of bluster in Washington, this time the threats seem serious and worrisome. By my count, over 18 pieces of antitrade legislation have been introduced in the first nine months of the 110th Congress. In almost all cases, the target—either explicitly or implicitly—is China.

Nor has this outbreak of China bashing appeared out of thin air. In the previous two years, the 109th Congress floated some 27 anti-China proposals. The difference between the two sessions of Congress is troubling. In the end, the 109th Congress was all talk and no action. By contrast, two bills passed major Senate committees in 2007—finance and banking—with overwhelming bipartisan majorities. The risk, in my view, is that the

Stephen S. Roach is chairman of Morgan Stanley Asia.

110th Congress could well pass one of the measures currently in the legislative hopper with a large enough bipartisan margin to withstand the threat of a presidential veto.

Gary Hufbauer provides an insightful assessment of the potential ramifications of the three leading anti-China approaches currently under consideration in Congress—two very similar efforts in the Senate and a somewhat different approach in the House. It is difficult to say which, if any, of these versions will prevail in the end or what type of hybrid might emerge from a conference committee. But it is important to lay bare the assumptions embodied in Congress's penchant for China bashing to understand where the approach is coming from—and what unintended consequences it may well trigger.

First and foremost, the debate is grounded in very legitimate concerns over the increased economic insecurity of middle-class American workers. Real wage stagnation is at the top of the list. In the second quarter of 2007, inflation-adjusted median weekly earnings for full-time US workers were unchanged from levels prevailing seven years ago in the second quarter of 2000. Yet over that same period, productivity in the nonfarm business sector recorded a cumulative 18 percent increase. Contrary to one of the basic axioms of economics, American workers have not been paid their just reward as measured by their productivity contribution.

As voters, workers are holding their elected representatives accountable for the extraordinary disconnect between real wages and productivity, and politicians are scrambling to come up with both reasons and solutions. At the top of the political answer column is trade and globalization. Congress is presuming that the United States' record foreign trade gap—namely, an $838 billion deficit on merchandise trade in 2006—has been a decisive factor in squeezing both jobs and real wages of middle-class American workers. That supposition has dictated the politically expedient solution—of attacking the external imbalance by going after the so-called bad citizens among US trading partners.

That is, of course, where China enters the equation. The US bilateral trade deficit with China accounts for by far the largest slice of the overall imbalance: 28 percent of the total US merchandise trade deficit in 2006 and about 31 percent of the cumulative shortfall in the first eight months of 2007. Carrying the label of the Great Currency Manipulator seals China's fate in the eyes of Congress and many economists, some of whom attended and even hosted the conference that produced this volume. End of story for China bashers.

Not quite so fast. It does not take a rocket scientist to figure out that the United States has a multilateral trade problem. At least 40 countries were in deficit with the United States in 2006. Yes, China has the largest of the United States' bilateral trade deficits. But is that because of its currency policy? Or is it an outgrowth of a China-centric supply chain constructed by US multinationals desperately in search of efficiency solutions in an increasingly competitive world? Or does it reflect the simple and possibly related fact that China happens to produce—or assemble, to be more accurate—a broad cross-section of products that satisfies the tastes, pricing, and aspirational wants of over-extended American consumers?

Either way, the congressional math of the blame game is fatally flawed. Omitting the figures for China still leaves a US trade deficit of over $600 billion in 2006, a number nearly three times as large as the shortfall with China. So even if Congress fixes the Chinese piece of the US trade deficit—a dubious assumption, as I note below—that still leaves a rather large remainder for the US trade gap. What is the policy to address that? Is Congress telling us that China is merely first in line—that, one by one, it will go down the list of US trading partners and impose trade sanctions until the deficit has been eliminated?

It follows that the so-called currency fix that Congress is now contemplating is equally preposterous, assuming that pressure on a bilateral cross rate will solve a multilateral deficit. Such a fix will simply send a relative price signal that will shift the mix of the deficit elsewhere, most likely to a higher-cost producer. That is akin to rearranging the deck chairs on the Titanic. It is also the functional equivalent of a tax hike on middle-class Americans, the very group of US citizens the Congress is trying to protect.

The multilateral characteristics of the US trade deficit are the smoking gun to this problem. And it is painfully clear what the root cause is: an extraordinary lack of US domestic saving. According to US Department of Commerce statistics, the United States' net national saving rate—the combined saving of individuals, businesses, and governmental units, adjusted for depreciation—averaged a mere 1.4 percent of national income over the five years ending in 2006. That is the lowest national saving rate for a five-year period in modern US history and apparently the lowest saving rate for the hegemonic power in modern world history. Lacking in domestic saving, the United States must import surplus saving to grow and run massive current account and trade deficits to attract the capital.

That, I am afraid, is the real end of the story. If the United States wants to fix its trade deficit and relieve the concomitant pressures that are bearing down on middle-class workers, it must address its seemingly chronic saving deficit. I am highly critical of my macro brethren, several of whom are sitting in this room today, who only pay lip service to this critical aspect of the problem when appearing alongside me as expert witnesses in offering congressional testimony on these key issues.

Of course, in Washington, it has long been easy to duck the facts and weave a good yarn. China bashing is largely a by-product of that predilection. But it is actually far worse than that. Who is really to blame for inadequate saving, the root cause of the US trade deficit? In my opinion, Washington is at the top of that list, with its penchant for budget deficits, consumption incentives, and an asset-based saving mindset that has been underwritten by the Federal Reserve. The same Washington is utterly incapable of taking a deep look in the mirror and accepting responsibility for problems such as these. It is much easier to indulge in scapegoating and point the finger elsewhere. As underscored above, China is but the latest in a long line of such targets. Just ask Japan what it was like some 20 years ago—or India just a few years ago.

China bashing is also emblematic of a deeper problem that grips the United States body politic: an unwillingness to embark on the heavy lifting of education reform and other investments in human capital that are required to enable American workers to compete and prosper in today's increasingly competitive world. Instead of investing in a hard-pressed work force, Washington apparently believes more in shielding US workers from low-wage talent pools in the developing world.

The doubling of the world's labor supply that has occurred in the past two decades has evoked a response of fear and protectionism, putting the United States at grave risk of becoming more insular and inward looking. Yet over the long sweep of US economic history, its workers have actually done best when they are pushed to their limits by a risk-taking, entrepreneurial, and innovative society. By blaming others for our own shortcomings—especially on the saving and human capital fronts—the United States runs the very real risk of losing its most special edge, an indomitable economic spirit. By shirking its responsibility for putting US saving policy on a sound path, Congress is, instead, veering toward the slippery slope of protectionism.

Finally, a word about China, where I spend an awful lot of my time these days. China is a living miracle of economic development. The world has never seen anything like the transformation of the Chinese economy that has occurred over the past 15 years. This extraordinary development trajectory is based primarily on a steadfast commitment to market-based reforms—something that Washington as the bastion of capitalism should applaud, not criticize.

But China also has a new strength—one that takes a page from right out of the United States' own experience—as dynamic private companies are now springing up all over China. Of the 21 new Chinese companies that Morgan Stanley brought public in 2007, fully 19 of them were private. For China, the newfound spirit of its privately employed workers and businesspeople is contagious and very reminiscent of that which has long been central to the American dream.

Like any economy, China has its share of problems and risks, many of which have been emphasized in this conference volume. Structural imbalances, environmental degradation, and income disparities are all openly debated in China, especially now as the Party Congress convenes in Beijing. Currency policy has long been a topic of discussion in official Chinese policy circles as well. But despite its remarkable progress, China is still a very poor country with many important issues to deal with.

Therein lies a critical difference between the two perspectives. Washington's penchant for the quick fix singles out the Chinese currency as a lightning rod in the great middle-class globalization debate. China, by contrast, views the currency issue not as an end in and of itself, but as one of many pieces in a broad mosaic of financial reforms. These are two very different perspectives, which have now boiled over in the form of trade frictions.

Ironically, in contrast to US intransigence on the saving issue and the multilateral trade deficit it has spawned, China is making important progress in relieving this source of tension. As China puts its financial system increasingly on a market-based footing, its leaders have given every indication the currency regime will follow. The shift to a managed float in July 2005 was an important first step in that direction. At the same time, China is taking dead aim at the imperatives of a consumer-led growth dynamic, a very different economic structure that will boost imports and thereby reduce its destabilizing trade surplus.

China is considering the timing and sequencing of these moves with due deliberation, but mainly with an eye toward keeping its embryonic financial system stable. There are clear risks in this approach, excess liquidity and asset bubbles being the most obvious. But these are China's risks to accept and manage rather than our place to dictate the terms of engagement. China's pace may not fit US political imperatives, but that is not China's fault.

Globalization is not easy, and the win-win mantra long offered by the economics profession does this mega trend a great disservice. It oversimplifies the problems and overlooks the inherent tensions of a globalization that is now occurring at hyper speed, enabled by the new connectivity of information technology. Globalization is full of opportunity and challenge as well as fear and risk. But in the end, globalization is nothing more than trust—trust in economic partners to act out of collective interests in making the world a better and more prosperous place. I fear that a China-bashing Congress has lost sight of this noble objective at great peril.

7

Influence of the Renminbi on Exchange Rate Policies of Other Asian Currencies

TAKATOSHI ITO

The East Asian countries, most notably China, are often collectively described as managing, if not manipulating, their exchange rates to be undervalued. They are said to have maintained large current account surpluses and accumulated foreign reserves; along with oil-producing nations, they are a large piece in the puzzle of global imbalances.

However, despite this initial impression, the exchange rate regimes of East Asian countries are diverse and uncoordinated. Some currencies have appreciated more than 25 percent between July 2005 and November 2007, whereas China appreciated only 11 percent during the same period. The lack of exchange rate policy coordination among Asian countries tends to prevent rather than help the global exchange rate realignment and demand rebalancing that is essential to resolve global imbalances.[1] Countries that trade with China and compete with it in exports to third markets are keen not to allow too much appreciation of their own curren-

Takatoshi Ito, professor at the Graduate School of Economics, University of Tokyo, has taught extensively both in the United States and Japan, including at the University of Minnesota, Hitotsubashi University, and Harvard University. Helpful comments from participants of the Peterson Institute conference are gratefully acknowledged. The author is grateful to Junko Shimizu, Michiko Baba, and Hiroki Yoshida for their assistance in obtaining data and econometric analysis.

1. See Blanchard, Giavazzi, and Sa (2005) and Obstfeld and Rogoff (2005) for standard references for global imbalances and the necessity of exchange rate adjustment.

cies against the renminbi. When China allows its currency to appreciate only very gradually, the neighboring countries try not to allow sharp appreciation of their own currencies. However, the Asian emerging currencies appreciated more than the renminbi did from July 2005 to November 2007. Would the other Asian currencies have appreciated more if China had allowed more appreciation?

Currently, countries under a managed exchange rate regime, such as Korea, Singapore, and Thailand, tend to keep the trade-weighted exchange rate stable rather than the dollar peg. As the weights of China in exports and imports have increased in these countries, the influence of Chinese exchange rate policy on these currencies is considered to have increased. The trend is fairly certain, but the variations are diverse. In the past several years, appreciations of the Korean won and the Thai baht have been much more pronounced than the renminbi's very gradual appreciation. However, that Thailand decided on but shortly thereafter rescinded capital controls in December 2006 is circumstantial evidence that these countries do not welcome too great an appreciation against the renminbi or the US dollar.

In turn, China seems to be very much worried about its export competitiveness. Despite US pressure to allow faster appreciation, China has allowed appreciation by only about 11 percent since July 2005—as of November 7, 2007 the exchange rate stood at RMB7.44 to the US dollar, compared with RMB8.28 to the dollar on July 20, 2005. Chinese officials often cite low profit margins of exports, especially textiles and agricultural goods, but the appreciation would be easier to swallow if China were sure that other Asian currencies would follow the renminbi if it appreciated faster.

China most likely is more willing to accept renminbi appreciation if neighboring countries, in addition to Korea and Thailand, allow faster appreciation as well. For their part, East Asian countries definitely are more willing to allow appreciation if renminbi appreciation accelerates. If all of the countries concerned desire joint appreciation but cannot realize it due to a lack of communication and commitment, this can be considered a coordination failure.

I would argue that if the East Asian countries manage to coordinate their exchange rate regimes, the pace of Asian currencies' appreciation against the US dollar, when necessary to resolve global imbalances, will accelerate. One of the possible mechanisms of such coordination is to adopt an Asian currency unit (ACU), with each country aiming at a stable relationship with it. Various research institutes in the East Asian region, including Ogawa and Shimizu (2005) and the Asian Development Bank (ADB), have explored the possibility of an ACU.

The rest of this chapter is organized as follows. The following section reviews the lessons of the Asian currency crisis regarding exchange rate regimes. The second section explains the exchange rate regimes in East Asia, including the results of regression analysis. The third section reviews various basket currency proposals, while the fourth discusses the political economy of the exchange rates. The fifth section discusses East Asia's role in resolving global imbalances. The final section concludes the chapter.

Overview of Exchange Rate Developments, 2004–07

This section surveys the trends in nominal exchange rate movements in Asia from January 2004 to July 2005 and July 2005 to November 2007. The currencies included are the Chinese renminbi, Korean won, Singaporean dollar, Thai baht, Malaysian ringgit, Philippine peso, and Indonesian rupiah. Figures 7.1 and 7.2 describe their nominal exchange rates against the US dollar for the respective subperiods.

The sample periods are divided on July 21, 2005, when the renminbi was reformed from the dollar peg to a more flexible regime. The exact announcements will be examined below. Figure 7.1 shows nominal exchange rate movements before the renminbi reform period (January 2004–July 2005), with a benchmark of 100 on January 1, 2004. Higher values denote appreciation and lower values denote depreciation. Four groups in terms of appreciation or depreciation against the US dollar can be identified: The Korean won appreciated by about 15 percent, the Indonesian rupiah depreciated by 15 percent, Malaysia and China explicitly pegged their currencies to the dollar, and the rest fluctuated around the dollar value of January 2004.

The appreciation of the Korean won was remarkable, especially after October 2004. There was strong pressure on the Korean won to appreciate starting in 2003, and the authorities had intervened to stabilize the won against the dollar for some period, but as the level of necessary intervention became large, the authorities decided to let go in the fall of 2004. The weakest currency was the Indonesian rupiah; political uncertainties and inflation are usually identified as contributing to its depreciation.

On July 21 the Chinese authorities announced that they would revalue the renminbi by 2.1 percent immediately and abandon the currency's US dollar peg.[2] Some Asian currencies appreciated along with the renminbi in the following days. Figure 7.2 shows nominal exchange rate movements from July 21, 2005 to November 7, 2007 from the benchmark of July 20, 2005. After a 2 percent jump on July 21, the renminbi appreciated steadily and gradually, and it has kept a pace of about 5 percent a year since then. There is very little fluctuation around the gradual accent path; the movement is best described as a crawling peg to the US dollar. On November 7, 2007, the renminbi was 11.2 percent above the July 20, 2005.

---

2. See People's Bank of China, Public Announcement of the People's Bank of China on Reforming the RMB Exchange Rate Regime, July 21, 2005, in appendix 7A to this chapter.

Figure 7.1 Asian currency movements vis-à-vis US dollar: Pre-renminbi reform, January 1, 2004–July 20, 2005

index (January 1, 2004 = 100)

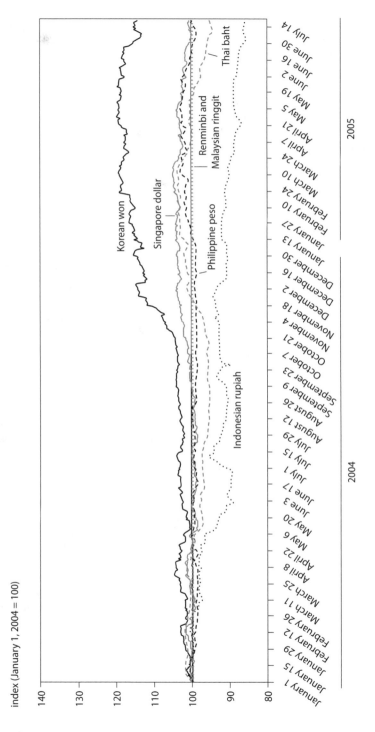

Note: Each exchange rate is the nominal exchange rate vis-à-vis the US dollar. The daily exchange rate is in the ratio of its rate on January 1, 2004.

Source: Datastream.

Figure 7.2   Asian currency movements vis-à-vis US dollar: Post-renminbi reform, July 21, 2005–November 7, 2007

index (July 20, 2005 = 100)

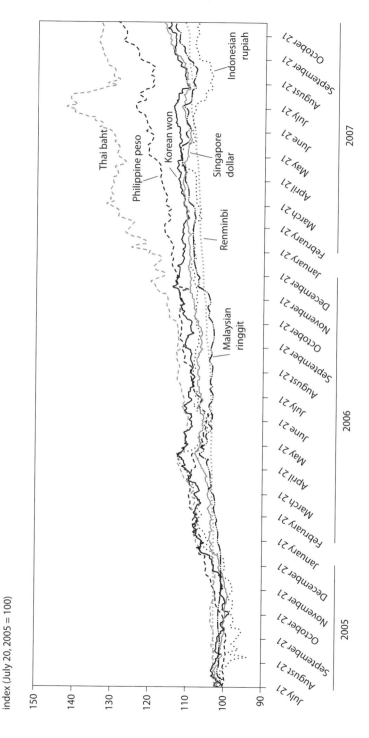

Note: Each exchange rate is the nominal exchange rate vis-à-vis the US dollar. The daily exchange rate is in the ratio of its rate on July 20, 2005.
Source: Datastream.

By contrast, most other Asian currencies appreciated much more than the renminbi after the renminbi reform. By November 7, 2007 the Thai baht had appreciated by 33 percent, the Philippine peso by 29 percent, the Singaporean dollar by 17 percent, the Korean won by 15 percent, and the Malaysian ringgit by 14 percent against their respective values on July 20, 2005. The Indonesian rupiah was the only currency that appreciated less than the renminbi did.

Two facts stand out. First, excepting the Indonesian rupiah, the renminbi was at the bottom of the appreciation ladder among East Asian emerging-market economies. In a sense, the renminbi tended to be a drag on the currency movement rather than a leader in it. This is contrary to the perception that the renminbi is a mover and shaker in emerging Asia. Second, Asian currencies other than the renminbi have become managed floaters. Since the renminbi reform, the Asian currencies have become much more flexible, contrary to the perception that they are collectively pegged to the US dollar for mercantilist motives, most notably expressed by those who advocate the so-called Bretton Woods II view.

A few more observations are also helpful in understanding the magnitude of the appreciations of the Thai baht and Philippine peso, which, at about 30 to 35 percent, are large even by the standards of Asian currencies. Comovements among the currencies of Singapore, Malaysia, and Korea have appeared lately, whether by an act of the market or an act of the monetary authorities.

Exchange Rate Regimes in East Asia

One of the important lessons that East Asian countries have learned from the Asian currency crisis of 1997–98 was that the type of exchange rate regime matters. There are two parts to this lesson. First, the well-known part is that a de facto fixed exchange rate regime tends to invite double mismatches and boom-and-bust cycles. Borrowers in an emerging market and lenders in advanced countries overlook the currency risk because of the peg, resulting in double mismatches on banks' balance sheets—that is, long-term local currency assets and short-term foreign currency liabilities. Second, the exchange rate regimes adopted by neighboring countries influence how a country chooses its own exchange rate regime. This aspect ties into the coordination failure of the exchange rate regimes in East Asia.[3] Thailand chose a de facto dollar peg because Malaysia, China, Indonesia, and other economically important neighbors were adopting a de facto dollar peg, as Thai exporters had to compete against neighboring exporters.

Due to the currency crisis of 1997–98, most Asian countries shifted their exchange rate regimes to managed float systems with varying degrees of

---

3. The coordination failure was first pointed out by Ito, Ogawa, and Sasaki (1998).

foreign exchange intervention, the notable exceptions being China, Hong Kong, and Malaysia. China had held the renminbi tightly fixed to the US dollar since 1994, through the turbulent period of the Asian currency crisis, until July 2005. On July 21, the People's Bank of China (PBC) changed its exchange rate regime, causing an immediate 2 percent appreciation, and moved to a more flexible regime. Later, the PBC allowed the renminbi to appreciate very gradually, by 2 to 3 percent a year. Hong Kong has maintained, until now, a fixed exchange rate against the US dollar. Malaysia first floated its currency with the Philippines and Indonesia, right after the Thai baht depreciated, but in September 1998 fixed its exchange rate to the US dollar. It quickly followed China in appreciation on July 21, 2005 and later added more flexibility than the renminbi has. China's exchange rate policy clearly influenced the Malaysian exchange rate regime on July 21, 2005, but Malaysia actually implemented flexible exchange rate management after the one-time jump better than China did.

At present, there are four exchange rate regimes in East Asia. Japan has adopted a free float; monetary authorities have not intervened in the yen since March 17, 2004. Second, Korea, Singapore, Thailand, Indonesia, Malaysia, and the Philippines have adopted managed floating regimes with varying degrees of basket currency features. Hong Kong and China have hard and crawling pegs, respectively, to the US dollar. Others have dollarized (Vietnam, Cambodia, and Laos), established a currency board against the Singaporean dollar (Brunei), and implemented multiple exchange rates with heavy controls (Myanmar), but this final group is out of the scope of analysis in this paper.

The diverse exchange rate regimes, unfortunately, are vulnerable to major global exchange rate shocks. Suppose that the US dollar depreciated against the yen by 10 percent overnight. Because the currencies in the region would react very differently, the currencies of some countries, such as China, would experience windfall gains in export competitiveness by moving more or less with the US dollar. Others would likely suffer appreciation in terms of the real effective exchange rate (REER) as neighbors (China) refused to appreciate against the dollar.

What would be an optimal collective arrangement of exchange rate regimes in East Asia? How much weight would China have in such an arrangement? Any proposed exchange rate regime should allow enough flexibility to adjust to external shocks and changes in fundamentals, but also keep volatility low. The volatility of the exchange rate should also be measured in terms of REER. As intraregional trade ratios have increased to levels comparable to the European Union, keeping REER stable means keeping bilateral exchange rates in the region relatively stable while they jointly float against outside currencies. Europe has pursued the concept of a joint float ever since the snake system of 1979, which led to the introduction of single currency, the euro.

Bilateral exchange rates in the region cannot be stabilized but float against the rest of the world unless the countries agree to keep their exchange rate regimes similar to one another. One way to achieve such a confluence of regimes is to adopt a basket currency system—that is, a country pursues a peg with a narrow band to a common basket comprised of outside currencies with weights roughly reflecting a region's average of trade weights. However, any proposal of a joint float or common basket system in Asia needs China to accept flexible management of the exchange rate in tandem with neighboring countries. More currencies in Asia seem to be accepting a loose basket system, most notably the Singaporean dollar; it is questionable whether China at this moment is embracing such a system as well.

Has China Moved to a Basket Currency?

The announcement of renminbi reform on July 21, 2005[4] was immediately greeted with a welcome note by the Group of Seven, which stated, "Starting from July 21, 2005, China will reform the exchange rate regime by moving into a managed floating exchange rate regime based on market supply and demand with reference to a basket of currencies." It contained three major elements: an immediate 2 percent appreciation of the renminbi to RMB8.11 to the dollar; a daily fluctuation of ± 0.3 percent allowed, with the closing rate being the central rate of the following day; and, as the announcement stated, "The RMB exchange rate will be more flexible based on market condition with reference to a basket of currencies."

A regression analysis can reveal from data whether China's regime moved away from a dollar peg and adopted a basket peg, as the PBC said it would. The following regression, first introduced by Jeffrey Frankel and Shang-Jin Wei (1994), is used to estimate the weight on the three major currencies if the Chinese renminbi is on the basket system:

$$\Delta CHY_t = \text{Const} + b_1 \Delta USD_t + b_2 \Delta JPY_t + b_3 \Delta EUR_t + e_t \quad (7.1)$$

where all currencies are in terms of one Swiss franc, CHY is the Chinese renminbi, USD is the US dollar, JPY is the Japanese yen, and EUR is the euro. The symbol Δ is the log difference operator, making the variable the (approximate) percentage change. In view of the renminbi reform and gradual change in implementation after the reform, regressions are conducted for the three periods: preform, from January 2, 2004 to July 18, 2005; Post-1, that is, the first year after reform, from July 19, 2005 to July

---

4. See People's Bank of China, Public Announcement of the People's Bank of China on Reforming the RMB Exchange Rate Regime, July 21, 2005, in appendix 7A to this chapter.

Table 7.1 Basket regression for the Chinese renminbi

Currency	Prereform	Post-1	Post-2
US dollar	1.000	0.938	0.967
Standard error	0.000	0.018	0.015
(t)	6007.43	53.56	64.51
Probability	0.000***	0.000***	0.000***
Yen	0.000	0.070	−0.016
Standard error	0.000	0.018	0.010
(t)	0.08	3.94	−1.55
Probability	0.938	0.000***	0.122
Euro	0.000	0.022	0.007
Standard error	0.000	0.055	0.029
(t)	−0.66	0.39	0.26
Probability	0.508	0.697	0.797
Constant	0.000	−0.020	−0.020
Standard error	0.000	0.008	0.005
(t)	−0.05	−1.80	−4.07
Probability	0.962	0.073	0.000***
$\bar{R}^2$	1.00	0.95	0.96

*** = Estimate is statistically significant at 1 percent level.
Prereform = January 2, 2004 to July 18, 2005
Post-1 = First year after reform (July 19, 2005 to July 18, 2006)
Post-2 = Second year after reform (July 19, 2006 to November 7, 2007)

18, 2006; and Post-2, that is, the second year after reform, from July 19, 2006 to November 7, 2006.

Table 7.1 shows the results. For the prereform period, the renminbi was on the dollar peg, so that the weight of the US dollar is measured as one. Even after the reform, the dollar weight remained very high, though the hypothesis that it equals one is refuted (i.e., the standard error is small). The weight is estimated as 94 percent in the first year after the reform and 97 percent in the second year after the reform. In the first year after the reform, the Japanese yen was estimated to have a weight of 7 percent, although most of this power comes from the July 21 jump of the renminbi and yen together (not shown). The euro also appears to have some weight, but it is not statistically significant. In the second year after the reform, the statistical significance of the Japanese yen disappears. The renminbi hews very close to the dollar peg.

However, in figure 7.2, we also observe that the renminbi became a crawling peg rather than remaining fixed to the dollar, as the value of the renminbi against the dollar climbs steadily over time, at an almost constant but slightly accelerating slope. To confirm this observation, the fol-

Table 7.2   Crawling peg regression for the Chinese renminbi

	Prereform	Post-1	Post-2
Constant	8.2771	8.1260	8.0002
Standard error	0.0000	0.0023	0.0016
(t)	4756.93	3528.32	4922.93
Probability	0.000***	0.000***	0.000***
Trend	0.0000	−0.0005	−0.0015
Standard error	0.0000	0.0000	0.0000
(t)	−26.08	−33.81	4922.93
Probability	0.000***	0.000***	0.000***
$\bar{R}^2$	0.63	0.81	0.99

*** = Estimate is statistically significant at 1 percent level.
Prereform = January 2, 2004 to July 18, 2005
Post-1 = First year after reform (July 19, 2005 to July 18, 2006)
Post-2 = Second year after reform (July 19, 2006 to November 7, 2007)

lowing crawling peg regression is conducted. The level of the renminbi/US dollar exchange rate is regressed on the constant and time.

$$(CHY_t / USD_t) = Const + d_1 t + e_t \qquad (7.2)$$

Table 7.2 shows that the model has quite a good fit. In the period before reform, the slope is zero, as the renminbi was pegged to the dollar at the time. In the first year after reform, the daily appreciation speed is estimated as 0.05 renminbi to the dollar each day. The speed of appreciation in the second year accelerated to 0.15 renminbi to the dollar each day, three times as fast as the first year. The second year $\bar{R}^2$ is very high, suggesting that the Chinese authorities implemented a crawling peg with very few fluctuations around the constant slope.

In sum, examining table 7.1 leads us to confirm that the renminbi is hardly a basket currency. Table 7.2 confirms our prior guess from figure 7.2 in that the renminbi has become instead a crawling peg against the US dollar, with little flexibility, after the July 2005 reform.

Basket Currencies in Asia

The preceding subsection confirms that the renminbi is still closely tied to the US dollar. This subsection applies the Frankel-Wei basket currency regressions to other Asian currencies:

$$\triangle ASIA_{it} = Const + b_1 \triangle USD_t + b_2 \triangle JPY_t + b_3 \triangle EUR_t + e_{it} \qquad (7.3)$$

where ASIA$_i$ is the Asian currency of country i against the Swiss franc. The countries included in the sample are Indonesia, Korea, Malaysia, the Philippines, Singapore, and Thailand. These countries are categorized as emerging Asia countries.

Table 7.3 presents the estimation results for the Prereform, Post-1, and Post-2 periods. Before the renminbi reform of July 2005, Malaysia's currency was pegged to the dollar just as the renminbi was. This is evident in the estimated coefficient, 1.00, of the US dollar. Other currencies in the sample were the basket currencies between the US dollar and the yen. Weights varied from country to country, with the weight of the yen higher for Singapore (30 percent), Korea (22 percent), and Thailand (21 percent). During the Post-1 period, the basket regimes seemed to have been less relevant. The coefficient of determination is uniformly lower. Singapore and Thailand seemed to have developed a genuine basket system weighting all of the three major currencies. Both Singapore and Thailand suppressed the dollar weight below 65 percent and increased the weights of the yen and euro. During the Post-2 period, three changes occurred: The dollar weight increased, the yen weight lowered, and the euro weight increased. No currency had statistically significant weight in the yen. The number of countries with statistically significant weight in the euro increased from two in the Post-1 period to four in Post-2. The Asian currencies behaved quite differently from the renminbi.

In sum, even after the renminbi reform, the Asian currencies have much lower weights on the US dollar than does the Chinese renminbi. Some currencies in some time periods, such as Singapore and Thailand in Post-1, show the character of a basket currency linked to the yen and euro as well as the US dollar. The estimation results of table 7.3 corroborate with figure 7.2.

Renminbi's Influence on Asian Currencies

After the renminbi reform, several observers speculated that Chinese currency movements would have a spillover effect on other Asian currencies. If China allowed the renminbi to appreciate, the currencies of other Asian countries would appreciate as well. Figure 7.2 shows that this speculation was not firmly grounded, at least in the magnitude of appreciation, as other Asian countries allowed their currencies to appreciate more than China did. A more formal analysis to examine the renminbi effect on other Asian currencies would be helpful, but because the Chinese currency has moved closely with the US dollar even after the renminbi reform, econometric problems arise: The simultaneous presence of the US dollar and renminbi as explanatory variables may cause multicollinearity.[5]

---

5. Shimizu (2008) estimated the movement of an Asian currency in response to the yen, euro, and renminbi, excluding the US dollar. Naturally, the weight of the renminbi turned out to be very large.

Table 7.3   Basket regressions for Asian currencies

Currency	Indonesia	Korea	Malaysia	Philippines	Singapore	Thailand
Prereform						
US dollar	0.765	0.675	1.003	0.885	0.560	0.711
Standard error	0.047	0.041	0.002	0.023	0.019	0.023
(t)	16.2	16.63	578.19	39	30.19	30.32
Probability	0.000***	0.000***	0.000***	0.000***	0.000***	0.000***
Yen	0.178	0.215	−0.002	0.092	0.297	0.213
Standard error	0.045	0.039	0.002	0.022	0.018	0.022
(t)	3.95	5.56	−1.44	4.25	16.81	9.53
Probability	0.000***	0.000***	0.152	0.000***	0.000***	0.000***
Euro	0.131	0.215	0.000	0.035	0.130	0.150
Standard error	0.131	0.113	0.005	0.063	0.052	0.065
(t)	1	1.91	-0.06	0.56	2.52	2.29
Probability	0.32	0.057*	0.953	0.578	0.012**	0.022**
$\bar{R}^2$	0.65	0.69	1.00	0.90	0.90	0.88
Post-1						
US dollar	0.638	0.699	0.888	0.869	0.597	0.633
Standard error	0.121	0.054	0.051	0.040	0.026	0.041
(t)	5.27	12.97	17.33	21.47	23.14	15.44
Probability	0.000***	0.000***	0.000***	0.000***	0.000***	0.000***
Yen	0.021	0.132	0.045	0.046	0.301	0.236
Standard error	0.123	0.055	0.052	0.041	0.026	0.042
(t)	0.17	2.42	0.86	1.12	11.52	5.67
Probability	0.866	0.016**	0.388	0.263	0.000***	0.000***
Euro	0.284	0.293	0.221	−0.064	0.258	0.379
Standard error	0.381	0.170	0.161	0.127	0.081	0.129
(t)	0.75	1.73	1.37	−0.5	3.17	2.94
Probability	0.456	0.085*	0.173	0.615	0.002***	0.0004***
$\bar{R}^2$	0.17	0.60	0.69	0.76	0.87	0.73
Post-2						
US dollar	0.820	0.810	0.781	0.827	0.734	0.889
Standard error	0.062	0.047	0.044	0.077	0.031	0.130
(t)	13.29	17.07	17.76	10.73	23.57	6.84
Probability	0.000***	0.000***	0.000***	0.000***	0.000***	0.000***
Yen	−0.046	0.022	0.020	−0.050	0.029	−0.067
Standard error	0.042	0.033	0.030	0.053	0.021	0.089
(t)	−1.11	0.66	0.66	-0.95	1.36	−0.75
Probability	0.269	0.508	0.512	0.343	0.174	0.452
Euro	0.560	0.430	0.530	0.382	0.406	−0.057
Standard error	0.120	0.092	0.085	0.149	0.060	0.252
(t)	4.69	4.67	6.22	2.56	6.73	−0.23
Probability	0.000***	0.000***	0.000***	0.011**	0.000***	0.82
$\bar{R}^2$	0.57	0.68	0.71	0.43	0.81	0.18

Prereform = January 2, 2004 to July 18, 2005
Post-1 = First year after reform (July 19, 2005 to July 18, 2006)
Post-2 = Second year after reform (July 19, 2006 to November 7, 2007)

Note: Estimated statistics of the constant term are not reported in this table. Asterisks denote that the estimate is statistically significant at the 10 percent (*), 5 percent (**), or 1 percent (***) level.

Table 7.4 shows the result of the following regression:

$$\Delta ASIA_{it} = Const + b_1 \Delta USD_t + b_2 \Delta JPY_t + b_3 \Delta EUR_t + b_4 \Delta CHY_t + e_{it} \qquad (7.4)$$

The variable CHY is added on the right-hand side. As predicted, the estimates show some instability. Either USD or CHY may be statistically significant, but not both. Table 7.3 poorly estimates some equations. It may be concluded that because the renminbi is basically a crawling peg, its influence on Asian currencies is not well separated from the US dollar's influence on Asian currencies.

Basket Currency Proposals

Several institutions and individuals have proposed the creation of a basket currency unit in Asia. One early official document was a Japanese-French discussion paper submitted to an Asia Europe Meeting (ASEM) in January 2001 (see Ministry of Finance, Japan and Ministry of Finance, France 2001), which discussed the virtue of a managed exchange rate with reference to a basket currency value for East Asian countries excluding Japan.

Later, basket currency proposals in the region shifted to those including the yen inside the basket. The ACU proposal, first put forward by the ADB in late 2005 and taken over by the finance ministers' process in the Association of Southeast Asian Nations (ASEAN)-plus-three[6] in the ADB annual meeting in May 2006, explicitly included the yen in the basket. The following section discusses two different kinds of baskets. One excludes the yen and the other includes it.[7]

YES Basket: Yen, Euro, and US Dollar

The YES basket consists of the yen, euro, and US dollar. According to the ASEM document of 2001, "Basket currency regimes including the dollar, the yen and the euro would better suit the geographical structure of the balance of payments and would foster stability."

Using a basket that includes the yen implicitly assumes that Japan is outside the region that would pursue a basket currency. The basket is formed by the three major global currencies: the dollar, euro, and yen. Suppose that one YES unit is equivalent to 100 yen, 1 US dollar, and 1 euro.

---

6. That is, 10 ASEAN countries plus Japan, China, and Korea.

7. See Ito (2004) for a proposal of creating a basket bond that is a bond of value with weighted average of underlying national currency–denominated bonds.

Table 7.4 Basket regressions for Asian currencies, renminbi added

Currency	Indonesia	Korea	Malaysia	Philippines	Singapore	Thailand
Post-1						
US dollar	0.575	0.331	0.834	0.862	−0.014	−0.138
Standard error	0.423	0.187	0.179	0.141	0.081	0.134
(t)	1.36	1.77	4.66	6.09	−0.18	−1.03
Probability	0.175	0.077*	0.000***	0.000***	0.858	0.302
Yen	0.016	0.105	0.041	0.045	0.256	0.178
Standard error	0.127	0.056	0.054	0.042	0.024	0.040
(t)	0.13	1.87	0.76	1.07	10.56	4.44
Probability	0.899	0.063*	0.446	0.284	0.000	0.000
Euro	0.283	0.285	0.219	−0.064	0.244	0.362
Standard error	0.382	0.169	0.162	0.128	0.073	0.121
(t)	0.74	1.69	1.36	−0.5	3.34	2.99
Probability	0.459	0.093*	0.176	0.615	0.001	0.003
Renminbi	0.067	0.392	0.057	0.008	0.652	0.822
Standard error	0.432	0.191	0.183	0.144	0.083	0.137
(t)	0.16	2.06	0.31	0.06	7.9	6.01
Probability	0.876	0.041**	0.756	0.956	0.000	0.000
$\bar{R}^2$	0.17	0.61	0.69	0.76	0.90	0.76
Post-2						
US dollar	0.677	0.119	0.371	0.482	0.782	1.237
Standard error	0.226	0.169	0.159	0.281	0.114	0.475
(t)	3	0.7	2.33	1.71	6.87	0.474797
Probability	0.003***	0.482	0.020**	0.088*	0.000***	0.010**
Yen	−0.044	0.033	0.027	−0.044	0.028	−0.073
Standard error	0.042	0.032	0.030	0.053	0.021	0.089
(t)	−1.05	1.03	0.89	−0.84	1.32	−0.81
Probability	0.296	0.301	0.377	0.402	0.188	0.416
Euro	0.559	0.424	0.527	0.379	0.406	−0.055
Standard error	0.120	0.090	0.084	0.149	0.060	0.252
(t)	4.67	4.73	6.24	2.54	6.73	−0.22
Probability	0.000***	0.000***	0.000***	0.012**	0.000***	0.829
Renminbi	0.147	0.715	0.425	0.357	−0.050	−0.360
Standard error	0.224	0.168	0.159	0.280	0.113	0.472
(t)	0.66	4.25	2.68	1.27	−0.44	−0.76
Probability	0.512	0.000***	0.008***	0.204	0.661	0.446
$\bar{R}^2$	0.57	0.70	0.72	0.43	0.81	0.18

Post-1 = First year after reform (July 19, 2005 to July 18, 2006)
Post-2 = Second year after reform (July 19, 2006 to November 7, 2007)

Note: Asterisks denote that the estimate is statistically significant at the 10 percent (*), 5 percent (**), or 1 percent (***) level.

If the exchange rate is 1 US dollar = 1 euro = 100 yen, then YES 1 has a value of 3 US dollars = 3 euros = 300 yen.

Suppose that the yen-dollar and dollar-euro exchange rates become 120 yen = 1 US dollar and 1.4 US dollars = 1 euro. Then YES 1 has a value of

388 yen, 3.23 US dollars, or 2.31 euros. If all Asian currencies aim to keep parity with YES, then Asia jointly appreciates against the yen, depreciates slightly against the US dollar, and depreciates most against the euro.

The YES basket makes sense if the Asian countries export and import from the three advanced regions—the United States, European Union, and Japan—with significant shares and want to keep the average nominal effective exchange rate stable.

Asian Monetary Unit Basket: ASEAN-Plus-Three ACU

The ASEAN-plus-three countries have studied the benefits of having a 13-country weighted basket currency. The weight of each currency can be calculated from the average of the share of trade and the share of GDP, by market exchange rate or purchasing power parity (PPP) exchange rate. The benchmark can be chosen as a year when imbalances in current accounts were relatively small.

Such an indicator has been developed, calculated, and updated every week by Professors Eiji Ogawa and Junko Shimizu at the Research Institute of Economy, Trade, and Industry (RIETI)–Hitotsubashi University.[8] For weights, they chose the arithmetic average of the share of GDP based on a PPP exchange rate and the share of total trade, exports and imports, in the basket region. According to these criteria, China has the largest share in country weight (37 percent), followed by Japan (26 percent), Korea (10 percent), Singapore (6 percent), Malaysia (5 percent), Thailand (5 percent), Indonesia (4.9 percent), and the Philippines (2.8 percent). Other countries—Brunei, Cambodia, Laos, Myanmar, and Vietnam—had shares of less than 2 percent.

Currently, Ogawa and Shimizu are using the Asian monetary unit to indicate whether and how much the exchange rate of a county deviates from the weighted average of the region's currencies. If all currencies were to peg to the basket with a narrow band, it would work just as the European currency unit did before the euro was introduced.

Political Economy

Currency coordination, not to mention adoption of a single currency, cannot be achieved without political leadership and commitment to shared values—namely, democracy—similar income levels, using income transfer if necessary, and free movement of capital and labor. The challenges in East Asia to creating such conditions appear to be insurmountable at

---

8. See Ogawa and Shimizu (2005) for the construction of the database. See www.rieti.go.jp for updates.

this point. In East Asia, economic integration is well ahead of political convergence.

Many observers who are familiar with European experiences are skeptical at best about currency coordination in East Asian any time soon.[9] They emphasize that, in Europe, political leadership moved countries toward economic integration and a single currency. Such political resolve is quite important, and admittedly, political cohesiveness in East Asia is very weak. All economists can hope for at this point is to prepare economic tools and instruments to be used readily if the political winds blow in the right direction in favor of economic integration and currency coordination in the future.

Global Imbalances and East Asia

Global imbalances—large US current account deficits corresponding to large current surpluses in China, other Asian economies, and oil-producing nations, with capital inflows to the United States supporting the US dollar—have dominated discussions in international financial institutions. One obvious answer to large US current account deficits is to engineer a US dollar depreciation that would force expenditure switching from imports to domestically produced goods for US residents. However, a slowdown in the US economy may cause a worldwide recession rather than rebalancing demand around the world.

US dollar depreciation also means that some currencies will appreciate. However, if many currencies maintain a dollar peg or a very gradual crawling peg, then the burdens of appreciation would concentrate on freely floating currencies. This seems to be a serious worry for Europeans, as the euro has appreciated markedly in the past two years while the appreciations of major East Asian currencies are very gradual at most. The yen has not appreciated remarkably due to a low interest rate and the private sector's investing abroad without intervention since March 2004.

Although intraregional trade of semifinished goods has increased tremendously, it is a serious concern for East Asian policymakers that their economies depend on exports of final products to the United States. A sharp depreciation of the US dollar against the East Asian currencies would put more dampening effects on the East Asian economies. However, a slowdown of the US economy, depreciation of the dollar, and decline in US imports—or an increase in US exports to East Asia, Europe, and oil-producing nations—is an essential part of global demand rebalancing, and the majority of the impact of a decrease in US imports will hit Asia.

---

9. Wyplosz (2006) attempted to draw lessons from the European integration process as a blueprint for other regions, especially Asia.

There are two ways to mitigate the adverse effects of possible dollar depreciation against East Asian currencies. First, the exchange rate policies of the East Asian countries could be better coordinated so that the exchange rates jointly float against the US dollar and other major currencies outside the region. The East Asian economies have integrated enough that the intraregional trade ratio is as high as it is among EU countries, about 50 percent. A sharp fall in the US dollar would cause large changes in intraregional exchange rates (e.g., yen-renminbi, yen-won, baht-yen) unless the Chinese monetary authorities allowed much more flexibility for their currencies. One way to ensure that East Asian currencies move in a coordinated fashion is to adopt a common-basket band regime, under which East Asian currencies maintain stability with each other but float jointly against outside currencies.[10]

Second, economic policies in East Asia can be relaxed in anticipation of pressures for dollar depreciation. However, fiscal spending may not be a wise choice in some of the East Asian countries. With a very large level of government debt, Japan has little room for fiscal stimuli. Instead, monetary policy in Japan has room to maneuver, as the threat of inflation is remote. Moving out of deflation, monetary policy can be behind the curve to make sure that economic recovery lifts the economy from its 15-year stagnation and 8-year deflation. Similarly, deficit spending by the government may not be wise in Korea, Thailand, Indonesia, and the Philippines, as they are still extricating themselves from the fiscal deficit problems posed by their management of the 1997 crisis. Only China and Malaysia have some room to stimulate their economies through fiscal policy.

Concluding Remarks

The East Asian region contains countries with different exchange rate regimes. The yen operates under a clean float. Among managed floats, the Singaporean dollar, Thai baht, and Korean won have been managed as genuine currency baskets. The Asian currencies also influence each other. If one currency appreciates or depreciates, the others tend to move in the same direction.

It is crucially important that East Asian currencies coordinate better to lessen chaos and disorderly reactions if and when the US dollar depreciates in the resolution of global imbalances. However, such a resolution must come with private-sector initiatives and adjustments, rather than officials simply pushing around a few currencies.

---

10. Proposals based on a basket, band, and crawl proposal and its variants for East Asia have been around for some time. See Ito, Ogawa, and Sasaki (1998), Ogawa and Ito (2002), and Williamson (2000) for details.

Despite the July 2005 PBC declaration that it would move the renminbi to a managed exchange rate with reference to a currency basket, the new regime can be regarded as having a crawling peg to the US dollar—no room for flexible management. No influence on other currencies is detected, although it is difficult to estimate the influence of the renminbi and that of the US dollar separately as determinants of baskets of other managed float currencies in the region.

When China truly liberalizes its capital controls, say, in 10 years, the renminbi's influence in the region will be much greater. In 10 years the GDP of the Chinese economy measured by the market exchange rate will surpass that of Japan. Currencies of countries with strong ties with China will naturally have incentives to keep their bilateral exchange rates against the renminbi more stable. Gradually the renminbi will become a key regional currency. At present, the renminbi's influence on the currencies in the region appears quite limited. The East Asian currency movements after the Chinese reform of the exchange rate system on July 21, 2005 shows that the degree of appreciation by China is the second least (after Indonesia). There is a possibility that China is setting the floor of appreciation in East Asia. The coordination among the East Asian countries, aiming at a joint float against the dollar and the euro may bring less turmoil in the intraregional trading relationship if and when the dollar depreciates sharply against free or managed float currencies.

References

Blanchard, Olivier, Francesco Giavazzi, and Filipa Sa. 2005. The US Current Account and the Dollar. *Brookings Papers on Economic Activity 2005*, no. 1: 1–66.

Frankel, Jeffrey, and Shang-Jin Wei. 1994. Yen Bloc or Dollar Bloc? Exchange Rate Policies of the East Asian Economies. In *Macroeconomic Linkage: Savings, Exchange Rates, and Capital Flows*, ed. Takatoshi Ito and Anne O. Krueger. Chicago: University of Chicago Press.

Ito, Takatoshi. 2004. Promoting Asian Basket Currency Bonds. In *Developing Asian Bond Markets*, ed. Takatoshi Ito and Yung Chul Park. Canberra: Asia Pacific Press at the Australian National University.

Ito, Takatoshi. 2006. A Case for a Coordinated Basket for Asian Countries. In *A Basket Currency for Asia*, ed. Takatoshi Ito. London: Routledge.

Ito, Takatoshi, Eiji Ogawa, and Yuri Nagataki Sasaki. 1998. How Did the Dollar Peg Fail in Asia? *Journal of the Japanese and International Economies* 12, no. 4 (December): 256–304.

Ministry of Finance, Japan, and Ministry of Finance, France. 2001. Exchange Rate Regimes for Emerging Market Economies. Paper presented at the Third ASEM Finance Ministers' Meeting, Kobe, Japan, January 13–14. Available at www.mof.go.jp (accessed on December 26, 2007).

Obstfeld, Maurice, and Kenneth S. Rogoff. 2005. Global Current Account Imbalances and Exchange Rate Adjustments. *Brookings Papers on Economic Activity 2005*, no. 1: 67–123.

Ogawa, Eiji, and Takatoshi Ito. 2002. On the Desirability of a Regional Basket Currency Arrangement. *Journal of the Japanese and International Economies* 16, no. 3 (September): 317–34.

Ogawa, Eiji, and Junko Shimizu. 2005. *A Deviation Measurement for Coordinated Exchange Rate Policies in East Asia.* RIETI Discussion Paper Series 05-E-017. Tokyo: Research Institute of Economy, Trade, and Industry.

Shimizu, Junko. 2008. On the Asian Monetary Unit (in Japanese). *Meikai Economic Review* (forthcoming).

Williamson, John. 2000. *Exchange Rate Regimes for Emerging Markets: Reviving the Intermediate Option.* POLICY ANALYSES IN INTERNATIONAL ECONOMICS 60. Washington: Institute for International Economics.

Wyplosz, Charles. 2006. Deep Economic Integration: Is Europe a Blueprint? *Asian Economic Policy Review* 1, no. 2: 259–79.

Appendix 7A
Public Announcement of the People's Bank of China on Reforming the RMB Exchange Rate Regime, July 21, 2005

With a view to establish and improve the socialist market economic system in China, enable the market to fully play its role in resource allocation as well as to put in place and further strengthen the managed floating exchange rate regime based on market supply and demand, the People's Bank of China, with authorization of the State Council, is hereby making the following announcements regarding reforming the RMB exchange rate regime:

1. Starting from July 21, 2005, China will reform the exchange rate regime by moving into a managed floating exchange rate regime based on market supply and demand with reference to a basket of currencies. RMB will no longer be pegged to the US dollar and the RMB exchange rate regime will be improved with greater flexibility.
2. The People's Bank of China will announce the closing price of a foreign currency such as the US dollar traded against the RMB in the interbank foreign exchange market after the closing of the market on each working day, and will make it the central parity for the trading against the RMB on the following working day.
3. The exchange rate of the US dollar against the RMB will be adjusted to 8.11 yuan per US dollar at the time of 19:00 hours of July 21, 2005. The foreign exchange designated banks may adjust quotations of foreign currencies to their customers.
4. The daily trading price of the US dollar against the RMB in the interbank foreign exchange market will continue to be allowed to float within a band of ±0.3 percent around the central parity published by the People's Bank of China, while the trading prices of the non-US dollar currencies against the RMB will be allowed to move within a certain band announced by the People's Bank of China.

The People's Bank of China will make adjustment of the RMB exchange rate band when necessary according to market development as well as the economic and financial situation. The RMB exchange rate will be more flexible based on market conditions with reference to a basket of currencies. The People's Bank of China is responsible for maintaining the RMB exchange rate basically stable at an adaptive and equilibrium level, so as to promote the basic equilibrium of the balance of payments and safeguard macroeconomic and financial stability.

Comment
The Regional Currency Unit and Exchange Rate Policy Cooperation in East Asia

YUNG CHUL PARK

As part of the effort to promote cooperation for financial and monetary integration in East Asia, in 2006 policymakers from the Association of Southeast Asian Nations (ASEAN)-plus-three—China, Japan, and Korea—agreed to explore steps to create regional currency units (RCUs) as a sequel to two other regional initiatives, the Chiang Mai Initiative and Asian Bond Market Initiative. This agreement was preceded by a proposal to create an Asian currency unit (ACU), forwarded by the Asian Development Bank (ADB) and a number of Japanese economists, among them Mori, Kinukawa, Nukaya, and Hashimoto (2002), Ogawa (2006), and Ogawa and Shimizu (2006a).

Yung Chul Park is a distinguished professor at the Division of International Studies, Korea University. This comment draws on Park (2007).

1. In the Ogawa (2006) construction, the 13 ASEAN-plus-three currencies are weighted by their relative GDPs valued in terms of purchasing power parity (PPP) and total trade volumes, the sum of exports and imports. To reflect the most recent trade relationships and economic trends, Ogawa (2006) uses the averages of these variables for the most recent three years for which data are available. The value of the AMU is then quoted in terms of a weighted average of the two major international currencies, the US dollar and the euro. The weights of the two currencies are the shares of the United States and the euro area in the total trade of the ASEAN-plus-three countries and set at 65 percent and 35 percent, respectively. The benchmark period of the AMU exchange rate against the dollar and euro, for which the

Both the ADB and Ogawa (2006) define the ACU, or Asian monetary unit (AMU), as a basket of the 13 currencies of the ASEAN-plus-three member countries weighted by their relative importance in terms of GDP, trade volume, population, and the degree of capital account liberalization.[1]

If the ACU is an Asian version of the European currency unit (ECU), it is an accounting unit. However, it is suggested that

- the unit could assist ASEAN-plus-three policy authorities in their conduct of exchange rate policy and be a surveillance indicator for regional coordination of exchange rate policy in East Asia;[2]

- the ACU could be adopted as an internal common currency basket to which the ASEAN-plus-three members, except Japan, could link their currencies (Ogawa and Shimizu 2006);

- the ACU could facilitate the creation of a regional market for basket bonds denominated in the ACU;[3] and

- the ACU could be an intermediate step toward making the yen the anchor currency for the member states of ASEAN-plus-three (Ogawa and Shimizu 2006b)

Such additional functions make the ACU more than a simple numeraire, understandably generating a certain amount of confusion about its possible role in the East Asia.

ACU as a Regional Accounting Unit

How does creating the ACU contribute to exchange rate policy coordination and monetary integration in East Asia? The European Union's experience with the ECU may provide both lessons and answers.

The ECU was a political gesture toward monetary union. As a unit of account, it was symbolic, just as the special drawing right (SDR) is a symbol for a future world currency. The ECU was used as an internal accounting unit for all official EU transactions and accounts, although the member central banks did not use it in their own transactions. As seen

AMU exchange rate is set at unity, is chosen for a period (2000–2001) when the total trade balance of the 13 countries with the rest of the world and the total trade balance of ASEAN-plus-two (excluding Japan) with Japan are relatively close to zero.

2. See Haruhiko Kuroda, Towards Deeper Asian Economic Integration: Progress and Prospects, speech at the Asia Business Conference, Harvard University, Boston, February 11, 2006; Haruhiko Kuroda, Challenges of Regional Cooperation and Integration in Asia, speech at the Symposium on Perceptions on Asian Economic Cooperation, Tokyo, January 25, 2006.

3. See Haruhiko Kuroda, "The Conundrums of Global Bond Markets—An Asian Perspective," address at the Global Bond Summit, Hong Kong, November 16, 2005.

from the management of the European Monetary System (EMS), the ECU played no particular role in stabilizing the intramember exchange rates of the constituent currencies, although it was one of the four elements of the EMS in addition to the grid, mutual support, and a commitment to joint decision of realignments (Baldwin and Wyplosz 2004, chapter 12).

Initially, the ECU was expected to impose a symmetric burden on both weak and strong currencies, preventing them from intervening in the market to serve their own interests. In reality, countries with weak currencies intervened in the market well before the limits of the system were reached, so the burden was largely asymmetric. The only real lasting effect of the ECU is that when the euro became the European Monetary Union's new unit of account, its conversion rate was one ECU to one euro, an obscure stipulation of the Maastricht Treaty.[4]

ACU as the Numeraire for Asian Basket Bonds

In the past a few attempts to issue bonds denominated in a basket of currencies in Europe have been unsuccessful. Debt instruments denominated in the ECU were issued in Europe, but Dammers and McCauley (2006) show that these instruments owed their limited success in the 1980s and 1990s to restrictions on internationalization of the Deutsche mark and speculative investments. Certainly the European Union did not encourage or render any institutional support for developing a market for bonds denominated in the ECU.

Notwithstanding the European experience, the advocates of Asian basket bonds, however denominated, should be able to justify public sector involvement in creating a market for such an instrument. It is unclear what the advantages are of holding basket bonds over bond portfolios consisting of bonds in different currencies. Market participants may prefer bond portfolios diversified across currencies to basket bonds, as they are more flexible in managing return and risk profiles of their investments. If there is demand for basket bonds, it is reasonable to argue that private institutions would not leave the market opportunity unexploited. That is, investment banks and securities firms would be prepared to create and market bonds denominated in many different baskets of different currencies as long as there is demand for them. The absence of a regional accounting unit does not stand in the way of developing markets for basket bonds.

Failures of the market, regulatory controls, or the insufficiency of market infrastructure may have prevented the development of markets for basket bonds in Asia. If that is the case, advocates of Asian basket bonds should identify what these impediments are and how they could be mitigated before proposing public sector involvement in fostering basket bond markets in Asia.

---

4. The author owes this point to Charles Wyplosz.

**Figure 7.C1   Asian monetary unit (AMU) in terms of the euro
and US dollar, 2001–07**

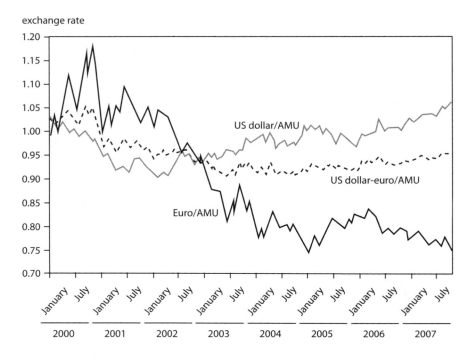

Note: Benchmark year = 2000/2001; basket weight = 2003–05.

Source: Ogawa (2006).

ACU as a Surveillance Indicator for Exchange Rate Policy Coordination

The role of the ECU in EU monetary unification makes it clear that simply creating the AMU will not strengthen exchange policy coordination in East Asia. What is needed for coordination in East Asia is a collective regional exchange rate regime, such as the exchange rate mechanism adopted by the European Community as part of the EMS or a common basket pegging. This can be seen from recent movements of some of the key East Asian currencies against the US dollar, euro, and AMU.

Figure 7.C1 depicts changes in the AMU exchange rate in terms of the US dollar and euro. It has appreciated slightly against the dollar and depreciated a great deal against the euro since mid-2002, largely because of the weakening yen and inflexibility of the dollar/renminbi exchange rate. Because ASEAN-plus-three as a group has been running sizable surpluses in trade with both the United States and European Union, which have be-

Figure 7.C2 Nominal exchange rates of the yen, renminbi, and won against US dollar, 1994–2007

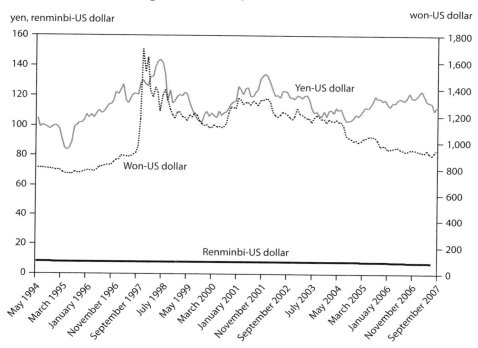

yen, renminbi–US dollar

won–US dollar

Source: Bank of Korea.

come the major sources of global imbalance, it may be in the interest of ASEAN-plus-three to let the AMU appreciate against the dollar and euro. What could these countries do collectively to bring about such an adjustment? The yen is a component currency of the AMU. But because it is a free floating currency, Japanese authorities are not likely to intervene in the dollar/yen market. This means that other members of ASEAN-plus-three will have to adjust their exchange rates, although the yen is largely responsible for the weakening of the AMU against the dollar and the euro.

Except for Japan and Singapore, the other member countries of ASEAN-plus-three do not have a domestic currency/yen market and their currencies are largely nonconvertible. As a result, the only way they can engineer an appreciation of the ACU against the dollar or euro is to intervene in their local currency/dollar markets to induce an appreciation of their currencies against the dollar. If they do, then their currencies will strengthen further against the yen while Japan is running a surplus with them.

As figure 7.C2 shows, the won appreciated against the dollar by 11.6 percent and the renminbi by 9.3 percent, while the yen depreciated by 12 percent between early 2005 and September 2007. These changes in the

Figure 7.C3 Asian monetary unit (AMU) exchange rates (renminbi, yen, and won): Real AMU deviation indicators, 2000–2007

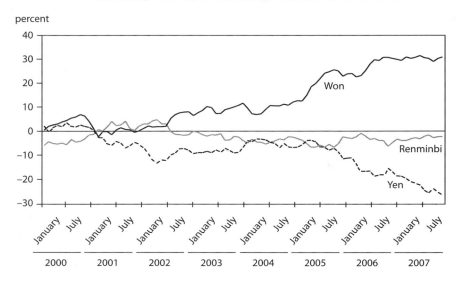

Note: Benchmark year = 2000/2001; basket weight = 2000–2004, monthly.

Source: Research Institute of Economy, Trade, and Industry, Tokyo.

dollar exchange rates of the three currencies have led to widely divergent movements of their ACU exchange rates, as figure 7.C3 shows.

Figure 7.C3 tracks the movements of the yen, renminbi, and won against the ACU estimated by Ogawa (2006). Compared with the base period, by the end of September 2007 the won appreciated by almost 20.7 percent against the ACU while the yen depreciated by more than 6 percent and the renminbi returned to parity after a period of depreciation. The major cause of these large and varying deviations was the depreciation of the yen against both the renminbi and the won.

Under such circumstances, if China and Korea were to stabilize their AMU exchange rates to coordinate their exchange rate polices, they would have to intervene jointly in their local currency/dollar markets. China would have to strengthen its currency against the dollar, whereas Korea would need to bring about a depreciation of the won against the dollar. If China does not let the renminbi appreciate, Korea will have to assume a greater burden of adjustment, even though it is running a surplus in its US trade. Thus countries such as Korea and Thailand are thrown into an impossible situation in which they must weaken their currencies against the dollar to keep their currencies in line with the AMU but let their dollar exchange rates appreciate for the AMU to appreciate against the dollar as well.

As long as the yen remains a free-floating currency and China is reluctant to revalue its currency, the AMU will be of little use as a surveillance indicator for regional exchange policy coordination. It also cannot provide any useful guidelines to individual members of ASEAN-plus-three in formulating their exchange rate policies. In the highly unlikely case in which China, Japan, and Korea intervened to stabilize their AMU exchange rates in term of the dollar or euro, they would have to agree beforehand to a set of rules governing intragroup exchange rate adjustments. What is needed is a collective regional exchange regime.

ACU as a Common Basket of Internal Currencies for ASEAN-Plus-Three

The regime shift in both China and Malaysia to a basket arrangement in 2004 has underscored the need for closer coordination of exchange rate policy in East Asia. As Kawai (2002) notes, South Korea and Thailand have shifted to a de facto currency basket arrangement similar to Singapore's managed float since the 1997–98 crisis. The movements of both the nominal and real effective exchange rates of Indonesia and the Philippines also indicate that their currencies are linked to a basket of the currencies of their major trading partners. Practically all seven emerging economies in East Asia—the original five ASEAN countries, China, and South Korea—are now explicitly or implicitly on a variety of basket arrangements.

Now that the seven Asian economies have all adopted a similar basket arrangement, they will probably monitor changes in the nominal and real effective exchange rates of other members to make sure there is no erosion in their relative export competitiveness. If any one of the seven ASEAN-plus-three members moves to weaken its currency against the dollar, it will set off a competitive devaluation throughout the region. Therefore, the seven countries have a common interest in adopting a collective exchange rate regime to prevent such competitive skirmishes.[5]

According to Williamson (2005), the seven emerging economies will benefit more from adopting a common basket of external currencies, including the dollar, the euro, and the yen, than from adopting different baskets.[6] Common basket pegging would not only reduce room for competitive devaluation for export promotion but also help adjust dollar ex-

---

5. With a new regime in place and its growing economic influence in the region as leverage, China may be in a position to initiate the discussion on coordinating exchange rate policies among the seven countries.

6. Several Japanese economists have also advocated similar arrangements for East Asia's emerging economies. See Ito and Ogawa (2002), Kawai (2002), and Kawai and Takagi (2000). These economists now argue that the ACU is a more appropriate common basket for ASEAN-plus-three.

change rates simultaneously and improve the chance for cooperation on monetary integration in the long run.

Ogawa and Shimizu (2006b) argue that the AMU they propose can be a common basket for the ASEAN-plus-three countries, except Japan. According to their proposal, the ACU will not be entirely an internal basket to ASEAN-plus-three, as the yen will remain outside of the pegging arrangement as a free-floating currency. However, the yen will dominate, more so if the weights of the constituent currencies are calculated in terms of nominal GDP instead of the GDP at purchasing power parity (PPP). With the yen in the basket, a great deal of variations of the ACU against the dollar and euro would result from changes in the dollar/yen or euro/yen exchange rates.

Most of the changes in the ACU exchange rates of the 12 countries of ASEAN-plus-three will also be caused by changes in their bilateral exchange rates against the yen, as has happened in recent years. The 12 members may then ask why the yen, which will increase the variability of the ACU against the dollar and euro as well as that of their ACU exchange rates, should be included in a common basket to be chosen for exchange rate policy cooperation. In theory, the common pegging to the AMU may serve as a mechanism for internal exchange rate adjustments among the ASEAN-plus-three members if Japan forgoes its free-floating status. But even in this case, it is highly uncertain whether the member countries could agree to a complicated and elaborate mechanism of intragroup exchange rate adjustments that a common pegging would entail.

If Japan cannot or does not want to give up its free-floating status, the preceding analysis does not suggest that the ACU without the yen would be a more viable basket for ASEAN-plus-two. An ACU composed of the ASEAN-plus-two currencies would be dominated by the renminbi, as China is by far the largest economy in the group. The ASEAN five and Korea, not to mention ASEAN latecomers, would be marginalized in such an ACU; in reality, its creation would be equivalent to making the renminbi a regional anchor currency and forming a de facto renminbi bloc. Whatever the economic rationale behind such a currency bloc, ASEAN-plus-Korea will find it politically unacceptable to join the renminbi bloc.

The preceding analysis raises serious doubts as to the viability of the ACU as either a common internal basket for or an indicator monitoring changes in the exchange rate policies of the ASEAN-plus-three countries. Why, then, is Japan at the forefront in advocating the creation of the ACU, knowing it cannot be part of the arrangement? Ogawa and Shimizu (2006b) offer an answer: In their view, the ACU can be an intermediate regime to creating a yen bloc in East Asia. In their proposal, ASEAN-plus-two members tie their currencies to the AMU first; after a period of experimentation with common pegging, they choose the yen as the anchor currency. Ogawa and Shimizu do not explain why the yen should be the key regional currency, although it has become less attractive than the British pound as a reserve currency in recent years.

In conclusion, creating a regional currency unit, as proposed by ASEAN-plus-three, will be mostly a symbol that the member states are committed to monetary cooperation and integration in East Asia as a long-run objective. In this regard, the creation will be a welcome development. However, following the European model, unless it is followed by the establishment of a mechanism for exchange rate policy coordination and mutual support among the members, the ACU will end up as only a political gesture.

References

ASEAN Plus Three. 2006. Joint Ministerial Statement of the ASEAN Plus Three Finance Ministers Meeting. Presented at the ninth ASEAN+3 finance ministers meeting, Hyderabad, India, May 4.

Baldwin, Richard E., and Charles Wyplosz. 2004. *The Economics of European Integration.* London: McGraw-Hill.

Dammers, Clifford R., and Robert McCauley. 2006. Basket Weaving: The Euromarket Experience with Basket Currency Bonds. *BIS Quarterly Review* (March): 79–89.

Frankel, Jeffrey, and Andrew Rose. 1998. The Endogeneity of the Optimum Currency Area Criteria. *Economic Journal* 108, no. 449: 1009–25.

Fratzscher, M. 2001. *Financial Market Integration in Europe: On the Effects of EMU on Stock Markets.* Working Paper Series no. 48. Frankfurt: European Central Bank.

Ito, Takatoshi, Eiji Ogawa, and Yuri N. Sasaki. 1998. How Did the Dollar Peg Fail in Asia? *Journal of the Japanese and International Economies* 12: 256–304.

Ito, Takatoshi, and Eiji Ogawa. 2002. On the Desirability of a Regional Basket Currency Arrangement. *Journal of Japanese and International Economies* 16: 317–34.

Kawai, Masahiro. 2002. Exchange Rate Arrangements in East Asia: Lessons from the 1997–98 Currency Crisis. Paper presented at the tenth International Bank of Japan conference, Exchange Rate Regimes in the 21st Century, sponsored by the Institute for Monetary and Economic Studies, Bank of Japan, Tokyo, July 1–2.

Kawai, Masahiro, and Shinji Takagi. 2000. *Proposed Strategy for a Regional Exchange Rate Arrangement in Post-Crisis East Asia.* World Bank Policy Research Working Paper 2503. Washington: World Bank.

Mori, Junichi, Maoyoshi Kinukawa, Hideki Nukaya, and Masashi Hashimoto. 2002. *Integration of East Asian Economics and a Step by Step Approach Towards a Currency Basket Regime.* IIMA Research Report 2 (November). Institute for International Monetary Affairs.

Murase, Tetsuji. 2004. The East Asian Monetary Zone and the Roles of Japan, China, and Korea. Kyoto University. Photocopy.

Ogawa, Eiji. 2006. *AMU and AMU Deviation Indicators.* Tokyo: Research Institute of Economy, Trade and Industry.

Ogawa, Eiji, and Junko Shimizu. 2006a. *AMU Deviation Indicator for Coordinated Exchange Rate Policies in East Asia and Its Relation with Effective Exchange Rates.* RIETI Discussion Paper Series 06-E-002 (January). Tokyo: Research Institute of Economy, Trade, and Industry.

Ogawa, Eiji, and Junko Shimizu. 2006b. Progress toward a Common Currency Basket System in East Asia. Paper presented at the 5th Asia Pacific Economic Forum, sponsored by Kangwon National University, Chuncheon, Korea, July 5–6.

Park, Yung Chul. 2007. Whither Financial and Monetary Integration in East Asia? *Asian Economic Papers* 6, no. 3: 95–128.

Williamson, John. 2005. *A Currency Basket for East Asia, Not Just China.* Policy Briefs in International Economics 05-1. Washington: Institute for International Economics.

Comment
The End of Europe's Long-Standing Indifference to the Renminbi

JEAN PISANI-FERRY

Is the renminbi's exchange rate an important issue for Europe? For a long time, it seemed as though it was not. As recently as 2006–07, when Henry Paulson, secretary of the US Treasury, was calling the US-China economic relationship the most important in the world and no less than three congressional bills envisaged potential trade retaliation against an allegedly deliberate currency undervaluation, Europe was surprisingly silent. It apparently had no strong views on either the exchange rate regime or the valuation of the renminbi.

Ministries of finance and the European Central Bank (ECB) investigated the issue and discussed it in contacts with Chinese counterparts, but it was not prominent on policymakers' agendas and was hardly discussed publicly. When asked, officials either referred to the latest Group of Seven (G-7) communiqué or replied that the issue was best dealt with behind closed doors in discussions between ministers or among central bankers. Europe was apparently relying on the implicit assumption that, to it, the issue was second order, and in any case, its interests coincided with those of the United States. Therefore, Europe could rely on US activism for all practical purposes.

Jean Pisani-Ferry is director of Bruegel, a Brussels-based economics think tank, and professor at Université Paris-Dauphine. The author is grateful to Jérémie Cohen-Setton for his assistance in preparing this comment and to Frank Moss for discussions on a previous version of it.

The situation began to change only in autumn 2007 as the Eurogroup, an informal gathering of euro-area finance ministers, began a more in-depth discussion of the matter. On October 8, 2007 the group issued a statement that "in emerging countries with large and growing current account surpluses, especially China, it is desirable that their effective exchange rates move so that necessary adjustments occur" and decided to initiate direct discussion with China's leadership. At the end of November, Eurogroup President Jean-Claude Juncker, ECB President Jean-Claude Trichet, and European Commissioner Joaquín Almunia were sent to Beijing for the first direct bilateral consultations on monetary and exchange rates matters. The Europeans, however, remain guarded in expressing their views on China's exchange rate policy.

Is there a rationale for this difference in attitudes between the two sides of the Atlantic? Or is the euro area only slower in reacting to China's emergence as a major surplus country in the world economy? This is the issue I intend to investigate in this paper. To this end, I examine five potential explanations of transatlantic differences of view: that China does not matter that much to Europe; that the renminbi-US dollar exchange rate is a bilateral issue; that the alternatives are worse; that the Europeans have divergent interests; and that the euro area does not have an exchange rate policy. After examining these five potential explanations, I conclude this comment in the last section.

China Does Not Matter That Much to Europe

Many observers would suggest that Europe behaves as it does because China is a much more important economic partner for the United States than it is for Europe. This is a widely held perception, probably attributable to the rather smooth development of EU-China relations. In contrast with the emotional, generally politicized, and sometimes tense character of US-China relations, EU-China relations have only recently become a matter of public interest in Europe.[1] Previously, the international rise of China and its global economic implications had long remained underestimated, sometimes almost unnoticed. In the 1990s and early 2000s, political energy was essentially devoted to addressing internal issues, such as the creation of the single market and the euro or enlargement.

To further illustrate the apparent neglect, in 2000, in response to the perceived challenge of that time—the emergence of the so-called new economy in the United States—Europe adopted a new economic strategy, the Lisbon agenda, which essentially ignored the various opportunities and

---

1. The first EU policy paper on China was issued in 1995, almost two decades after the Chinese economy had begun its transformation. The first EU-China summit meeting occurred in 1998.

Figure 7.C4 Goods and services trade deficit with China, 1986–2006

billions of US dollars

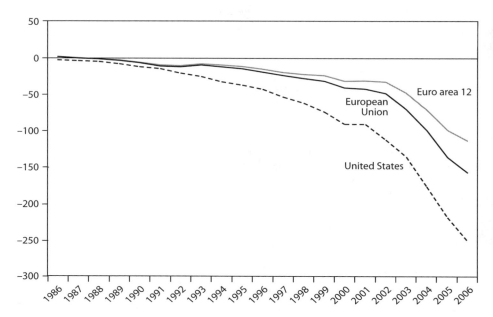

Source: International Monetary Fund, *Direction of Trade Statistics*, various years.

challenges that China's growth and development posed. Since then, perceptions have changed, and initial inattention has started to be corrected, but European interest in and concern about China remain strikingly less intense than the US fascination with it.

However, this asymmetry in perceptions is not supported by numbers. In 2006 EU exports to China exceeded those of the United States by 45 percent and its imports from China were only 23 percent lower than those of the United States. Its trade deficit is certainly lower, but it trails that of the United States by only about two years (figure 7.C4). The euro area is in a very similar situation. As a consequence, European policymakers have started to indicate that they could soon lose patience. As Trade Commissioner Peter Mandelson said in November, "the number that preoccupies Europe these days is $20 million. Because that is how fast the EU-China trade deficit is growing every single hour. Fast enough to catch up with the US-China trade deficit in the next year or so."[2]

---

2. Europe and the US: Confronting Global Challenges, speech at the Carnegie Endowment for International Peace, Washington, November 8, 2007.

Figure 7.C5 China's weight in effective exchange rates
(based on 2002–04 trade)

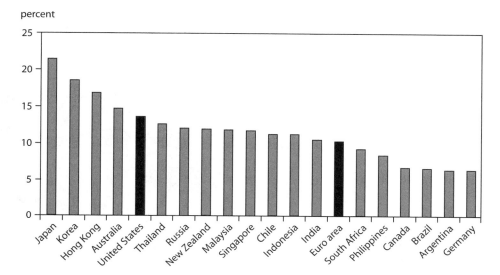

percent

Source: Bank for International Settlements.

The transatlantic difference does not become wider when competition in third markets is accounted for, such as by using Bank of International Settlements measures of effective exchange rates (EERs): China's weight in the euro area's EER is only somewhat lower that its weight in the US EER (figure 7.C5). Clearly, no number supports the view that the intensity of US economic relations with China is of a different order of magnitude than those of the European Union or euro area.

Second View: The Dollar-Renminbi Exchange Rate Is a Bilateral Issue

The second potential explanation for Europe's relative detachment from the renminbi issue is that the European currencies are in a floating exchange rate regime against the dollar. Thus, while the renminbi-dollar exchange rate is not market determined, the exchange rate of European currencies against the renminbi is indirectly market determined. This asymmetry is indisputable.

What the asymmetry may imply can be best understood by imagining the United States and China as partners in a de facto currency union. Accordingly, it should not be the US or Chinese current account balance that

Figure 7.C6 Current account balances, 1983–2008

billions of US dollars

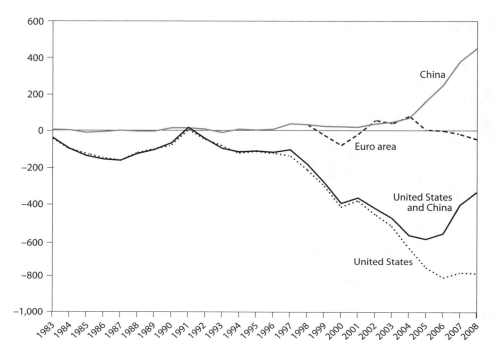

Sources: International Monetary Fund, Balance of Payments Statistics; International Monetary Fund, *World Economic Outlook.*

matters but rather the aggregate US-China current account balance or that of a wider dollar zone, in the same way that what matters for the exchange rate of the euro is neither the Spanish deficit nor the German surplus but the aggregate balance, which is close to equilibrium. The aggregate US-China balance, while still far from equilibrium, has improved somewhat in recent times and is set to improve further in 2008 (figure 7.C6).[3] Also, the bilateral trade balance of the euro area regarding the United States and China combined is very close to zero.

The trade balance figures suggest that the dollar peg of the renminbi and its undervaluation might result in the euro being stronger against the dollar and weaker against the renminbi than would be the case if the renminbi were to float, with no clear consequences in effective terms. This type of reasoning is consistent with the revived Bretton Woods approach of Doo-

---

3. Forecasts for 2007 and 2008 are from the IMF, based on the conventional assumption of stable exchange rates throughout the forecast period.

ley, Folkerts-Landau, and Garber (2003), who emphasise that emerging countries have entered a stable fixed exchange rate arrangement with the dollar; it may also have underpinned the view frequently held in the early 2000s that the euro had no stake in global adjustment because it was itself close to equilibrium in effective terms.

For this view to be justified, however, the United States and China would have to form a true monetary union or to be expected eventually to create one. In that case, market participants could and actually would be wholly indifferent to the two countries' individual balances. But because they do not expect the peg to last forever, they still regard each country's intertemporal budget constraints as meaningful and, accordingly, monitor their national current accounts and net foreign asset positions.

If the US current account matters, rather than the current account of a wider aggregate comprising China, then it follows that a renminbi undervaluation has strong consequences for the euro-dollar exchange rate. For a given equilibrium exchange rate of the US currency, the more the renminbi is undervalued, the more the euro needs to appreciate in bilateral and effective terms. This type of reasoning underpins most evaluations of equilibrium exchange rates, including those of the International Monetary Fund (IMF 2006). Such evaluations generally conclude that, although the effective exchange rate of the US dollar was above equilibrium in 2007, there was no need for the euro to appreciate further in effective terms (Ahearne et al. 2007).

Following this line of reasoning, the Europeans should have every interest in pushing for an appreciation of the renminbi because such a move would reduce the upward pressure on their own currency and the risk of it becoming clearly overvalued in effective terms, at significant macroeconomic cost. It would also reduce its required appreciation against the US dollar (Ahearne et al. 2007), and to the extent that the Europeans are sensitive to the dollar exchange rate because the United States is their direct competitor in certain industries, most notably aerospace, the latter is something they should be sensitive to.

Third View: The Alternatives Are Worse

The third reason for Europe's caution regarding the reform of the Chinese exchange rate regime may be an aversion to the risk of unintended adverse consequences. Better the devil you know than the devil you do not. Europeans might fear that a Chinese move toward a more flexible exchange rate regime would result in an appreciation of the euro as China diversifies its reserves away from US dollar assets and, at least partially, into European currencies. The reasoning here starts from the financial account rather than the current account, resulting in the opposite conclusion. Thus, there seems to be an inconsistency between the so-called trade

Figure 7.C7 Effects of a renminbi float on the euro-dollar exchange rate

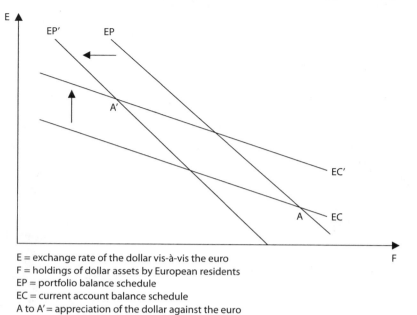

E = exchange rate of the dollar vis-à-vis the euro
F = holdings of dollar assets by European residents
EP = portfolio balance schedule
EC = current account balance schedule
A to A' = appreciation of the dollar against the euro

view and the so-called financial account view of Europe's relationship to the renminbi issue.

The model of Blanchard, Giavazzi, and Sa (2005) helps to clarify the reason for the inconsistency, as it encompasses both views. It can be summarized in two long-term relations between the exchange rate (E)[4] and the external debt (F) of the United States, represented by current account balance (EC) and a portfolio balance (EP) schedules (figure 7.C7). Both slope downward: In the steady state, a higher debt implies a more devalued exchange rate, resulting in a larger trade surplus, which allows for servicing of the debt. Higher debt also implies that nonresidents hold more dollar assets, which they are inclined to do if a lower dollar makes those assets cheaper.[5]

Suppose now that E represents the exchange rate of the dollar against the euro and that F represents the holdings of dollar assets by European residents. A Chinese move to a floating exchange rate regime means two things: first, an appreciation of the renminbi resulting in an outward shift of the EC curve (because for a given level of debt, the same US current account balance can be achieved with a higher bilateral euro-dollar exchange rate); and second, the removal of a marginal buyer of US dollar assets, which moves the EP curve inward (because for a given level of debt,

---

4. A rise in E represents an appreciation.

5. Returns on dollar and nondollar assets are supposed to be identical.

the dollar needs to depreciate as Europeans have to hold more of it in their portfolios). In the long run, the result of the two moves is unambiguously an appreciation of the dollar against the euro (a move from A to A' in figure 7.C7).

In the short term, however, the dynamics are likely to imply a depreciation of the US dollar against the euro (see Blanchard, Giavazzi, and Sa 2005), as for a given level of debt and US current account deficit, an end to Chinese intervention implies a lower demand for dollar-denominated assets, which implies a further depreciation of the US currency.

The issue for the Europeans is therefore one of time preference. The renminbi peg on the dollar has the advantage of avoiding too sharp a depreciation of the US currency in the short run, but it also contributes to the buildup of US external debt and thus to an eventually lower dollar in the long run.

Fourth View: The Europeans Are Divided

A factor often mentioned to explain why the Europeans have difficulty defining a stance on the Chinese exchange rate is that they are internally divided. This is both true and unconvincing.

Certainly the Europeans hold different views. In autumn 2007 German Finance Minister Peer Steinbrück notoriously claimed "love"[6] for the strong euro at the same time that French President Nicolas Sarkozy was lamenting its detrimental effects on the aerospace industry. At the root of this divergence are strongly divergent performances in world trade, the determinants of which can be found in structural factors and the evolution of the real exchange rate of the participating countries against their partners in the euro zone since the start of the monetary union.

Figure 7.C8 illustrates those diverging trends. For each of the euro-area member countries, the X-axis plots the deviation since 1999 of the real exchange rate from the euro area average, and the Y-axis plots the deviation of exports from the euro area average. Countries in the southeast quadrant, most notably Germany, have experienced real depreciation and an improvement in their relative export performance. Countries in the northwest quadrant, especially Italy, Portugal, and Spain, have experienced the opposite development. France also belongs to this category. Ireland has experienced both a sharp real appreciation and a structural improvement in its relative export performance. The extent of divergence over a rather short time span is striking. These developments have taken policymakers by surprise, contributing to an explanation for why national ministers have different views on the exchange rate of the euro.

---

6. Declaration on July 9, 2007 at the Eurogroup meeting: "I am not worried about a strong euro—I love a strong euro."

Figure 7.C8   Real exchange rate and export performance divergence within euro area, cumulative change between 1999 and 2006

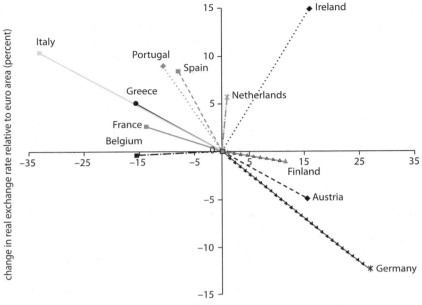

change in real exchange rate relative to euro area (percent)

export growth (excess over euro area average; percent)

Source: Bruegel calculation based on Eurostat and DG ECFIN (European Commission).

Other reasons why the Europeans react differently have to do with the wide dispersion of geographical and sectoral trade patterns, resulting in different sensitivity to exchange rate changes.

However, the Europeans are no less divided on trade matters—largely for the same reasons—but they nevertheless have a common trade policy that makes the European Union one of the few key players in international trade negotiations. Divergence within can explain external paralysis only if governance mechanisms are too weak to ensure that a common stance is defined and implemented. After all, US states also have strongly divergent interests regarding the appropriate level of the exchange rate, yet the federal government can define its stance and communicate it. At any rate, the straightforward tone adopted in official declarations since autumn 2007—"We want an end to a managed currency in China," as Mandelson said that November[7]—indicates that divisions do not hamper common positions any more.

7. "Europe and the US: Confronting Global Challenges," speech at the Carnegie Endowment for International Peace, Washington, November 8, 2007.

Fifth View: The Euro Area Does Not Have an Exchange Rate Policy

This leads to the examination of a fifth potential factor behind the Europeans' lack of assertiveness on the renminbi issue: that they do not have a proper exchange rate policy. The treaty provisions for exchange rate matters are notoriously complex and ambiguous, as they result from a compromise between German and French views (Henning 2007). The issue here is one of vertical division of labor between the European Union or the euro area, which logically has competence on exchange rate matters, and the member states, which participate individually in the G-7, Group of 20, and the IMF. It is also one of horizontal division of labor between the ECB and the Eurogroup, not to mention the European Commission. Both insiders (Bini Smaghi 2006) and observers (Ahearne and Eichengreen 2007) have assessed those arrangements as a drag on the definition and effective expression of common views on international monetary and financial matters. Such arrangements certainly make it difficult to decide who sets the objective (the Eurogroup or the ECB?), who speaks (de facto everybody), and who acts (often nobody). The fact that trade policy is an EU-27 competence, while exchange rate matters are dealt with by the 15-member-strong euro area, and structural reforms are primarily a national competence further complicates the issue.

Defining a stance and a strategy on the renminbi was bound to entail entering unexplored territory. The arrangements for exchange rate policy enshrined in the Maastricht Treaty had been drafted with a view to deciding how to intervene on exchange markets, manage target zones, or enter into formal agreements with third countries, not anticipating the delicate issues of financial diplomacy raised in any dialogue with Chinese authorities. By nature, a conversation about the renminbi has to include both the Eurogroup, because only governments speak to governments, and the central bank, because of its extensive responsibility on exchange rate matters. Against the background of controversies about the monetary stance of the ECB, such a conversation is also bound to be regarded as a test of the central bank's effective independence. All these factors may have contributed to delaying Europe's response to the renminbi issue.

However, the communiqué of October 2007 and the decision to send a mission to Beijing indicate that the complexity of internal arrangements is not an insurmountable impediment to expressing views any more. It probably signals the end of Europe's long-standing benign neglect toward the renminbi.

Conclusion

There is no convincing reason for the Europeans to be more indifferent than are Americans regarding the Chinese exchange rate policy. Of all the possible explanations we have examined—that China matters less for Europe than it does for the United States, that the exchange rate of the renminbi is a bilateral issue, that alternatives to the dollar peg can only be worse, that the Europeans are divided, and that they do not have a proper exchange rate policy—none provides a compelling motive for indifference.

What remains as a hypothesis to explain the difference between US and EU attitudes is probably that the Europeans are slower to react to external developments. The absence of significant external deficit, doubts about which policy stance is desirable, internal disagreements, an untested governance of exchange-rate relations, and a habit of following US leadership may have all contributed to a slow European response. That said, the Europeans have recently woken up to the issue as the euro has appreciated quickly against both the dollar and the renminbi, and they can be expected to adopt an increasingly active stance on China's exchange rate policy.

References

Ahearne, Alan, William R. Cline, Kyung Tae Lee, Yung Chul Park, Jean Pisani-Ferry, and John Williamson. 2007. *Global Imbalances: Time for Action*. Bruegel Policy Brief 2007/02 (March). Brussels: Bruegel.

Ahearne, Alan, and Barry Eichengreen. 2007. External Monetary and Financial Policy: A Review and a Proposal. In *Fragmented Power: Europe and the Global Economy*, ed. André Sapir. Brussels: Bruegel.

Bini Smaghi, Lorenzo. 2006. Powerless Europe: Why is the Euro Area Still a Political Dwarf? *International Finance* 9, no. 2: 1–19.

Blanchard, Olivier, Francesco Giavazzi, and Filippa Sa. 2005. The US Current Account and the Dollar. *Brookings Papers on Economic Activity 2005*, no. 1: 1–66.

Dooley, Michael, David Folkerts-Landau, and Peter Garber. 2003. *An Essay on the Reinvented Bretton-Woods System*. NBER Working Paper 9971 (September). Cambridge, MA: National Bureau of Economic Research.

Henning, Randall. 2007. Organizing Foreign Exchange Intervention in the Euro Area. *Journal of Common Market Studies* 45, no. 2: 315–42.

IMF (International Monetary Fund). 2006. Methodology for CGER Exchange Rate Assessments. Washington. Photocopy (November 8).

8

IMF Surveillance over China's Exchange Rate Policy

MICHAEL MUSSA

In the revisions to its Articles of Agreement, approved in 1976 and formally ratified in 1978, the International Monetary Fund (IMF) is charged under Section 3(a) of Article IV with the responsibility to "oversee the international monetary system in order to insure its effective operation" and with the more specific responsibility to "oversee the compliance of each member with its obligations under Section 1 of this Article." To fulfill these functions, the Fund is instructed in Article IV, Section 3(b) to "exercise firm surveillance over the exchange rate policies of members, and . . . adopt specific principles for the guidance of all members with respect to those policies."

The provisions of the revised Articles of Agreement had two intentions: to maintain the Fund as the key international institution for establishing and enforcing reasonable rules for the operation of the international monetary system, especially the exchange rate and related policies of its members; and to adapt the policies and practices of the Fund in this vital area to the evolving character of the international monetary system that replaced the system of pegged-but-adjustable par values for national currencies prescribed by the original Bretton Woods agreement of 1946. Building on earlier experience and analytical work, much was done in the mid-to-late 1970s and early 1980s to adapt the Fund to its new responsi-

Michael Mussa, senior fellow at the Peterson Institute since 2001, served as economic counselor and director of the research department at the International Monetary Fund from 1991 to 2001.

bilities and authorities under the revised Article IV, including the establishment of the 1977 Guidelines for Exchange Rate Policies of Members.[1]

By the late 1980s, however, the Fund's role as arbiter of issues related to exchange rate policies and the functioning of the international monetary system had atrophied, as both the Group of Five (G-5) and Group of Seven (G-7) countries and the European countries participating in the Exchange Rate Mechanism (ERM) of the European Monetary System largely excluded the Fund from their deliberations. Most developing countries also resisted Fund involvement in decisions regarding their exchange rate policies. Facing nearly universal lack of support from member countries, Fund staff and management effectively abandoned vigorous efforts to implement firm surveillance over members' exchange rate policies, and related analytical work lost priority.

However, the ERM crisis of the early 1990s and the fall of the dollar in early 1995 brought renewed activity and interest in IMF surveillance over exchange rates. This activity and interest deepened as a number of important emerging-market countries faced foreign exchange crises from the mid-1990s through 2003. The recent evaluation of the Fund's policy advice on exchange rate and related issues by the IMF's Independent Evaluation Office (IEO 2007) testifies to the importance of this work and offers a critical appraisal. Even more impressive, for the first time in 30 years, in 2006–07 the IMF undertook a comprehensive review of the 1977 Surveillance Decision of the Executive Board. After extensive analysis and debate, the Board agreed to revisions of this important decision that many inside the Fund hope will improve the effectiveness of exchange rate surveillance.

Of all of the issues for which IMF exchange rate surveillance is relevant in the new millennium, two stand out as of particularly great importance. One is the general problem of global payments imbalances, in particular, the large and, until very recently, rising current account deficit of the United States and the corresponding surpluses of a number of other countries. On this issue, Fund surveillance has been effective in both recognizing the problem as it develops and promoting an agreed global strategy to address the problem.

In stark contrast to this success in Fund global surveillance stands the catastrophic failure of Fund surveillance in the critical case of China, now the third-largest trading economy in the world and a vital driver of global economic growth. Since 2002 the Chinese authorities have used massive and largely sterilized official intervention to resist substantial, economi-

---

1. The Fund has done much work on exchange rate issues under the par value system of the original Articles of Agreement, during the interregnum when the Second Amendment was being debated and agreed, and in the late 1970s and the early-to-mid 1980s. This included a good deal of work in the Research Department that found significant practical application, including in the actual setting of exchange rates. The histories of the Fund prepared by Margaret de Vries (1976, 1985) describe some of these activities. Jacques Polak's essay (1994) provides an excellent survey.

cally warranted appreciation of the renminbi against the US dollar. With the substantial appreciation of many other currencies against the dollar as well, the real effective exchange rate of the renminbi has depreciated significantly since 2002.[2] Meanwhile, China's current account balance, which typically ran a modest surplus of one to two percent of GDP in the decade through 2002, exploded to over 9 percent of GDP by 2006 and appears to be headed significantly higher in 2007. Beyond any reasonable doubt, the renminbi's exchange rate has become substantially undervalued and is being kept in this position by Chinese policies that powerfully resist, and are intended to resist, significant appreciation. Indeed, China is the one major country for which exchange rate policy and current account performance are clearly operating strongly in the wrong direction with respect to reducing major global payments imbalances, which the Fund has identified as a major concern for the world economy.[3]

Yet, in their surveillance of China's exchange rate and related policies before the summer of 2006, IMF staff reports and executive board deliberations speak only vaguely about the desirability of "greater flexibility" in the renminbi's exchange rate—not of the increasingly urgent need for a major appreciation of the renminbi. IMF Managing Director Rodrigo de Rato emphasized that the IMF was not the official "umpire" of exchange rate issues and that gentle persuasion—generally not in public—was the IMF's only appropriate means of dealing with the Chinese authorities on the sensitive issue of their exchange rate policy. Neither the managing director nor key IMF staff cared to point out forcefully to Chinese authorities the specific and general obligations regarding their exchange rate policy under Article IV, either in public, in executive board discussions, or in private.

In my view, the IMF's approach to the application of surveillance to China's exchange rate policy constitutes gross misfeasance, malfeasance, and nonfeasance by the managing director and the IMF more generally. Included in this indictment are key members of the staff—especially in the Asia and Pacific Department (APD)—much of the executive board, and the national authorities of leading members, most importantly senior officials of the US Treasury (with the notable exception of former Undersecretary Timothy Adams).

---

2. The extent of the real depreciation of the renminbi since early 2002, when the US dollar was at its peak on a real effective basis, depends on the particular measure that is used. If one accounts for rapidly rising productivity in Chinese manufacturing and rapidly falling unit-labor costs in this critical tradable goods sector, the real effective depreciation of the renminbi could easily be as large as 20 to 25 percent.

3. Several major oil-exporting countries, most notably Russia and Saudi Arabia, have seen recent major increases in their current account surpluses while resisting substantial exchange rate appreciations. However, in contrast with China, the enormous and relatively sudden rise in world oil prices accounts for these current account gains, and based on past behavior these surpluses may reasonably be expected to erode over time.

To support this conclusion, this essay takes up the following issues. First, it critically assesses Fund surveillance of China from 2001 to 2006. Using the 1977 Surveillance Decision, which was in force until the new decision was adopted in June 2007, this assessment details how and why China's exchange rate and related policies violated that country's specific and general obligations laid out in Article IV. Second, to provide further insight into how China's exchange rate and related policies have produced such untoward results, a traditional analytical tool developed in the Fund and elsewhere—the monetary approach to the balance of payments—is applied. This helps to explain some important and otherwise puzzling features of the recent spectacular surge in China's balance-of-payments surplus and the enormous rise in its saving-investment balance. Third, the essay reviews the general problem of global imbalances and the strategy that the Fund developed to address that problem. China's glaring failure to play its proper role in this strategy is highlighted. Fourth, the issue of what to do now regarding China's exchange rate and related policies is discussed. Finally, the essay appraises the accountability for the failures of Fund surveillance in the case of China.

China's Exchange Rate Policy

Following the unification of the Chinese exchange rate regime at the beginning of 1994, the nominal exchange rate of the renminbi against the US dollar fluctuated within a relatively narrow range before being pegged quite rigidly at 8.28 renminbi to the dollar in 1996. It was kept at this pegged rate until July 2005. Subsequently, it moved gradually to about 7.50 renminbi to the dollar as of October 2007. While the renminbi's nominal exchange rate against the dollar has been quite stable, its real effective exchange rate fluctuated over a fairly wide range, as shown in figures 8.1 and 8.2.

The Chinese economy grew rapidly from 1993 through 2002, with annual real GDP growth averaging 9½ percent and not falling below 7½ percent. Chinese trade with the rest of the world grew at one-and-a-half times this pace, transforming China from the tenth- to the fourth-largest trading economy in the world. Chinese imports grew at nearly the same pace as Chinese exports, and Chinese trade and current account balances as shares of Chinese GDP were in moderate surplus, without pronounced and persistent tendencies to move into substantial surpluses, as shown in figures 8.3 and 8.4. During this period, official holdings of international reserves grew substantially, rising from $22 billion at end-1993 to $291 billion at end-2002; half of this increase occurred in 2001 and 2002 (see table 8.1). Reserve holdings were already relatively high at 5.4 months of imports even in 1994. Over the next eight years, they rose to 8.9 months of imports in 2002.

Consistent with the well-known Balassa-Samuelson effect, movements in China's real effective exchange rate and current account balance from

Figure 8.1   Real effective exchange rate of the renminbi (Citigroup and International Monetary Fund data), January 1994–September 2007

index (January 1994 = 100)

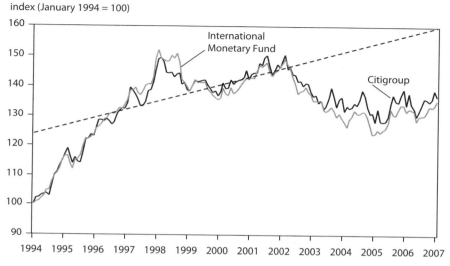

Sources: Citigroup and International Monetary Fund.

Figure 8.2   Real effective exchange rate of the renminbi (JPMorgan data), January 1994–September 2007

index (January 1994 = 100)

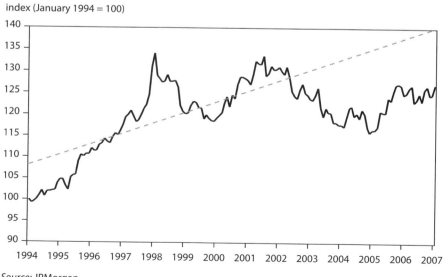

Source: JPMorgan.

Figure 8.3 Real effective exchange rate of the renminbi (IMF/Citigroup data) and China's current account balance

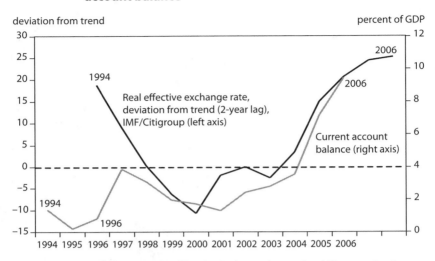

Sources: China State Administration of Foreign Exchange; International Monetary Fund; and Citigroup.

Figure 8.4 Real effective exchange rate of the renminbi (JPMorgan data) and China's current account balance

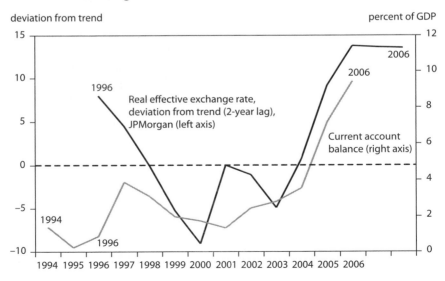

Sources: China State Administration of Foreign Exchange; JPMorgan.

Table 8.1   Indicators of reserve adequacy, 1994–2006

Year	Nongold reserves (billions of dollars)	Ratio of reserves to GDP (percent)	Reserves as months of imports (months)	Ratio of reserves to monetary base (percent)
1994	53	9.5	5.5	25.9
1995	75	10.4	6.4	30.2
1996	107	12.5	9.3	33.0
1997	143	15.0	12.0	38.7
1998	149	14.6	12.8	39.4
1999	158	14.6	9.6	38.8
2000	168	14.0	9.0	38.2
2001	216	16.3	8.9	44.8
2002	291	15.1	8.9	40.2
2003	408	24.9	12.1	64.0
2004	614	31.1	11.0	85.2
2005	822	36.6	14.8	103.0
2006	1,068	40.4	16.2	108.1

Source: Data are from International Monetary Fund, *International Financial Statistics Yearbook,* 2007 and earlier years.

1994 to 2002 suggest that the long-run equilibrium path for China's real exchange rate has a moderate upward tilt of about 2 percent per year.[4] In figures 8.1 and 8.2, this is indicated in two panels by a rising path for an artificially constructed estimate of the longer-run equilibrium exchange rate with a positive tilt of 2 percent per year.[5] The actual real exchange

---

4. See Balassa (1964) and Samuelson (1964). Impressive work that has demonstrated the general relevance of the Balassa-Samuelson idea that nominal exchange rates normally diverge from levels suggested by purchasing power parities (PPP) was presented by Kravis, Heston, and Summers (1978). Further development of the work by these and other scholars, with substantial support from the World Bank, has refined the initial analysis and extended the range of countries. This work provided the foundation for the innovation introduced in the IMF's *World Economic Outlook,* beginning in May 1993, of using PPP-based exchange rates to aggregate different countries' GDP growth rates to obtain a world total.

5. The IMF measure of the real effective exchange rate and the Citigroup measure are sufficiently similar that the same assumed path for the longer-run equilibrium real effective exchange rate of the renminbi makes sense. The behavior of the JPMorgan measure of the renminbi's real effective exchange rate is sufficiently different from the other two measures that a different path for the renminbi's longer-run equilibrium exchange rate is appropriate, also with a 2 percent upward tilt. There is no inconsistency in having different estimates for the longer-run equilibrium path of the real effective exchange rate associated with different measures of the actual behavior of this real effective exchange rate. The relevant question is whether the position and upward tilt of the assumed paths for the longer-run equilibrium real effective exchange rates reflect reasonably justified assumptions. I believe that they do. The general evidence supporting the Balassa-Samuelson effect and its likely relevance to

rate started out below this long-run equilibrium path in 1994–95. With the usual lag of about two years, the undervaluation was reflected in an improvement in the current account, from a surplus of about 0.8 percent of GDP in 1994–96 to a surplus of about 3½ percent of GDP in 1997–98. By 1997 the cumulative effects of somewhat higher inflation in China than in partner countries had pushed China's real effective exchange rate from below its long-run equilibrium path to modestly above it, and the collapse of a number of Asian emerging-market currencies in the crises of 1997–98 pushed China's real effective exchange rate even higher.

With a lag of about two years, which is common for many countries, the consequences of substantial movements in China's real exchange rate relative to its assumed longer-run trend are reflected in movements in China's current account, as figures 8.3 and 8.4 illustrate. Consistent with the assumed lagged effect of movements in the real effective exchange rate relative to its equilibrium path, the current account shows modest (below average) surpluses in 1994–96. The surplus expands significantly in 1997–98, reflecting, with a lag, the real undervaluation of the renminbi in 1994–96. This undervaluation resulted from rapid inflation in China and a relatively weak US dollar against other key currencies. By 1999–2001, the effects of the Asian crisis of 1997–98 and the moderate overvaluation of the renminbi from mid-1998 through 2000 contributed to declines in China's current account surplus. After 2001, the real effective exchange rate of the renminbi fell ever further below its longer-run equilibrium path, and this is reflected in a progressive widening of the current account surplus. At the same time, private capital flows into China began to pick up, with the result that the official settlements balance (or overall balance) increased even more rapidly than the current account balance. This was reflected in increasingly massive inflows of foreign exchange reserves, which reached 9 percent of China's GDP (as an annual flow) in 2006 and pushed China well ahead of Japan as the world's largest holder of reserves in 2007.

The above facts suggest that the Chinese renminbi has become substantially undervalued since 2002. It has been kept in this position by deliberate policies of the Chinese authorities. They intervened massively in the foreign exchange market to keep the exchange rate of the renminbi against the US dollar at a pegged rate of RMB8.28 until July 2005. Since then, they have used even larger intervention to limit appreciation of the renminbi-dollar exchange rate to no more than about 5 percent per year. To offset the effect that this enormous intervention would otherwise have

China is quite strong, and the 2 percent upward tilt of the path of the longer-term equilibrium rate is reasonable in light of the evidence. The choice of the vertical position of the two longer-run equilibrium paths is suggested by the behavior of China's current account balance. However, there should be no illusion. The assumed paths of the longer-run equilibrium real effective exchange rates are based on assumptions that I believe are well-justified, but that others might dispute.

had on China's domestic money supply and price level, the authorities have engaged in massive sterilization operations, in which the net domestic assets of the People's Bank of China (PBC) have been reduced from half of the monetary base at end-2001 to negative 10 percent of the monetary base at end-2006. The exceptional nature, scale, and duration of these policies, together with the extraordinary upsurge in China's balance of payments surplus over the past five years, necessarily raises a serious question as to whether China is violating its specific obligation under Article IV, Section 1 (iii) of the IMF Articles of Agreement, to "avoid manipulating exchange rates or the international monetary system in order to prevent effective balance of payments adjustment or to gain unfair advantage over other members."[6]

Applying the Fund Guidelines

To address the question of whether China should be judged in violation of Article IV, Section 1 (iii) of the IMF Articles of Agreement, it is appropriate to look to the executive board's 1977 decision on Surveillance over Exchange Rate Policies.[7] Two key parts of the decision are particularly relevant.

The Principles for the Guidance of Member's Exchange Rate Policies (PGM) are:

A. A member shall avoid manipulating the exchange rate or the international monetary system in order to prevent effective balance of payments adjustment or to gain unfair competitive advantage over other members.

B. A member should intervene in the foreign exchange market if necessary to counter disorderly conditions which may be characterized inter alia by disruptive short-term movements in the exchange value of its currency.

C. Members should take into account in their intervention policies the interests of other members, including those of the countries in whose currencies they intervene.

---

6. Formal consideration by the executive board of a violation of obligations under Article IV and the recommendation for such consideration by the managing director should only come after all other vigorous efforts at persuasion have been rejected without plausible justification. Unfortunately, in the case of China, the IMF did not begin these efforts when it should have in 2004 and 2005, and there is little indication that appropriately vigorous efforts at persuasion have so far been attempted.

7. In June 2007 the Executive Board adopted a new decision on bilateral surveillance over members' policies, which revised the 1977 decision. The new decision does not materially change the old decision in ways that are relevant to the present discussion, and it is the old decision that is relevant to the period under discussion here. For a discussion of the old and the new surveillance decisions, see IMF (2006a, 2006b, 2007a, 2007b).

The Principles of Fund Surveillance over Exchange Rate Policies (PFS) are:

1. The surveillance of exchange rate policies shall be adapted to the needs of international adjustment as they develop. The functioning of the international adjustment process shall be kept under review by the Executive Board and Interim Committee [now the International Monetary and Finance Committee] and the assessment of its operation shall be taken into account in the implementation of the principles set forth below.

2. In its surveillance of the observance by members of the principles set forth above, the Fund shall consider the following developments as among those which might indicate the need for discussions with a member:

(i) protracted large-scale intervention in one direction in the exchange market;

(ii) an unsustainable level of official or quasi-official borrowing, or excessive and prolonged short-term official or quasi-official lending, for balance of payments purposes;

(iii) (a) the introduction, substantial intensification, or prolong maintenance, for balance of payments purposes, of restrictions on, or incentives for, current transactions or payments, or (b) the introduction or substantial modification for balance of payments purposes of restrictions on, or incentives for, the inflow or outflow of capital;

(iv) the pursuit, for balance of payments purposes, of monetary and other domestic financial policies that provide abnormal encouragement or discouragement to capital flows; and

(v) behavior of the exchange rate that appears to be unrelated to underlying economic and financial conditions including factors affecting competitiveness and long-term capital movements.

3. The Fund's appraisal of a member's exchange rate policies shall be based on an evaluation of the developments in the member's balance of payments against the background of its reserve position and its external indebtedness. The appraisal shall be made within the framework of a comprehensive analysis of the general economic situation and economic policy strategy of the member, and shall recognize that domestic as well as external policies can contribute to timely adjustment of the balance of payments. The appraisal shall take into account the extent to which the policies of the member, including exchange rate policies, serve the objectives of the continuing development of the orderly underlying conditions that are necessary for financial stability, the promotion of sustained sound economic growth, and reasonable levels of employment.

In the PGM, principle A simply reiterates Article IV, Section 1 (iii). Principle B is irrelevant to China because China's massive intervention cannot plausibly be justified as necessary to counteract disorderly conditions in exchange markets. Principle C raises a serious issue for China because China's massive and protracted intervention has clearly not accounted for the interests of other members, especially those of the country (the United States) in whose currency the Chinese authorities primarily conduct their exchange market interventions.

The PFS expounds on the key points that the Fund is supposed to examine in determining whether a member's exchange rate and related policies may violate its obligations under the IMF articles. In applying the PFS to China, it is efficient to look at points 1 and 3 and then turn to the list of items under point 2.

Point 1 is highly relevant to China.[8] The executive board and the International Monetary and Financial Committee (IMFC) have kept the functioning of the international adjustment process under close and continuous review. As discussed in detail below, they have concluded that global payments imbalances are a major concern and have espoused a strategy to deal with this concern that clearly involves China and its exchange rate and related policies—specifically, the need for China, as a major surplus country, to adapt its policies to reduce rather than further increase its balance of payments surpluses. Bilateral surveillance over China should have taken account of these systemic concerns.

Point 3 is also highly relevant to China. Recent developments in China's balance of payments and reserve positions have certainly been remarkable and present clear evidence of serious external payments disequilibrium. As expressed in the Outline of the 11th Five Year Plan approved by the Central Committee of the Chinese Communist Party, China's stated policy objectives include maintaining rapid growth of output and employment with low inflation and financial stability. They also include a clearly stated preference and intention to achieve better-balanced growth and economic development; specifically, a shift of growth toward lesser reliance on the tradable-goods sector and the coastal regions, where development has been very rapid, and greater expansion of consumption and more rapid development of the country's interior regions.[9] That this latter objective is not being achieved, the essential linkage of this failure to China's growing external payments disequilibrium and its exchange rate and related policies (as discussed further below) is further reason for the Fund to call for reform of these policies.

Turning to the subpoints under point 2 of the PFS, item (v) is directly concerned with the exchange rate and whether it is misaligned with "underlying economic and financial conditions including factors affecting competitiveness and long-term capital movements." When this language was drafted in the mid-1970s, the idea was that a country's exchange rate was reasonably aligned with relevant economic fundamentals if the current account deficit or surplus was financed by sustainable longer-term capital in-

---

8. It is highly relevant in other cases as well. Resolution of the problem of global payments imbalances requires efforts by many countries that should be examined in the context of the Fund's bilateral surveillance. Taking an earlier example, the Fund did not regard the strong dollar and the large and rising US current account deficit as an immediately pressing problem in the late 1990s because the international adjustment process generally benefited from a strong US economy that could absorb the improvements that other, more weakly performing economies needed to make in their current accounts.

9. For further discussion of the Chinese government's economic priorities and how they might better be achieved, see Bergsten et al. (2006, chapter 2) and Lardy (2006).

flows or outflows. In such circumstances, at the prevailing exchange rate, the current account imbalance would not give rise to unsustainable official settlements deficits or surpluses. However, if the current account balance associated with the prevailing exchange rate was unduly large relative to the sustainable level of longer-term capital flows, this was a key indication of a seriously misaligned exchange rate—"a fundamental disequilibrium," in the language of the original Article IV—and, accordingly, a strong reason for the Fund to question whether the country's exchange rate and related policies were consistent with Article IV, Section 1 (iii).

That China's exchange rate has become substantially undervalued is abundantly clear and has already been amply discussed. The massive increases in China's foreign exchange reserves and current account surplus since 2002 leave no doubt on this issue. That this undervaluation is to an important extent the consequence of China's exchange rate and related policies, rather than some fortuitous accident, is also quite clear. It is synonymous with the conclusion (discussed below) that an alternative feasible path of China's exchange rate and related policies would have produced much a smaller accumulation of reserves and a much smaller rise in China's current account surplus since 2002.

Items (ii), (iii), and (iv) are included on the list under point 2 of the PFS to deal with situations in which a country pursues policies that indirectly induce a seriously misaligned exchange rate without direct intervention into the foreign exchange market. Such policies include official or quasi-official borrowing, which does not show up in official reserves, government-sponsored incentives or restraints that affect trade flows or capital flows, and "monetary and other domestic financial policies that provide abnormal encouragement or discouragement to capital flows." As these policies generally have a variety of legitimate purposes from the Fund's perspective, the qualifying language that these policies are being pursued "for balance-of-payments purposes" is included in all three of these items.

For China, some concerns could be raised under items (ii), (iii), and (iv). In particular, on some occasions, the Chinese authorities apparently have sought to limit reported increases in official reserves by inducing Chinese banks to hold the proceeds of capital flows offshore. Such operations may have amounted to $50 billion of disguised reserve accumulation in 2006 and a similar or possibly greater amount in 2007. However, it is not essential to focus a great deal of attention on this issue because the Chinese authorities have relied primarily on direct intervention in the foreign exchange market to implement their exchange rate policy, and the massive scale of these operations leaves no room for reasonable dispute about the inconsistency of Chinese policies with obligations under Article IV, Section I (iii).

Indeed, on the list of factors that the Fund should consider in assessing whether there are serious problems with a country's exchange rate and related policies, the first item is "(i) protracted large-scale intervention in one direction in the exchange market." This item has pride of place for very good reason: Official intervention in the foreign exchange market corresponds precisely to a key measure of a country's balance of payments, namely, the official settlements balance. Even before the adoption of the Second Amendment in 1978 and the Bretton Woods conference in 1944, it was understood that protracted large-scale deficits or surpluses in the official settlements balance are, by themselves, a clear indicator of disequilibrium in a country's international payments and a critical signal that adjustments are required in policies that affect the balance of payments. Moreover, in contrast with other policies that may influence a country's exchange rate for reasons ancillary to their main intended purposes, official intervention in the foreign exchange market is, by its very nature, intended to influence the exchange rate and the official settlements balance. It is always carried out "for balance-of-payments purposes."

A nonreserve-currency country that persistently runs official settlement deficits will ultimately run out of reserves, rapidly so if the official settlements deficits are large. The result will almost always be a sharp depreciation of the exchange rate in the midst of a foreign exchange crisis, as speculation mounts against the currency peg and reserve outflows become very large. In such cases, protracted large-scale intervention to support an exchange rate is, by itself, a clear indicator that an exchange rate is seriously overvalued, and thus, the policy that is used to keep it overvalued—protracted large-scale intervention—is by its very nature an exchange rate policy pursued to prevent effective balance-of-payments adjustment, in contravention of Article IV, Section 1 (iii).

For countries with pegged or tightly controlled exchange rates and persistent official settlements surpluses, such as China at present, the judgment on whether this signals a significantly undervalued exchange rate and an important failure to allow appropriate adjustment in the balance of payments is somewhat more complicated. Countries with pegged or quasi-pegged exchange rates generally need foreign exchange reserves to operate their chosen exchange regimes, and prudent holdings of reserves tend to grow with the size of the economy and the volume of trade. Reserves significantly below prudent standards signal potential problems, including the risk of a disruptive foreign exchange crisis and a sudden large depreciation. Conversely, countries that continue to accumulate reserves when they are already well above prudent standards are not only frustrating adjustment of their own balance of payments, but they are also making it more difficult for countries that need to reduce their deficits to make the necessary and appropriate adjustments. It is relevant in this regard that the Fund's executive board has repeatedly expressed concern about persistently large and growing US balance-of-payments deficits. In accord with principle 1 of the PFS, these concerns imply that the Fund should not apply an overly lax standard in assessing when official settlement surpluses of countries like China have become too large and persisted too long.

In looking at the circumstances of individual countries, the Fund has long maintained that foreign reserves equivalent to about three months of imports are prudent. Reserves of up to six months of imports probably should not be regarded as excessive. As table 8.1 reports, China's foreign exchange reserves stood at about 6 months of imports in 1994–95. They rose to almost 13 months of imports in 1998 before this ratio fell back to about 9 months of imports from 2000 through 2002. Subsequently, reserves surged to 16 months of imports by 2006, and reserve and trade data so far available for 2007 indicate a further rise in this ratio. This is massively beyond any reasonable standard of prudence for a country like China.

Another important standard for judging whether reserve accumulation is excessive is to look at its monetary implications (discussed in greater detail in the next section). A country with a pegged or tightly managed exchange rate normally wants to have reserves equal to a reasonable fraction of its monetary base, and it acquires additional reserves corresponding to a reasonable fraction of the annual increase in the domestic monetary base. As table 8.1 reports, China maintained a ratio of reserves to its monetary base of between 25 and 45 percent between 1994 and 2002. Annual increases in the monetary base during this period were supplied about equally by increases in foreign exchange reserves and increases in the PBC's net domestic assets. Since 2002, however, that situation has changed dramatically, with reserves rising to more than 100 percent of the monetary base and net domestic assets declining by nearly RMB3 trillion as a result of sterilization operations. From a monetary perspective, this clearly indicates that China has been maintaining a substantially undervalued exchange rate and that its exchange rate and related policies have frustrated balance-of-payments adjustment.

Applying the PFS, nothing more really needs to be said to conclude that China's exchange rate and related policies stand in violation of China's obligations under Article IV, Section I (iii). The facts concerning China's massive, protracted, one-way intervention to resist appreciation of the renminbi are, by themselves, overwhelmingly sufficient to make the case. There is no question that the Chinese authorities intended to do precisely what they did do. They intervened persistently and massively in the foreign exchange market to resist strong pressures for appreciation of the renminbi, and they sterilized much of the monetary effect of this intervention to avert real appreciation of the renminbi through the alternative mechanism of upward increases in China's domestic price level.

Unfair Competitive Advantage?

That the Chinese government is using massive, protracted, sterilized intervention to resist appreciation of the renminbi, resulting in massive increases in official reserves and the current account surplus, is more than enough to conclude that China's policies are inconsistent with its obligations under Article IV, Section 1 (iii). There is no question of the intent of China's policies: Protracted, large-scale intervention in one direction in the foreign exchange market is indisputably intended to affect the exchange rate and the balance of payments. Such a policy is always pursued "for balance-of-payments purposes."

To conclude that China's policies are in violation of Article IV, Section 1 (iii), it is not necessary to go further to establish that the policies are intended to create unfair competitive advantage. There are, however, important grounds for the Fund to find the requisite intent.

First, some Chinese authorities and other commentators have argued that China faces a critical problem of assuring growing employment opportunities that will enable millions of workers in the rural and poorly developed sectors of the Chinese economy to move to the more modern sectors. However, while achievement of high levels of employment and employment growth is a domestic policy objective that is lauded by the Fund, there is one means for achieving this goal that is specifically prohibited by the Fund's Articles of Agreement. Purpose (iii) in Article 1 and the strictures in Article IV Section 1(iii) make clear that "competitive depreciation" is banned as a means for achieving domestic employment objectives. The assertion by Chinese officials that China is using its exchange rate and related policies for the purpose of stimulating domestic employment is a confession of guilt to violation of Article IV Section 1 (iii).

Second, aside from an explicit admission of guilt to pursuing a policy of competitive depreciation, the fact that the Chinese authorities have persisted for a number of years to maintain a substantially undervalued exchange rate that confers competitive advantage on Chinese producers relative to foreign rivals is important evidence that this effect is not unintentional. If the Chinese authorities are pursuing their exchange rate and related policies with the clear effect, but not the intent, of conferring competitive advantage on Chinese producers, then they owe the Fund and the world a convincing explanation for why this is not an meaningful part of what they intend their policies to achieve.

Third, the Fund needs to weigh carefully its responsibilities to the international economic system when considering how much deference to give to members' assertions that they are not pursuing policies of competitive depreciation when that is clearly the policies' effect. Supervising of the international trading system is not the responsibility of the Fund, but the effective operation of that system is one of the Fund's important concerns. If, with substantial justification, people and businesses in other countries see themselves as the victims of substantial and prolonged competitive depreciation practiced by the Chinese authorities, and if the Fund does not even acknowledge the problem, then the disaffected will seek redress through other channels and will be justified in doing so. The result could ultimately be that, disgusted with the Fund's failure to fulfill its assigned responsibilities, others will be given the job. In view of countries' use and abuse of antidumping and countervailing duties to address other trade complaints, it is worrying to contemplate that similar mechanisms could substitute for more assiduous action by the Fund to deal with cases that appear to involve substantial and prolonged competitive depreciation.

Explaining China's Policy

If the purpose of China's policy is not actively to pursue unfair competitive advantage to boost domestic employment, one might well ask why the Chinese authorities have engaged for so long in such massive and largely sterilized intervention to resist appreciation of the renminbi.

The answer to this intriguing question was provided by the Fund's long-time and highly distinguished economic counselor, Jacques Polak, at virtually the same time that China embarked on its present exchange rate policy. In an essay on the occasion of the 50th anniversary of the Fund in 1994, Polak concluded with the following trenchant observation:

> Taking the past fifty years as a whole, the exchange rate problems that the Fund has had to deal with in connection with requests for use of its resources, or more generally in the surveillance of the policies of the great majority of its members, have been problems of overvaluation. In policy advice handed out by the Fund, "exchange rate flexibility" has almost always served as only a slightly veiled euphemism for devaluation or depreciation. In the most recent years, however, this has no longer necessarily been so. As an increasing number of developing countries are faced with large inflows of capital, some real appreciation of their currencies can usually not be avoided. . . . A few developing countries . . . have in recent years taken steps toward some revaluation of their currencies. These steps, however, have been quite modest, *providing confirmation of an asymmetry in countries exchange rate policy that can be observed over the entire period covered by this paper: countries often fail to take action needed to improve competitiveness, but they hesitate to take any action that would reduce it* [emphasis added]. (Polak 1994)

This conclusion accords perfectly with my experience as the Fund's economic counselor from 1991 to 2001. I had serious discussions with senior officials of a number of countries, both industrial and developing, that had clearly overvalued exchange rates. These officials advanced all sorts of arguments for why their exchange rates were not significantly overvalued. Ultimately, only collapse of these overvalued exchange rates proved to be a convincing argument. In my more limited experience with countries that had clearly undervalued exchange rates, I found officials at least equally determined to deny any significant undervaluation.

I believe that the fundamental reason for the officials' determination is that changing an exchange rate that is pegged, either de jure or de facto, is almost always seen as a defeat for the government officials involved, as they have been forced to change their policy. More than that, a change in an exchange rate is a price change that always hurts somebody, even as it benefits others. When an exchange rate is changed as a visible act of government policy, the government is blamed by those who are hurt and gets little credit from those who benefit.

The Monetary Approach: Explaining Some Chinese Puzzles

To provide further insight into how China's exchange rate and related policies have driven recent developments in China's balance of payments, it is useful to consider these issues from the perspective of the monetary approach to the balance of payments.

The Basic Ideas of Monetary Approach to the Balance of Payments

In spirit, the monetary approach to the balance of payments dates back to David Hume's (1752) brilliant explanation of the price-specie-flow mechanism, and it can be traced through the writings of prominent economists well into the 20th century. The modern formulation of the monetary approach owes much to work done in the Research Department at the Fund, most notably by Jacques J. Polak.[10] In the early-to-mid-1970s, the monetary approach enjoyed a resurgence of interest in the academic community, particularly among economists associated with the University of Chicago, but interest in the approach waned with the shift to floating exchange rates among the major currencies.[11] Inside the Fund, key elements of the monetary approach continued to be applied, especially to countries to which the Fund was providing financial support (IMF 1987, Mussa and Savastano 1999, Robichek 1967).

The essential ideas of the monetary approach that are relevant to the present discussion can be exposited relatively concisely. In all countries, domestic residents demand domestic money, in both currency and bank

---

10. A useful and concise exposition of the monetary approach and a review of work done at the Fund on this subject are provided in Polak (1998). A number of the papers produced by IMF staff over the years up to the mid-1970s are collected in IMF (1977), including Polak (1957) and Polak and Boisenneault (1960).

11. A number of the Chicago papers dealing with the monetary approach are collected in Frenkel and Johnson (1976). Several of Dornbusch's insightful papers reappear in various chapters in Dornbusch (1980). The work of Mundell (1968) and Johnson (1958) provided much of the stimulus for many who worked on the monetary approach at the University of Chicago, including my colleague on the faculty at Chicago and my immediate predecessor as the Fund's economic counselor, Jacob Frenkel (1971, 1976) and my long-time friend Alexander Swoboda (1973). For a general description of the monetary approach and its field of relevance, see Mussa (1974, 1979) and Frenkel and Mussa (1985).

deposits, for use in transactions and as a liquid reserve or form of savings. The quantity of money demanded, M, depends on the level of real income, general domestic price level, interest rates, and other factors, including the degree of financial development in the country. For present purposes, it costs little and is convenient to assume that demand for money is proportional to nominal GDP, that is, $M = kY$, where k is the multiplier that summarizes all factors affecting money demand other than nominal GDP, denoted by Y. It is also convenient and costs little to assume that domestic residents want to hold currency, C, as a fixed fraction, a, of their total money holdings, $C = aM$, with the rest held as bank deposits, $D = (1 - a)M$. Banks need to hold reserves, R, with the monetary authority equal to a fraction, r, of their deposition: $R = rD$. It follows that the effective demand for base money, $B = C + R$, is given by $B = C + rD = aM + r (1 - a) M = (a + r [1 - a]) M = (a + r [1 - a]) kY = bY$, where $b = (a + r[1 - a])k$.

Base money is the liability of the domestic monetary authority. Corresponding to this liability, two items appear on the asset side of the (consolidated) balance sheet of the monetary authority: foreign exchange reserves, F, which are foreign assets held by the monetary authority; and N, net domestic assets held by the monetary authority. By definition, the net domestic assets of the monetary authority are all of the assets held by the monetary authority, except F, less all of the liabilities and capital (and any other items net) of the monetary authority, except base money, B. Thus, as a fact of accounting, $F + N = B = C + R$.

It follows that, for the monetary base to meet the effective demand for base money, $B = bY$, we must have $F + N = bY$. In precisely the spirit of David Hume's analysis, this equation should be viewed as an economic equilibrium condition. If $F + N$ is not equal to bY, then either the monetary authority needs to adjust $F + N$ or allow $F + N$ to adjust, or the public's effective demand for base money, bY, needs to change. In the latter case, if b is a constant, then Y has to change through changes in either real output or the general price level. For example, if $F + N < bY$ and the monetary authority refuses to allow any increase in $F + N$, then the public scrambles to acquire the base money they want to hold by cutting back on spending, putting downward pressure on output and the price level, and therefore on Y, until monetary equilibrium is achieved. Alternatively in this situation, if the monetary authority did not want to force a contraction in Y, it could issue additional base money and use it either to buy foreign exchange, F, or acquire more net domestic assets, N.

Applying the Monetary Approach to China

In principle, the monetary approach can be applied to countries that run either pegged or floating exchange rate regimes, but it is particularly relevant to countries with pegged or tightly managed exchange rates. This is because the monetary approach is fundamentally attuned to explaining the behavior of a country's official settlements balance, which corresponds to the net gain of official loss of foreign exchange reserves.[12] The approach can also be useful in understanding the behavior of the current account balance, especially for countries with pegged exchange rates and limited openness to international capital flows. It is typically not very helpful in analyzing the behavior of the current account for countries that maintain floating exchange rates with little or no official intervention and have quite open capital accounts.

For example, using the monetary approach to explain the evolution of the US current account balance since the early 1990s does not get us very far. It is US policy to allow the exchange rate of the dollar to float freely, and exchange market intervention by US authorities has been sporadic and very small, relative to the size of the US economy. The monetary base in the United States is also relatively small, amounting to only about 6 percent of US GDP. Moreover, it is the policy of the US Federal Reserve to adjust the interest rate in the federal funds market to keep inflation low and help control fluctuations in economic activity. The supply of base money adjusts automatically through changes in the net domestic assets of the Federal Reserve to whatever the demand for base money may be. Hence, in accord with the monetary approach, the US official settlements balance does not deviate far from zero. But this is not helpful in explaining the behavior of the US current account, which has moved into increasingly massive deficit since the early 1990s. But differences between the growth in demand for US base money and the supply made available through increases in the net domestic assets of the Federal Reserve—which have been effectively zero—have played no meaningful role in determining the US current account. Instead, as described in detail in Mussa (2005), the evolution of the US current account balance involves the general equilibrium interactions of complex forces in the US economy and the rest of the world, which have influenced levels of spending relative to income (in the United States and in the rest of the world), the associated movements in both trade flows and international flows of capital (private and official), and the (mainly market-determined) movements of exchange rates against the US dollar.

By contrast, China's economy is quite different from the US economy in ways that make applying the monetary approach to explain developments in China's balance of payments far more relevant and fruitful. China runs a pegged exchange rate regime and uses massive official intervention to

---

12. The particular relevance of the monetary approach to explaining the behavior of the official settlements balance has been much emphasized in the literature; see, e.g., the introductory chapter by Rudolph Rhomberg and Robert Heller in IMF (1977), Johnson (1958), and Mussa (1974).

Table 8.2   China's monetary aggregates, 1993–2006 (billions of renminbi)

Year	Nominal GDP (Y)	Monetary base (B)	Ratio of (B) to (Y) (b)	Foreign assets (F)	Net domestic assets (N)	Money (M1)	Money plus quasi money (M2)
1993	3,533	1,315	.372	155	1,160	1,676	3,568
1994	4,820	1,722	.357	445	1,277	2,154	4,692
1995	6,079	2,076	.342	667	1,409	2,308	6,074
1996	7,118	2,689	.378	956	1,733	2,756	7,609
1997	7,897	3,063	.388	1,345	1,718	3,481	9,187
1998	8,440	3,134	.371	1,376	1,758	3,869	10,556
1999	8,968	3,362	.375	1,486	1,876	4,698	12,104
2000	9,922	3,649	.368	1,558	2,091	5,454	13,596
2001	10,966	3,985	.363	1,986	1,999	6,169	15,641
2002	12,033	4,514	.371	2,324	2,190	7,088	18,501
2003	13,582	5,284	.389	3,114	2,171	8,412	22,122
2004	15,988	5,886	.368	4,696	1,190	9,582	25,305
2005	18,387	6,434	.350	6,344	90	10,690	29,838
2006	21,087	7,776	.369	8,577	−801	12,604	34,609

Sources: Data are from International Monetary Fund, *International Financial Statistics Yearbook,* 2007 and earlier years; GDP data are from China's National Bureau of Statistics, based on estimates of national production.

keep the exchange rate of the renminbi against the US dollar from moving far from its policy-determined level, which has been allowed to appreciate very slowly since July 2005. Unlike the US Federal Reserve, Chinese monetary authorities do not automatically adjust their net domestic assets to meet fluctuations in the demand for base money. Rather, they adjust the growth of net domestic assets to offset increases in the supply of base money resulting from foreign reserve inflows that exceed China's monetary policy objectives. In recent years, this has required massive sterilization of very large foreign exchange inflows. Also, as reported in table 8.2, monetary aggregates in China are very large relative to the size of the economy, especially compared with those of the United States. Broad money in China is about 150 percent of GDP versus about 50 percent of GDP in the United States, and the monetary base in China runs about 37 percent of GDP versus only 6 percent of GDP in the United States. Moreover, with the annual growth rate of nominal GDP in China running about 16 percent versus about 6 percent in the United States, annual growth of demand for base money in China has averaged almost 6 percent of GDP, 20 times larger than the growth of base money as a share of US GDP.

In China the official settlements balance has not been virtually zero in recent years. Indeed, foreign reserve inflows (which correspond to the official settlements surplus) have ranged from a low of RMB31 billion, or

Table 8.3   Changes in China's GDP and monetary aggregates from the preceding year, 1994–2006

Year	GDP growth (percent)	Base growth (percent)	Change in monetary base (dB) (billions of renminbi)	Change in net domestic assets (dN) (billions of renminbi)	Change in foreign assets (dF) (billions of renminbi)
1994	36.4	30.1	407	117	290
1994	26.1	20.6	354	132	222
1996	17.1	29.5	613	324	289
1997	10.9	13.9	374	−15	389
1998	6.9	2.3	071	40	031
1999	6.3	7.3	228	118	110
2000	10.5	8.5	287	215	072
2001	10.5	9.2	336	−92	428
2002	9.7	13.3	529	191	338
2003	12.9	17.1	770	−19	790
2004	17.7	11.4	602	−981	1,582
2005	15.0	9.3	548	−1,100	1,648
2006	14.7	20.1	1342	−891	2,233

Source: Table 8.2.

0.4 percent of GDP in 1998, to RMB2,233 billion, or 10.6 percent of GDP in 2006. Clearly, for China the behavior of the official settlements balance is something that merits analysis and explanation.

The monetary approach provides the relevant framework for such analysis and explanation. For China the data in table 8.2 reveal a remarkably stable relation between base money and nominal GDP, with their ratio, b, averaging 0.369 and moving in a very narrow range between 0.342 and 0.389. It is noteworthy that b remains remarkably stable given the following: a more than a quadrupling of nominal GDP; considerable variations in the annual growth rates of nominal GDP, real GDP, and price level; and very large variations in the two factors—foreign exchange reserves and net domestic assets—that determine increases in the supply of base money. We may conclude with considerable confidence that demand for base money in China is highly stable, characterized by a nearly constant ratio of base money to nominal GDP of about 0.369. Applying the principles of the monetary approach, we may use this demand function for base money both to analyze what actually transpired in China's official settlements balance and to consider the implications of counterfactual experiments of what would have been different under alternative policy scenarios.

Consider first what actually happened from 1994 through 1999. As table 8.3 reports, from 1994 through 1996, Y rose very quickly, reflecting both rapid real growth and high inflation. Correspondingly, the demand for base money grew quite rapidly. The Chinese monetary authorities met about half of this rising demand for base money through increases in the PBC's net domestic assets. To maintain the exchange rate of the renminbi, the authorities were also compelled to increase foreign exchange reserves by the amount corresponding to the rest of the increase in the demand for base money. The word "compelled" is used advisedly, as the authorities could have intervened less in the foreign exchange market if they had been willing to allow the renminbi to appreciate—which would have affected the behavior of Y. Alternatively, the authorities could have met a larger fraction of the increasing demand for base money by expanding net domestic assets or done something else to change the behavior of nominal GDP. However, given the behavior of Y, the growth of demand for base money was determined by the stable demand function, and the authorities had to meet this growing demand with either increases in net domestic assets or official intervention that increased in foreign reserves.

From 1997 through 1999, growth of nominal GDP slowed considerably, reflecting both slower real growth and much lower inflation. Correspondingly, the demand for base money grew much more slowly than in the preceding three-year period, only 25 percent compared with 104 percent in the earlier three years. Increases in net domestic assets also slowed in percentage growth, providing about one-third of the increase in the total supply of base money. Increases in foreign exchange reserves resulting from intervention to maintain the exchange rate peg were also somewhat smaller than in the earlier three years, accounting for about two-thirds of the increase in the supply of base money. The slower growth of China's nominal GDP in this period reflects both Chinese government efforts to reduce inflation, which are reflected in the slower growth of net domestic assets, as well as some negative impact on China's economy from the crises affecting a number of Asian emerging-market economies. The Chinese authorities' decision to hold the exchange rate peg of the renminbi in the face of large depreciations of a number of other Asian currencies helped to transmit some negative effects to China's GDP growth. Thus, as in the earlier period, the behavior of Y was not entirely exogenous with respect to the exchange rate and related policies pursued by Chinese authorities. Nevertheless, given the behavior of Y and the increase in demand for base money it implied, the Chinese authorities were compelled to intervene in the foreign exchange market to the extent necessary to meet that part of the growing demand for base money that they chose not to meet with increases in net domestic assets.

The three years from 1999 though 2002 saw China's nominal GDP grow by 34 percent, with the GDP deflator rising cumulatively by only 3 percent. Characteristically, base money expanded proportionally with nominal GDP by 34 percent, but net domestic assets supplied none of this increase. Instead, the authorities were compelled, in the sense already defined, to meet the rising demand for base money by acquiring additional foreign exchange reserves through their interventions to prevent the renminbi from appreciating against the US dollar. Again, of course, the behavior of the Chinese economy was not entirely exogenous to the authorities' policy. For example, with the exchange rate pegged, suppose that net domestic assets had been expanded by half of the actual increase in base money of RMB1,152 billion. This increase in N would have been only partly offset by a decline in acquisition of foreign exchange rate reserves. Base money would have risen by significantly more than RMB1,152 billion. The more rapid growth of base money—and of other money and credit aggregates—would have been reflected in somewhat higher inflation and probably a temporary stimulus to stronger real growth. With downward pressure on the real effective exchange rate of the renminbi from higher Chinese inflation, and with somewhat stronger growth of domestic demand in China, the current account surplus would have been somewhat smaller, implying less need to intervene in the foreign exchange market to maintain the exchange rate peg.

In the four years since 2002, China's nominal GDP has risen cumulatively by 75 percent, and base money expanded by 72 percent. In this period, as previously discussed, the real effective exchange rate of the renminbi became increasingly undervalued relative to its longer-run equilibrium path, despite modest nominal appreciation of the renminbi against the dollar beginning in July 2005. This increasing undervaluation contributed to significant expansion of China's current account surplus. Especially in 2004, increasing private capital inflows added to upward pressures on the exchange rate of the renminbi. To hold the exchange rate, the authorities intervened in increasingly massive amounts in the foreign exchange market. To prevent this massive intervention from being fully reflected in growth of the supply of base money and ultimately in an upsurge of inflation, the Chinese authorities engaged in massive sterilization operations, reducing net domestic assets by almost RMB3 trillion between end-2002 and end-2006. To meet the rising demand for base money implied by the growth of China's nominal GDP, Chinese residents compelled the authorities to intervene in the foreign exchange market to the extent that such interventions both met the rising demand for base money and offset the reductions in the supply of base money induced by the authorities' sterilization operations.

Thus the monetary approach explains the explosion of China's official settlements surplus from 2002 through 2006: The explosion was the direct consequence of the exchange rate and related policies pursued by Chinese authorities in the face of exogenous factors that were affecting China's economic situation. China's policy of pegging the nominal exchange rate of the renminbi against the US dollar, together with the upward trend in the longer-run equilibrium real effective exchange rate of the renminbi and the depreciation of the US dollar against many currencies beginning in early 2002, induced an expanding surplus in China's current account. The policy of sterilizing an important part of the increase in base money that would otherwise have resulted from exchange market intervention had the intended effect of limiting domestic inflation, and thereby, also forestalled adjustment of the renminbi's real effective exchange rate through David Hume's classic price-specie-flow mechanism. In addition, as is argued below, these operations probably depressed spending relative to income in China, contributing directly to an expanding current account surplus and official settlements surplus.

Of course, if circumstances had been different, the results of China's exchange rate and related policies would have been different. Experience provides many examples of countries that have sought to maintain pegged nominal exchange rates through extensive exchange market intervention, sterilizing much of the effect of such intervention on the domestic monetary base. In many of these cases, the exchange rate is or becomes substantially overvalued, leading to rapidly expanding official settlements deficits and ultimately a crisis in which the country is forced to adopt sharply contractionary domestic credit policies, devalue, or both. Cases like China, in which a country seeks to maintain an exchange rate peg that becomes increasingly undervalued, are relatively rare. But economic logic implies that such cases must be possible. The facts demonstrate that China's recent experience in one such case.

It is also clear that China's exchange rate and related policies must be treated as a package. The policy of pegging the nominal exchange rate of the renminbi tightly to the US dollar is linked to the policy of intervening in the foreign exchange market as required to keep the exchange rate on its prescribed path. These interventions are tied to the policy of offsetting the expansion they imply in the domestic monetary base by adjusting the behavior of net domestic assets. Changing an element of this policy package affects the other elements and the consequences of the policy package. The only way to speak of the effects of the policy package in an analytically meaningful way is to consider the counterfactual of how things would have been different if an alternative package of policies had been pursued.

In this regard, it is relevant to consider what would likely have happened if the Chinese authorities had maintained the same path for the nominal exchange rate of the renminbi against the dollar from 2002 through 2006 and had intervened as required to do so, but had not sterilized the effect of reserve inflows on the growth of the monetary base. Instead, suppose that Chinese authorities expanded net domestic assets to retain the same ratio of N to B, 48.5 percent, that prevailed at the end of 2002. Assuming for a moment that reserve inflows remained unchanged under this alternative policy scenario, the monetary base would have expanded from RMB4,514 billion at end-2002 to RMB17,669 billion—a whopping 2.72 times larger than the actual monetary base of RMB7,776 billion at end-2006.

One does not need to be a devout monetarist to understand that in view of Chinese residents' desire to maintain a ratio of base money to nominal GDP of 37 percent, this massive supposed increase in the monetary base could only have been consistent with a massively higher level of nominal GDP than the actual level of RMB21,087 billion in 2006. Correspondingly, there would have been a huge increase in China's price level between 2002 and 2006.

Of course, the outcome under the alternative policy scenario would not have been quite so extreme. Substantially greater money and credit expansion beginning in 2003 would have started to push up the Chinese price level even during that year and during the years that followed. The real effective exchange rate of the renminbi would have depreciated considerably due to this more rapid inflation, leading to significantly smaller current account and official settlements surpluses. China's foreign exchange reserves would have risen by substantially less than the actual increase (RMB6,253 billion), leaving the level of reserves well below the actual level of RMB8,577 billion.

Assuming, for concreteness and simplicity, that the reserve gain would have been cut in half, the implied level of reserves at end-2006 is RMB5,461 billion. With the PBC keeping net domestic assets at 48.5 percent of the monetary base, the implied size of the monetary base is RMB10,604 billion, 36 percent above the actual figure of RMB7,776 billion but well below the initially hypothesized figure of RMB17,669 billion. This significantly larger monetary base implies increases in China's nominal GDP and price level of about 36 percent by 2006. With such inflation inducing real effective appreciation of the renminbi by 36 percent, China's current account surplus in 2006 would have been substantially less than the actual level of $240 billion. Combined with the 36 percent rise in China's GDP, measured in dollars, the result would probably have been a current account surplus of no more than 3 to 4 percent of China's nominal GDP in 2006, rather than the actual surplus equal to 9 percent of China's GDP.

There is no escape from the conclusion that, in the circumstances that have confronted China's economy since 2002, the Chinese authorities' package of exchange rate and related policies induced massive official settlements surpluses. The usual objection to the monetary approach—that there is insufficiently stable demand for base money—is clearly irrelevant for China. The issue is not whether there is some variation in the ratio of base money to GDP indicating flexibility in the demand for base money but rather whether there is credible evidence of sufficient stability in the demand for base money to support the conclusion that a significantly different package of exchange rate and related policies than that actually pursued by Chinese authorities would have led to substantially different behavior in China's balance of payments.

Indeed, the only situation in which the above analysis applying the monetary approach to recent developments in China would be invalid is if China was operating in conditions approximating a liquidity trap in which fluctuations in the supply of base money would have been willingly accepted without any meaningful change in the factors that are normally thought to affect the demand for base money.[13] But the evidence contradicts any notion of a liquidity trap in China. That the ratio of base money to nominal GDP is highly stable across a wide range of variation in growth rates of nominal GDP and the price level—and in the face of vast differences in the factors accounting for the growth of the supply of base money—points unequivocally to a reasonably stable demand for base money.[14] The gross magnitudes of the variables that the monetary approach relies upon to explain the behavior of the official settlements balance are so large that they overwhelm any concerns about minor instabilities in the money demand function or money supply process. If, at an unchanged nominal exchange rate path, Chinese authorities had increased net domestic assets *pari passu* with the increases in international reserves that actually occurred between end-2002 and end-2006, no competent economist could doubt that this would have led to vastly higher inflation in China, a substantially appreciated real exchange rate, and a significantly smaller current account surpluses.

Moreover, the argument that the monetary approach is all a tautology or the result of reverse causation is clearly nonsense. It was not by accident or whim that Chinese authorities engaged in massive sterilization to offset much of the rapid rise in the monetary base that would otherwise have resulted from massive foreign reserve gains. They understood fully that allowing such increases in the monetary base would have pushed up

---

13. Japan in recent years provides the unique recent example of a major economy operating in conditions of a liquidity trap, in which fluctuations in the supply of base money have little effect on anything. Under a monetary policy by which the Japanese authorities pushed the nominal interest rate in the short-term interbank market down to zero and engaged in massive quantitative easing to force large increases in excess reserves (up to 30 trillion yen during 2005), it should be expected that large fluctuations in foreign exchange market intervention, as occurred in 2004 when the Japanese authorities suddenly stopped massive intervention to depress the exchange value of the yen, would have little or no effect. The situation in China, however, was in no way comparable to Japan's very peculiar situation.

14. Anderson (comment to chapter 1) notes that the ratio of currency to base money in China has not been constant and that Chinese banks have sometimes held substantial excess reserves. These facts do not undermine the present analysis using the monetary approach. It is not unusual for currency to decline somewhat as a ratio of total money demand, nor for the demand for broad money to rise relative to income as income rises in a country such as China. To the extent that Chinese banks voluntarily decide to hold excess reserves, this is a component of the demand for base money. To the extent that the government requires banks to hold higher required reserves or persuades them to hold excess reserves, this too is a component of the demand for base money. The fact is that the ratio of base money to nominal GDP has been highly stable, indicating quite stable demand for base money. This observed stability is far beyond the minimum required to demonstrate that the demand for base money is sufficiently stable to rule out the anomaly of the liquidity trap and validly apply the basic principles of the monetary approach to the balance of payments.

inflation to uncomfortable rates. China's experience in the mid-1990s demonstrated this effect. The understandable desire to avoid rapid domestic inflation, however, is not a reason to deny the analytical conclusion that the package of exchange rate and related policies pursued by Chinese authorities generated enormous official settlements surpluses and frustrated appreciation of the real exchange rate of the renminbi, through both nominal appreciation against the dollar and through the operation of Hume's price-specie-flow mechanism. Any economist who does not understand this essential point should retire permanently from commenting on issues related to exchanges rates and the behavior of the balance of payments.

The Monetary Approach and China's Current Account

While application of the monetary approach convincingly explains why China's package of exchange rate and related policies generated huge official settlements surpluses after 2002, it leaves open an important question: How did Chinese policies induce the reduction of national spending relative to national income that is necessarily the counterpart to China's rising current account surplus?

The theoretical literature on the monetary approach has elaborated several mechanisms to explain this phenomenon. In circumstances such as those in China, where the growing demand for base money is not met by increases in net domestic assets, Rudi Dornbusch's classic hoarding function is highly relevant (Dornbusch 1973a, 1973b, 1974; Dornbusch and Mussa 1975). Chinese households own much of the currency and bank deposits that constitute the money supply. Lacking other financial alternatives, much of the saving of Chinese households takes the form of increased money holdings. The part of these increased money holdings arising from household savings that is not base money gets recycled as loans by the banking system and ultimately contributes to somebody's spending. The part of increased money holdings that is sequestered into base money does not get recycled (except to the extent that the authorities expand their net domestic assets); the monetary authorities impound it and add it to an already huge hoard of foreign exchange reserves. The mechanisms through which this sequestration is achieved are generally opaque. For example, the income that Chinese residents earn on their massive bank deposits is very low. Real interest rates paid to depositors have typically been negative in recent years, partly because Chinese banks are required to hold significant reserves against their deposit liabilities, which depresses the returns they can afford to pay to depositors. As the income that deposit holders should receive never appears, we do not see the national savings that result because the government effectively collects this income and uses it to acquire foreign exchange assets. Nevertheless, the effect is essentially the same as if the government imposed a tax on bank deposits and used the proceeds to buy foreign exchange assets.

More generally, the Chinese government earns substantial seigniorage from its monopoly over the creation of base money. Since 2002 it has used all of this seigniorage to buy additional foreign exchange reserves. It has also borrowed an additional RMB3,000 billion from the Chinese people—corresponding to the reduction in monetary authorities' net domestic assets—to finance purchases of foreign exchange assets. Suppose instead that the government made the seigniorage revenues available to the Chinese people through transfer payments (or, equivalently, lowered taxes while maintaining the level of government expenditure). Suppose further that the government did not borrow from the people to finance reserve accumulation but instead imposed an explicit tax to finance its accumulation of foreign exchange reserves, amounting cumulatively to RMB6,253 billion between 2002 and 2006. The effects of this alternative would have been essentially the same as what actually happened in China. But with reserve accumulation financed by an explicit tax, it would be much clearer why spending by Chinese residents was depressed relative to income as the counterpart of the large increase in the current account surplus.

To develop a more formal analysis of how the monetary approach helps to explain the increase in the current account surplus after 2002, it is useful to return to our earlier notation and formulas. When China's GDP rises by an amount dY, where d stands for the change, the demand for base money by Chinese residents rises by bdY, where b is the desired ratio of base money to nominal GDP explained earlier. There are two ways in which the supply of base money may rise to meet this increased demand: (1) from an expansion of the net domestic assets of monetary authorities, dN; or (2) from increases in base money that the monetary authorities must issue as the counterpart to increases in their foreign exchange reserves, dF.

The increase in foreign exchange reserves corresponds to China's official settlements balance, which must equal the sum of China's current account balance, CA, and the net capital inflow into China (other than accumulation of official foreign reserves), dK; that is, $dF = CA + dK$.[15] For the increase in the supply of base money to meet the increase in demand, we must have $bdY = dN + CA + dK$.

If the rules of accounting are properly implemented, a country's current account balance must correspond to the country's net saving, S, which in turn must equal the excess of national income, Q, over national expenditure, E; that is, $CA = S = Q - E$. National income, Q, differs (modestly) from

---

15. In the data reported in the IMF's *International Financial Statistics*, there are modest differences between the level of China's foreign exchange reserves (valued in renminbi) and the value of foreign assets of the PBC. For annual changes, differences between the official settlements balance (valued in renminbi) and the change in foreign assets of the PBC are significant in some years.

GDP, Y, to the extent that a country's residents receive net income from the rest of the world: $Q = Y + Nfi$. For this purpose, net foreign income, Nfi, is defined to include both private and official international transfers, which are part of a country's balance of payments receipts but not counted in the usual national income aggregate of gross national product or gross national income. National expenditure on goods and services, E, is comprised of consumption, Cn, investment, Iv, and government spending on goods and services, G; that is, $E = Cn + Iv + G$. As GDP $= Y = Cn + Iv + G + (Ex - Im)$, we may immediately conclude that $CA = S = Q - E = (Ex - Im) + Nfi$; that is, the current account balance is, as it should be, the sum of net exports plus net income, including transfers from abroad.

In applying the monetary approach to analyzing the current account, the monetary activities of monetary authorities are distinguished from the economic and financial activities of the aggregate of all other Chinese residents and from the activities of the rest of the world. The monetary activities of the monetary authority consist precisely and exclusively of expanding (contracting) the supply of base money, B, in exchange for increases (decreases) in the authority's holdings of foreign exchange assets, F, and net domestic assets, N. These activities are summarized by the equation $dB = dF + dN$.

All domestic residents other than the monetary authority have a flow of current receipts $Q + dK + dN$ consisting of national income plus net inflows of capital from abroad plus the proceeds of net sales of domestic assets to the monetary authority. These current receipts must all be spent either on current purchases of goods and services, $E = Cn + Iv + G$, or on the acquisition of additional base money, dB. As previously emphasized, the essential idea of the monetary approach is that the amount of current receipts that is devoted to acquiring additional base money does not float freely in the breeze and automatically accommodate to whatever additional base money the monetary authority may decide to supply. Instead, there is a reasonably well-defined demand for additional base money, bdY, that depends to an important degree on the growth of nominal GDP. To the extent that current receipts must be devoted to satisfying the demands of domestic residents for additional base money, these receipts are not available to pay for spending on goods and services. Because current receipts include net capital inflows, dK, and the proceeds of net sales of domestic assets to the monetary authority, the amount that is available to finance domestic spending, E, after satisfying the demand for additional base money, is given by $E = Q + dK + dN - bdY$. As the current account, CA, is equal to $Q - E$, this condition implies that

$$CA = Q - E = (bdY - dN) - dK.$$

Using this formula, movements in the current account balance may be decomposed into movements of two factors: a monetary factor, $bdY - dN$, which measures the excess of growth of demand for base money over the increase of net domestic assets of the monetary authorities; and a capital flow factor, $-dK$, which corresponds to the net capital outflow, excluding official reserve transactions.

Unlike the United States, for China the behavior of the monetary factor is highly relevant to explaining the evolution of China's current account, especially the upsurge of the current account surplus in recent years, but it clearly falls short in explaining everything important about the behavior of China's current account. Table 8.4 helps to illuminate these conclusions. The first two columns report China's current account balance, CA, in billions of renminbi and as a share of China's GDP (the current account as a share of national income, CA/Q, is very similar to CA/GDP). The next two columns report the capital flow factor, $-dK$, in billions of renminbi and as a share of China's GDP.[16] It is apparent that, although China maintains significant restrictions on private capital flows, the magnitude of these flows and fluctuations in them is quite substantial. Capital flowed into China from 1995 through 1997, leaving a current account surplus that was somewhat smaller than that implied by the monetary factor. From 1998 through 2000, capital flowed out of China, probably partly reflecting spillovers from the crises in other Asian emerging-market economies, and this was associated with current account surpluses that were larger than the monetary factor implied. Since 2001 capital inflows have returned to China, with a very large inflow in 2004 probably related to speculation that the renminbi might be revalued.[17] Correspondingly, in recent years the current account surplus has been somewhat smaller than the monetary factor implied. This probably reflects efforts to circumvent the government's policy of repressing increases in the supply of base money and the supply of credit inside China. In other words, some Chinese residents have decided to exploit their access to foreign capital rather than reducing their spending and raising their saving as the means of acquiring additional base money.

A key consequence of the fluctuations in capital flows is that the influence of the monetary factor on China's current account is not one to one; movements in the monetary factor cannot explain everything that is im-

---

16. The figures for the capital account factor are the sum of the capital account balance, the financial-account balance, and net errors and omissions in China's balance-of-payments accounts as reported by the IMF. Net errors and omissions are included here because, for many countries, they appear to reflect primarily unrecorded capital flows, although they also surely include some misreported trade flows.

17. The sharp falloff in capital inflows in 2006 partly reflects efforts by Chinese authorities to persuade Chinese banks to hold the proceeds from foreign investment inflows in external accounts, with the result that these inflows were not recorded in the balance of payments and did not require explicit PBC sterilization to forestall their effect in raising the monetary base. Through these efforts the Chinese authorities effectively engaged in disguised foreign exchange market intervention to help limit the appreciation of the renminbi.

Table 8.4   Monetary factors and the current account in China, 1994–2006

Year	Current account balance (CA) (billions of renminbi)	Current account balance relative to GDP (CA/Y) (percent)	Net capital inflow (–dK) (billions of renminbi)	Net capital inflow relative to GDP (–dK/Y) (percent)	Change in monetary factor (dB – dN) (billions of renminbi)	Change in monetary factor relative to GDP (dB – dN)/Y (percent)	Change in monetary factor (bdY – dNa) (billions of renminbi)	Change in monetary factor relative to GDP (bdY – dNa)/Y (percent)
1994	60	1.2	203	4.0	290	5.8	288	5.7
1995	14	0.2	174	2.8	222	3.5	341	5.4
1996	60	0.8	203	2.7	289	3.9	151	2.0
1997	306	3.8	–9	–0.1	384	4.7	134	1.6
1998	261	3.1	–209	–2.4	31	0.4	189	2.2
1999	130	1.4	–58	–0.6	110	1.2	116	1.3
2000	170	1.7	–81	–0.8	72	0.7	186	1.9
2001	144	1.3	249	2.3	428	3.9	324	3.0
2002	293	2.4	329	2.7	338	2.8	345	2.9
2003	380	2.8	585	4.3	790	5.8	488	3.6
2004	568	3.5	1,137	7.1	1,582	9.9	1,390	8.7
2005	1,318	7.0	381	2.0	1,648	8.7	1,928	10.2
2006	1,992	9.4	–24	–0.1	2,233	10.1	1,995	9.0

Sources: International Monetary Fund, *International Financial Statistics Yearbook*, 2007 and earlier years, and author's calculations; GDP data are "production estimates" from China's National Bureau of Statistics.

portant in the behavior of China's current account. This relates to the point made above that the monetary approach is fundamentally a framework for analyzing and understanding the behavior of the official settlements balance, and in turn, its relevance and usefulness in explaining the behavior of the current account—or other subaccounts of the overall balance of payments—depends on the circumstances of particular countries, especially in their arrangements regarding international capital mobility.

The next two sets of columns in table 8.4 report two alternative measures of the monetary factor, in billions of renminbi and as shares of GDP. The first of these measures, $dB - dN$, is simply the change in the monetary base less the change in the PBC's net domestic assets, measured using year-end data. The argument for using this measure is that in annual data, the actual change in base money is a good proxy for the change in the demand for base money, and $dB - dN$ is therefore a reasonable measure of excess growth of demand for base money over the supply that the monetary authority provides through acquiring net domestic assets. Comparing the movements in this measure of the monetary factor with movements in the current account, as reported in table 8.4, the series for both $dB - dN$ and CA are consistently positive and have similar average ratios to GDP: 4.4 percent versus 3 percent. The ratio $(dB - dN)/Y$ also varies considerably over the period, ranging from under 1 percent in 2000 to over 9 percent after 2003. Thus—in contrast to the monetary factor in the United States, which is always essentially zero—it is at least possible that movements in the monetary factor for China might help to explain something important about the behavior of the current account, or might fail dramatically to provide a relevant explanation if the scale and pattern of movements in the monetary factor were decisively different from those of the current account.

As the monetary approach implies, movements in $dB - dN$ show some rough correspondence to movements in the current account, especially for the large upsurges in both $(dB - dN)/Y$ and CA/Y after 2003. This rough relation applies not only to the general pattern of movements of the two time series but also to similar absolute scales of the movements in the two series. If the theory is right, then movements in the monetary factor should drive movements of the same sign and similar scale in the current account, not movements of the opposite sign or a much greater or smaller scale.

The rough relation between $(dB - dN)/Y$ and CA/Y works best when movements in the monetary factor are related to movements in the current account balance a year or so later. The relatively high levels of $(dB - dN)/Y$ in 1995–97 are reflected in relatively high values of CA/Y in 1997–98; the much lower values of the monetary factor in 1998–2000 are reflected in the lower levels of CA/Y in 1999–2001; and the upsurge in the monetary factor that begins in 2003 and strengthens significantly in 2004 is followed one year later by an upsurge in the current account surplus, which also grows through 2006. Data so far available for 2007 indicate that the further rise in the monetary factor to 10.1 percent of GDP in 2006 will be reflected in a further rise in the current account surplus this year.

The timing in the relation between movements in the monetary factor, $(dB - dN)/Y$, and the current account balance, CA/Y, as well as the rough correspondence of the gross magnitudes of these two series, is important evidence there is some causal effect running from movements in $dB - dN$ to subsequent movements in the current account. There is also a mechanism of reverse causation—or, more appropriately, simultaneous causation—through which movements in the current account balance lead to changes in the supply of base money and, particularly in recent years, to sterilization operations, by which the monetary authorities reduce net domestic assets to prevent undesired increases in the supply of base money. But this alternative mechanism clearly does not explain the lead in the apparent relationship of changes in $(dB - dN)/Y$ ahead of changes in CA/Y. Thus, as the monetary approach implies, the monetary factor $dB - dN$ appears to be driving at least an important part of the developments in China's current account; the relation is not predominantly the other way around.

The second measure of the monetary factor reported in the final two columns of table 8.4 provides an alternative approach to addressing the issue of possible reverse or simultaneous causation. For these columns, the alternative monetary factor, $bdY - dNa$, is calculated as follows. It is assumed that the growth of demand for base money for a given year may be reasonably approximated by the average ratio of base money to GDP, $b = 0.37$, multiplied by the change in Y from its level the preceding year. Because the data for Y are year-average figures and the data for N are year-end figures, it is not appropriate simply to subtract dN from bdY to calculate the alternative monetary factor. Instead, a series for the average level of N during the year, Na, is calculated by taking the average between N at the end of the year and N at the end of the preceding year; then dNa is calculated as the change in Na from the preceding year to the current year. This procedure for calculating the monetary factor $dbY - dNa$ forecloses any channel for reverse causation as far as the measure of change in demand for base money, dbY, is concerned but still leaves partially open the channel for some reverse causation affecting dNa.

Comparing the behavior of the alternative measure of the monetary factor $bdY - dNa$ with that of the current account yields essentially the same conclusions as does the comparison using the monetary factor $dB - dN$. The two series have similar average magnitudes and are uniformly of the same sign. There is also a rough correspondence of their movements that works best when movements in the monetary factor have a lead over movements in the current account. Again, the monetary approach appears to contribute something useful to the explanation of the behavior of China's current account balance, especially the remarkable upsurge in the surplus after 2003.

Of course, this conclusion must be interpreted with due caution. As previously emphasized, the monetary factor does not perfectly explain the behavior of the current account; other forces that are not captured by the monetary factor are clearly important. Also, in considering the relation between the monetary factor and the current account, there is surely some reverse or simultaneous causation. With their policy of resisting appreciation of the renminbi, Chinese authorities automatically respond to upward pressures on the exchange rate with official intervention, and they tend to sterilize this intervention to the extent that its effects in increasing base money threaten to generate too much domestic inflation. Thus the authorities' reaction to a rising current account surplus tends to push up the monetary factor, $dB - dN$, in reaction to increases in CA, creating a process of reverse causation. The timing of the relation between movements in the monetary factor and movements in the current account shows that causation cannot be going only in this reverse direction. There must be significant causation going in the primary direction—from movements in the monetary factor to subsequent movements in the current account.

Moreover, the presence of an important mechanism of reverse causation—from the current account to the monetary factor—does not in any way weaken the primary mechanism of causation from the monetary factor to the current account. The authorities' reaction to large foreign exchange inflows with sterilization operations affects the behavior of the monetary factor. But whatever the reasons for the authorities' actions, Chinese residents adjust their behavior to the fact that the authorities' increases in net domestic assets are supplying them with less of an increase in base money than they desire. Chinese residents thus reduce their spending relative to their income or seek additional foreign capital inflows to acquire the additional base money. Thus, causation runs in both directions in what has become a vicious spiral, as ever more vigorous efforts to resist appreciation and sterilize the domestic monetary consequences of official reserve accumulation leads to stronger efforts by Chinese residents to raise saving to acquire the additional base money they require, generating ever-larger current account surpluses.

Explaining Some of the Chinese Puzzles

The above analysis of how monetary factors have influenced China's current account is helpful in explaining some otherwise very puzzling features of the evolution of China's economy in recent years.

First, the rise in China's current account surplus is exceptionally large: from about 2 percent of GDP in 2002 to over 9 percent of GDP in 2006 and probably to about 12 percent of GDP in 2007. Moreover, this rise in the current account surplus has occurred despite two factors that should have pushed China's current account toward deficit: (1) growth of China's economy that has substantially exceeded the growth of its trading partners; and (2) large increases in the prices of China's commodity imports, especially energy. The depreciation of China's real effective exchange rate relative to a plausible estimate of its longer-run equilibrium path can rationalize an important part of the improvement in China's current account improvement—but not all of it.

Second, China's current account surplus is necessarily equal to its national savings–investment balance. A rising current account surplus necessarily corresponds to an equal increase in the excess of national saving over national investment. In China over the past four years, there has been an extraordinary boom in investment, as fixed investment has risen to over 40 percent of GDP and GNP, and the average annual growth rate of real fixed investment has outstripped significantly the average growth rate of China's real GDP. It is surprising, even bizarre, that with such rapid growth in investment, China's saving-investment balance has improved by 6 percentage points of GDP or GNP between 2002 and 2006, and probably by another 2 to 3 percent by 2007.

A third puzzle concerns the distribution of investment in China. Contrary to the proclaimed objectives of China's government, business investment has been particularly concentrated in the tradable-goods sector, related infrastructure, and real estate development in China's large commercial cities, rather than in the underdeveloped hinterland. Capital-intensive industries have seen large investments that have caused the capital-labor ratio in these industries to rise.[18] Total factor productivity growth in these industries appears to have been relatively poor, but labor productivity growth has benefited from rising capital-labor ratios, while employment growth in these sectors has been relatively meager.

The three puzzles are logically interconnected. The extraordinary rise in China's current account surplus is clearly linked both to the remarkable improvement in China's saving-investment balance and to the extraordinary rise in productive capacity in China's tradable-goods industries. Hence, an explanation of these puzzles that relies entirely on the coincidental effects of special factors is neither satisfying nor convincing. Rather, it is relevant to ask whether there is a common factor that helps to explain at least an important part of all of the puzzles.

The preceding discussion of applying the monetary approach to China provides such a common factor. It explains how the government's policy of resisting renminbi appreciation through massive and largely sterilized official intervention has induced large increases in net saving as Chinese residents seek to acquire the additional base money that they want to hold in a rapidly growing economy. It also helps to explain why the Chinese current account balance has improved substantially more than would normally be expected from only the real effective depreciation of the ren-

---

18. See Lardy (2007a) for further discussion of these phenomena.

minbi. Increases in net saving automatically tend to improve the current account by reducing import demand, even if the exchange rate does not change.

The remarkable combination of an enormous investment boom and substantial improvements in China's net saving-investment balance reflects the effect of China's exchange rate and related policies in putting strongly biased downward pressure on consumption spending while stimulating investment, especially by businesses in the tradable-goods sector. These policies force Chinese households to restrain spending growth if they want to accumulate additional currency and bank deposits, or they achieve the same result from depressing the incomes that households would otherwise receive on their huge money holdings. By contrast, many Chinese businesses have favorable access to credit from domestic banks at real interest rates that are kept artificially low. Those with such favorable access can afford to invest. Much more than Chinese households, Chinese businesses also enjoy access to foreign capital inflows, much of which come in the form of financing for direct investment. Thus business investment has another important avenue to escape the downward pressure on domestic spending exerted by the government's exchange rate, intervention, and sterilization policies.

Some businesses are much more advantaged than others, and these businesses tend to be linked to the tradable-goods sector of the Chinese economy, including related infrastructure and real estate in China's large commercial centers. The policy of keeping the renminbi substantially and increasingly undervalued is an important part of this special advantage. This policy keeps the prices of the outputs of firms in the tradable-goods sector high relative to output prices for firms in the nontradable-goods sector. This situation tends to make firms in the tradable-goods sector more profitable, and hence, both more able to generate internal funds to finance investment and more attractive to domestic lenders and to domestic and foreign investors. Also, as Nicholas Lardy (2007b) has argued recently, the situation tends to enhance the real effective undervaluation of the renminbi, measured using unit-labor costs rather than consumer prices.[19] The

---

19. In contrast to consumer price indices, which are essentially universally available, consistent measures of unit-labor costs in tradable-goods industries are not generally available for a wide range of countries. Also, relative unit-labor costs in manufacturing—the key tradable-goods industries for most countries—have some deficiencies of their own when used in calculating real exchange rates. Nevertheless, where reliable measures of unit-labor costs are available, they can be very useful. In measuring real exchange rates within the euro area, the nominal exchange rate between different member countries has been fixed since the start of 1999. Inflation rates measured by consumer price indices have moved somewhat differently in different euro-area countries, but these differences do not indicate large changes in real exchange rates. Hence, consumer price index–based measures of euro-area real exchange rates are not very useful in explaining the quite wide divergences in the current account performances of different euro-area countries, in particular the large growth of Germany's surplus versus the growth of Italy's deficit. In contrast, measures of real exchange

effective output subsidy for capital-intensive firms in the tradable-goods sector does this directly. In addition, increases in capital intensity normally increase labor productivity by raising the capital-labor ratio.

It would be an exaggeration to suggest that the monetary approach explains almost all of the puzzles described earlier. However, the approach clearly helps to provide a unified explanation for phenomena that are logically linked, while leaving considerable room for a variety of special factors that are not part of the monetary approach. The most worrying feature of this explanation is not that it is incomplete, but rather that it suggests that the phenomena of China's rising current account surplus and its interaction with the policies of the Chinese authorities to resist appreciation of the renminbi through increasingly massive, increasingly sterilized foreign exchange market intervention has a self-reinforcing internal dynamic. China started down the path of a substantially undervalued renminbi by deciding to maintain the renminbi's nominal peg against the US dollar as the dollar depreciated substantially against many other important currencies. This policy is now operating like a huge snowball rolling rapidly downhill, augmenting in size and increasing in speed as it goes.

A Digression on Accounting

Before leaving the monetary approach, it is (unfortunately) necessary to clarify certain points concerning the accounting for aggregates that appear, or should appear, in a comprehensive statement of national income and expenditure accounts. As explained in the above discussion, net national saving S is defined as the excess of national income Q over gross national expenditure $E = Cn + Iv + G$, where Q is gross domestic product $Y = Cn + Iv + G + Ex - Im$ plus the net foreign income of Chinese residents Nfi. Net national saving is explicitly not attributed to particular sectors of the Chinese economy.

Jonathan Anderson (in his comment on chapter 1 in this volume) has raised the objection that the empirical application of the monetary approach to explain an important part of the recent behavior of China's current account is flawed because there has been no significant increase in the saving rate of Chinese households in recent years corresponding to the rise in China's current account surplus. Instead, much of the increase in saving in China has been in business saving, that is, the profits retained by corporate businesses and state enterprises that are not distributed to shareholders or paid as taxes. This is correct if we apply the usual measure of household saving as the excess of household disposable income

---

rates based on relative unit-labor costs in manufacturing show more than 30 percent real depreciation of Germany's exchange rate vis-à-vis Italy. This helps considerably in explaining why Germany's current account has moved into substantial surplus in recent years while Italy's deficit has grown.

Yhd over consumption spending *Cn*, and if we account separately for saving in the business sector *Sb*.

The above analysis does not follow such an approach, as doing so requires description and analysis of dozens of the details of national-income accounting that are required to deal with the multifaceted economic and financial transactions among the many sectors of China's economy. For China, at a minimum, sectors of interest include households; private businesses, both incorporated and unincorporated; state enterprises; state banks and financial institutions; private banks and other private financial institutions; securities markets; government operations, including production and purchase of goods and services from business, households, and foreigners, direct and indirect taxation of households, business, and foreigners, transfers and subsidies paid to household, business, and foreigners, and issuance of public debt and payment of interest thereon; the nonmonetary operations of the monetary authority; the monetary operations of the monetary authority; and transactions with the rest of the world. Getting into this morass is tedious, confusing, and unnecessary for the purposes of establishing the main points of the present discussion. Instead, we focus attention on just three sectors: (1) the aggregate of all Chinese residents except the monetary operations of the monetary authority; (2) the monetary expectations of the monetary authority (summarized by the relation $dB = dN + dF$); and (3) the rest of the world. In this simplified framework, the following points are essential.

First, there is the essential idea of a reasonably stable demand for base money. This means that for a given behavior of Y (nominal GDP), the quantity of base money B cannot float freely in the breeze. More specifically, with the monetary authority holding the exchange rate to a fixed path, if the monetary authority expands its net domestic assets N, thereby tending to generate an expansion in the supply of base money, then either foreign exchange reserves F are forced to flow out to keep the monetary base from expanding or an increase in Y is induced that raises the level of demand for base money to the higher level of supply. Nothing about the details of multisector national income accounting changes this principle.

Second, Chinese residents (exclusive of the monetary authority) can obtain the additional base money that they effectively demand as Y rises from only three sources: (1) increases in N that the central bank pays for by issuing base money; (2) net inflows of foreign capital K that Chinese residents exchange with the monetary authority for additional base money, as the monetary authority intervenes to keep the nominal exchange rate on its desired path; and (3) reductions in gross national expenditure $E = Cn + Iv + G$ relative to national income, $Q = Y + Nfi = Cn + Iv + G + Nfi$, that result in a current account surplus, $CA = Q - E = Ex - Im + Nfi$, and a corresponding inflow of foreign exchange that the monetary authority absorbs by issuing additional base money. Given a reasonably stable demand for base money, it follows that movements in the monetary factor $bdY - dN$—the difference between growth of demand for base money and growth of net domestic assets—must be reflected in the sum of the current account and private net capital flows, that is, $bdY - dN = CA + dK$. Nothing about the details of multisector national income accounting changes any of this.

Third, China is partially open to private international capital flows, and there is little doubt that movements in dK have absorbed part of the impact of movements in the monetary factor $bdY - dN$ on the current account. However, the flexibility of private net capital flows into China is sufficiently limited that movements in the monetary factor have also been reflected to a significant extent in movements in China's current account balance. Details concerning the functioning of China's multisector economy are probably of some importance in understanding how capital flows have responded to movements in $bdY - dN$ and how much this has affected particular sectors. But they do not alter the basic result that the current account has absorbed a substantial part of the movements in $bdY - dN$.

Fourth, movements in the current account balance, $CA = Ex - Im + Nfi$, necessarily correspond to movements in the difference between national income $Q = Y + Nfi = Cn + Iv + G + Ex - Im + Nfi$ and gross national expenditure $E = Cn + Iv + G$, as emphasized by the fact that $CA = Q - E$. Given the value of Nfi, which is small relative to Q and Y, it follows that significant movements in the ratio of the current account to Q, that is, $CA/Q = (Q - E)/Q = 1 - (Cn/Q) - (Iv/Q) - (G/Q)$, must be reflected in significant movements in one or more of the ratios: Cn/Q, Iv/Q, or G/Q. Therefore, movements in the monetary factor $dbY - dN$ that induce significant movements in CA—and hence, CA/Q—must also be reflected in significant movements in one or more of the ratios of consumption spending, investment spending, or government spending to Q. Nothing yet says which of these ratios will move or by how much, but one or more of them must move. Nothing about the details of China's multisector economy alters this general conclusion either, although the details may be relevant to which ratios move and how much.

Regarding the explanation of how the ratios Cn/Q, Iv/Q, and G/Q moved in China between end-2002 and end-2006 as CA/Q rose sharply, the analysis above does suggest reasons why Cn/Q declined significantly while Iv/Q rose. As table 8.5 indicates, this is what happened.[20] The share of consumption spending in Q fell by 8 percentage points, from 43.7 to 35.7 percent, while the share of investment spending in Q rose by 4 percentage points, from 37.9 to 41.9 percent. The share of government spending in Q fell by 2.4 percentage points, from 15.9 to 13.5 percent. The sum

---

20. The GDP data used to construct table 8.5 are the "demand side" series that is released with a lag of about one year (after the standard series used in earlier tables). This series for GDP provides a breakdown into the main components of GDP: consumption, government spending, and net exports.

Table 8.5   Movements in ratios of consumption, investment, and government spending to GNP, 1994–2006

Year	Gross national income (Q) (billions of renminbi)	Consumption (Cn) (billions of renminbi)	Cn/Q (percent)	Investment (Iv) (billions of renminbi)	Iv/Q (percent)	Government spending (G) (billions of renminbi)	G/Q (percent)
1994	5,018	2,184	43.5	2,074	40.5	740	14.8
1995	6,236	2,837	45.5	2,547	40.8	838	13.4
1996	7,330	3,346	45.6	2,878	39.3	996	13.6
1997	8,117	3,692	45.5	2,997	2997	36.9	13.8
1998	8,551	3,923	45.9	3,131	36.6	1,236	14.4
1999	9,033	4,192	46.4	3,295	36.5	1,372	15.2
2000	9,806	4,586	46.8	3,484	35.5	1,566	16.0
2001	10,808	4,921	45.5	3,977	36.8	1,766	16.3
2002	12,018	5,257	43.7	4,556	37.9	1,912	15.9
2003	13,701	5,683	41.5	5,596	40.8	2,062	15.1
2004	16,488	6,387	38.7	6,917	42.0	2,320	14.1
2005	19,165	7,122	37.2	7,957	42.1	2,660	13.9
2006	22,443	8,012	35.7	9,410	41.9	3,029	13.5

Sources: China's National Bureau of Statistics for GDP data and its composition; International Monetary Fund, *International Financial Statistics Yearbook,* 2007 and earlier years, for data on net foreign income included in (Q).

of the changes in the three ratios, of course, corresponds (with sign reversed) to improvements in the ratio of the current account to Q.

Especially in light of Anderson's criticisms, it should be reemphasized that the ratio of consumption spending referred to here is the ratio of Cn to Q, not the ratio of Cn to household disposable income Yhd. In recent years, consumption in China has not fallen to a substantial degree relative to Yhd, but growth of Yhd has been suppressed relative to the growth of Q. This has happened through a multiplicity of channels that would take far too much space to attempt to elaborate in any detail and would probably more confuse than clarify. An example, however, helps to illuminate the matter. Disposable income of Chinese households is repressed because the interest paid to households on their large holdings of bank deposits is kept very low, and they receive no interest at all on holdings of currency. The repression of interest paid to households enables banks to hold large (low-interest) reserves without suffering corresponding reductions in their profits. It also enables banks to charge relatively low interest rates to borrowers. Businesses in both the state and private sectors benefit from relatively low real borrowing costs and their profits reflect this benefit. Higher profits for banks and businesses enable higher levels of business saving, while household saving, although not necessarily the saving rate as a percentage of Yhd, is constrained by the repression of Yhd.

Of course, this does not entirely explain why the growth of household disposable income in recent years has been repressed relative to the growth of Q. And not all of the reasons that Yhd growth has been repressed relative to the growth of Q can necessarily be related to the effects of Chinese exchange rate and related policies. But the notion that all of this is merely a fortuitous accident does not pass the smell test. At the aggregate level, we know that the effect of China's exchange rate and related policies, given the circumstances of recent years, must have been to depress the ratio of gross national expenditure to Q, and hence, to depress the sum of the ratios Cn/Q, Iv/Q, and G/Q. It is not merely happenstance that Cn/Q has fallen substantially while Iv/Q has risen significantly. This result also must have been driven to a meaningful extent, if not exclusively, by the interaction of China's exchange rate and related policies with other features of the Chinese economy.

The Problem of Global Imbalances

The large and growing US current account deficit and the significant apparent overvaluation of the US dollar relative to medium-term economic fundamentals were already a matter of concern to the Fund in the late 1990s. This concern, however, was primarily forward looking. In the second half of the 1990s, the strong US dollar and the rising US current account deficit were more of a solution to the world's economic problems than a cause of them, even if the US external deficit and the dollar's over-valuation would eventually need to be corrected.

In recent years, however—and especially since 2002—the large and (until 2007) growing US current account deficit and the corresponding surpluses of a number of countries have been seen as an important concern, part of the problem of global payments imbalances and the worry that their correction might become rapid and disorderly. In particular, the IMF executive board, which is under international law the adjudicator of issues concerning the effective operation of the international monetary system, has found repeatedly in connection with its semiannual assessments of the *World Economic Outlook* (WEO) that the large US external payments deficit and the corresponding surpluses of several other countries, including China, are a major issue. The executive board has also elaborated a strategy for addressing this concern, including the contributions that should be made by various members of the Fund. In view of this agreed strategy, it is relevant to examine the efforts to implement it.

The United States

While further progress in improving the structural fiscal position would be desirable, the US federal budget deficit has contracted from 3.6 percent of GDP in FY2004 to 1.2 percent in FY2007. Also, in recent quarters, growth of domestic demand in the United States has slowed, from more than 3½ percent annually from mid-2003 through mid-2006 to around 2 percent annually since the first quarter of 2006. Sharp declines in residential investment and slowing consumption growth linked to falling home values point to likely continuing improvements in the private-sector savings-investment balance.

As table 8.6 indicates,[21] except for the Japanese yen, the real exchange rates of industrial-country currencies against the US dollar have all appreciated substantially since 2002. The current accounts of Australia, the euro area, and the United Kingdom have moved in the direction consistent with reducing the US deficit. The improvements in Canada's and Norway's current accounts reflect higher world energy prices. For Switzerland and to a lesser extent Sweden, there might be more of a question about the contribution to reducing global imbalances, but large real exchange rate appreciations indicate that these countries are not resisting necessary adjustments. For Japan, there is more of an issue. The yen has depreciated since 2002 from a level that was already probably somewhat undervalued, and the

21. In this table, nominal exchange rate changes are measured from end-2001. Real exchange rate changes are calculated by adjusting the nominal exchange rate change for the ratio of the rise in consumer prices from 2001 to 2006 for the country (or region) in question to that of the United States. GDPs for 2005 are converted into US dollars using the average exchange rate for 2005.

Table 8.6   Exchange rate and balance-of-payments developments: United States and industrial countries

Country	Change in exchange rate versus US dollar (percent)	Change in consumer prices (percent)	Change in real exchange rate versus the United States (percent)	Current account balance (billions of dollars) 2002	Current account balance (billions of dollars) 2006	Nominal GDP, 2005 (billions of US dollars)
United States	—	13.9	—	−472	−857	12,456
Australia	55.0	15.1	56.6	−16	−41	685
Canada	36.7	11.6	33.9	13	21	1,130
United Kingdom	35.3	14.3	35.9	−25	−80	2,232
Euro area	49.4	11.4	46.1	51	−20	9,609
Germany	49.4	7.9	41.6	41	147	2,787
France	49.4	9.9	44.2	11	−28	2,137
Italy	49.4	12.7	47.9	−9	−28[a]	1,770
Spain	49.4	17.1	53.6	−22	−106	1,125
Netherlands	49.4	9.6	43.8	10	57	629
Belgium	49.4	10.2	44.7	12	7	372
Norway	44.0	8.3	36.9	24	56	296
Sweden	55.4	7.8	47.1	13	24[a]	357
Switzerland	37.4	2.0	23.1	25	63	366
Japan	10.7	−1.1	−1.7	112	171	4,549

a. Figure is from 2005.

Note: Exchange rate change is cumulative from end-2001 to end-2006; positive indicates appreciation.

Source: International Monetary Fund, *International Financial Statistics Yearbook,* 2007.

current account surplus has expanded by about $50 billion. But excluding Japan, the non-US industrial countries have generally made important contributions to the strategy for reducing global payments imbalances.

Meanwhile, the current accounts of major oil exporters generally have moved into massive surpluses over the past five years, as world oil prices have nearly quadrupled.[22] When world oil prices rise sharply, exporters initially find it difficult to spend all of the increased export revenues, and foreign assets are accumulated.[23] However, oil exporters do increase their spending relatively rapidly, and their current account surpluses conse-

22. As noted in the earlier quotation from the Summing Up of the Executive Board discussion, chapter 2 of the April *2006 World Economic Outlook* provides a detailed analysis of the effects of oil price shocks.

23. There was considerable concern after the first world oil price shock over whether the surpluses of the major oil exporters could be recycled efficiently to countries that raise their spending (in reasonable and productive ways) to offset the negative impact that higher savings by oil exporters would otherwise have on world aggregate demand, and hence, on world output and employment. This has not been a significant concern in the present round of oil price increases, although it is still possible that the very low interest-rate environment to which increased savings by oil exporters have contributed may yet lead to important difficulties.

quently decline. This is what is happening in the present round of world oil price increases. Russia's imports have surged upward by 160 percent between 2002 and 2006. In Saudi Arabia, imports rose by 150 percent between 2002 and 2006. Once world oil prices stop rising rapidly, import spending may reasonably be expected to catch up with much if not all of the increase in revenues of oil exporters. The rest will be saved in accumulations of foreign assets, and this increased saving will be relatively efficiently recycled by the international financial system. So far at least, the process has operated effectively.

Table 8.7 reports key results regarding developments in the trade and current account balances and exchange rates from 2002 through 2006 for important emerging-market countries that are not significant oil exporters. Leaving aside China, Hong Kong, Malaysia, and Singapore, all but two of the countries covered in table 8.7 share two general characteristics: Their current accounts are either in deficit or in modest surplus as shares of their respective GDPs, and their exchange rates have appreciated significantly against the US dollar since 2002. For these countries, these developments indicate that they are not making the problem of global payments imbalances any worse, and in many cases, are making modest contributions to resolve this global problem.[24]

Developments in the balance of payments and exchange rates of Hong Kong, Malaysia, and Singapore raise important concerns that these economies are not making the appropriate contributions to resolving the problem of global imbalances. Adding in Taiwan, which is not a member of the Fund, the combined current account surplus of the four economies rose from about $80 billion in 2002 to $120 billion in 2006. A reduction of this combined surplus by about one-third would provide the counterpart to about 10 percent of the needed reduction in the US current account surplus—not small for countries with combined GDPs that equal about 6 percent of that of the United States.

Even though China is a major oil importer, its current account surplus rose by $200 billion from 2003 to 2006 and appears headed for a further $80 billion rise in 2007. As previously emphasized, China's exchange rate and related policies have clearly played a central role in stimulating this massively rising current account surplus.

Thus, in assessing implementation of the agreed strategy for reducing global payments imbalances espoused by the Fund in connection with its responsibility to "oversee the international monetary system in order to ensure its effective operation," the following conclusion is justified: China is the one major player in the world economy that is making large and growing negative contributions toward resolving the problem of global

---

24. For Chile, the rise in the current account surplus reflects surging world copper prices. For Argentina, there is more of a question about whether policies are appropriate from both a domestic and international perspective.

**Table 8.7   Exchange rate and balance-of-payments developments:
United States and selected emerging-market countries**

Country	Change in exchange rate versus US dollar (percent)	Change in consumer prices (percent)	Change in real exchange rate versus the United States (percent)	Current account balance (billions of dollars) 2002	Current account balance (billions of dollars) 2006	Nominal GDP, 2005 (billions of US dollars)
United States	—	13.9	—	−472	−857	12,456
Asia						
China	6.0	7.6	1.4	46	250	2,278
Hong Kong	nil	−3.1	−14.9	12	21	178
Malaysia	7.6	11.3	5.1	7	26	131
Singapore	20.5	3.2	9.2	12	36	117
India	8.9	18.6	18.6	7	−13	809
Korea	41.3	15.8	43.7	5	6	801
Philippines	4.7	29.2	18.8	0	5	99
Thailand	22.7	15.2	24.1	5	3	177
Latin America						
Argentina	−67.1	81.4	−47.6	9	8	177
Brazil	8.6	47.8	40.9	−8	13	882
Chile	22.8	13.4	22.3	−1	5	119
Colombia	3.4	32.1	19.9	−1	−3	123
Mexico	−16.0	23.9	−8.6	−14	−2	768
Other regions						
Czech Republic	73.4	9.5	66.7	−4	−5	124
Hungary	45.6	26.6	61.8	−5	−6	119
Poland	40.0	9.9	35.1	−5	−8	304
Turkey	2.8	144.3	120.5	−2	−32	363
South Africa	74.0	16.1	77.4	1	−16	242
Oil exporters						
Indonesia	15.3	58.3	91.1	8	10	281
Nigeria	−11.9	88.8	46.0	1	24[a]	95
Russia	14.5	80.3	81.2	29	95	764
Saudi Arabia	nil	4.0	−8.7	12	87[a]	316

a. Figure is from 2005.

Note: Exchange rate change is cumulative from end-2001 to end-2006; positive indicates appreciation.

Source: International Monetary Fund, *International Financial Statistics Yearbook, 2007.*

payments imbalances. In so doing, China is clearly failing to meet its general obligation under Article IV to "collaborate with the Fund and with other members" in implementing the agreed-upon strategy, espoused and repeatedly reaffirmed by the Fund.

What To Do Now

In view of the above conclusions concerning China's failure to meet both its specific and general obligations under Article IV of the IMF Articles of

Agreement, it is relevant to ask what should be done about the substance of Chinese policies that are problematic.

Reduction of the Chinese current account surplus to reasonable proportions will require reduction from about 12 percent of China's GDP in 2007 to no more than about 3 percent of GDP within five years or so. This will need to be accompanied by a very substantial real effective appreciation of the Chinese renminbi, probably on the order of 20 to 30 percent over a number of years. Appreciation of the renminbi against the US dollar will need to be even larger, though appreciation against some Asian currencies, including the Japanese yen, should be quite limited.

It is important not to try to be too precise about such figures and not to be either too lax or too ambitious about the pace of achieving them. China clearly has a long way to go. How far cannot be estimated very precisely now, but it will become clearer as China moves along the adjustment path. Indisputably, the pace of adjustment implicit in Chinese policy since July 2005—of very gradual appreciation of the renminbi against the US dollar and continued massive intervention to prevent more rapid appreciation—is woefully inadequate. This is apparent from the continued massive expansion of China's current account surplus. China needs a policy that will stop this expansion and bring about its gradual decline.

That said, the desired policy is surely not an abrupt end to all intervention and a sudden massive appreciation of the renminbi that could impart a sharp negative shock to the Chinese economy. Rather, the best policy would be something like that suggested by my Peterson Institute colleagues, most prominently, C. Fred Bergsten, Morris Goldstein, and Nicholas Lardy: a step appreciation of the renminbi sufficiently great—probably between 10 and 15 percent—to stop the further widening of China's current account surplus and to permit a meaningful scaling back of intervention; a refocusing of exchange rate policy on a suitable basket of foreign currencies; further gradual appreciation of the renminbi to bring its value up to a plausible estimate of longer-run equilibrium within a period of three to five years;[25] and various other measures to redirect and strengthen growth of domestic demand in China. Eventually, China should move to a market-determined exchange rate after critical reforms of the Chinese financial system are implemented.[26]

---

25. This part of the policy is tricky to implement because predictable appreciation of the renminbi tends to induce capital inflows. If these inflows are large, then allowing them to come in without sterilization can generate excessive inflation, while sterilizing their monetary effect can, as has been discussed, contribute to other problems.

26. A properly functioning (mainly) market-determined exchange rate requires market makers (usually banks and other financial institutions) that can take large long and short positions in domestic and foreign currencies and that have some efficient way of laying off part of the risks associated with such positions. To be willing to operate on any significant scale, market makers generally need credible assurance that the government will not suddenly step in (with intervention or regulation) because it does not like the way the exchange rate

In such a strategy, sufficiently large initial real appreciation of the renminbi is essential to get the dynamic of China's current account operating in the right direction. Sufficient appreciation would forestall further rises in China's current account. Once this was accomplished, the rapid growth of China's nominal GDP and the appreciated value of the renminbi relative to the US dollar would automatically reduce significantly China's current account surplus as a share of GDP. Suppose that real effective appreciation of the renminbi and scaling back of intervention and sterilization were sufficient to stabilize China's current account surplus approaching a level of $400 billion in 2007. Assuming that China's nominal GDP grows at a compound annual rate of 12 percent, which is below recent growth rates, in five years nominal GDP would rise by 75 percent— even more measured in dollars, as the renminbi's exchange rate continues its moderate adjustment. Without any decline in its dollar value, China's current account surplus as a share of China's GDP would fall from 12 percent to barely more than 5 percent in 2012. A decline in the dollar value of the surplus from $320 billion in 2007 to $200 billion in 2012 would reduce the surplus to about 3 percent of China's nominal GDP in 2012. This is an achievable outcome without the prospect of serious damage to the growth of China's economy.

Accountability

"Mistakes were made," Ronald Reagan famously observed in connection with the Iran-Contra controversy. The same may be said about China's exchange rate policy over the past five years and about Fund surveillance of that policy. These mistakes were the errors and omissions of particular people in specific positions of responsibility who failed to do their jobs as they should have been done.

Officials of China's Government

Senior officials of the Chinese government have authority over the substance of China's exchange rate and related policies and must take responsibility for them. These officials have received a wide array of advice concerning these policies from inside China and a host of outside commentators, including Fund staff and management and officials from various national governments. Often the advice has been inconsistent and, not infrequently, conflicting. But like key policymakers in other governments,

---

is moving, or for some other reason. In view of the Chinese government's long history of intervention and regulation in markets of all sorts, and the fact that it will undoubtedly retain huge foreign exchange reserves, it may well prove somewhat difficult to make commitments that potential market makers will find credible.

senior Chinese policymakers have the responsibility to sort through the chatter and arrive at appropriate conclusions. In fact, they have stubbornly adhered to a policy of resisting anything more than very modest nominal appreciation of the renminbi against the dollar through massive, largely sterilized official intervention, and through this policy, they have begot an increasingly undervalued real exchange rate, an increasingly massive current account surplus, and severe distortions of the direction of the Chinese economy's development. Although advice has been conflicting, enough of it has been sound that, together with the plain facts of what has been happening and available analyses, senior Chinese officials cannot be excused on the basis of ignorance or other grounds for persisting in their policies and producing the results that these policies continue to yield.

Other National Authorities

Senior officials of other national governments also have some responsibility for the problems that have arisen from China's exchange rate and related policies and the failure of Fund surveillance to recognize and emphasize these problems and press for actions to correct them. Fund staff and management have always found it difficult to press a member on sensitive surveillance issues, especially exchange rate policy, if they do not enjoy the support of the Fund's key members. And in the end, it is the executive board, which is appointed or elected by member countries and responsible to them, that determines the position of the Fund on all key issues.

In both of these respects, the United States is usually the most important member of the Fund. The US Treasury is primarily responsible for international economic policy issues and relations with the IMF inside the US government, and the performance of its top officials on the issue of China's exchange rate policy has been erratic. Through 2004, the attitude of the key Treasury official, the undersecretary for international affairs, was that China should gradually allow greater flexibility of its exchange rate to respond to market forces, leading ultimately to a fully flexible, market-determined exchange rate. This may be a fine idea for the long run, when China has advanced to the point where it can successfully operate a fully flexible exchange rate. But it was irrelevant to China's situation in 2001–04, is still irrelevant today, and will be irrelevant for a number of years to come.

With the arrival of a new undersecretary, Timothy Adams, US policy became much more focused on getting Chinese authorities to allow their currency to appreciate and on getting the Fund to press China on this issue (Adams 2006). The thrust behind this approach, however, dissipated after Adams' departure. The new Treasury secretary, Henry Paulson, has instituted a strategic economic dialog with senior Chinese officials in which

China's exchange rate policy is one of many issues being discussed. Top priority, however, has not consistently been given to this critical issue. Moreover, in its most recent report to Congress on exchange rate policies under the Exchange Rate and Economic Policy Coordination Act of 1988, the Treasury once again declined to name China as an exchange rate manipulator, citing as its reason the lame excuse that it was not clear—to the Treasury or the IMF—that Chinese authorities intended to do what they clearly were doing with their exchange rate policy.[27]

Other members of the Fund have been even less forceful than the United States on the issue of China's exchange rate policy. Because the exchange rate of the yen is also very weak and China is a very important customer for Japanese exports, it is not particularly surprising that Japan has not been a critic of China's exchange rate policy. It is more surprising that, until the autumn of 2007, the European Union was virtually silent on the issue, only periodically expressing concern about the weak dollar and the weak yen. Among emerging-market countries, even those that are clearly suffering from intense competition from Chinese exports are reluctant to press on the issue of China's exchange rate policy. Perhaps this reflects the not entirely unreasonable concern that their own exchange rate policies could come under more intense Fund scrutiny.

The IMF Executive Board

Until 2006, Fund staff, in the published versions of the Chinese Article IV staff reports, spoke only of the desirability for a more flexible exchange rate policy, not about the urgent need for a significant appreciation of the renminbi. The managing director, Rodrigo de Rato, explicitly denied that the Fund was the umpire of exchange rate issues in the international monetary system and decried the notion that the Fund should pressure the Chinese authorities to appreciate the renminbi.

Not surprisingly, in view of the performance of Fund staff and management, the executive board did not press the Chinese authorities on the issue of their exchange rate policy. The Chairman's Summing Up of Board Discussion of recent Chinese Article IV consultations generally endorse "greater exchange rate flexibility" but place no urgency on either accelerating the pace of appreciation of the renminbi or scaling back the immense magnitude of (largely sterilized) official intervention that resists such appreciation. The relevant paragraph from the 2006 discussion reads as follows:

---

27. See Mark Sobel, Statement before the Joint Hearing on Currency Manipulation and Its Effects on US Business and Workers, Committee on Ways and Means, Committee on Energy and Commerce, and Committee on Financial Services, United States House of Representatives, Washington, May 9, 2007.

Many Directors found it appropriate for China to continue to allow greater flexibility in its exchange rate in a gradual and controlled manner. They shared the authorities' concern that accelerating exchange rate flexibility could have an adverse impact on macroeconomic stability. Some Directors also viewed that the exchange rate adjustment alone would have a limited impact on external imbalances. A number of other Directors, however, stressed that the flexibility afforded by the current strength of the Chinese economy provides a favorable context for adjustment and should serve to alleviate the authorities concerns about potential adverse economic effects. Directors noted that greater exchange rate flexibility, along with other policy changes and reforms in China, will aid in rebalancing the economy over the medium term, and will contribute to orderly resolution of the global current account imbalance, in conjunction with concerted policy efforts by other key economies.[28]

Such mush—and the even more equivocal language in the Summing Up of Executive Board discussion of China Article IV consultations of earlier years—clearly does not convey to Chinese authorities any notion that the Fund's executive board has serious and urgent concerns about China's exchange rate policy and is looking for decisive and expeditious actions to begin correcting an important exchange rate misalignment and massively and increasingly unbalanced balance-of-payments account position. Moreover, because of politeness, fear of giving offense, raising the specter of criticism of their own policies at present or in the future, or simple lack of understanding of the issues, other national authorities have generally not pressed the Chinese on their exchange rate policy.

Fund Staff

Like most bureaucracies, the Fund is quite poor at recognizing that serious mistakes have been made, at identifying the people who made them, and at holding these people accountable. Tilting the analysis and assessment in Fund surveillance or program cases in the direction that suits the sensitivities of the countries under review, and that serves the objectives or predilections of Fund management, often tends to be career enhancing. The ability to get along well with the authorities of the Fund's members is a very highly valued skill for Fund staff, especially in the area departments, and is much appreciated in and by Fund management. Provided "clientitis" does not go too far, it facilitates the Fund's ability to work with its members. However, Fund surveillance over members' economic policies inherently involves the possibility of serious tension and disagreement, particularly when a member's exchange rate policy is rightly subject to Fund criticism. In such situations, the strong tendency of Fund staff

---

28. From the Summing Up of the 2006 Article IV consultation with China, discussed by the executive board on July 31, 2006; see IMF Public Information Notice (PIN) No. 06/103, released on September 11, 2006. Available at www.imf.org (accessed on February 10, 2008).

to sympathize with the authorities and ignore, play down, or explain away important problems undermines the Fund's capacity to fulfill key responsibilities mandated by the Articles of Agreement.

Largely out of frustration with the reluctance of Fund management to face up to such problems and be more forthcoming in recognizing mistakes and more aggressive in seeking to correct them, the executive board established in 1999 the Fund's Independent Evaluation Office (IEO 2007), which has conducted a number of important evaluations of Fund work in various areas, including a recent assessment of Fund surveillance over exchange rates. But this assessment did not look specifically at the recent case of China. Pending such an assessment by the IEO, I offer the following observations.

The Research Department (RES) is primarily responsible for preparation of the WEO and other materials relevant to analysis and assessment of the problem of global payments imbalances. Any fair reading of the WEOs of the past six years (since I left the Fund) will find that the RES has done a good job of analyzing and explaining a variety of important issues related to global payments imbalances, and, as evidenced by the Summing Up of Executive Board discussions of the WEO, this work has provided an excellent foundation for the board to establish an agreed strategy for reducing global imbalances.

The Policy Development and Review Department (PDR) has many important responsibilities, including that of ensuring reasonable consistency across Fund staff in work on surveillance. If, as appears to be the case, the RES was making the case in the context of the WEO that substantial exchange rate adjustments were needed as an important part of the strategy to reduce global imbalances, and the APD was simultaneously taking the position that there was no clear case for renminbi appreciation, then the PDR should have noted this inconsistency and insisted that it be resolved.

Within Fund staff, primary responsibility for surveillance work on individual members rests with the various area departments; China is covered by the APD. We know from the published Article IV staff reports that the APD did not press Chinese authorities on the issue that their exchange rate was substantially undervalued. The desirability of greater exchange rate flexibility was mentioned in 2004 and 2005 as a gentle suggestion that adjustment of China's exchange rate would be desirable. Explicit mention of the appropriate direction of that adjustment, appreciation, only comes in 2006, and without any clear indication of magnitude or urgency.

This analysis and advice is far too timid and late for the IMF staff principally responsible for surveillance work on China's exchange rate and related policies. My colleagues at the Peterson Institute, Morris Goldstein and Nicholas Lardy, began a series of papers in 2003 that analyzed clearly the issue of the undervaluation of the Chinese renminbi (see Goldstein 2004, 2006a, 2006b, 2007; Goldstein and Lardy 2003, 2005, 2006), and most of their work was widely known and discussed before its formal publication. Other work on exchange rate issues at the Peterson Institute during this period strongly endorsed the Goldstein-Lardy conclusions (see Bergsten et al. 2006; Bergsten 2007; Cline 2005, 2007; Mussa 2004, 2005, 2007; Williamson 2004, 2007). Moreover, while some disputed the initial Goldstein-Lardy analysis, such disputes became increasingly unreasonable in 2004 and beyond, especially for IMF staff.[29] By 2004 China's current account surplus rose to 3.6 percent of GDP, well above its average in the preceding decade. Monthly figures on China's trade indicated that this surplus was continuing to grow very rapidly. Also the IMF executive board had concluded by 2002 that the large and growing US external payments deficit was an important concern as a key part of the problem of global imbalances, and it was clear that substantial real effective depreciation of the dollar would be an essential part of resolving this problem. This necessary correction of the real effective exchange rate of the dollar could not plausibly exclude significant appreciation of the renminbi against the dollar, along with significant appreciations of other key currencies. However, the Chinese renminbi remained pegged to the dollar until July 2005 and depreciated significantly in real effective terms from its level at the beginning of 2002. The implications of this real effective depreciation of the renminbi—versus the rising real equilibrium value of the renminbi—should have been clear to IMF staff. The IMF staff should have been at the forefront in pointing out to the Chinese authorities, at the earliest possible moment, the implications of these developments for the unsuitability of China's exchange rate policy.

IMF staff did not take such actions. In the staff reports on Article IV consultations presented to the executive board, and presumably in its confidential discussions, the APD did not press the Chinese authorities on the urgent need to allow the renminbi to appreciate significantly. Nor does it appear that Chinese authorities were advised that their exchange rate and related policies—specifically the policy of resisting appreciation of the renminbi through massive, protracted, and heavily sterilized intervention—could be easily seen as violating China's obligations under Article IV. The department head of the APD, the senior immediate office staff (B4s) responsible for China, and the division chief for China, in that order, are most responsible for these failures.

---

29. The Deutsche Bank trio—Michael Dooley, David Folkerts-Landau, and Peter Garber (2003)—argue in a series of papers that under the so-called Bretton Woods II system, there is a symbiotic relationship in which China and other developing countries maintain undervalued exchange rates and run substantial current account surpluses that, in turn, finance a substantial continuing US current account deficit and help to maintain an overvalued dollar. Goldstein and Lardy (2005) provide an extensive critique of the Bretton Woods II theory applied to China. I would note that whatever sense this theory might have made in 2003, with a Chinese current account surplus at 2.8 percent of GDP, it makes no sense as an explanation and justification for the massive increase in the surplus since that time.

The Renminbi Stops with the Managing Director

The foremost responsibility for the Fund's failure in the case of surveillance over China's exchange rate and related policies resides with Fund management. The deputy managing directors who were involved in the China case, especially the first deputy managing director, deserve some of the blame. In a management team where disagreements over a variety of issues were not unknown, there was no indication that deputy managing directors were anything other than fully on board with a see-no-evil, gentle-persuasion approach to the issue of China's exchange rate policy.

The primary responsibility, however, must rest with the managing director. Horst Kohler succeeded Michel Camdessus as managing director in May 2000. In the face of considerable and not entirely justified dissatisfaction among some of the Fund's Asian members about how countries in the region were treated during the Asian crisis, Kohler took a conciliatory approach. Asian countries were not challenged when they unfairly criticized the Fund for its deficiencies during the Asian crisis and ignored the fact that the problems were largely of their own making. Nor were Asian countries pressed on current policy issues, including the extraordinary rise of their foreign exchange reserves well beyond reasonable standards of prudence. Beginning in 2002, as the renminbi remained pegged to the dollar and the dollar began to depreciate significantly against most industrial currencies, the Fund should have raised the issues of China's exchange rate policy and its accelerating reserve accumulation. The concerns expressed by the Fund on these issues should have intensified in 2003 and 2004. Kohler did not press these issues in public, and there is no indication that he did so in private.

He resigned as managing director in May 2004 to become president of Germany. By that time, China's exchange rate and related policies were clearly becoming a major problem and the Fund should have been pressing the Chinese authorities to modify their policies. The Fund's next managing director, Rodrigo de Rato, faced this critical challenge. Like his predecessors, de Rato exercised immense authority over Fund staff and held the position of leadership of the executive board. He had the authority and the responsibility to push Fund surveillance to the forefront on the issue of China's exchange rate and related policies. Under his direction and leadership, the Fund could have fulfilled its mandated responsibilities for exchange rate surveillance under Article IV. Without his direction and leadership, failure by the Fund was inevitable.

de Rato's publicly announced positions on the issue of China's exchange rate and related policies are simply extraordinary. He denied that the Fund was or should be anything more than a confidential adviser using gentle persuasion to coax its members to adopt better policies. He failed to recognize that under the provisions of Article IV, the Fund has the responsibility both to oversee the international monetary system in order to ensure its effective operation and to oversee members' compliance with general and specific obligations under this article and is supposed to exercise "firm surveillance over the exchange rate policies of members." The Fund is supposed to police the international monetary system, and the managing director is the top cop, with the Executive Board serving as a final resort for those rare and highly regrettable cases where all vigorous but less extreme efforts at persuasion have failed.

de Rato should not have been managing director. Fortunately, he has left. Unfortunately, he leaves his successor, Dominique Strauss-Kahn, with a real mess to straighten out and a real challenge to restore order to, and instill confidence in, the Fund's essential surveillance activities.

The issue of how the Fund should address the issue of necessary adjustments in China's exchange rate and related policies is clearly key. With China's current account surplus continuing to surge upward, the time for gentle persuasion of Chinese authorities concerning the need for substantial modification of their exchange rate and related policies has long since passed. However, after five years in which the Fund has failed to press the issue clearly and forcefully, it would be premature for the executive board suddenly to proclaim that China stands in violation of general and specific obligations under Article IV. Rather, the current need is for the Fund and its key members to speak to Chinese authorities with a clear and unified voice that China's exchange rate and related policies are, in fact, seriously inconsistent with their international responsibilities and a key impediment to the strategy to which all countries have agreed for reducing global payments imbalances. It is in China's best interest, in the broader interests of the international community, and necessary to a properly functioning international monetary system that China adjust its policies in a sufficiently aggressive manner as to start its current account surplus on a downward path to a sustainable share of GDP within about five years. This will require a significant scaling-back of official intervention to resist renminbi appreciation and a significant acceleration of the pace of the real effective appreciation of the renminbi, preferably beginning with a step appreciation of at least 10 percent.

References

Adams, Timothy. 2006. The IMF Back to Basics. In *Reforming the IMF for the 21st Century*, ed. Edwin Truman. Washington: Institute for International Economics.

Balassa, Bela. 1964. The Purchasing Power Parity Doctrine: A Reappraisal. *Journal of Political Economy* 72.

Bergsten, C. Fred, Bates Gill, Nicholas R. Lardy, and Derek J. Mitchell. 2006. *China The Balance Sheet: What the World Needs to Know Now About the Emerging Superpower*. New York: Public Affairs for the Center for Strategic and International Studies and the Institute for International Economics.

Bergsten, C. Fred. 2007. The Dollar and the Renminbi. Statement before the Hearing on US Economic Relations with China: Strategies on Exchange Rates and Market Access. Subcommittee on Security and International Trade and Finance, Committee on Banking, Housing and Urban Affairs, United States Senate, Washington, May 23.

Cline, William R. 2005. *The United States as a Debtor Nation*. Washington: Institute for International Economics.

Cline, William R. 2007. Estimating Reference Exchange Rates. Paper presented at a workshop on policy to reduce global imbalances, sponsored by Bruegel, Korea Institute for International Economic Policy, and Peterson Institute for International Economics, Washington, February 8–9.

De Vries, Margaret. 1976. *The International Monetary Fund 1966–1971: The System under Stress*, volumes 1 and 2. Washington: International Monetary Fund.

De Vries, Margaret. 1985. *The International Monetary Fund 1972–1978: Cooperation on Trial*, volumes 1 to 3. Washington: International Monetary Fund.

Dooley, Michael P., David Folkerts-Landau, and Peter Garber. 2003. *An Essay on the Revived Bretton Woods System*. NBER Working Paper 9971 (September). Cambridge, MA: National Bureau of Economic Research.

Dornbusch, Rudiger. 1973a. Currency Depreciation, Hoarding, and Relative Prices. *Journal of Political Economy* 81: 893–915.

Dornbusch, Rudiger. 1973b. Money, Devaluation, and Nontraded Goods. *American Economic Review* 63: 871–80.

Dornbusch, Rudiger. 1974. Real and Monetary Aspects of Exchange Rate Changes. In *National Economic Policies and the International Financial System*, ed. Robert Z. Aliber. Chicago: University of Chicago Press.

Dornbusch, Rudiger. 1980. *Open Economy Macroeconomics*. New York: Basic Books.

Dornbusch, Rudiger, and Michael Mussa. 1975. Consumption, Real Balances, and the Hoarding Function. *International Economic Review* 16: 415–21.

Frenkel, Jacob A. 1971. A Theory of Money, Trade, and the Balance of Payments in a Model of Accumulation. *Journal of International Economics* 1: 159–87.

Frenkel, Jacob A. 1976. Adjustment Mechanisms and the Monetary Approach to the Balance of Payments: A Doctrinal Perspective. In *Recent Issues in International Monetary Economics*, ed. Emile Classen and Pascal Salin. Amsterdam: North Holland.

Frenkel, Jacob A., and Harry G. Johnson, eds. 1976. *The Monetary Approach to the Balance of Payments*. London: Allen and Unwin.

Frenkel, Jacob A., and Michael Mussa. 1985. Asset Markets, Exchange Rates, and the Balance of Payments. In *Handbook of International Economics*, vol. 2, ed. Ronald W. Jones and Peter B. Kenen. Amsterdam: Elsevier Science Publishers.

Goldstein, Morris. 2004. *Adjusting China's Exchange Rate Policies*. Working Paper 04-1. Washington: Institute for International Economics.

Goldstein, Morris. 2006a. Renminbi Controversies. *Cato Journal* 26, no. 2 (Spring/Summer).

Goldstein, Morris. 2006b. Currency Manipulation and Enforcing the Rules of the International Monetary System. In *Reforming the IMF for the 21st Century*, ed. Edwin M. Truman. Washington: Institute for International Economics.

Goldstein, Morris. 2007. *A (Lack of) Progress Report on China's Exchange Rate Policies*. Working Paper 07-5. Washington: Peterson Institute for International Economics.

Goldstein, Morris, and Nicholas R. Lardy. 2003. "A Modest Proposal for China's RMB," *Financial Times*, August 26.

Goldstein, Morris, and Nicholas R. Lardy. 2005. *China's Role in the Revived Bretton Woods System: A Case of Mistaken Identity*. Working Paper 05-2. Washington: Institute for International Economics.

Goldstein, Morris, and Nicholas R. Lardy. 2006. China's Exchange Rate Policy Dilemma. *American Economic Review* 96, no. 2 (May): 422–26.

Goldstein Morris, and Michael Mussa. 2005. "The Fund Appears to Be Sleeping at the Wheel," *Financial Times*, October 3.

Hume, David. 1898 [1752]. Of the Balance of Trade. In *Essays, Moral, Political and Literary*, vol. 1. London: Longmans Green. Excerpts reprinted in *International Finance*, ed. N. Cooper (Harmondsworth: Penguin Books, Ltd., 1969).

IEO (Independent Evaluation Office). 2007. *IMF Exchange Rate Policy Advice*. Washington: International Monetary Fund.

IMF (International Monetary Fund). 1977. *The Monetary Approach to the Balance of Payments*. Washington.

IMF (International Monetary Fund). 1987. *Theoretical Aspects of the Design of Fund Supported Adjustment Programs*. IMF Occasional Paper 55. Washington.

IMF (International Monetary Fund, Legal Department). 2006a. *Article IV of the Fund's Articles of Agreement: An Overview of the Legal Framework* (June 28). Washington.

IMF (International Monetary Fund, Policy Development and Review Department). 2006b. *Review of the 1977 Decision on Surveillance over Exchange Rate Policies: Preliminary Considerations, Background Information, and Summing Up of the Board Meeting* (June 19). Washington.

IMF (International Monetary Fund, Policy Development and Review Department and Legal Department). 2007a. *Review of the 1977 Decision on Surveillance over Exchange Rate Policies: Further Considerations, and Summing Up of the Executive Board Meeting* (February 14).

IMF (International Monetary Fund, Policy Development and Review Department and Legal Department). 2007b. *Review of the 1977 Decision—Proposal for a New Decision, and Public Information Notice* (June 21). Washington.

Johnson, Harry G. 1958. Towards a General Theory of the Balance of Payments. In *International Trade and Economic Growth*. London: George Allen and Unwin.

Kravis, Irving, Alan Heston, and Robert Summers. 1978. Real Per Capita GDP for More than 100 Countries. *Economic Journal* 88: 215–41.

Lardy, Nicholas R. 2006. *China: Toward a Consumption-Driven Growth Path*. Policy Briefs in International Economics 06-6. Washington: Peterson Institute for International Economics.

Lardy, Nicholas R. 2007a. China: Rebalancing Economic Growth. In *The China Balance Sheet in 2007 and Beyond*. Compendium of papers released at the conference sponsored by the Center for Strategic and International Studies and the Peterson Institute for International Economics, Washington, May 2, 2007.

Lardy, Nicholas R. 2007b. Note on Export Prices, Productivity Growth, and Renminbi Appreciation. Washington: Peterson Institute for International Economics (April).

Mundell, Robert A. 1968. *International Economics*. New York: Macmillan Publishing Company.

Mussa, Michael. 1974. A Monetary Approach to Balance of Payments Analysis. *Journal of Money, Credit, and Banking* 6, no. 3 (August): 333–51.

Mussa, Michael. 1979. Macroeconomic Interdependence and the Exchange Rate Regime. In *International Economic Policy: Theory and Evidence*, ed. Rudiger Dornbusch and Jacob Frenkel. Baltimore: Johns Hopkins University Press.

Mussa, Michael. 2004. Exchange Rate Adjustments Needed to Reduce Global Imbalances. In *Dollar Adjustment: How Far? Against What?* ed. C. Fred Bergsten and John Williamson. Special Report 17. Washington: Institute for International Economics.

Mussa, Michael. 2005. Sustaining Global Growth while Reducing External Imbalances. In *The United States and the World Economy: Foreign Economic Policy for the Next Decade*, ed. C. Fred Bergsten. Washington: Institute for International Economics.

Mussa, Michael. 2007. The Dollar and the Current Account: How Much Should We Worry? *Journal of Policy Modeling* 29: 691–96.

Mussa, Michael, and Miguel Savastano. 1999. The IMF Approach to Economic Stabilization. In *NBER Macroeconomics Annual*, ed. Ben Bernanke and Julio Rotemberg. Boston: MIT Press.

Polak, Jacques J. 1957. Monetary Analysis of Income Formation and Payments Problems. *IMF Staff Papers* 6: 1–50. Reprinted in *The Monetary Approach to the Balance of Payments* Washington: International Monetary Fund.

Polak, Jacques J. 1994. Fifty Years of Exchange Rate Research and Policy at the International Monetary Fund. *IMF Staff Papers* 42: 734–61. Reprinted in *Economic Theory and Financial*

Policy: Selected Essays of Jacques J. Polak 1994–2004, ed. James Boughton. Armonk, NY and London: M. E. Sharpe.

Polak, Jacques J. 1998. The IMF Monetary Model at 40. *Economic Modeling* 15: 395–410. Reprinted in *Economic Theory and Financial Policy: Selected Essays of Jacques J. Polak 1994–2004*, ed. James Boughton. Armonk, NY and London: M.E. Sharpe.

Polak, Jacques J., and Lorette Boisonneault. 1960. Monetary Analysis of Income and Imports and Its Statistical Application. *IMF Staff Papers* 7: 349–415. Reprinted in *The Monetary Approach to the Balance of Payments*. Washington: International Monetary Fund.

Robichek, E.W. 1967. *Financial Programming Exercises of the International Monetary Fund in Latin America*. Washington: International Monetary Fund.

Samuelson, Paul A. 1964. Theoretical Notes on Trade Problems. *Review of Economics and Statistics*: 145–54.

Swoboda, Alexander. 1973. Monetary Policy under Fixed Exchange Rates: Effectiveness, Speed of Adjustment, and Proper Use. *Economica* 40: 136–54.

Williamson, John. 2004. Current Account Objectives: Who Should Adjust? In *Dollar Adjustment: How Far? Against What?* ed. C. Fred Bergsten and John Williamson. Special Report 17. Washington: Institute for International Economics.

Williamson, John. 2007. *Reference Rates and the International Monetary System*. POLICY ANALYSES IN INTERNATIONAL ECONOMICS 82. Washington: Peterson Institute for International Economics.

Comment
The IMF's Approach to Surveillance

STEVEN DUNAWAY

I would like to explain the approach of the International Monetary Fund (IMF) to surveillance of China's economy. I am not the IMF truth squad, sent to correct factual errors made by Michael Mussa. However, I must admit that I do not understand the basis for Mussa's assertion that essentially everyone but him and possibly Timothy Adams have been wrong in their approach to surveillance of China's exchange rate. When I sort through the Mussa paper and pare its arguments down to their essence, I am not surprised to find that he is simply advocating the traditional IMF approach to surveillance, which is exactly what we have been doing for the last several years.

In looking at what the IMF has done, one must keep in mind that the public record on IMF work is really just the tip of the iceberg. A significant part is done out of the public eye. It has to be that way if the IMF is to play a role as a trusted policy adviser—to have a seat at the table, as Mussa puts it—especially on a sensitive issue such as the exchange rate. As a consequence, the IMF at times makes a handy target and a convenient scapegoat.

In broad policy terms, the staff report on the Multilateral Consultation exemplifies where the IMF stands on surveillance of the economic policies of the major economies that participated in that exercise (China, the euro area, Japan, Saudi Arabia, and the United States). The policy plans laid out in that context were judged to meet the objective set by the Interna-

Steven Dunaway is deputy director of the International Monetary Fund's Asia and Pacific Department.

tional Monetary and Financial Committee (IMFC) of bringing about an orderly adjustment in global imbalances over time through policies that were in each individual countries' own interest. But those policy plans did not come out of thin air; to a significant extent, they reflect results from the IMF's regular bilateral and multilateral surveillance work.

In the case of China, since 1999—long before there were any questions about the value of the exchange rate—the IMF was pressing the Chinese authorities to increase the exchange rate's flexibility. The record on the IMF's position is reflected in public statements by IMF management and senior staff in various venues. Managing Director Rodrigo de Rato made several trips to China during his tenure, meeting with Premier Wen Jiabao on three occasions. During each trip and in subsequent public statements and remarks, he stressed the need for greater exchange rate flexibility and an appreciation in the renminbi.

A clearer view on the IMF's position comes from the staff reports for the annual Article IV consultations with China, which became publicly available starting in 2004. These reports reflect how the staff's position on the renminbi has evolved in line with economic developments in China. In the 2004 report, the staff said:

> The staff continued to stress that greater exchange rate flexibility would enhance China's ability to pursue an independent monetary policy.
> The staff also maintained its view that it is difficult to find persuasive evidence that the renminbi is substantially undervalued. [The report in other parts, however, makes clear that the renminbi was undervalued and the exchange rate needed to be adjusted.]
> While recent strong capital inflows potentially complicate the introduction of flexibility, it is best for China to move from a position of strength, which should serve to limit adverse effects, and a move to greater exchange rate flexibility should not be unduly delayed.

With the current account widening further in 2005, the report said:

> Although it is difficult to reach firm conclusions about its extent, the continued strengthening of the external balance points to increased undervaluation of the renminbi, adding to the urgency of making a move.
> Greater exchange rate flexibility continues to be in China's best interest, with an early move desirable.
> The continued strengthening of China's external position has added to the urgency of making a move.
> The costs associated with a continued delay in moving toward greater exchange rate flexibility are growing.

The above statements were written in June 2005; China's new exchange rate regime was introduced that July. At that time, the IMF said that the change represented a move in the direction of greater exchange rate flexibility, and we encouraged the authorities to utilize fully the scope for flexibility in the new exchange arrangement.

In 2006, the staff report said that

> developments point to the currency as being undervalued and that this underval-
> uation has increased further since last year's Article IV consultation.
>   Now is the time to more fully utilize the flexibility afforded by the current ex-
> change rate system and allow greater movement in the renminbi-US dollar ex-
> change rate and a further significant appreciation of the currency in nominal effec-
> tive terms.

Given the above record, I admit to being absolutely puzzled about how Mussa concludes that the IMF has not pressed China on the exchange rate issue and that the IMF "speaks only vaguely about the desirability of greater exchange rate flexibility." His comments give the distinct impression that he is not completely familiar with what the IMF has publicly released on this subject.

Because China has persisted in heavily managing its exchange rate, it has created for itself a major problem with macroeconomic control. Trying to contain investment and credit growth has been the major preoccupation of macroeconomic policy over the past four years. It has not and will not be possible to solve this problem without a faster pace of renminbi appreciation to provide scope for monetary policy to operate.

Maybe part of what bothers Mussa about the IMF's performance on China—or a potential source of his misunderstanding—is the IMF's emphasis on the fact that, while appreciation of the exchange rate is important, it alone is not enough. Only by rebalancing its economy away from heavy reliance on investment and exports for growth toward consumption will China be able to sustain rapid growth and provide a permanent contribution to resolving global imbalances.

The exchange rate is only one of several key prices in China that are badly distorted. Energy, other utilities, land, and pollution are others. But above all, the cost of capital in China is very low. We have laid out the impact of these price distortions on investment in a working paper (Aziz 2006), we have looked at the effects on consumption in another working paper (Aziz and Cui 2007), and the overall case for rebalancing the economy is laid out in a September 2007 *Finance and Development* article by Aziz and Dunaway.

The exchange rate and the cost of capital are linked. There can be no meaningful increase in the cost of capital without an appreciation of the exchange rate. If the cost of capital and the exchange rate are raised, credit and investment growth will be slowed and the composition of investment will shift away from producing tradable goods. If at the same time, bank intermediation is improved and the capital markets are permitted to develop further, capital will be better allocated.

One key element in financial-market reform is removing the ceiling on bank deposit rates in China, which—with appreciation of the currency—will raise household real incomes and boost consumption over time. The government also has to play a major role in rebalancing the economy by removing uncertainties that have contributed to very high precautionary savings, particularly in the areas of education, health care, and pensions.

The authorities recognize that China's economy needs to be rebalanced along these lines, and this is reflected in China's policy plans put forth in the context of the Multilateral Consultation. The IMF also has argued that it is critical to maintain focus on the appropriate primary objective, which is rebalancing China's economy. Reducing the current account surplus should not be the goal, however; as mentioned above, only by rebalancing the economy will a permanent reduction in the current account surplus be achieved.

So we agree on the basic policies. The key remaining difference between the IMF staff and the Chinese authorities is the speed of implementation. The IMF continues to warn the Chinese that it is not costless to them to delay reform. Distortions in the economy grow day by day. By proceeding slowly, they also test the patience of the rest of the world. So the IMF closely monitors the situation and continues to push for speedy implementation of reforms.

References

Aziz, Jahangir. 2006. *Rebalancing China's Economy: What Does Growth Theory Tell Us?* IMF Working Paper 06/09. Washington: International Monetary Fund.

Aziz, Jahangir, and Li Cui. 2007. *Explaining China's Low Consumption: The Neglected Role of Declining Household Income.* IMF Working Paper 07/181. Washington: International Monetary Fund.

Aziz, Jahangir, and Steven Dunaway. 2007. Rebalancing China's Economy. *Finance and Development* (September). Washington: International Monetary Fund.

9

Commentary

ANDREW CROCKETT

In my reading of the papers and comments on China's exchange rate policy, some points are agreed on, some are not agreed on, and some are not adequately recognized.

Starting with the points that are agreed on, I do not see any real dispute now that the Chinese exchange rate will have to appreciate over time and become more flexible. Any Chinese commentator would agree on that.

Second, on the points that are not agreed on—and Steven Dunaway made this point (in his comment on chapter 8)—there is huge variation between the different estimates of the degree of undervaluation of the renminbi. In assessing the equilibrium exchange rate at a given point in time, much depends on the structure of the economy and the incentives to save and invest. These factors change over time. So there is no real agreement on the degree of undervaluation of the renminbi.

The next point that is not really agreed on is, given the need for a higher exchange rate and greater flexibility, how does one get from here to there—in large jumps, small jumps, more rapidly, or more slowly? And how does one do all of the things required to make a flexible exchange rate system stable and sustainable?

Andrew Crockett has been president of JPMorgan Chase International since 2003. Fan Gang is a professor at the Chinese Academy of Social Sciences and director of National Economic Research Institute of the China Reform Foundation. C. Fred Bergsten has been director of the Peterson Institute for International Economics since its creation in 1981. Lawrence H. Summers, US secretary of the treasury from 1999 to 2000, was the 27th president of Harvard University (2001–06) and former Nathaniel Ropes Professor of Political Economy. He has been the Charles W. Eliot University Professor at Harvard University since 2007.

Turning last to the points I find insufficiently recognized in the literature and the political debate, perhaps the most important is what Simon Johnson (see comment on chapter 4) referred to as the general equilibrium nature of the issue. The current account imbalances are not simply a US-China problem, and they are not simply a question of relative exchange rates. Relative exchange rates are part of the story, but a country like China has many imbalances it needs to correct. It is undergoing perhaps the most significant economic reform process of any country, both in size and complexity. It is facing issues of employment generation, income distribution, pollution control, and many others.

Dealing with these issues will require not only macroeconomic and regulatory policies but also targeted fiscal policies that will affect the balance of payments and the equilibrium exchange rate. So when we talk about the need for China to adjust the exchange rate, we need to look at all of the adjustments that need to take place in other areas as well. We need to recognize the fact that the balance of payments is the difference between saving and investment, and we should be looking at the factors that underlie saving and investment decisions. We know that China's saving rate is enormously high. Why? Some people say that is hard to determine, but there are ways in which expenditure, particularly consumption expenditure, can be encouraged. It is hard to believe that consumption rates as low as China's—some estimate household expenditure to be under 40 percent of GDP—are in keeping with the experience of other countries or the needs and aspirations of the Chinese population itself. Why is consumption so low?

It is often pointed out that the social safety net in China is such that it encourages very high levels of private saving. It would seem clearly in the interest of the Chinese people for China to create a social safety net that meets their aspirations and needs. Such a social safety net would have an impact on household expenditure. It would thereby influence the saving-investment balance and, with or without accommodating exchange rate moves, would have an impact on the balance of payments. So it is very important to look at these factors in a more general equilibrium framework than has characterized the debate so far.

It is also important to recognize that exchange rate manipulation is not as easy to define as it seems. Exchange rates are influenced by many factors besides the state of the balance of payments and the intervention policy of the authorities. I was at a meeting in mid-2007 at the Bank for International Settlements and the subject of imbalances and exchange rate management came up. Of course, China and the United States were talked about as examples of evident imbalances. Then the Swiss governor pointed out that Switzerland had a current account surplus in the high teens, and its exchange rate was depreciating with no intervention. New Zealand's governor said they had the opposite problem: They had a deficit almost as big, their exchange rate was appreciating, and they were also not intervening.

Is there a case in saying that either of these countries is manipulating the exchange rate? Clearly not. They have hands-off policies with regard to the exchange rate, but they do have sets of policies that generate very high current account surpluses or deficits, as the case may be. So one has to look at "inadvertent generation of unsustainable exchange rate patterns" as a result of other sets of policies or the behavior of the private sector.

I have just put out as a question whether one can define manipulation, or potentially unsustainable exchange rate policies, as being derived only from policies that are directly aimed at the exchange rate or also from policies that have some other legitimate purpose but nevertheless affect the exchange rate.

I turn next to practical issues of what can be done about the Chinese exchange rate against the background of what I have said so far. First, it is clearly in China's own interest to act to reduce excess saving in the domestic economy. This can be done in different ways. I would encourage consumer expenditure. This is very much in the interest of the Chinese population and very much in conformity with the Chinese government's own professed desire to encourage harmonious development.

Next, what can we say about the speed of adjustment? The Chinese authorities tend to say, "We are moving in the right direction even if we are moving gradually." I think there is a potential flaw in such incrementalism. It is a bit like going up an escalator that is going down. If you are not moving up the escalator faster than it is going down, you are not making progress. This is relevant in two aspects in China: First, interest rate adjustments, if they take place too gradually, can fall behind acceleration of the rate of inflation. Insofar as that is happening, it is not using the interest rate mechanism as a means of controlling demand in the desired direction. Real interest rates are actually declining.

Second, with exchange rates, the Chinese will say—and it is true—that they have already moved the renminbi by 9 percent. But if 9 percent is against depreciating currency, it is rather obvious that the net real effect of appreciation is much less. And most estimates find the adjustment in China's real effective exchange rate since it moved to greater exchange rate flexibility has not been very different from zero. So I would encourage the Chinese to think in terms of a benchmark for interest rate and exchange rate adjustments that ensures genuine economic adjustment in these variables.

In other words, is the exchange rate moving in real effective terms in the desired direction? I thought the basket approach that China adopted would have been a means of making sure that happened. But of course we know that if there is a basket, the weight of the US dollar must be pretty close to one in that basket, and therefore it is not nearly as effective as it should be. I do not see why the Chinese should not, as suggested in one of the papers for this conference, move to a true basket that reflects all competitive currencies and not just the US dollar.

Let me say a little more about how domestic steps to increase consumption can be implemented. In my new capacity working for a large international bank looking at opportunities in China, I have become very aware of how undeveloped consumer finance is in China. There is quite a lot of scope for making financial instruments available to Chinese households that would help increase the rate of spending and lower saving.

Also—as China moves toward greater flexibility in its exchange rate—the financial sector has to evolve faster. We know that the financial sector is repressed in many ways. For that reason, it would be a mistake to immediately liberalize interest rates and exchange rates without taking the necessary steps to strengthen the financial system.

Of course, this can become a recipe for paralysis if you say that one cannot be moved without moving the other. Such reasoning should obviously be avoided. But a mistake can also be made in the other direction if liberalization takes place without the necessary preparation. So another aspect of reform acceleration is to make sure that the financial system is strengthened.

I believe, however, that the banking system in China is stronger than is appreciated by people outside China. I serve on the advisory council of the China Banking Regulatory Commission, and I do feel that enormous strides have been made in supervision, and as a consequence the banking system is not nearly as bad as is sometimes believed outside China. But the financial system does not yet have a panoply of risk management tools in the capital markets that is needed to establish a stable environment for the financial system as a whole.

Regarding my last point on the question of what should be done with the exchange rate, I think that it is well nigh impossible to expect the Chinese to make a substantial sudden move. Morris Goldstein and Nicholas Lardy (chapter 1) make a very persuasive case for a substantial initial "down payment."

The Chinese, as we all know, have the saying of crossing the river by feeling the stones, and I think incrementalism is so deeply ingrained. The leadership believes they have done pretty well by moving gradually. The likelihood of deviating from that approach is small. But that does not mean that they cannot move faster, significantly faster, than they have. It would be desirable to increase the rapidity of appreciation from where they are now and to do it, as I said earlier, not on the basis of a comparison with the US dollar but with the real effective exchange rate. This and the increased encouragement to raise spending in the domestic economy would create a situation in which the Chinese authorities would be willing to move faster, the recent rapid expansion in the current account surplus would taper off, and the protectionist pressures from outside China would be reduced.

FAN GANG

Listening the whole day to all the fascinating papers, comments, and debates, I cannot help thinking how difficult it is for a developing country like China to grow in today's world. It is facing new challenges every day, and it seems it is not doing anything right. But we need to think of China from the perspective of a developing country that is so far behind a developed country.

From that perspective, all the problems in China that we have been talking about are not really unfamiliar to us. Historically, developing countries—those catching up—have faced the same problems. Of course, if a country grows to reach a per capita income level of $2,000 to $3,000 and continues to grow, it will have to appreciate its currency. Rising productivity is the major reason for such growth.

I agree with Morris Goldstein and Nicholas Lardy that the hidden productivity theory is one of explanations for a number of things taking place in China, including lower inflation and high profitability of Chinese corporations. Actually, my institute is finalizing research on growth accounting using 2005 revised data, which show that the total factor productivity growth in the past 20 years was an average of 4 percent, 4.4 percent in the 1990s, and 3.5 percent between 2000 and 2005.

This really is the explanation, and from this point of view, the country should revalue its currency. The only questions are how fast it should revalue and how it should deal with the issues around this revaluation.

With improvement in productivity and competitiveness, China is also experiencing import substitution. This explains why China's imports are stagnating, while exports are growing. We have not talked much about it today. It is really a serious issue for China.

Another issue we have not touched on today is that nobody wants to sell what China wants to buy—I mean high-technology and military products. We all know why this is: There is a high-tech embargo in today's trade relationship. And we all know that for developing countries, the purchase of weapons and computers is the major part of balancing trade. When there is import substitution of not only materials but also machinery, and at the same time there is a high-tech embargo, then for Chinese companies and China as a nation, the question really is what to buy—except for Boeing aircraft, as some papers already pointed out.

Then there is trade friction, which is also normal. But as many papers have pointed out, what is unprecedented is the size of the problem, the size of the surplus, the size of the $1.5 trillion foreign exchange reserves, and overliquidity in the economy.

But we also need to think about several other unprecedented developments in China: first, the size of the population and the labor force. What is unprecedented is that 1.3 billion people now come into the labor market, consumer market, and the global resources market. From this point of view, we need to think hard about how difficult it is for such a big economy, a big labor force, to reach full employment. The difficulty is unprecedented in some sense. After 28 years of high growth, 35 percent of the labor force is still in agriculture, underemployed, and needs jobs.

Second, the pattern of China's growth is unprecedented. China has grown with globalization and foreign direct investment. But Japan, Korea, and some Latin American countries did not grow as much with as much foreign investment. All the multinationals are now in China, but all aim to export to the international market: 60 percent of China's exports is from multinationals, either joint ventures or foreign investment companies. That is the fundamental reason for this lasting trade surplus. Although growing for 26 years, China's per capita income is $2,000. But 20 years ago, it was only $200. The purchasing power of consumers was then very limited. So this growth pattern with foreign direct investment is really a new phenomenon. India is also big and attracting foreign direct investment and will face such problems in the future—trade frictions, trade surplus, and currency issues. These problems will come up for all economies with a growth pattern similar to China's.

Last, but not least, what is unprecedented is that this is the first time a large country like China has developed and grown under a global monetary system of the dollar standard, not the gold standard. This means that being the currency anchor, or a reserve-currency country, the United States may be able to run higher trade deficits for a longer time. In such a global currency system, disequilibrium in nonreserve-currency countries is equilibrium in a reserve-currency country. China has had a big trade surplus for only a couple of years. But the United States has run deficits (against various economies since 1970) for quite a long time.

So, taken together, it is a problem of the global monetary system and is unprecedented. Of course, the United States does not have a currency policy, but the relaxed monetary policy and fiscal deficits may lead to dollar devaluation, which will become a problem of currency revaluation for other countries, particularly developing countries. So from that point of view, it is not only an issue for China but also for developing countries around the world. As more developing countries come up, we will see more such issues in the future.

C. FRED BERGSTEN

I want to make three or four points by way of takeaways from the day's discussion. In doing so, I very much agree with what Fan Gang was just saying about the uniqueness of China, not just in today's world economy but also in the history of the world economy. China is the first global economic superpower that is at the same time still a poor country, not yet by any means a full market economy, and certainly not a political democracy. Therefore, its integration into the world system poses a very unique set of problems that have to be addressed in unique ways.

At the same time, we cannot accept what Stephen Roach said about China being just one little piece of the global payments imbalance, one of 39 countries, as he put it, that is running counterpart surpluses to the US deficit. Many others today have repeated the forecast that China's global current account surplus in 2007 will approach $400 billion. That means it will represent more than half the global current account deficit of the United States. That means there is no possible correction of the US deficit without a substantial correction of the Chinese surplus. They go hand in hand as mirror images, and the only issue is how it happens, through what techniques, who takes the initiatives, and the like.

Point one is that China obviously has to be a central part of the global adjustment. Simon Johnson reminded us to put all of this in a multilateral context. That is right. We all agree here that the dollar is still substantially overvalued and that it is part of the mirror image of China's undervaluation. Both exchange rates will have to move as part of the correction.

Second is the point emphasized by Michael Mussa, and perhaps surprisingly, not as much by others, that China—this very large player in the global economy—is violating some of the crucial international rules of the game: prominently, for this purpose, the International Monetary Fund (IMF) rules about competitive undervaluation and large protracted one-way intervention in the currency markets. Our friends from the Congress did not really mention it too much, but one issue frequently cited in the Congress is not just the size of the Chinese surplus and its alleged impact on the US economy but also the fact that China is participating in an unfair manner in the global economic system. It is already the world's most competitive economy, for a variety of reasons, but it compounds that with official policy that clearly violates the international rules of the game and therefore conveys a concept of unfairness in addition to sizable disequilibrium.

Our Japanese friends will recall all too well that it was the combination of large imbalances and a perception of unfairness that really roiled the political debate and the backlash against Japan in the United States. The backlash is even stronger, if possible, against China now than it was against Japan in the 1980s.

I would reiterate the factual point I made at the outset and put to Madame Wu Xiaoling, who did not really respond directly, that China announced over two years ago that it was moving to a more market-oriented exchange rate system. But today its monthly intervention to prevent appreciation of the renminbi is about double what it was when it made that announcement. So, on that metric, China's exchange rate policy is about one-half as market-oriented as it was two years ago. That is not moving in the right direction, let alone beginning to resolve the problem. That violation of international rules creates a sense of unfairness, which I think clearly is a big part of the issue.

Just to state the obvious, neither I nor anybody at this Institute believes that revaluing the exchange rate is the only answer to the problem. It is certainly not a panacea as people have said all day. It has got to be part of a broader rebalancing strategy, as Nicholas Lardy has laid out for well over a year, but it is an essential part of the issue. Without it, the problem cannot be resolved.

My third point is to hopefully clear up some facts. Questions have been raised in this conference, as elsewhere, as to whether even a large appreciation of the renminbi would have much impact on reducing the global imbalances. Morris Goldstein and Lardy cite some estimates in their paper (chapter 1). I mentioned them briefly before. The conclusion is that if the renminbi rose by 30 percent—the real effective rate that they have proposed—and half to all of the other Asian currencies were brought along with it, as Takatoshi Ito's paper (chapter 7) suggested would be the case, then between $100 billion and $200 billion per year would be taken off the US global current account deficit.

That needs to be measured against the targets we have at the Institute of cutting the US deficit about in half, from $800 billion to $400 billion, so we get something like one-quarter to one-half of the needed adjustment from that set of contributions to the overall process. Obviously, these numbers are rough. I would not submit them in a PhD dissertation, but they are the best estimates that we can make and that others have made, and I think they do suggest that we are talking about big numbers and big contributions. None of this is trivial in the context of the overall issue that we discussed.

Finally, what about Andrew Crockett's question on how to get this to happen? The answer, of course, is that we hold this conference and, as the Party Congress now comes to an end, the Chinese will adopt the Goldstein-Lardy three-step process and everything will be sweetness and light. However, assuming that will not quite happen, a systemic defense question comes up. Assume with me for the moment that this is important not only for maintaining the stability of the world economy and financial flows but also for avoiding a major backlash that could jeopardize the openness of the global trading system over time. So it is a systemic defense question.

Suppose that the multilateral institutions that we all agree should be the first responder, and the appropriate answer to the problem, fail. Then do we simply throw up our hands and say there is nothing to do, or do we take unilateral action?

The same question comes up in terms of nuclear proliferation. If you cannot get the UN Security Council to act on Iran, for example, do you, if you are Israel or the United States, take unilateral action to defend your own interests—but at the same time the interests of the system, whether it is global security in that case or in the case we talk about today, the world economy?

The conceptual question that underlies the congressional issue, in the face of revealed failure by the IMF and the US administration, is whether Congress should attempt to take additional action to put pressure on the outcome. There are all sorts of questions as to whether its action would be effective, but again, since everything else is failing, maybe it should be tried. I argued before, and would reiterate, that I do not think any of the bills in Congress now can fairly be labeled as protectionist. They might be ineffectual, but I do not think it would be fair to charge any of them with being protectionist.

I would go beyond what Gary Hufbauer said (chapter 6). He noted the traditional division between the World Trade Organization (WTO) for trade and the IMF for finance including exchange rates. But here we have a classic case where the need to integrate the financial and trade mechanisms must be addressed. That is true between treasuries and trade ministries within governments, and it is now true at the multilateral level.

Certainly, the WTO will and should go to the IMF for a finding as to whether the renminbi is undervalued if somebody brings a trade case to the WTO. Suppose the IMF finds, as it already has, that the renminbi is undervalued. Will the WTO then be able to handle the issue? This requires cooperation between the Fund and the WTO, but it seems to me that is perfectly appropriate in this case, and the next systemic test would then be whether the WTO could work it out. As long as Congress essentially votes to activate that process and pushes the US government to go to the multilateral institutions to try to generate that kind of process, it seems to me it is very hard to call it protectionist. We do not know how the WTO process will turn out, but I think that is the right way to go at this stage, and it is certainly better than doing nothing.

If the WTO then were also to punt, and if the problem is still not resolved, Congress would come back and have second thoughts. But the same issue would then arise as to what would be the appropriate role of an individual country, particularly the country that still purports to be the systemic leader and defender of openness of the global economic system.

LAWRENCE H. SUMMERS

Let me make four observations that are helpful in thinking about the Chinese exchange rate problem. First, the Chinese exchange rate has not caused the primary economic problems of American workers. They are caused by issues that shape productivity growth and income distribution in the United States. They are caused by inevitable features of a world trading system where substantially more low-wage labor is involved in international trade. They are caused by low saving rates in the United

States, which contribute to the current account deficit, but at any of a number of levels. The current account deficit is not the primary source of economic insecurity or slow growth in wages of American workers. China's exchange rate is not the primary source of the US current account deficit. All approaches that seek to blame Chinese exchange rate policy for the concerns of US middle class workers are founded on economic judgments that the vast majority of those who have seriously studied the question would not agree with, and to pretend otherwise is to be misleading.

My second observation, which you will recognize, has a rather different flavor, but I think it is important to keep these things straight. China's international economic policies, principally its exchange rate regime; the way it has driven its currency though its intervention policy; and the ways in which the need to maintain given levels of exchange rates, particularly in the face of a falling dollar, have all led to endogenous adjustments in China's levels of saving and investment. This combination of Chinese economic policies centered on the exchange rate and an export-led growth strategy has been as large a contributor to potential economic instability and difficulties in the global economic and financial system as we have seen in many years. They are an appropriate cause for concern because of what they mean for global economic imbalances and for global financial conditions and because of what they represent in prospect, given the trends that we have seen toward rising trade surpluses and increasing rates of reserve accumulation. They are properly a matter of multilateral concern.

My third broad observation is that there are dozens of well-documented instances of exchange rates in international economic history that were managed and kept stable for too long, to the detriment of the financial authorities involved, the countries involved, and the global economy. The losses suffered by the British Treasury and the fixed exchange rates that collapsed with tremendous consequences during the Asian financial crisis are just two of many examples. I am aware of no convincingly documented case in which an exchange rate that had been maintained as fixed or relatively fixed was adjusted in response to market pressures in a way that was judged ex post to have been erroneous.

My prediction is that having put forth Summers law that there are no such examples—this will be the only time I put it forth—I will be confronted afterwards with any number of you here—and I can see John Williamson, who unlike me knows what happened in Colombia in 1988, is constructing examples—with four examples to which I will not be able to answer and so I will have to fall back on the vast preponderance of errors, which have taken the form of maintaining fixed exchange rates.

It is useful to think about the international mechanisms we have for addressing these issues and to recognize that there is an enormous human tendency for such potentially wrenching adjustments to be delayed for too long. So arguments that an error—which has been made by national economies and the international system on dozens of occasions before—is being made again seem to me to have more presumption in their favor than arguments that are in the other direction.

I would never have thought of uttering a sentence like this, but I think it is possible that Michael Mussa (chapter 8) may have understated the case against the International Monetary Fund (IMF) in recent years. If one is to take seriously the notion that there is a global, multilateral agency tasked with the preservation of international financial stability, with special emphasis on aspects of policy that have international ramifications, the job the Fund has done over the last four years is indefensible, and the culture of the Fund, with respect to these things, needs to be radically altered.

One aspect that struck me, which may well have been in Mussa's paper, was that the IMF—here we are in the 21st century—largely ducked the exchange rate issue in its November 2006 report, explaining that its conclusions were based on data available as of May 14, when the IMF surveillance mission was completed. This is a fundamental indication of nonseriousness in the 21st century. I am not a big believer in litmus tests, but I am struck that in the substantial discussion that surrounded the appointment of a new IMF managing director, to my knowledge, no one raised the question of whether the new managing director would be committed to a more robust approach to these issues than his predecessor had been. His nationality was a matter of great and enduring importance, but no one in the broad government community thought that his view on multilateral surveillance of China was an important qualification. It would not have been inconsistent with the extant political understandings for the US Treasury to have said that it recognized the potential desirability of respecting international understanding and choosing a European, but it wished that a European who was committed to taking this issue seriously be chosen.

This is not a trivial problem, and it is easy to suggest that the Fund does need to maintain relations with everybody. It is true that China, in believing that the Fund has no business messing with its policies, is following in the tradition of all great nations previously, all of whom have been of the view that the Fund had no business messing with their policies. But at a minimum, given the level of seriousness that has surrounded the Fund's discussion of these issues and the desire to seek mealy-mouthed muddled formulations where China is concerned, the IMF in the wake of recent difficulties could think of nothing more creative or interesting than to reinforce the importance of fiscal consolidation. Has there ever been an event that did not leave the IMF to conclude reinforcing the case for fiscal consolidation? If an economy booms, the IMF reinforces the importance of fiscal consolidation. If it contracts, it reinforces the importance of fiscal consolidation. This seems to be a very poor show.

An important role of an international institution should be to respond to that reality—that exchange rate adjustments are systematically delayed rather than advanced—and I would argue that a reasonable case can be made that the IMF over the last 25 years has contributed to, rather than reduced, that problem. What did it do to quiet efforts to persuade Mexico of the need to adjust its exchange rate in 1994, for the IMF to hold it up as a poster child of skilled macroeconomic management in the summer of 1994?

Every government that has maintained an inappropriate exchange rate has been able to point to its involvement with the IMF international surveillance process. I have always been skeptical of Alan Greenspan's view that regulating something creates moral hazard, because people rely on the regulation, and you therefore undermine other kinds of market discipline. I think the surveillance process has run some of those risks.

I do not think any of us have figured out the right answer, and it is untenable to imagine the IMF seeking to destabilize fixed exchange rates by warning that they are basically untenable and are going to need to be adjusted at some point.

I do not have all the answers, and certainly, there are plenty of cases—Stanley Fischer knows of all of them and certainly more than I do—when the IMF was doing just the right thing in private but faced very serious questions as to what it was able to do in public.

But if you take as a given that it is wrong to blame China for the problem of America's workers, but it is right to be deeply concerned about China's surpluses, the logic points you very strongly toward the right processes of working through these issues—multilateral and international, rather than bilateral and US-led, particularly bilateral and US-led by those like Congress, whose record on protection can be questioned, or those like the Bush administration, whose questions on issues like fiscal probity can also be challenged.

My fourth observation is that it would be in China's interest to pursue more aggressive exchange rate adjustment than it has to date. However, one does need to exercise caution, as a policymaker who was very proud to be part of a period when his economy had grown at 3½ percent, about lecturing policymakers in countries that have maintained 10 or 11 percent growth for decades about what their appropriate policies should be. Similar caution also applies to those who study these issues from external perspectives and comment on what is in the interest of other countries.

That said, the combination of asset price effects, problems in the financial system, and distorted patterns of economic activity, summarized in the Goldstein-Lardy paper (chapter 1), does lead me to believe that questions of protectionism apart, China would likely be better off with an exchange rate that adjusted more rapidly.

But it is important to recognize—and I think this nuance in the dialogue is very hard to manage—that two styles of argument can be made externally, and they are both problematic. One argument is that it is in your interest to adjust, and we are just going to explain to you why it is in your interest to adjust. This argument is a little problematic for policymakers in countries that are growing at 3 percent who are reading briefing papers that were handed to them three days before the meeting and speaking with policymakers who have been managing the Chinese economy at 11 percent growth for 20 years.

The other argument is that it is your international obligation to do this for the sake of the system, and the world requires that this be done, whether it is in your interest or not. This argument encounters the hypocrisy problem: Few policymakers have the moral standing that comes from being able to say, "My country responded to international imperatives."

So it is very important to be mindful of this difficulty. That said, I think the preponderance of evidence, as I read it, suggests that the issue goes in the direction I suggest, but one should be cautious.

A poll of Nobel Prize winners, weighted by their actual knowledge of what is going on in China on the exchange rate question, Robert Mundell and Joseph Stiglitz's skepticism about the desirability of revaluation, multiplied by the amount of time they spend in China, would actually bulk pretty large compared with the diverse set of views that exist among others, most of whom have very little familiarity with Chinese exchange rate details.

So, it is important to recognize that the narrow question of what is in China's interest is somewhat more vexed than is often suggested in these discussions.

Which way from here? I have already suggested that the IMF's approach ought to change. I detect very little interest in the United States in multilateralizing the approach to China, which is likely to make any approach substantially more effective and which is more resonant of the actual problems—except for reasons that are not entirely admirable. It is not entirely clear why congressional legislation does not take the form of the sense of the Congress that there needs to be much more aggressive engagement through the IMF and that the sense of the Congress's support for the IMF needs to be such and such.

Even if one accepts the argument that global and US Treasury efforts have been inadequate, the proposals in Congress have more protectionist energy behind them and therefore undermine their effectiveness relative to what would be ideal.

It has always struck me as a bit of an irony in the current political debate that in the traditional security realm of foreign policy, America needs to become much more multilateralist than it has been, but that there is great reluctance to carry the same principle into the economic area, which is something that I would like to see in the future.

To sum up, it is the beginning of wisdom to distinguish the global problem, which is real, from blaming China for America's problems, which is largely unreal. If that crucial distinction is made, much of the rest—a more appropriate multilateralist policy and the like—is likely to follow.

Keynote Address
China's Exchange Rate Policy
and Economic Restructuring

WU XIAOLING

I am very glad that the Peterson Institute has offered to me this opportunity to share my views on two issues of interest to you: China's foreign exchange and monetary policies. I believe the reason we have difficulties and controversies is because of lack of communication. If we can enhance communication between people, we can solve these problems.

I will first discuss the relationship between China's foreign exchange policy and the balancing of the Chinese economy. In recent years, with the increasing openness of China's economy and its rapid economic growth, China's trade surplus has been growing as well. Figure 1 shows the evolution of China's trade balance with the United States, Western Europe, East and Southeast Asian countries, and the resource-exporting economies of Saudi Arabia (oil) and Brazil (iron ore and soybeans). The figure shows that some of the surpluses are transferred from other countries. Because of multilateral companies' allocation of resources, the manufacturing industry is moving to emerging markets. Thus China has a growing surplus with the advanced economies of Europe and North America but runs increasing deficits with the East and Southeast Asian economies and

Wu Xiaoling, deputy governor of the People's Bank of China at the time of the conference, is the vice chairperson of the Finance and Economic Committee of the National People's Congress, the executive vice chairperson of the Finance and Banking Society of China, and the chairwoman of the Financial Accounting Society of China.

the resource- and energy-rich emerging-market countries such as Brazil and Saudi Arabia.

Figure 2 shows the sources of the trade deficit of the United States. In 1998 China accounted for 27 percent of the US trade deficit. By 2005 China's share had risen to 42 percent. Meanwhile, the US trade deficit with Japan and East and Southeast Asian countries in 1998 was much larger than it is with those countries today. This corroborates my conclusion that some of China's surplus has been transferred from other countries, especially those in East and Southeast Asia.

China's international trade imbalance actually reflects an imbalance in China's internal economic structure. The major symptoms are high saving and investment rates coupled with low consumption. China's national saving rate in 2002 was close to 50 percent of GDP. Its investment rate was around 42 percent of GDP. The difference between savings and investment, of course, is made up in trade surplus.

Furthermore, within total savings, household savings is actually declining. Figure 3 shows that in 1992 household savings accounted for 52.4 percent of national savings. In 2005 it accounted for 38.9 percent. Meanwhile, the shares in total savings of corporate (or enterprise) and government savings increased relatively quickly. Because China's investment rate is already very high, further investment is constrained by resource and environmental concerns. Thus, a lack of sufficient consumption results in a large surplus for China.

In the current international monetary system, the US dollar is the world's reserve currency, and many emerging markets have increased their dollar holdings. It is only natural for the United States to run a trade deficit with other countries. However, this deficit cannot be unsustainably large. I have to admit that China's large trade surplus and its increasing foreign exchange reserves do not benefit China, because the return on the investment in the foreign exchange reserves, specifically US treasuries, is far lower than the return on capital investment in China.

We believe that the exchange rate plays only a limited role in balancing international trade and reducing the trade surplus. Exchange rate changes will play only some role in restraining China's exports and controlling inflation. However, the exchange rates of the deutsche mark (1971–2006) and Japanese yen (1977–2006) against the US dollar show that currency appreciations do not necessarily result in reduced trade surpluses.

Figure 4 shows the exchange rate of the deutsche mark and Germany's trade balance. There is no apparent correlation between the two. Similarly, the yen has appreciated over the years, but this appreciation does not change Japan's trade surplus (figure 5).

For these reasons, we say that China's trade surplus is the result of three factors: China's economic structure, adjustments in the location of international production, and the international monetary system. To reduce China's trade surplus, we have to restructure the Chinese economy.

Now I'd like to discuss the restructuring of macroeconomic policies. Actually, in recent years, we have implemented a number of measures to increase exchange rate flexibility, reform the foreign exchange regime, and relax some capital control measures. To be more specific, these measures include reviewing policies originally designed to encourage exports and restrain imports; improving the pricing mechanism of resources; reinforcing environmental regulations; boosting household consumption; improving government income-transfer policies; encouraging enterprises to invest overseas; and relaxing foreign exchange controls. We have already seen the preliminary effects of these restructuring policies. In September 2007, exports grew by 22.8 percent. This was the second consecutive month that export growth ran lower than the average of 28.6 percent in the first seven months of the year.

Moving the exchange rate in the absence of economic restructuring policies will hurt China's economy and thus the global economy, as China is one of its driving forces. For this reason, we decided to reform our foreign exchange regime in a controlled manner, on our own initiative, and in a gradual fashion. This is not a manipulation of the exchange rate but rather shows China fulfilling its responsibility as a large emerging-market country.

Now I would like to discuss China's monetary policy. The growing trade surplus, admittedly, results in increased foreign exchange reserves for China. In recent years, using open-market operations and increases in the required reserve ratio, the People's Bank of China (PBC) has been effectively controlling the growth of base money as well as the liquidity of the banking sector (see figure 6).

Figure 7 shows the excessive reserves of China's banking sector, representing its liquidity. At the moment, excess reserves stand at around 2.5 percent of deposits. China's money supply has been also under control. However, within the money supply, M1 has grown faster than M2 (see figure 8) due to the rapid development of the equity market. Because of the booming equity market, a large number of households turned their savings into investments in the equity market, resulting in a surge of M1.

In recent years, China has maintained GDP growth of 10 to 11 percent, and in May 2007, the consumer price index (CPI) stood at under 3 percent: a high growth and low inflation situation. However, starting in June 2007 China experienced increasing inflationary pressure. With China's current CPI, such pressure is still controllable. In August the CPI grew by 6.5 percent and in September by 6.2 percent. Since 2004, housing prices in China have been rising very quickly, and since 2007, the equity market also has been expanding rapidly (figure 9). The PBC will work to monitor very closely the financial risk related to a potential asset-market correction.

Figure 1   China's trade balance with East Asia, the United States, and the European Union, 1998–2005

billions of US dollars

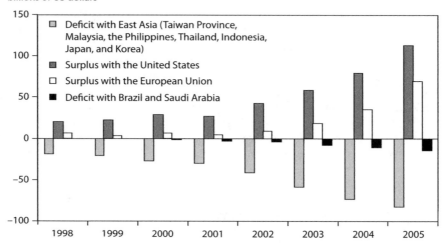

Sources: CEIC data; International Monetary Fund, *Direction of Trade Statistics;* Chinese Ministry of Commerce website, http://english.mofcom.gov.cn.

Figure 2   Breakdown of US trade balance (US statistics), 1998 and 2005

percent

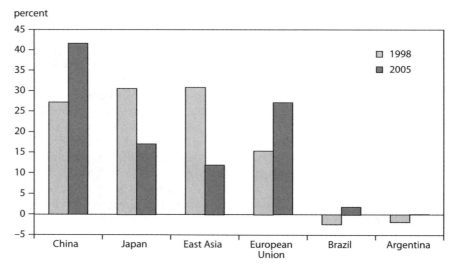

Note: East Asia includes Malaysia, the Philippines, Indonesia, Korea, and Singapore.

Source: People's Bank of China.

Figure 3 Share of savings of all sectors in national savings, 1992–2005

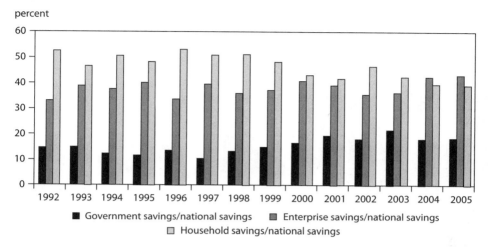

percent

■ Government savings/national savings   ■ Enterprise savings/national savings
□ Household savings/national savings

Source: People's Bank of China.

Figure 4 Deutsche mark exchange rate and Germany's trade surplus, 1971–2006

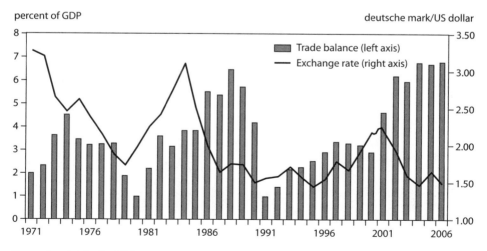

percent of GDP   deutsche mark/US dollar

■ Trade balance (left axis)
— Exchange rate (right axis)

Source: People's Bank of China.

Figure 5 Yen exchange rate and Japan's trade surplus, 1977–2005

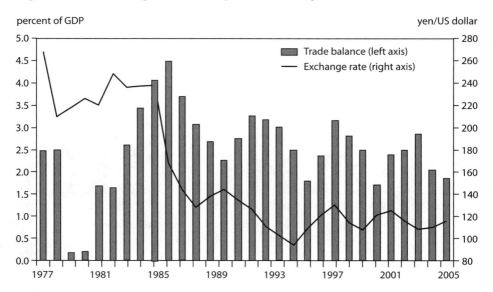

Source: People's Bank of China.

Figure 6 Comparison of the growth of renminbi equivalent of foreign exchange purchase and growth of base money, 1997 to June 2007

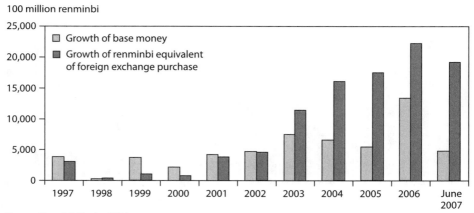

Source: People's Bank of China.

Figure 7   Excess reserve ratio, 2002 to July 2007

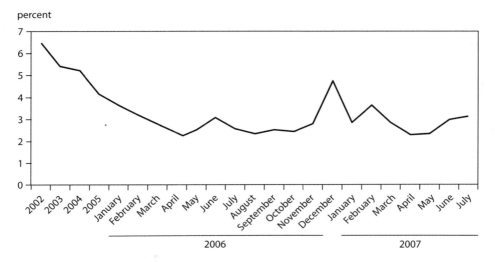

Source: People's Bank of China.

Figure 8   Growth of money supply, 2002 to July 2007

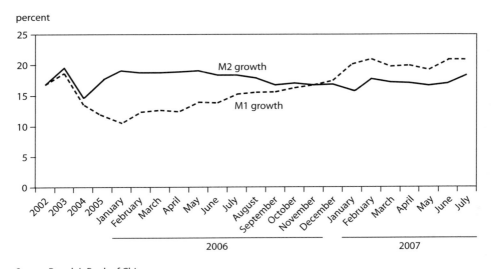

Source: People's Bank of China.

Figure 9   Movement in Shanghai Stock Exchange A Share Index, 2004 to June 2007

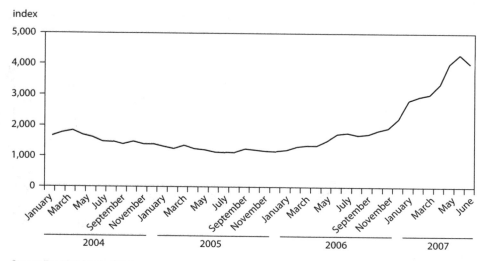

Source: People's Bank of China.

About the Contributors

Jonathan Anderson is managing director, Global Emerging-Markets Economist at UBS Investment Bank. Before joining UBS in 2003, he worked at Goldman Sachs. He also spent eight years at the International Monetary Fund, including three years as resident representative in China and three years as resident representative in Russia. From 2003 through 2007, he was chief Asian economist for UBS. He is coauthor of *The Five Great Myths About China and the World* (PPP Company Limited, 2003). He received his MA degree and PhD candidacy in economics from Harvard University.

C. Fred Bergsten has been director of the Peterson Institute for International Economics since its creation in 1981. He was assistant secretary for international affairs of the US Treasury (1977–81); assistant for international economic affairs to Dr. Henry Kissinger at the National Security Council (1969–71); and a senior fellow at the Brookings Institution (1972–76), the Carnegie Endowment for International Peace (1981), and the Council on Foreign Relations (1967–68). He is co-chairman of the Private Sector Advisory Group to the United States–India Trade Policy Forum. He was chairman of the Competitiveness Policy Council, which was created by Congress, throughout its existence from 1991 to 1995; and chairman of the APEC Eminent Persons Group throughout its existence from 1993 to 1995. He has authored, coauthored, or edited 38 books on international economic issues including *China: The Balance Sheet* (2006), *The United States and the World Economy: Foreign Economic Policy for the Next Decade* (2005), *Dollar Adjustment: How Far? Against What?* (2004), *Dollar Overvaluation and the World Economy* (2003), *No More Bashing: Building a New Japan-United States Economic Relationship* (2001), and *The Dilemmas of the Dollar* (2d ed., 1996).

Barry Bosworth is a senior fellow in the Economic Studies Program (the Robert V. Roosa Chair in International Economics) at the Brookings Institution, where he has been a senior fellow since 1979 and served as a research associate from 1971 to 1977. He was director of the President's Council on Wage and Price Stability in 1977–79; visiting lecturer at the University of California, Berkeley (1974–75); and assistant professor, Harvard University (1969–71). His publications include *Services Productivity in the United States: New Sources of Economic Growth* (Brookings, 2004), *Aging Societies: The Global Dimension* (Brookings, 1998), and *Coming Together? Mexico-U.S. Relations* (Brookings, 1997). He received his PhD from the University of Michigan in 1969.

Claire Brunel is a research assistant at the Peterson Institute for International Economics. Her areas of research at the Institute include trade issues, particularly relating to North America, China, and the European Union. Before joining the Institute, she worked at the European Commission in the Economics and Financial Affairs DG, for BNP Paribas in macroeconomic studies, and for Schroeder Salomon Smith Barney in mergers and acquisitions. She received her BS degree in mathematics and economics from Georgetown University and an MPhil in economics from the University of Oxford.

William R. Cline is a senior fellow jointly at the Center for Global Development and the Peterson Institute for International Economics. He has been a senior fellow at the Institute since its inception in 1981. During 1996–2001, while on leave from the Institute, he was deputy managing director and chief economist at the Institute of International Finance. He was a senior fellow at the Brookings Institution (1973–81); deputy director of development and trade research, office of the assistant secretary for international affairs, US Treasury Department (1971–73); Ford Foundation visiting professor in Brazil (1970–71); and lecturer and assistant professor of economics at Princeton University (1967–70). His publications include *Global Warming and Agriculture: Impact Estimates by Country* (2007), *The United States as a Debtor Nation* (2005), *Trade Policy and Global Poverty* (2004), *Trade and Income Distribution* (1997), *International Debt Reexamined* (1995), *International Economic Policy in the 1990s* (1994), and *The Economics of Global Warming* (1992).

Andrew Crockett has been president of JPMorgan Chase International since 2003. He served as general manager of the Bank for International Settlements from 1994 to 2003 and as chairman of the Financial Stability Forum from 1999 to 2003. Earlier in his career, he held appointments at the International Monetary Fund and the Bank of England. He was chairman of Working Party Three of the Organization for Economic Cooperation and Development. He serves as chairman of the Per Jacobsson Foundation; trustee of the American University of Beirut; director of the International Centre for Leadership in Finance in Kuala Lumpur; and member of the International Advisory Council of the China Development Bank and of the China Banking Regulatory Commission.

Steven Dunaway is deputy director of the International Monetary Fund's Asia and Pacific Department. Since November 2001, he has directed the International Monetary Fund's country work and headed the consultation missions with China. Prior to his current assignment, he was head of the North American Division in the IMF's Western Hemisphere Department and managed the IMF's consultations with the United States and Canada. During his 24-year career at the IMF, he has had a variety of other country assignments, including Australia and New Zealand, Indonesia, and the Philippines. In addition, during the mid-1990s, he directed the IMF's research on private capital flows to developing countries and handled IMF support for Brady debt deals for Ecuador, Panama, and Peru. Prior to coming to the IMF, he worked for 10 years at the Bureau of Economic Analysis. He received his PhD in economics from the George Washington University.

Mohamed A. El-Erian is co-chief executive officer and co-chief investment officer of Pacific Investment Management Co. (PIMCO). He previously served as president and CEO of Harvard Management Company and as a member of the faculty of Harvard Business School. He spent 15 years at the IMF before moving to the private sector, where he served as managing director at Salomon Smith Barney/Citigroup in London. He has served on several boards and committees, including the Emerging Markets Traders Association and the IMF's Committee of Eminent Persons. He is a board member of the International Center for Research on Women and the Peterson Institute for International Economics. He is also a member of the US Treasury Borrowing Advisory Committee and chairs Microsoft's Investment Advisory Committee. He earned his bachelor's degree in economics from Cambridge University and master's and doctorate degrees in economics from Oxford University.

Fan Gang is a professor at the Chinese Academy of Social Sciences, a government think tank overseeing numerous research institutes, and director of National Economic Research Institute of the China Reform Foundation. He also serves as an adviser to the Chinese government and consultant to a number of international organizations. He earned his PhD in economics from the Graduate School of the Chinese Academy of Social Sciences.

Jeffrey A. Frankel is James W. Harpel Professor of Capital Formation and Growth at Harvard University's Kennedy School of Government. He also directs the National Bureau of Economic Research's program in International Finance and Macroeconomics and is a member of the NBER Business Cycle Dating Committee, which officially declares US recessions. He served in the White House as a member of President Clinton's Council of Economic Advisers (1996–99), with responsibility for international economics, macroeconomics, and the environment. Before that, he was professor of economics at the University of California, Berkeley. He was a frequent visiting fellow at the Institute for International Economics between 1984 and 1996 and is a member of the Institute's Advisory Committee. His Institute books include *Regional Trading Blocs* (1997) and *Does Foreign Exchange Intervention Work?* (1993). Other recurrent visiting appointments include with the International Monetary Fund. He is a member of the Bellagio Group and of advisory boards of the New York and Boston Federal Reserve Banks. He received his PhD in economics from MIT.

Morris Goldstein, Dennis Weatherstone Senior Fellow since 1994, has held several senior staff positions at the International Monetary Fund (1970–94), including Deputy Director of its Research Department (1987–94). He is the author of *Managed Floating Plus* (2002), *The Asian Financial Crisis: Causes, Cures, and Systemic Implications* (1998), *The Case for an International Banking Standard* (1997), *The Exchange Rate System and the IMF: A Modest Agenda* (1995), coeditor of *Private Capital Flows to Emerging Markets after the Mexican Crisis* (1996), coauthor of *Controlling Currency Mismatches in Emerging Markets* (2004) with Philip Turner and *Assessing Financial Vulnerability: An Early Warning System for Emerging Markets* with Graciela Kaminsky and Carmen Reinhart (2000), and project director of *Safeguarding Prosperity in a Global Financial System: The Future International Financial Architecture* (1999) for the Council on Foreign Relations Task Force on the International Financial Architecture.

Bert Hofman is the country director for the World Bank in the Philippines. At the time of writing, he was chief of the Economics Unit at the World Bank office in Beijing, where he led analytical and policy advisory work of the World Bank in China. He was also lead economist at the World Bank office in Jakarta, where he spent more than five years leading a team of professionals focusing on fiscal policy, decentralization, financial sector, poverty analysis, and governance. He has worked for the World Bank on Brazil, South Africa, Mongolia, Zambia, and Namibia. Before joining the World Bank, he was a researcher at the Kiel Institute of World Economics; the Organization for Economic Cooperation and Development in Paris; ING Bank; and Erasmus University, Rotterdam. He holds degrees in economics from Erasmus University, Rotterdam, and the Christian Aelbrechts University, Kiel.

Gary Clyde Hufbauer resumed his position at the Peterson Institute as Reginald Jones Senior Fellow in 1998. Previously he was the Marcus Wallenberg Professor of International Financial Diplomacy at Georgetown University and served in the US Treasury Department from 1974 to1980. His coauthored publications include *Economic Sanctions Reconsidered*, 3d ed. (2007), *US Taxation of Foreign Income* (2007), *US-China Trade Disputes: Rising Tide, Rising Stakes* (2006), and *NAFTA Revisited: Achievements and Challenges* (2005). He holds an AB from Harvard College, a PhD in economics from King's College at Cambridge University, and a JD from Georgetown University Law Center.

Takatoshi Ito, professor at the Graduate School of Economics, University of Tokyo, has taught extensively both in the United States and Japan, including at the University of Minnesota, Hitotsubashi University, and Harvard University. He also served as senior advisor in the IMF's Research Department (1994–97) and as deputy vice minister for international affairs at the Ministry of Finance, Japan (1999–2001). He was appointed as a member of the Council of Economic and Fiscal Policy in October 2006. The council, which consists of 11 members including the prime minister and finance minister, decides the framework of the budget each year. He was the president of the Japanese Economic Association in 2004. He also serves on the Peterson Institute's Advisory Committee. He is the author of *The Japanese Economy* (1992) and coauthor of *A Vision for the World Economy* (MIT Press, 1996), *Political Economy of Japanese Monetary Policy* (MIT Press, 1997), *Financial Policy and Central Banking in Japan* (MIT Press, 2000), and *No More Bashing: Building a New Japan–United States Economic Relationship* (2001).

Jin Zhongxia has been the chief representative of the Representative Office of the People's Bank of China for the Americas since June 2006. He was the director of the International Monetary Fund Division, International Department, People's Bank of China (2004–06); technical assistant, IMF's China executive director's office (2002–03), and consultant with the World Bank (1996–97). He has published articles on international economics and the renminbi exchange rate in both Chinese and English. His current research interests include international economic issues and Chinese economic and financial issues. He graduated from Beijing University with BA and MA degrees in international economics and management economics, respectively. He pursued a PhD in economics at the University of Hawaii.

Simon Johnson is economic counselor and director of the Research Department at the International Monetary Fund, on leave from the Sloan School of Management at MIT, where he was the Ronald A. Kurtz Professor of Entrepreneurship. Over the past 20 years he has worked on crisis prevention and mitigation, as well as economic growth issues in advanced, emerging-market, and developing countries. His work focuses on how policymakers can limit the impact of negative shocks and manage the risks faced by their countries. He received his PhD in economics from MIT, MA degree from the University of Manchester, and BA degree from the University of Oxford.

Louis Kuijs has been a senior economist at the World Bank's China office in Beijing since September 2004. He is the main author of the Bank's *China Quarterly Update*. Before joining the Bank, he served at the European, African, and Fiscal Affairs Departments at the International Monetary Fund. Before joining the Fund in 1997, he worked at Oxford Economic Forecasting (Oxford, UK) on macroeconomic modeling and forecasting for industrialized countries and emerging markets. He also served at the University of Amsterdam, the Hypo Vereinsbank (Munich), and the Economist Intelligence Unit (London). He received his undergraduate degree in economics from the University of Amsterdam and his master's degree in economics from the London School of Economics.

Nicholas R. Lardy, senior fellow at the Peterson Institute since 2003, was a senior fellow in the Foreign Policy Studies Program at the Brookings Institution from 1995 to 2003. He was the director of the Henry M. Jackson School of International Studies at the University of Washington from 1991 to 1995. From 1997 through the spring of 2000, he was the Frederick Frank Adjunct Professor of International Trade and Finance at the Yale University School of Management. His publications include *China: The Balance Sheet* (2006), *Prospects for a US-Taiwan Free Trade Agreement* (2004), *Integrating China into the Global Economy* (Brookings Institution Press, 2002), *China's Unfinished Economic Revolution* (Brookings Institution Press, 1998), *China in the World Economy* (Institute for International Economics, 1994), *Foreign Trade and Economic Reform in China, 1978–1990* (Cambridge University Press, 1992), and *Agriculture in China's Modern Economic Development* (Cambridge University Press, 1983).

Michael Mussa, senior fellow at the Peterson Institute since 2001, served as economic counselor and director of the research department at the International Monetary Fund from 1991 to 2001. He served as a member of the US Council of Economic Advisers from August 1986 to September 1988, and was a faculty member of the Graduate School of Business of the University of Chicago (1976–91) and the department of economics at the University of Rochester (1971–76). He is the editor of *C. Fred Bergsten and the World Economy* (2006) and author of *Argentina and the Fund: From Triumph to Tragedy* (2002).

Yung Chul Park is a distinguished professor at the Division of International Studies, Korea University. He was a member of the National Economic Advisory Council (2003–04) and ambassador for International

Economy and Trade, Ministry of Foreign Affairs and Trade (2001–02). He previously served as the chief economic adviser to the president of Korea (1987–88), as president of the Korea Development Institute (1986–87), as president of the Korea Institute of Finance (1992–98), and as a member of the Central Bank of Korea's Monetary Board (1984–86). He is has written and coedited several books, including *Economic Liberalization and Integration in East Asia* (Oxford University Press, 2006), *A New Financial Structure for East Asia* (Edward Elgar, 2006), and *China, Asia, and the New World* (Oxford University Press, 2008).

Jean Pisani-Ferry is director of Bruegel, a Brussels-based economic think tank, and professor at Université Paris-Dauphine. He is a member of the European Commission's Group of Economic Policy Analysis and of the French prime minister's Council of Economic Analysis. In 1983 he was appointed as head of the macroeconomic department in the Centre d'études prospectives et d'informations internationales (CEPII). In 1989, he joined the European Commission as economic adviser to the Director-General of DG ECFIN. From 1992 to 1997 he was the director of CEPII. In 1997, he became senior economic adviser to the French minister of finance. He was executive president of the French prime minister's Council of Economic Analysis (2001–02). In 2002–04, he was senior adviser to the director of the French Treasury. He has held teaching positions with various universities including the Ecole polytechnique in Paris and the Université libre de Bruxelles. In 2002–03, he was a member of the Sapir Group appointed by the president of the European Commission.

Eswar S. Prasad is the Tolani Senior Professor of Trade Policy in the Department of Applied Economics and Management at Cornell University. He was chief of the Financial Studies Division in the International Monetary Fund's Research Department and, before that, was the head of the International Monetary Fund's China division. He is one of the lead authors of a recent IMF study on financial globalization and has edited IMF books and monographs on China, Hong Kong, and India. His current research interests include the macroeconomics of globalization, the relationship between growth and volatility, and the Chinese and Indian economies. He has served as the coeditor of *IMF Staff Papers*, was on the editorial board of *Finance & Development*, and was the founding editor of the quarterly *IMF Research Bulletin*. He has been a research fellow of IZA (Institute for the Study of Labor, Bonn) since 2002. He received his PhD from the University of Chicago.

Stephen S. Roach is chairman of Morgan Stanley Asia. Prior to this appointment, he was Morgan Stanley's chief economist, heading up the firm's global team of economists located in New York, London, Frankfurt, Paris, Tokyo, Hong Kong, and Singapore. His recent research has focused on globalization, the emergence of China and India, and the capital market implications of global imbalances. He has long advised governments and policymakers around the world and frequently presents testimony to the US Congress. Before joining Morgan Stanley in 1982, he was vice president for economic analysis for the Morgan Guaranty Trust Company. He also served in a senior capacity on the research staff of the Federal Reserve Board from 1972 to 1979. Prior to that, he was a research fellow at the Brookings Institution. He holds a PhD in economics from New York University and a bachelor's degree in economics from the University of Wisconsin.

Kenneth Rogoff has been a professor of economics at Harvard University since September 1999 and the Thomas D. Cabot Professor of Public Policy there since January 2004. He was vice president of the American Economic Association (2007). He was the chief economist and director of research, International Monetary Fund (2001–03); director of the Harvard Center for International Development (2003–04); professor of economics and international affairs (1992–94) and Charles and Marie Robertson Professor of International Affairs at Princeton University (1995–99); professor of economics, University of California at Berkeley (1989–91); associate professor of economics, University of Wisconsin-Madison (1985–88); economist, International Finance Division, Board of Governors of the Federal Reserve System (1980–83) and section chief, Trade and Financial Studies Section (1984); and economist at the IMF's Research Department (October 1982–September 1983). His books include *Foundations of International Macroeconomics* (MIT Press, 1996), *Workbook for Foundations of International Macroeconomics* (MIT Press, 1998), and *Handbook of International Economics*, volume 3 (Elsevier, 1995). He received his PhD from MIT in 1980.

Brad Setser is a fellow at the Greenberg Center for Geoeconomic Studies at the Council on Foreign Relations. He previously worked as a senior economist at RGEMonitor, an online financial information service. He served in the US Treasury Department from 1997 to 2001, where he concluded his tenure as the acting director of the Office of International Monetary and Financial Policy, and spent 2002 as a visiting scholar at the International Monetary Fund. He is the coauthor of *Bailouts or Bail-ins? Responding to Financial Crises in Emerging Economies* (2004) with Nouriel Roubini.

Lawrence H. Summers, US secretary of the treasury from 1999 to 2000, was the 27th president of Harvard University (2001–06) and former Nathaniel Ropes Professor of Political Economy. He has been the Charles W. Eliot University Professor at Harvard University since 2007. He received his PhD degree in economics from Harvard in 1982, by which time he had taught for three years as an economics faculty member at MIT, where he was named assistant professor in 1979 and associate professor in 1982. He then went to Washington as a domestic policy economist for the President's Council of Economic Advisers. In 1983, he returned to Harvard as a professor of economics. In 1987 he became the first social scientist ever to receive the annual Alan T. Waterman Award of the National Science Foundation. In 1993 he was awarded the John Bates Clark Medal. In 1993 he was named as the nation's undersecretary of the treasury for international affairs, and on July 2, 1999, he was confirmed by the Senate as secretary of the treasury. After leaving the treasury in January 2001, he served as the Arthur Okun Distinguished Fellow in Economics, Globalization, and Governance at the Brookings Institution. His many publications include *Understanding Unemployment* (1990) and *Reform in Eastern Europe* (1991).

Edwin M. Truman, senior fellow at the Peterson Institute since 2001, was assistant secretary of the Treasury for international affairs (1998–2000). He directed the Division of International Finance of the Board of Governors of the Federal Reserve System from 1977 to 1998. He is the author of *A Strategy for IMF Reform* (2006) and *Inflation Targeting in the World Economy* (2003), editor of *Reforming the IMF for the 21st Century* (2006), and coauthor of *Chasing Dirty Money: The Fight Against Money Laundering* (2004).

Shang-Jin Wei is professor of finance and economics and the N. T. Wang Professor of Chinese Business and Economy at Columbia University's Graduate School of Business. He was assistant director and chief of the trade and investment division in the IMF's Research Department, chief of the IMF Mission to Myanmar (Burma), the New Century Chair Senior Fellow at the Brookings Institution, advisor at the World Bank, and associate professor at Harvard University's Kennedy School of Government. His research on the global economy has been featured in the *Economist, Business Week, Financial Times, Wall Street Journal*, and other media outlets and published in leading academic journals.

John Williamson, senior fellow at the Peterson Institute, has been associated with the Institute since 1981. He was project director for the UN High-Level Panel on Financing for Development (the Zedillo Report) in 2001; on leave as chief economist for South Asia at the World Bank during 1996–99; economics professor at Pontificia Universidade Católica do Rio de Janeiro (1978–81), University of Warwick (1970–77), Massachusetts Institute of Technology (1967, 1980), University of York (1963–68), and Princeton University (1962–63); adviser to the International Monetary Fund (1972–74); and economic consultant to the UK Treasury (1968–70). He is author, coauthor, editor, or coeditor of numerous studies on international monetary and development issues, including *Reference Rates and* *the International Monetary System* (2007), *Curbing the Boom-Bust Cycle: Stabilizing Capital Flows to Emerging Markets* (2005), *Dollar Adjustment: How Far? Against What?* (2004), and *After the Washington Consensus: Restarting Growth and Reform in Latin America* (2003).

Wu Xiaoling, former deputy governor of the People's Bank of China (PBC), is the vice chairperson of the Finance and Economics Committee of the National People's Congress, the executive vice chairperson of the Finance and Banking Society of China, and the chairwoman of the Financial Accounting Society of China. She started her career at the PBC in 1985, when she was appointed deputy director of the Office for Applied Theoretical Research at the PBC's Research Institute. In 1994, she was appointed as director general of the PBC's Research Bureau. She was promoted to deputy administrator of the State Administration of Foreign Exchange (SAFE) under the PBC in 1995 and then the administrator of SAFE in April 1998. In November 1998, she was appointed as president of the PBC's Shanghai branch. She has been a professor and a tutor of doctoral candidates at seven universities in China. She received the Sun Yefang Economics Prize, the highest Chinese award in the field, in 1994. She ranked 18 on *Forbes*'s 100 Most Powerful Women 2007. She was included in the Top 50 Women to Watch, released by the *Wall Street Journal* on November 8, 2004. Among the 24 women in the category of In Line to Lead, she ranked 18. She graduated from the Graduate School of the PBC in 1984.

Index

Abu Dhabi Investment Authority (ADIA), 37, 179, 185, 198, 202
Abu Dhabi Investment Corporation (ADIC), 179
accountability
   for IMF surveillance, 325–32
   of sovereign wealth funds (*See* transparency and accountability)
ACU. *See* Asian currency unit
ADB. *See* Asian Development Bank
ADIA. *See* Abu Dhabi Investment Authority
ADIC. *See* Abu Dhabi Investment Corporation
Advisory Committee on International Exchange Rate Policy, 230
Agreement on Subsidies and Countervailing Measures (ASCM), 222, 229
Agricultural Bank of China, 35, 176, 211
agriculture, productivity gap for, 117, 121, 121*n*
air pollution, 114–15, 117, 121, 124
Alaska Permanent Fund (US), 185*n*
Alberta Heritage Savings Trust Fund (Canada), 185*n*
AMU. *See* Asian monetary unit
annual reports, sovereign wealth funds, 189*t*, 192
antidumping (AD) remedies, 222, 227–30, 232, 294

APD. *See* Asia and Pacific Department (IMF)
appreciation (currency)
   in Asian economies, 33, 239–40
   bank reform and, 13
   consumption demand and, 10
   costs of, 22–23, 71–72
   against dollar, 2, 2*n*, 28–35, 52, 70–75, 81, 83*f*
   effectiveness of, 20–21, 343
   foreign pressure for, 22, 53–54, 56, 91
      (*See also* congressional bills)
   global imbalances and, 26, 28–35, 87*n*, 348
   gradual, 50–52, 324, 332, 343, 344, 357
   IMF surveillance and, 281, 324–25
   international reserves and, 217
   needed to eliminate undervaluation, 131–32, 133*t*, 149*f*–150*f*, 149–53
   strategy for, 12, 324–25, 341, 343–44
   tax and tariff substitutes for, 51
   underestimation of, 104, 105*f*
Article IV (IMF), 19, 39, 227–28, 228*n*, 279, 287
   staff reports, 337–38
   violation of, 287*n*, 287–92, 293, 323, 327, 330, 332, 347–48
Article XV(4) frustration case (GATT), 222, 227–30
ASCM. *See* Agreement on Subsidies and Countervailing Measures

ASEAN-plus-three economies
  regional currency units (*See* Asian
    currency unit)
  trade surpluses, 262–65
ASEM. *See* Asia Europe Meeting
Asia. *See also specific country*
  current account balances, 216, 322, 323*t*
  exchange rate regimes in, 31–33, 216,
    239–40, 244–51
  global imbalances and, 254–55
  intraregional trade ratios, 245, 255, 355,
    358*f*
Asia and Pacific Department (IMF), 281,
  329, 330
Asia Europe Meeting (ASEM), 251
Asian Bond Market Initiative, 33, 259
Asian currencies. *See also specific currency*
  basket proposals, 33, 251–53, 252*t*
  basket regressions, 248–49, 249*n*, 250*t*,
    251, 252*t*
  benchmark for, 29–30
  influence of renminbi on, 33, 54, 216,
    249–51, 252*t*, 256
  movements vis-à-vis US dollar, 241–44,
    242*f*–243*f*, 256
  multilateral misalignment in, 139
Asian currency unit (ACU), 33, 240, 251,
  253, 259–67
  as common basket of internal
    currencies, 265–67
  as numeraire for Asian basket bonds,
    261
  as regional accounting unit, 260–61
  as surveillance indicator, 262*f*–264*f*,
    262–65
Asian Development Bank (ADB), 157,
  158*n*, 240, 251, 259
Asian economic integration, 246, 259–67.
  See also basket currency system
  benefits of, 240, 255
  global imbalances and, 255
  lack of, 239, 244, 244*n*
  political economy of, 253–54
  surveillance indicator for, 262*f*–264*f*,
    262–65
Asian financial crisis (1990s), 72, 173, 244,
  255, 286, 300, 350
Asian monetary unit (AMU), 259,
  259*n*–260*n*
  real deviation indicators, 264, 264*f*
  in terms of euro and US dollar, 262, 262*f*
asset diversification, for international
  reserves, 178, 199, 202, 209, 216–17
asset price bubbles, 89

Association of Southeast Asian Nations.
  See ASEAN-plus-three economies
audits, sovereign wealth funds, 190*t*, 193
Australia, Future Fund, 185*n*
auto industry, 231

balance of payments, 81, 82*t*, 342. *See also*
  current account balance
  errors and payments category, 87*n*
  exchange rate policy and, 291, 301–302,
    315
  global developments in, 320–22, 321*t*,
    323*t*
  monetary approach to (*See* monetary
    approach to balance of payments)
Balassa-Samuelson effect, 132, 282, 285*n*
  in enhanced-PPP approach, 132–34,
    137, 140–42, 156–60
Bank for International Settlements (BIS),
  173, 342
  REER data, 104, 105*f*, 152
banking system, 12–16. *See also* state-
  owned banks; *specific bank*
  base money multiplier, 68
  capital controls and, 86, 89
  excess reserves in, 304*n*
  foreign assets of, 206–207
  importance of, 12
  inefficiency of, 78, 85
  liquidity of, 357, 360*f*
  profitability of, 14, 16, 53
  reform of (*See* financial reform)
  sterilization operations and, 14, 16,
    52–53
  tax on, 6, 6*n*–7*n*, 53
Bank of Thailand, 216
base money, 298*t*–299*t*, 298–301, 357, 360*f*
  monetary policy and, 26–28, 53, 67–68,
    292, 296, 302–303
  ratio to nominal GDP, 303, 304, 304*n*
  savings rate and, 307
  sources of, 316–17
  stability of, 303–304, 316
  sterilization operations and, 27–28, 67,
    292, 304–305
  US, 297
basket bonds, 251*n*, 260, 261
basket currency system, 33, 246, 248–49,
  249*n*, 250*t*. *See also* Asian economic
  integration
  Chinese involvement in, 246–48,
    247*t*–248*t*, 343
  global imbalances and, 254–55
  proposals for, 251–53, 252*t*, 259–67

computable general equilibrium (CGE)
    model, 116, 119, 124, 125, 341–42
congressional bills, 44–49, 54, 71, 219–38,
    347
    2003 (S 1586), 219
    2007 (HR 2942), 221–22, 223*t*–225*t*, 230
    2007 (S 1607), 220–22, 223*t*–225*t*, 230
    2007 (S 1677), 221–22, 223*t*–225*t*
    action horizon, 226
    criticism of, 226, 236–38
    mirror legislation and, 232–33
    number of, 234
    as part of multilateral approach, 227,
        352–53
    political factors and, 45–46, 234–38
    as protectionism, 45, 47, 49, 237, 349,
        353
    and role of Congress, 230–32
    WTO involvement and, 222, 225*t*,
        227–30, 349
consumer price index (CPI), 5, 14, 14*n*,
    314, 314*n*, 357
    real effective exchange rate and, 105,
        106*f*
consumer price inflation, 98, 98*f*
consumption
    contribution to growth, 64, 79
    lack of, 342, 356
    promotion of, 9–10, 343–44
    ratio to GNP, 317–19, 318*t*
    share of GDP, 10, 64
consumption demand, 9–10
corporate goods price index, 5, 5*n*
corporate responsibility, sovereign wealth
    funds, 189*t*, 191
corporate savings. *See* enterprise savings
countervailing duty (CVD) laws, 222,
    227–30, 232, 294
CPI. *See* consumer price index
credit. *See also* loans
    allocation efficiency, 5
    development of, 14, 344
    growth tools, 85
cross-border assets. *See* international
    reserves
currency composition, of SWF
    investments, 190*t*, 192
Currency Exchange Rate Oversight
    Reform Act of 2007 (S 1607), 220–22,
    223*t*–225*t*, 230
currency manipulation, 38–43, 73–74
    congressional oversight issues, 231, 231*n*
    definition of, 38, 40, 41, 342–43

explanations for, 294–95
    IMF surveillance and, 281
    intent test, 222, 222*n*, 293, 342–43
    versus misalignment, 231, 231*n*
currency misalignments, 73. *See also*
    overvaluation; undervaluation
    bank vulnerability to, 13, 13*n*
    congressional oversight issues, 231,
        231*n*
    estimation of, 18–19
    IMF surveillance and, 289–90
    versus manipulation, 231, 231*n*
    unintentional, 342–43
currency reform, 1–2. *See also* appreciation
    gradual, 50–52, 324, 332, 343, 344, 357
    macroeconomic policy and, 77–108
    need for, 239, 239*n*, 341–42, 352–53
    risks of, 71–72
    speed of, 343–44, 353–54
    strategies for, 87–89, 343–44, 356–57
        three-stage, 54–56, 348
        two-stage, 51
Currency Reform and Financial Market
    Access Act of 2007 (S 1677), 221–22,
    223*t*–225*t*
Currency Reform for Fair Trade Act of
    2007 (HR 2942), 221–22, 223*t*–225*t*,
    230
current account balance. *See also* trade
    balance
    Asia, 216, 322, 323*t*
    behavior of, 297
    capital flow factor, 308*n*, 308–10, 309*t*
    Europe, 272, 272*f*
    international reserves and, 171*t*, 171–72
    Japan, 159, 231, 232*n*
    monetary factors, 307–12, 309*t*, 317
    oil-exporting countries, 281*n*, 321*n*,
        321–22
    US (*See* US current account deficit)
current account surplus (China), 2, 2*n*, 81,
    82*t*, 95, 97*f*, 112*t*, 112–14, 355, 358*f*
    appreciation and, 20–21, 343
    base money supply and, 27–28, 292, 303
    causes of, 23–28, 62, 346, 356–57
        cyclical, 25–26, 144, 147, 152, 159,
            162–63
    flexible exchange rate and, 93–95
    IMF surveillance and, 282, 284*f*, 285–86,
        323–25
    monetary approach to, 305–12
    movements in, 23, 23*n*, 126, 147, 281,
        286, 312–13

Government Investment Corporation (Singapore), 36, 37, 179n, 185, 198, 202, 214
government officials, policy accountability, 325–26
government role, in SWF investment strategy, 189t, 191
Graham, Lindsey, 44, 221
Grassley, Charles, 44, 220
Greenspan, Alan, 352
Group of Five (G-5), 280
Group of Seven (G-7), 37, 197, 202, 246, 268, 280
Group of Twenty (G-20), 142
GSDEER model, 143
Gulf funds, 218. *See also specific fund*
  demand for US equities, 213–14, 214n, 215f

harmonious society, 9, 117, 118, 343
heavy industry. *See also* excess capacity; manufacturing
  investment and capacity boom in, 61–69, 111–14, 313–14
  reliance on, 111–14
hedge funds, versus sovereign wealth funds, 196, 199
hedging instruments, 13, 15
high-tech embargo, 345
hoarding function, 305
Hodrick-Prescott filter, 146
Hong Kong, 245, 322
household registration system *(hukou)*, 116, 116n
household savings. *See also* saving rate
  versus enterprise savings, 11, 28, 63, 68, 79–81, 83, 112, 112t, 124, 315, 319
  and growth pattern predictions, 113t, 116–17, 117n, 126–27
  monetary approach to, 305–12, 315–16
House of Representatives, 2007 bill (HR 2942), 221–22, 223t–225t, 230
Hu Jintao, 9
human capital, 110t, 111, 237

ICP. *See* International Comparison Programme
IMF. *See* International Monetary Fund
IMFC. *See* International Monetary and Financial Committee
import(s)
  growth of, 62, 127
  price elasticities for *(See* trade elasticities)

import processing, restricted list for, 51–52
import substitution, 345
income
  disposable, 319
  from interest earnings, 9–10
  spending relative to, 305–12, 317
income inequality
  appreciation and, 23
  rising, 115–17, 124
incrementalism, 50–52, 324, 332, 343, 344, 357
Independent Evaluation Office (IMF), 38, 280, 329
India
  currency regime, 216
  foreign direct investment in, 346
  international reserves, 175n, 175–76
  PPP line, 140, 167
  scapegoating and, 234, 237
Indonesia, monetary policy, 255
Indonesian rupiah
  basket regressions, 249, 250t, 251, 252t
  exchange rate regime, 244, 245, 265
  movements in, 241, 242f–243f, 244
industry
  in emerging markets, 355
  investment boom in, 61–69, 111–14, 313–14
  production growth, 111–14
  reliance on, 11, 109, 111–14
  share in GDP, 111, 111n, 116, 119
inflation
  banking system and, 14
  consumer price, 98, 98f
  control of, 81
  euro-area countries, 314n–315n
  GDP growth and, 300, 303, 305, 357
  objective, 89–90, 98
  undervaluation and, 286, 301
institutional reforms, 118
interest income, tax on, 9–10
interest rates
  adjustments in, 343
  central bank bills, 85, 86f
  central bank management of, 15, 88
  deposit, 5–7, 9, 16, 78, 79, 80f, 85, 85n, 124, 305, 319, 338
  loans, 5, 16, 79, 80f, 319
  parity, versus foreign exchange reserve growth, 103, 103f
  sterilization operations and, 14–15
  US, 52, 208–209, 210f

Japan
ACU creation advocated by, 265n, 266
attitude toward renminbi, 327
auto industry, 231
current account surplus, 159, 231, 231n,
255, 356, 360f
economic conditions (1980s), 72
international reserves, 203, 205f
monetary policy, 255, 304n
PPP/er ratio, 135–37, 136f
scapegoating and, 234, 237, 347
Japanese yen
as Asian benchmark, 29–30, 260, 266
basket proposal, 251–53, 252t, 260,
263–66
basket regression, 246–48, 247t–248t
exchange rate regime, 245, 255, 265–66
misalignment of, 231, 231n
movements in, 263–64, 263f–264f, 356,
360f
JPMorgan, 211, 285n

KIA. See Kuwait Investment Authority
King, Mervyn, 38
knowledge economy, promotion of, 119,
125
Kohler, Horst, 331
Korea, monetary policy, 255
Korean won
basket regressions, 249, 250t, 251, 252t
exchange rate regime, 240, 245, 255,
264, 265
movements in, 241, 242f–243f, 244,
263–64, 263f–264f
Krugman, Paul, 162n
Kuwait Investment Authority (KIA), 37,
198

labor force, size of, 345–46
labor movement, restrictions on, 118
labor productivity growth, 110t, 111, 121
capital account and, 313–15, 314n
land transactions, restrictions on, 118
Laos, 245
Latin America, balance of payments, 322,
322n, 323t
liquidity trap, 304, 304n
Lisbon agenda, 269–70
loans, 12, 14. See also credit
to foreign borrowers, 176, 176n
interest rates, 5, 16, 79, 80f, 319
logarithms, use of, 155–56

Maastricht Treaty, 261, 277

macroeconomic policy, 81–86, 342, 356
alternative strategies for, 118–25, 120t
effect of flexible exchange rate on,
95–98
IMF surveillance and, 338–39
restructuring of, 356–57
Malaysia
balance of payments, 322
monetary policy, 255
Malaysian ringgit
basket regressions, 249, 250t, 251, 252t
exchange rate regime, 241, 244, 245, 265
movements in, 241, 242f–243f, 244
manager's role, in SWF investment
strategy, 189t, 191
Mandelson, Peter, 270, 276
manufacturing. See also industry
in emerging markets, 355
reliance on, 11, 109, 111–14
manufacturing wages, competitiveness
and, 20–21
market-oriented transition, 72, 79
Marshall-Lerner conditions, 21, 148
Mexico, 352
Oil Income Stabilization Fund, 179n
Middle East funds, 218. See also specific fund
demand for US equities, 212–14, 214n,
215f
military products, 345
monetary approach to balance of
payments, 26–28, 67–68, 282, 295–319
aggregate accounting, 298t, 298–301,
299t, 315–19
applied to China, 296–305
basic ideas of, 295–96
current account surplus and, 305–12
monetary base. See base money
monetary factors, in current account
balance, 307–12, 309t, 317
monetary policy, 357
alternative framework for, 89–90, 98
Asian economic integration and, 255
base money demand and, 26–28, 53,
67–68, 292
consumption demand and, 9
effectiveness of, factors affecting, 8,
87–88, 102–104
independence of, 4–9, 56, 77–108
open economy trilemma, 100–108, 102f
as part of rebalancing strategy, 342
monetary union. See Asian economic
integration; basket currency system
money supply, 73–74, 357, 361f
moral hazard, 74, 352

mortgage-backed securities, 208
movers, 31–32
Multi-Fiber Arrangement, 159
multilateral approach, 226–27
  versus bilateral approach, 352–53
  congressional bills as part of, 227,
    352–53
  to global imbalances, 34, 144, 167, 347–50
  mechanisms for, 350–51
  to US trade balance, 235–36
Multilateral Consultation, 336, 339
multilateral misalignment, versus
  bilateral, 131n, 131–32, 139, 149,
  149f–150f, 271–73
Mundell-Fleming model, 104
Myanmar, 245

national expenditure on goods and
  services, 307
national interest waiver, 224t, 226
National People's Congress, 109n, 118
net domestic assets (NDA), 67, 296,
  298t–299t, 298–300, 303
net foreign assets (NFA), 67, 142, 143, 168
net foreign income, 307
net national saving, 315
New Zealand, 342
  Superannuation Fund, 179, 179n, 185n
NiGEM model, 148
Nixon Shock, 73
nominal effective exchange rate, 81, 83f,
  94, 282
nondilemma situation, 18
Norway, Government Pension Fund,
  36–37, 179, 179n, 185n, 193, 212, 214,
  218

official settlements balance, 297, 297n
  China, 298–303
  savings rate and, 306–307
  US, 297, 310
oil-exporting countries, current account
  surpluses, 281n, 321n, 321–22
oil funds, demand for US equities,
  213–14, 214n
Omnibus Trade and Competitiveness Act
  of 1988, 44, 46
open economy trilemma, 100–108, 102f
Organization for Economic Cooperation
  and Development, 146
overvaluation
  definition of, 134, 134n
  estimation of, 137, 139
  exchange rate peg and, 302

Paulson, Henry, 46, 220, 226, 232, 268, 326
PBC. *See* People's Bank of China
pension funds, national, 185n
People's Bank of China (PBC), 5
  bills (*See* central bank bills)
  CIC coordination with, 38, 203, 216–17
  foreign assets of, 306n
  interest rate management, 88
  international reserves maintained by,
    67, 357
  renminbi float by, 245, 258
  sterilization operations (*See* sterilization
    operations)
  SWF established by, 169
per capita income, 117, 135, 346
  China versus US, 157, 158n
  PPP/er and, 133–34, 134f
PGM. *See* Principles for the Guidance of
  Members' Exchange Rate Policies
  (IMF)
Philippines, monetary policy, 255
Philippine peso
  basket regressions, 249, 250t, 251, 252t
  exchange rate regime, 245, 265
  movements in, 241, 242f–243f, 244
Phillips curves, 138, 161
physical capital, investment in, 79–81
Policy Development and Review
  Department (IMF), 329
political factors
  Asian currency coordination, 253–54
  congressional currency bills, 45–46,
    234–38
  international reserves, 176–78, 197, 203
  lending decisions, 16
  renminbi revaluation, 71
pollution, 114–15, 117, 121, 124
Polonius principle, 162
population size, 345–46
portfolio diversification, for international
  reserves, 178, 199, 202, 209, 216–17
poverty, 110, 118, 148
PPP approach. *See* purchasing power
  parity
PPP/er. *See* purchasing power
  parity/market exchange ratio
price distortions, on investment, 338
price elasticities
  of demand, 21, 21n
  for exports and imports (*See* trade
    elasticities)
price reforms, 118
price-specie-flow mechanism, 295, 302,
  305

Other Publications from the Peterson Institute

International Debt Reexamined*
William R. Cline
February 1995   ISBN 0-88132-083-8
American Trade Politics, 3d ed.
I. M. Destler
April 1995   ISBN 0-88132-215-6
Managing Official Export Credits:
The Quest for a Global Regime*
John E. Ray
July 1995   ISBN 0-88132-207-5
Asia Pacific Fusion: Japan's Role in APEC*
Yoichi Funabashi
October 1995   ISBN 0-88132-224-5
Korea-United States Cooperation in the New
World Order* C. Fred Bergsten and Il SaKong, eds.
February 1996   ISBN 0-88132-226-1
Why Exports Really Matter!*   ISBN 0-88132-221-0
Why Exports Matter More!*   ISBN 0-88132-229-6
J. David Richardson and Karin Rindal
July 1995; February 1996
Global Corporations and National Governments
Edward M. Graham
May 1996   ISBN 0-88132-111-7
Global Economic Leadership and the Group of
Seven   C. Fred Bergsten and C. Randall Henning
May 1996   ISBN 0-88132-218-0
The Trading System after the Uruguay Round*
John Whalley and Colleen Hamilton
July 1996   ISBN 0-88132-131-1
Private Capital Flows to Emerging Markets
after the Mexican Crisis*
Guillermo A. Calvo, Morris Goldstein,
and Eduard Hochreiter
September 1996   ISBN 0-88132-232-6
The Crawling Band as an Exchange Rate Regime:
Lessons from Chile, Colombia, and Israel
John Williamson
September 1996   ISBN 0-88132-231-8
Flying High: Liberalizing Civil Aviation
in the Asia Pacific*
Gary Clyde Hufbauer and Christopher Findlay
November 1996   ISBN 0-88132-227-X
Measuring the Costs of Visible Protection
in Korea*   Namdoo Kim
November 1996   ISBN 0-88132-236-9
The World Trading System: Challenges Ahead
Jeffrey J. Schott
December 1996   ISBN 0-88132-235-0
Has Globalization Gone Too Far?
Dani Rodrik
March 1997   ISBN paper 0-88132-241-5
Korea-United States Economic Relationship*
C. Fred Bergsten and Il SaKong, editors
March 1997   ISBN 0-88132-240-7
Summitry in the Americas: A Progress Report
Richard E. Feinberg
April 1997   ISBN 0-88132-242-3
Corruption and the Global Economy
Kimberly Ann Elliott
June 1997   ISBN 0-88132-233-4

Regional Trading Blocs in the World
Economic System   Jeffrey A. Frankel
October 1997   ISBN 0-88132-202-4
Sustaining the Asia Pacific Miracle:
Environmental Protection and Economic
Integration   Andre Dua and Daniel C. Esty
October 1997   ISBN 0-88132-250-4
Trade and Income Distribution
William R. Cline
November 1997   ISBN 0-88132-216-4
Global Competition Policy
Edward M. Graham and J. David Richardson
December 1997   ISBN 0-88132-166-4
Unfinished Business: Telecommunications
after the Uruguay Round
Gary Clyde Hufbauer and Erika Wada
December 1997   ISBN 0-88132-257-1
Financial Services Liberalization in the WTO
Wendy Dobson and Pierre Jacquet
June 1998   ISBN 0-88132-254-7
Restoring Japan's Economic Growth
Adam S. Posen
September 1998   ISBN 0-88132-262-8
Measuring the Costs of Protection in China
Zhang Shuguang, Zhang Yansheng,
and Wan Zhongxin
November 1998   ISBN 0-88132-247-4
Foreign Direct Investment and Development:
The New Policy Agenda for Developing
Countries and Economies in Transition
Theodore H. Moran
December 1998   ISBN 0-88132-258-X
Behind the Open Door: Foreign Enterprises
in the Chinese Marketplace   Daniel H. Rosen
January 1999   ISBN 0-88132-263-6
Toward A New International Financial
Architecture: A Practical Post-Asia Agenda
Barry Eichengreen
February 1999   ISBN 0-88132-270-9
Is the U.S. Trade Deficit Sustainable?
Catherine L. Mann
September 1999   ISBN 0-88132-265-2
Safeguarding Prosperity in a Global Financial
System: The Future International Financial
Architecture, Independent Task Force Report
Sponsored by the Council on Foreign Relations
Morris Goldstein, Project Director
October 1999   ISBN 0-88132-287-3
Avoiding the Apocalypse: The Future
of the Two Koreas   Marcus Noland
June 2000   ISBN 0-88132-278-4
Assessing Financial Vulnerability: An Early
Warning System for Emerging Markets
Morris Goldstein, Graciela Kaminsky,
and Carmen Reinhart
June 2000   ISBN 0-88132-237-7
Global Electronic Commerce: A Policy Primer
Catherine L. Mann, Sue E. Eckert,
and Sarah Cleeland Knight
July 2000   ISBN 0-88132-274-1

WORKS IN PROGRESS

DISTRIBUTORS OUTSIDE THE UNITED STATES

Australia, New Zealand,
and Papua New Guinea
D. A. Information Services
648 Whitehorse Road
Mitcham, Victoria 3132, Australia
Tel: 61-3-9210-7777
Fax: 61-3-9210-7788
Email: service@dadirect.com.au
www.dadirect.com.au

India, Bangladesh, Nepal, and Sri Lanka
Viva Books Private Limited
Mr. Vinod Vasishtha
4737/23 Ansari Road
Daryaganj, New Delhi 110002
India
Tel: 91-11-4224-2200
Fax: 91-11-4224-2240
Email: viva@vivagroupindia.net
www.vivagroupindia.com

Mexico, Central America, South America,
and Puerto Rico
US PubRep, Inc.
311 Dean Drive
Rockville, MD 20851
Tel: 301-838-9276
Fax: 301-838-9278
Email: c.falk@ieee.org

Asia (*Brunei, Burma, Cambodia, China,*
Hong Kong, Indonesia, Korea, Laos, Malaysia,
Philippines, Singapore, Taiwan, Thailand,
***and Vietnam*)**
East-West Export Books (EWEB)
University of Hawaii Press
2840 Kolowalu Street
Honolulu, Hawaii 96822-1888
Tel: 808-956-8830
Fax: 808-988-6052
Email: eweb@hawaii.edu

Canada
Renouf Bookstore
5369 Canotek Road, Unit 1
Ottawa, Ontario K1J 9J3, Canada
Tel: 613-745-2665
Fax: 613-745-7660
www.renoufbooks.com

Japan
United Publishers Services Ltd.
1-32-5, Higashi-shinagawa
Shinagawa-ku, Tokyo 140-0002
Japan
Tel: 81-3-5479-7251
Fax: 81-3-5479-7307
Email: purchasing@ups.co.jp
For trade accounts only. Individuals will find
Institute books in leading Tokyo bookstores.

Middle East
MERIC
2 Bahgat Ali Street, El Masry Towers
Tower D, Apt. 24
Zamalek, Cairo
Egypt
Tel. 20-2-7633824
Fax: 20-2-7369355
Email: mahmoud_fouda@mericonline.com
www.mericonline.com

United Kingdom, Europe
(*including Russia and Turkey*), Africa,
and Israel
The Eurospan Group
c/o Turpin Distribution
Pegasus Drive
Stratton Business Park
Biggleswade, Bedfordshire
SG18 8TQ
United Kingdom
Tel: 44 (0) 1767-604972
Fax: 44 (0) 1767-601640
Email: eurospan@turpin-distribution.com
www.eurospangroup.com/bookstore

Visit our website at:
www.petersoninstitute.org
E-mail orders to:
petersonmail@presswarehouse.com